Minorities in
California History

EDITED BY

George E. Frakes

AND

Curtis B. Solberg

Santa Barbara City College

MINORITIES
IN
California
History

RANDOM HOUSE · NEW YORK

ISBN: 0–394–31332–1

Library of Congress Catalog Card Number: 72–141961

Manufactured in the United States of America. Composed by H. Wolff Book Mfg.
Co., Inc., New York, N. Y. Printed and bound by Halliday Lithograph, Inc., West
Hanover, Mass.
Design by RONALD FARBER

First Edition
98765432

Contents

Introduction

California is widely believed to be a mirror of the nation. Since the turn of the century the Golden State has reflected and popularized national trends. Although well known for its fads, eccentricities, and new ideas, California is not so different from the rest of America. Indeed, the most populous state of the union may be considered to be a microcosm of American life, with all of its problems and promises exaggerated and projected to the rest of the nation and the world through motion pictures and the printed word. Perhaps it is this combination of exposure and national relevance that leads many to believe that the California way of life is the wave of the future.

As California is both a reflection and future projection of American life, minority groups in California play a particularly significant role in this new scene. But although every prominent American racial minority is represented, the percentages of blacks, Mexicans, Orientals, and Indians in California are larger than those of the nation as a whole. Another distinct segment of California's heterogeneous population is youth. Not a minority in the racial or ethnic sense, many California youth have established a way of life with new values that mark them as a group as far removed from the mainstream of American social, political, and economic life as any of the traditional minorities.

The purpose of this book of readings is twofold. The articles in the first section examine the part that minorities in California played in the historical development of the state until the end of World War II. The second section explores the contemporary minority situation in the state. The readings selected for both the historical and contemporary sections clearly suggest two prevailing themes concerning minorities. The first of these is that problems have always existed in California—severe problems that have been understood only partially by most of the population. These problems might be similar to those of other regions of America. The second theme is that although the problems persist, and in fact grow, there is a promise of a solution of minority problems in the West that may be applicable to the entire nation.

Why does this dichotomy between profound problems and the promise of solutions exist? Perhaps it is because in California everything seems to be magnified. Opportunities abound for many, yet this affluence seems to have eluded most minorities. The rich get richer, and the poor seem poorer in contrast. The plight of the poor is brought into sharper focus when one realizes that California's "GNP" is now sixth among all the nations of the world. This abundance is reflected by the standard of living enjoyed by a vast, prosperous middle class. In excellence and beauty California still boasts startling natural and man-made monuments that stand in contrast to the farm laborer's dilemma or the bleakness of Los Angeles' ghettos.

Another explanation for California's situation might be her newness and lack of well-developed traditions. These factors seem to promise success for all who wish to come. Indeed, there is a fluidity to the California social structure that sets it apart from some of the other sections of the nation. This absence of rigid class lines has contributed to California's aura of a free and open society. It is with these expectations that many of the minorities stream to the West from across the nation and from Mexico, only to nourish even greater disappointment and frustrations in the midst of unparalleled affluence.

Beginning in the 1960s California's minority problems, which heretofore had been largely overlooked, began to attract national interest. In fact, the rest of the nation was shocked by the news of the Berkeley student riots that began in the autumn of 1964 in a University well known for its liberalism, wealth, and scholarship. As surprising to many was the violence and destruction during the Watts riots in Los Angeles. It seemed impossible to many that such an explosion could occur in a state where traditional civil rights such as voting and nonsegregated public accommodations and schools were guaranteed to all citizens. In the months that followed, news of organized, militant youth and minority groups and of battles between minorities and police received national coverage by the media. The long and crippling strikes by Mexican-American grape pickers at Delano introduced still another issue of concern.

In order to place these isolated events in a meaningful perspective, they must be interpreted in the light of developments in recent California history. California since World War II has been characterized by rapid growth and change. More than 1,000 Americans migrate to California daily. They often come without an understanding of the state's history and hopeful for an escape from their own past. Yet most new Californians still retain many of their former social values. The result of this constant immigration is that California is a state with little sense of community or identity. This absence of a well-defined identity role has been a great handicap.

Many minority-group members believe it is impossible to achieve personal or collective group goals unless they know themselves. As never before, minorities in search of a sense of personal or collective identity hope to provide this first vital step as a prerequisite to solving the social problems of today. Certain minority leaders suggest that this search for identity has meaning beyond their own community. They imply that their values can contribute to altering a society that has in their judgment become so dehumanized, fragmented, and materialistic that it has lost its sense of community.

What the promise of identity will bring has been a matter of much discussion. Some minorities reject the older idea of America as a "melting pot." They are now challenging the notion that acceptance of the prevailing values of white America somehow makes them full participants in white-collar, middle-class society. For some, the melting pot has been a pressure cooker that has created new demands and yet has not produced enough benefits to make the effort toward assimilation worthwhile. Many minority spokesmen suggest that their only hope is to live in a culturally pluralistic society. In such a milieu, every racial and ethnic group would be able to maintain its own cultural identity and way of life without conforming to all the norms of the larger society. They maintain that this idea of cultural pluralism should be the final answer, because the traditional formula for assimilation has not worked. Other minority group members believe that understanding themselves can bring a sense of dignity, pride, and accomplishment in a pluralistic society. They feel that this step must precede their acceptance as equals by the Anglo majority. Still others, particularly members of the middle class who have become successfully assimilated, reject the concept of a separate identity entirely.

The stress on self-identity has developed only in recent times. Long before California entered statehood, the population included Indians, Mexicans, Spaniards, and blacks. In the years following the Hispanic and Mexican period, large numbers of Chinese, Japanese, and Filipinos immigrated, adding to the variety of races in the population. During the Gold Rush a floodtide of Anglo migrants came to California, drastically altering its ethnic and racial composition. These white men soon dominated the government, passing laws and writing a state constitution that reflected their racial and ethnic values and establishing a lasting influence on California society.

The articles in Part I of this book were selected to examine the historical role of minorities in California to 1945. Part II examines the search for identity among the four most prominent minorities: Indian, Mexican, black, and Oriental. After examining their quest for identity, the editors present the major sources of minority and youthful dissatisfaction in selections concerning law and order, jobs, welfare, and housing.

The selections in all chapters are only a brief sampling of a rich vein of literature that is only now attracting the attention of scholars and the wider reading public. Because of the book's necessary brevity, the editors are frankly interpretive and wish to remind the reader that these selections, although representative, do not pretend to be all-inclusive.

The selections included reflect the broad spectrum of sources available to the student of minority history, sociology, or ethnic studies, and to the student enrolled in the traditional survey courses in California and American history. The editors have selected material from such sources as the scholarly journals, ethnic and racial publications, the underground press, youth-oriented periodicals, and general newspapers and books. Some of the sources are national or regional publications that emphasize the interrelationship between minority groups in California and in the nation.

We would like to thank William Frohlich and Arthur Strimling, our editors at Random House, for their support; Peter Rose and William Goetzman for helpful criticism of the manuscript; and the many gracious authors and publishers who gave us permission to use their materials. We would also like to thank Susan Okada, Perry Kaufman, Frances Frakes, Dorothy Annable, and John Rowell for their assistance.

G.E.F.
C.B.S.

PART ONE

Minorities in the Years to 1945

Chapter 1

Minorities in the Hispanic Period,

1769-1846

The first minorities in California appeared during the Hispanic period. Although a number of minority groups can be identified in this era—Indians, Russians, Afro-Americans, mestizos, mulattoes, Anglo-Americans, Hawaiians, and others—two groups are of particular importance: Indians and blacks.

Since California and the other Spanish borderlands are approximately contemporary in colonial development with the Eastern United States, the treatment of these two minorities in California offers an excellent opportunity to compare Hispanic attitudes toward various racial groups with Anglo attitudes of the same era. In general, the Spaniards and the Mexicans were more tolerant than the English colonists and the Americans during this period. Hispanic customs and law permitted intermarriage and encouraged assimilation of Indians and blacks into society. This unbiased attitude toward racial differences was particularly noticeable in California because many of the Spaniards themselves and the Mexican pioneers after 1821 were persons of mixed racial background.

Greater tolerance and acceptance of non-Hispanic people in California did not mean, however, that minorities were necessarily the social and economic equals of Spaniards. The Spaniards usually held the important religious and administrative posts, and most of the largest landowners were mestizos, Spanish, or blacks. There was, however, opportunity for upward social mobility, because in the Spanish colonies a wealthy person of Indian or black ancestry could legally delete his true origins and gain Spanish status. Indeed, scholars of early California history believe that many of the most distinguished early "Spanish" families could also trace their family roots to Indian and African sources.

Another concern of historical authorities is the relationship of the Spaniards and, later, Mexicans with the largest minority group—the Indians. Many historians suggest that the major reason for the relative harmony between the Indians and the Spaniards and Mexicans prior to 1846 was the presence of the Catholic Church. In California, the Franciscan mission system was charged with many matters concerning the Indians. A chain of twenty-one missions stretched over 500 miles with thousands of Indian neophytes who were exposed to the paternalistic values employed by the Spanish padres. Apologists for the missions assert that Indians learned practical arts and skills, received the spiritual blessings of Christianity, and enjoyed a higher standard of living due to their mission experience. Critics of the mission system point to the limitations placed upon the freedom of Indians, who were in some cases confined to the missions. The critics also mention the number of Indian runaways, the widespread use of corporal punishment, and the Spaniards' authoritarian attempts to alter the Indians' way of life.

Although the debate continues, certain general patterns in Hispanic–minority group relations can be observed. Spanish attitudes toward minorities differed from those of the British colonists and Anglo-Americans. Early California society was more open and accepting of minorities and the children of mixed marriages than was the majority of Anglo America. Black pioneers played a more prominent role in early California and in the Spanish borderlands than is usually described in traditional American history textbooks.

In examining the selections in this chapter, there are a number of questions the reader might consider. Why are the missionaries considered to be both the destroyers and the saviors of the Indians? What were the differences in attitude toward minorities in Anglo America and Hispanic America, and why? Why were the black pioneers of the Hispanic period largely overlooked by historians?

1. THE INDIAN VERSUS THE SPANISH MISSIONS

SHERBURNE F. COOK

The Indian's life under the mission system is a matter that has stimulated much debate among scholars. Dr. Sherburne Cook, Emeritus Professor of the University of California, presents his critical interpretation of the impact of the European upon the indigenous population. Cook's analysis of the Indian's plight is relevant to contemporary concern over the issue of the first Americans.

Since no structural or functional adaptations could occur in the short space of two or three generations, the actual responses of the Indians to the mission system are restricted to visible activity by individuals or small groups and to population changes in the whole group. The visible activity with respect to the mission system could take but one of two forms: obvious opposition or acceptance. The positive aspect was manifested in an entirely unsensational manner, merely in carrying on the routine of daily life in the mission. The negative aspect, i.e., opposition, was made evident through either flight or rebellion. The extent of fugitivism and rebellion is then the key to the response of the individual, whereas population trends indicate the response of the group.

Population Changes in the Missions

In a recent paper[1] the data bearing on this question have been examined and critically analyzed. The chief conclusions were set forth as follows (p. 48):

> Primarily, as a result of consistent wholesale addition by conversion, the total population rose rapidly until approximately 1800. Thereafter the increase continued, but more slowly, up to an equilibrium point near 1820, subsequent to which a definite decline set in. These observed changes, which were based upon a large gentile immigration, mask the true situation with respect to the converted population. The latter was subject to a very great real diminution from the beginning. This is clear from the falling birth rate and the huge excess of deaths over births which was present throughout the mission era. Actually the critical and determining factor was the death rate, for it has been shown that the decline in gross or crude birth rate

[1] S. F. Cook, *Population Trends Among the California Mission Indians*, Univ. Calif. Publ., Ibero-Americana, No. 17 (Berkeley, 1940).

FROM Sherburne F. Cook, *The Conflict Between the California Indian and White Civilization* (Berkeley: University of California Press, 1943), Vol. 1, pp. 11–12, 64–72, 90, 94, 95–96, 98–100, 114, 122, 123, 145–146, 146–147, 153–154, 156–157. Reprinted by permission of The Regents of the University of California.

may be accounted for largely by the constantly increasing sex ratio (males to females). Since the latter was invariable at unity for children under ten, the change must have been due to a differential death rate between males and females during adolescence and maturity, which would result in a relative decline in the number of child-bearing women. The death rate as a whole was always remarkably high, even, for some as yet unexplained reason, at the very start of the missions. It tended definitely, however, to fall during the last thirty years and, at the existing rates of change, would probably have come into equilibrium with the birth rate ultimately. These aspects of the total death rate were due primarily to the state of the child death rate, since the adult death rate did not alter so materially in sixty-odd years.

The chief conclusion of a more general nature is that the Indian population, which presumably had been in a more or less steady equilibrium prior to missionization, underwent a profound upset as a result of that process, a process from which it was showing signs of recovery only at the time of secularization. The indications are, indeed, that several further generations would have been necessary to recast the race, as it were, and bring about that restoration of biotic equilibrium which eventually would have occurred.

.   .   .

The following items constitute the testimony of certain Indians who escaped but were caught. On their return each was asked to state why he absconded. The arabic numerals below indicate the individual reasons given:

1. He had been flogged for leaving without permission.
2. The same reason.
3. The same reason. Also, he ran away because he was hungry.
4. He had been put in jail for getting drunk.
5. He had run away previously and had been flogged three times.
6. He was hungry. He absconded previously and, when he returned voluntarily, he was given twenty-five lashes.[2]
7. He was frightened at seeing how his friends were always being flogged.
8. Because . . . of the great hunger he felt.[3]
9. When he wept over the death of his wife and children, he was ordered whipped five times by Father Antonio Danti.
10. He became sick.
11. His wife and one son died.
12. Because of hunger; also, he was put in the stocks while sick.
13. He wanted to go back to his country.
14. His wife, one son, and two brothers died.

[2] Nos. 1–6 inclusive are from a letter by Gutiérrez at Monterey, March 7, 1836, Prov. St. Pap. Ben. Mil., 81:44. Note that these incidents occurred after secularization when the mission (San Antonio) was in charge of an administrator.

[3] Nos. 7–8 from a *relación* by Argüello *et al.*, San Francisco, Aug. 9, 1797, Prov. St. Pap., 16:71. These Indians were new converts and ran away in a body shortly after conversion. They also participated in armed resistance to parties sent out to bring them back.

15. His wife and a son had run away to their country, and at the mission he was beaten a great deal.
16. Because of a blow with a club.
17. They beat him when he wept for a dead brother.
18. He went to see his mother.
19. His mother, two brothers, and three nephews died, all of hunger, and he ran away so that he would not also die.
20. Lorenzo went away.
21. His father died.
22. Being bad, they whipped him.
23. His wife sinned with a rancher, and the priest beat him for not taking care of her.
24. They made him work all day without giving him or his family anything to eat. Then, when he went out one day to find food, Father Danti flogged him.
25. His wife and two sons died, and he had no one to look after.
26. His little niece died of hunger.
27. He was very hungry.
28. After going one day to the presidio to find food, when he returned, Father Danti refused him his ration, saying to go to the hills and eat hay.
29. When his son was sick, they would give the boy no food, and he died of hunger.
30. Twice, when he went out to hunt food or to fish, Father Danti had him whipped.[4]

Much of the above-cited Indian testimony will obviously be heavily discounted. Several of the accusations are absurd, and many of the reasons advanced are trivial and irrational. Yet they ring true to the primitive psychology of the Indian, as most persons who have had dealings with this and similar races will admit, and they merit at least a fair examination.

If we examine the opinions expressed by competent white observers, we find that they exhibit a uniform trend. They all ascribe Indian aversion to mission life to love of liberty, distaste for their surroundings, longing for their native home, or revolt against all forms of restraint or compulsion. In other words, the white man, thinking of the Indians as a group, conceives their responses in terms of pure abstractions. These abstractions are those in which his own thoughts are likely to be cast. In the early nineteenth century the rights of man and human liberty were dominant among politico-social ideas. Hence the emphasis laid on them by the white commentators.

The Indian neophyte, on the other hand, possessed no such philosophical background nor such a ready-made system of concepts to which he might refer his condition and his actions. The new convert had no comprehension of liberty as opposed to servitude or slavery because he had known only one type of social status and had no basis for comparison

[4] Nos. 9–30 were with the same group as Nos. 7–8. Argüello, "Relación," San Francisco, Aug. 12, 1797, *ibid.*, p. 74.

with anything else. Furthermore, aside from small family or tribal affairs he had never encountered a situation which demanded expression in terms of abstract social concepts. Consequently, when called upon to give an account of his reasons for a specific line of conduct, he was totally unable to go beyond the concrete events of daily life. We must, therefore, regard Indian testimony as rationalization of underlying discontent in terms of sharp personal experience with definite environmental factors. Viewed in this light, Indian testimony makes sense. Moreover, it is no longer incompatible with the testimony of the white man. Both groups approach the same solution of the problem, but they approach it by different pathways and in different modes of expression. Where the Frenchman or the American assigns love of liberty as the cause for flight or resistance, the Indian says he ran away because he was put in jail. Where the white man talks about slavery, the Indian says he objected to being made to work by some individual, for instance, some particular father in the mission.

From the statements given here and many more which might be adduced certain factors emerge as possessing definite weight in the mission environment. The most important, and yet by far the most difficult to assess, is that called loss of liberty, by which is meant the restriction of the Indians' freedom of action, particularly with respect to the freedom they had previously enjoyed. Under the missions they were under no greater physical restraint or social compulsion than many civilized groups today; yet with their background the loss of personal license was a severe blow. Perhaps the best analogy is not that of slavery, which implies rigorous physical exactions, but captivity.

To summarize some of the foregoing discussion it may be stated that, apart from demographic changes, the missionized Indians responded to their environment primarily by numerous individual attempts to escape from it, or to resist it, in the physical sense. One group of factors which was at least partially responsible for the observed response was associated with the spatial restrictions imposed by the missions. In particular one may distinguish within this group: (1) emotional or material resistance to any type of compulsory conversion; (2) the emotional tendency to return to the familiar ancestral habitat which we have termed "homesickness"; (3) a revolt against overaggregation in the missions which ran counter to a centripetal drive on the part of the Indians or urge to reestablish the pristine, lower population density; and (4) a probable resistance to any confinement, especially to the custom of mass incarceration of both sexes at night. Further resolution of the components in this group of factors might be achieved if an exhaustive study were attempted.

In spite of individual differences arising from personal experiences or political bias all observers, not only those cited above but others as well, are agreed with respect to certain essential points. There can be no doubt that the standard working week consisted of from 5 to 6 days at 6 to 8 hours per day, let us say, 30 to 40 hours per week. Nowhere do we find any claims that more than 40 hours were required, except under extreme provocation. The actual tasks were those characteristic of rather primitive agriculture and strictly home industry. Much of this work would be classed today as light labor. It is very significant that even the bitterest opponents of the missions never accused the clergy of giving the Indians work which might cause either excessive fatigue through extremely long hours or physical injury through intense exertion and occupational hazard. The worst they could do was the charge that pregnant women were too severely treated. There is no doubt that by modern standards the work was very reasonable both as to hours and nature. . . . We may conclude immediately therefore that, as far as the adult neophyte was concerned, he was not obliged to perform labor which could in any way be injurious physically in either the individual or racial sense.

The only possible exceptions were the pregnant women and the children. Respecting the latter, all presidial commanders are in agreement that nothing more arduous was required of them than a little gardening and bird chasing. Overburden of pregnant women would be a serious charge, were it not for the fact that because of the low birth rate, as well as for religious reasons, the missionaries were exceedingly anxious for pregnancies and deliveries to be successful and would be most unlikely to jeopardize the issue. Finally, it must be remembered that in the California "Arcadia" no one did any really strenuous work, and what would be regarded by the Spanish white population as onerous labor would have been considered quite ordinary by the average American of the period. The purely physical effects of manual labor may therefore be dismissed as a factor effective in the racial disintegration of the mission Indian.

The mental and moral aspects of labor, however, belong in an entirely different category. The compulsion placed on the Indian, the restriction upon his daily activity through obligatory physical effort is important. But it is not the whole story. His reaction to labor itself, in the abstract, must be considered, since mental or bodily exertion of the type demanded by white civilization was completely new to him. It constituted an environmental factor, of the nonmaterial type, with which he had never come in contact and which therefore required an emotional and intellectual readjustment or adaptation very difficult for him to make. Labor, with its associated complex system of rewards and penalties, has perhaps constituted a more serious obstacle to the racial reorientation of the Indian than brutal but quite comprehensible physical conflict. We may focus attention on the aspect of compulsion in labor among the mission Indians, keeping continually in the background the idea that labor in any form was alien to their disposition, their social heritage, and their biological environment.

Despite innumerable lamentations, apologies, and justifications, there can be no serious denial that the mission system, in its economics, was built upon forced labor. Any cooperative system of support, any organization which is economically self-sustaining, as were the missions, must of necessity be founded upon the productive toil of its members. This very necessity is the primary compulsion, but if the corporate members are of sufficient intelligence, the compulsion becomes rationalized and there is an appearance of willingness and volition. On the other hand, if the mass is stupid and ignorant, then the hierarchy of authority at the top must exercise force, moral or physical, to obtain the essential effort on the part of the mass. Compulsion then becomes personal, and we begin to speak of "forced labor." Thus in its essence the mission system predicated forced labor by the neophytes. Understanding all this, the missionary fathers did their utmost to enlighten the neophytes, but with little success. The next step was moral suasion, and it must be admitted that, in general, such measures were adequate. When, however, they failed, physical means became necessary,[5] for the economic discipline of the community had to be maintained at all costs. It was very natural that many neophytes, not in the least comprehending the ideals of the Church and its servants or the complexities of administrative theory, should regard necessary "forced labor" as directed personally at themselves and should rebel against it. On the other hand, it is noteworthy that of all the complaints and grievances of the neophytes, relatively few were directed against the work itself.

.   .   .

Turning now to a more fundamental aspect of the labor problem, we observe that the California tribes shared with other Indians the characteristic, or the vice, of whole-hearted aversion to physical labor. Whether the labor was compulsory or voluntary, the Indian—at least at the time of his first contact with the white man—preferred not to perform it. Hence he has been universally termed lazy and indolent. Now there is very little to be gained by applying opprobrious epithets to a race or a group without analyzing, at least in a cursory fashion, the reasons for such inherent traits as call forth the epithets.[6]

In their wild state the Indians underwent extensive physical exertion.

[5] The term slavery has been uncritically applied to the mission social system. It should be pointed out that there was no implication of personal ownership whatever. Furthermore, in theory always, and in practice usually, the fruit of Indian labor was devoted to the welfare and improvement of the Indian himself. Any selfish enrichment of the mission was incidental and contrary to the tenets of the Church. The system was much closer to socialism or communism, in the Marxian sense, than slavery.

[6] A very restrained description of mission-Indian work habits is the following, taken from Lasuén's "Representación": ". . . besides those who have escaped or are away on leave, the sick and their caretakers. Those who are well are prone to offer some indisposition as a pretext, knowing that they are generally believed and that even in case of doubt the missionary always excuses them from work. Nobody hurries them; they sit down, they lie down and often leave to return whenever they see fit. When they work by the job [tarea] they are permitted to leave it unfinished and others, generally the majority, are urged not to exceed it. These tareas are customarily very moderate so that without more than the time necessary for common work and with only a little less indolence or with fair activity many are able to finish a whole day's work in the morning, and in three or four days that of a whole week to obtain recompense and have the rest of the time free."

Even in California, where life was easier than in the eastern forests or on the central plains, much hard work was devoted to the obtaining of food, whether through fishing and hunting or by gathering acorns, nuts, and other plant materials. The processes involved in preparing the food were likewise laborious and tedious. Furthermore, the building of shelters and the manufacture of clothing, utensils, and weapons demanded much time and effort. No Indian group ever survived a year in a state of complete indolence and inactivity. Indeed, among numerous tribes extraordinary exertions and hardships were necessary for simple survival. It is therefore inaccurate to assume that the Indian disliked to work simply because muscular exercise was involved. He disliked it because of the conditions under which it was performed. The whole basis of the aboriginal labor system was the idea of intermittent effort rather than steady, consistent exertion. This, in turn, was associated with the facts that, first, the food supply was highly seasonal and, second, no preparative measures were required. The fish ran at a certain time, the acorns were ripe in a definite month. Hence the native worked hard to accumulate these materials when they were available. He strove mightily and without stint for a brief period. Then he rested and loafed until his environment demanded another expenditure of energy. Even the women, upon whom devolved the domestic tasks, operated on much the same basis. Hence there was developed a tremendously powerful tradition of labor only when necessity demanded. There was no concept of continuous effort over a long period of time, directed toward a consistent production of commodities or an end to be achieved in the relatively distant future. In a sense the Indian style and method of labor was admirably adapted to his environment and to the needs of his way of life.

Now, place him in a so-called civilized environment, surrounded by a race with an utterly different tradition, that of the value of labor performed throughout the year. In order to conform to the new type of culture he is forced—in the widest sense—to alter his inherited method of work. Whether in a mission, on a reservation, or as an independent agent he is obliged to work every day, a certain number of hours, at tasks the immediate value of which are obscure to him. Since he sees no direct necessity for ploughing the wheat field or weeding the vegetable garden, he feels no internal compulsion to perform these tasks. He is thus regarded as lazy and improvident, and pressure is brought to bear from without. Since he cannot appreciate the value of the work, it becomes irksome to him, and he resents the pressure which forces him to do it. In other words, he tends to carry over into the new environment the habits of thought and the methods of labor which served him adequately under aboriginal conditions. As a result, not only the external compulsion but the labor itself acts as a stimulus which generates negative or adverse responses.

At this point a vicious cycle, similar to those already discussed, begins to form. In response to disinclination toward the new type of labor and to either impersonal economic compulsion or personal moral and physical pressure, the mission Indian takes one of two courses. He exercises passive resistance by stalling or "soldiering" on the job or by malingering and inventing all sorts of excuses for not working. Alternatively, he avails himself of the flight mechanism and runs away. No matter which course he adopts, he is regarded by the white race, clerical and secular alike, as indolent, improvident, and exasperatingly oblivious to his true economic welfare. To correct this failure in racial, social, and environmental adjustment, the missionaries, soldiers, and civilians respond by doing exactly the worst possible thing under the circumstances; increasing the extent and severity of the pressure, which in turn forces a little more labor from the Indian but also intensifies his own trend toward refusal to work or toward escape.

(Thus we see in seventy years of mission experience an irreconcilable conflict between the inborn, almost instinctive tendency of the Indian to work in his ancient way and the necessities of the European and American economic system.) Although, urged by compulsion of various categories, the Indian did perform a great deal of labor, this native, original tendency was substantially unaltered. Its tenacity was demonstrated by the fact that, when all compulsion was withdrawn at secularization but the opportunity for volitional labor and self-support was provided, the neophytes reverted in a body to their ancestral methods and disintegrated completely as an economic unit. As individuals, they either returned to the wild life among the heathen or subsisted miserably upon the thin charity of the white men, indulging in manual labor only to ward off acute, absolute starvation.

Apart from the strictly mission enterprise, as well as including it, the California Indian race proved itself a total failure as far as the labor system was concerned. From the point of view of population changes the race was doomed to severe depletion, if not extinction, in free competition with the whites simply because it could not sufficiently rapidly and successfully adapt itself to the labor system basic to white economy. This in turn is referable to the inherent attitude of the Indian toward consistent, long-continued physical exertion, an attitude built up through generations of adjustment to the wild environment, not to any genetically ingrained moral turpitude or reprehensible intellectual backwardness.

.   .   .

[The Indian's inability to adjust to the demands for his labor was paralleled by his] offenses against Spanish mission society through failure to conform to its specific or general requirements or through overt acts contrary to its interests. Here would be included all forms of fugitivism, apostasy, refusal to complete set tasks, conspiracies to overthrow the existing regime, theft or destruction of army or mission property (as contrasted with the robbery of personal goods), and finally armed opposition to the missionaries, soldiers, or even civilians. In short, the political offenses committed by the neophytes were of the same species as are perpetrated by every racial, political, or religious group which is at odds with the governing order at the time. Furthermore, it was as difficult for the Indian as for the members of any other repressed group to perceive the immorality or essential sinfulness of his behavior. His reaction to chastisement for such acts was a normal, healthy resentment, directed chiefly against the individuals who were personally instrumental in applying the chastisement, whom he endowed, by extension, with responsibility for all his woes, of whatever nature.

Punishment for offenses of both criminal and political categories was often carried out by the soldiers, in particular by imprisonment. This was natural, since the only quarters for confinement were in the presidios. Furthermore, the secular arm was entrusted with authority over ordinary criminal delinquencies. Moreover, actual military operations and expeditions were carried on by the armed forces. Since these frequently resulted in punishment meted out to gentiles as well as to renegade neophytes for acts of war or insurrection, stock stealing, and general raiding of the frontier, the soldiers functioned in a disciplinary capacity for the entire community. For these reasons it is difficult as well as unnecessary to dissociate the presidios and missions with respect to crime and punishment among the Indians.

.   .   .

The type of disciplinary measures was frequently degrading and offensive to the Indian. Corporal punishment, or flogging, was of course standard practice in the eighteenth century among all white civilizations, particularly when used upon so-called inferior races. Nevertheless it has been singularly ineffective for, unless the physical effects are so terrific as to break down utterly the spirit of a man, the result is usually to inspire him with an undying, implacable hatred, which in turn communicates itself to all his friends. Imprisonment, or other curtailment of liberty, if properly carried out, does not result in bodily harm, and is much more dreaded by a race to whom freedom means the breath of life. It was therefore unfortunate that the lash was so quickly resorted to by the Spanish administration and applied with such severity. . . .

Granting that discipline was often necessary and inevitable and that it took the form, as a rule, of confinement and whipping, we must inquire as to the extent and severity of the punishment inflicted. Quite obviously disciplinary measures of a conservative type, inflicted fairly and justly without personal spite for offenses generally conceded to be flagrant, would not be likely to affect the mass of the neophytes as adversely as irrational chastisement, administered for no good cause, in excessive amount, or by cruel methods. Now it so happened that this particular point was seized upon by the enemies of the mission system (both at the time and subsequently) as an argument against the missionaries. Consequently, the verbal testimony, from documentary sources, is conflicting in the extreme. In fact, some of the generalities set forth by the missionaries on the one hand and by some of the military men and civilians on the other are mutually exclusive. Moreover, individual cases have been cited which, perhaps, may have occurred but which alone by no means prove any rule.

Retention of Customs and Religion

Apart from law and language there exists in any society, primitive or otherwise, a vast body of traits which may for convenience be grouped under the terms customs and religion. Herein will be included the entire complex of beliefs, myths, and superstitions, on the one hand, and, on the other, the activities associated with them, such as costumes, rites, dances, ceremonies of all kinds, together with the necessary social structure for their administration. Needless to add, the entire group life is based upon and bound up in this interlocking set of traits. Furthermore, as the experience of centuries has demonstrated, it is extremely difficult to eradicate such traits from the collective mind of any human racial unit, and if the process is successful, it will probably be accompanied by the spiritual and intellectual disintegration of that unit. A people may achieve adaptation to a new physical environment, they may overcome obstacles of war, economics, and pestilence, but they are very likely to retain a considerable amount of their original nonmaterial culture.

The mission Indians appear to have been no exception to the general rule, despite the fact that great and peculiar difficulties were placed in their path. Over most of the continental United States, there was no spiritual conflict of serious magnitude between the white race and the Indians. This was due principally to the lack of interest shown by the whites. They literally did not care what the Indians believed, thought, or did, provided none of their own interests were affected. To be sure, a few ineffectual attempts at religious conversion have been attempted, and the modern Indian Service has tried to promote some education among the red men, but no wholesale, serious effort has ever been made to eradicate and destroy the aboriginal culture as inimical to civilized society. The Spanish missions were very different. Based entirely upon the premise of total conversion to orthodox Christianity, it was vitally necessary to extirpate those individual beliefs and tribal customs which in any way whatever conflicted with the Christian religion. Not only did this necessity apply to the doctrinal sphere, but it also extended to the administrative. The missionaries needed to erase, not only pagan or idolatrous tenets of belief, but also external manifestations like ceremonial rites. Not only did many gentile customs have to be suppressed, but, more important, all persons had to be eliminated who, under the gentile system, had exercised the slightest spiritual authority. Since the missionary was a spiritual as well as material dictator, it would have been fatal to his regime to permit any competition on the part of native strong men of the shaman class. The operation of the mission system, therefore, involved an immediate, powerful restriction on the social and intellectual expression of the Indians comparable with those previously discussed which affected liberty, space, diet, and sex relations. One might expect that the responses to this restriction would follow the same lines of resistance or escape as characterized the other types of restriction. Although this was doubtless true to some extent, the situation was modified by certain factors which did not operate in the other cases.

The first of these was the possibility of a new avenue of escape. Physical, spatial confinement could be enforced by purely corporal methods. Spiritual confinement, so to speak, provided the Indian was genuinely obdurate, could not be enforced at all. It was impossible to prevent the converted gentile from thinking of his folkways, from respecting the fellow neophyte who was a former shaman, from clandestinely carrying on his ancient ceremonies. Nor could the missionary prevent the Christian mother from passing on to her child the unforgotten lore and tradition of the tribe. The most elusive, the most tenacious thing in the social order of the world is tradition, which can be kept alive in the face of the bitterest persecution and which constitutes a region into which the most oppressed can always escape with impunity.

The second factor was the form of the Christian religion. It is no accident that Catholicism has been uniformly successful among primitive peoples. Its effective, simple dogma can be readily taught to minds of limited comprehension, and its system of observances can be dramatized so as to appeal to the primitive emotion. Moreover, the proselyting orders in the New World, through their vast experience were wonderfully adept at presenting their religion in its most attractive form. Christianity, therefore, i elf provided a line of escape from the restriction placed on the older gentile spiritual culture. It was the hope of the clergy that the Indians would all avail themselves of this resource, and it is to their credit that so many did. In theory, there was not a complete restriction but a redirection, a recanalization of social and emotional energy. Unfortunately, the process, actually, was too swift, too sudden, to be complete. The Indian mentality was too fixed and rigid to give ground, to make the shift and adapt itself within one or even two generations. Consequently, in many instances, the effect was one of absolute restriction rather than an easy redirection.

To what extent the course of conversion was complete—using conversion to imply conversion in the whole way of life rather than in the limited theological sense—can be judged only by those records of the missions which give evidence of tendencies to retain or revert to aboriginal custom. These records include only statements of opinion and overt acts of sufficient consequence to require official attention.

Concerning the general question of the retention of primitive belief and custom by the neophytes, we have two very authoritative sources. The first is Boscana, that thorough student of Indian religion. He says,[7] "Superstitions of a ridiculous and most extravagant nature were found associated with those Indians, and even now in almost every town or hamlet the child is first taught to believe in their authenticity." The second source is the "Contestación" of 1811. One of the questions asked was whether the neophytes adhered to their former customs. Six missions replied, the statements being unanimous that great tenacity in this respect was to be observed. Several other questions concerned specific cultural traits; the answers to these were, likewise, without exception in the same tenor. In fact, I know of no competent contemporary authority

[7] Geronimo Boscana, *Chinigchinich*, translated by Alfred Robinson, edited by P. T. Hanna (Santa Ana, 1933), p. 61.

who vouchsafed the unqualified assertion that the neophytes had to a significant degree given up the primitive customs and superstitions.

.   .   .

Assimilation of Christianity

Although, as has been stated, the Indian did not "surrender his ways" in order to substitute for them the introduced ritualism and religion, there is no a priori reason to assume that he may not have added some of the latter to his own system. The two are not mutually exclusive, as are Indian law and European law. Christianity of a sort can be superposed on a substratum of cultism and ceremonialism and indeed, in the long run, it can be incorporated with the primitive system.

.   .   .

. . . Did the mission group really assimilate Christianity to the extent that it in any way altered their belief or their spiritual equipment? This is an exceedingly difficult question to answer, and in fact probably cannot be answered at all. Obviously, there are no objective criteria; mere observance of form is no valid index to the spiritual motive behind the actions. Written opinion is untrustworthy, since it was difficult for a contemporary to go below the surface and since at that period every observer was influenced by racial, national, and religious prejudices. For manifest reasons the missionaries were prone to be optimistic concerning the success of their spiritual endeavors, although they did deplore the extent to which apostasy showed itself. Most of the Protestant Americans were contemptuous of both the missionaries and neophytes and suffered from a tendency toward extreme superficiality in their observations. It is probably best to attempt no categorical answer but to suggest that the neophytes must have absorbed a great deal of the form and spirit of Christianity. Moreover, it is highly probable that the ceremonial of the Catholic Church went far toward satisfying the innate love of the Indian for ritual.

.   .   .

If the concept of assimilation of religion by fusion is valid, it follows that racial conflict in this particular cultural sphere was resolved by adaptation in the reverse sense. That is, the primitive group adapted the introduced culture to fit its own mold, rather than changed its own culture to conform to the other. The pattern of religion, therefore, constitutes a noteworthy exception to the usual rule in the relations between the mission Indian and the white man.

In summary, it becomes evident that with respect to cultural factors the interracial contact or conflict led to quite different results, depending upon the degree to which a given cultural factor involved material relationships. In the field of personal relationships, laws and codes of behavior, the two systems were mutually exclusive and irreconcilable. For purely pragmatic reasons, the Indians were forced to make a rapid and very difficult adaptation which cost them dear in lives and suffering. With respect to religion (in its most general sense), ceremonialism, and shamanism, the opposite was true. Despite the most intensive moral suasion and pressure, the Indians retained the basic pattern of their culture intrinsically unaltered. Indeed, they went so far as to adopt and modify Christianity and to incorporate it in such a way as to conform to their own manner of thought. In this one respect, therefore, the Indians achieved an adaptational success, which stands unique in their history.

2. FONT'S DIARY

FRAY FATHER PEDRO FONT

The Spanish missionaries regarded their activities in California in a considerably different light from Professor Cook's point of view. Father Pedro Font, an eighteenth-century missionary and historian, describes mission life at Mission San Gabriel. In his description, the reader can discern Font's attitude toward the Indians and his feelings about the usefulness of the missionary effort.

After dinner I went with Father Sánchez to see the creek from which they made the acequia [a water ditch] for this mission of San Gabriel, and with which it has the best of conveniences. For, besides the fact that the acequia is adequate, and passes in front of the house of the fathers and of the little huts of the Christian Indians who compose this new mission (who must be some five hundred souls recently converted, counting large and small), it dominates all the plains of the immediate vicinity, which are suitable for planting or for crops, and for this reason the fields are near the pueblo. This mission has such fine advantages for crops and such good pastures for cattle and horses that nothing better could be desired. The cows which they have are very fat and they give much and rich milk, with which they make cheese and very good butter. They raise hogs and have a small flock of sheep, of which on our arrival they killed three or four wethers which they had. Their flesh was especially good, and I do not remember having eaten fatter or finer mutton. They also have a few hens.

The mission has plentiful live oaks and other trees for building timber, and consequently there is abundant firewood. It lacks only lime, which up to the present has not been found; but perhaps by careful search it will be found and will make possible the improvement of the buildings, which at present are partly adobe, but chiefly of logs and tule, and which for this reason are very insecure and exposed to fire. At present the buildings consist of a very long shed, all of one room with three divisions, which serves as a habitation for the fathers and for a granary and everything. Somewhat apart from this building there is a rectangu-

FROM Fray Father Pedro Font, "Diary of an Expedition to Monterey by Way of the Colorado River, 1775–1776," in Herbert E. Bolton (ed.), *Anza's California Expeditions* (Berkeley: University of California Press, 1933), Vol. IV, pp. 177–182. Reprinted by permission of The Regents of the University of California.

lar shed which serves as a church, and near this another which is the guardhouse, as they call it, or the quarters of the soldiers, eight in number, who serve the mission as guard; and finally, some little huts of tule which are the houses of the Indians, between which and the house of the fathers the acequia runs.

In the creek celery and other plants which look like lettuce, and some roots like parsnips, grow naturally; and nearby there are many turnips, which from a little seed which was scattered took possession of the land. And near the site of the old mission, which is distant from this new one about a league to the south, there is grown a great abundance of watercress, of which I ate liberally. In short, this is a country which, as Father Paterna says, looks like the Promised Land, although the fathers have suffered in it many hardships and toils, because beginnings are always difficult, especially in lands where formerly there was nothing; and besides, they suffered want because for two years the supplies failed them.

The converted Indians of this mission, who are of the Beñemé tribe, and also of the Jeniguechi[1] tribe, appear to be gentle, friendly, and of good hearts. The men are of medium stature, the women being somewhat smaller, round-faced, flat-faced, and rather ugly. The costume of the men in heathendom is total nakedness, while the women wear a bit of deer skin with which they cover themselves, and likewise an occasional cloak of beaver or rabbit skin, although the fathers endeavor to clothe the converted Indians with something as best they can.

The method which the fathers observe in the conversion is not to oblige anyone to become a Christian, admitting only those who voluntarily offer themselves, and this they do in the following manner: Since these Indians are accustomed to live in the fields and the hills like beasts, the fathers require that if they wish to be Christians they shall no longer go to the forest, but must live in the mission; and if they leave the ranchería, as they call the little village of huts and houses of the Indians, they will go to seek them and will punish them. With this they begin to catechize the heathen who voluntarily come, teaching them to make the sign of the cross and other things necessary, and if they persevere in the catechism for two or three months and in the same frame of mind, when they are instructed they proceed to baptize them.

The routine for every day is as follows: In the morning at sunrise Mass is regularly said; and at it, or without it if none is said, they assemble all the Indians. The father recites with all of them the Christian doctrine, which is concluded with the *Alabado*, which is sung in all the missions and in the same key. Indeed, the fathers sing it even though they may not have good voices, since uniformity is best. Then they go to eat their breakfast of *atole*, which is given to everybody, making the sign of the cross and saying the *Bendito*[2] before eating it. Afterward they go to work at whatever they can do, the fathers encouraging them and teaching them to labor by their example. At noon they eat their *pozole*, which is made in community for all, and then they work for another

---

[1] The Beñemé (Benyemé) and Jeniguechi are both classed by ethnologists as Serranos.

[2] Grace or Blessing.

spell. At sunset they again recite the doctrine and conclude by singing the *Alabado*.

The Christians are distinguished from the heathen in that an effort is made to have them go somewhat clothed or covered, so far as the poverty of those lands will permit. And in distributing the *pozole*[3] account is not taken of the catechumens unless it be that they are given some of what is left over. If any Indian wishes to go to the mountain to see his relatives or to hunt acorns, they give him permission for a specified number of days. As a rule they do not fail to return, and sometimes they come bringing some heathen relative, who remains for the catechism, either through the example of the others or attracted by the *pozole,* which they like better than their herbs and the foods of the mountain; and so these Indians are usually caught by the mouth.

The doctrine which is recited in all the missions is the short one of Father Castaño,[4] followed with complete uniformity, no father changing a single word or being permitted to add anything to it. It is recited in Castilian even though the fathers may be versed in the native tongue, as is the case at the mission of San Antonio, whose father minister, Fray Buenaventura Sitjar, understands and speaks well the language of the Indians of that mission. Nevertheless the doctrine is recited in Castilian, and although the father translated the doctrine into the native language,[5] the most that is done is to recite once each day in the vernacular and once in Castilian, thus conforming with what so many times has been ordered since the first Mexican Council, as is set forth by Señor Solózano, to the effect that the Indians shall be taught the doctrine in Castilian, and that effort shall be made to have them speak Castilian, since all the languages of the Indians are barbarian and very lacking in terms.

In the missions an effort is made to have the large unmarried girls sleep apart in some privacy. In the mission of San Luís[6] I saw that a married soldier served as the majordomo of the mission, thus giving the father some relief, while his wife looked after the unmarried girls, they being under her care and calling her *maestra.* In the daytime she had them with her, teaching them to sew and other things, and at night she locked them in a room where she had them secure against any insult, and for this reason they called them the nuns. This appeared to me to be a good arrangement.

In short, this method which the fathers observe in those new missions appeared to me to be very good; and I may note that what is done in one

[3] *Atole* is a name used in Cuba and Mexico for a sort of gruel made of ground maize or corn meal. In Perú it is called mazamorra. *Pozole* is an Aztec name for a porridge or stew made of barley, beans, or other ingredients.

[4] The reference is evidently to Father Bartolomé Castaño. In 1840 Juan Romualdo Amaro printed in Mexico the *Doctrina Extractada de los Catecismos Mexicanos de los Padres Paredes, Carochi y Castaño, autores muy selectos: traducida al Castellano para mejor instrucción de los Indios, en las Oraciones y Misterios principales de Doctrina cristiana.* I have not learned the exact title of the work by Castaño on which this catechism is based.

[5] *Vocabulario de la Lengua de la Mision de San Antonio* (New York, 1861).

[6] San Luís Obispo.

is done uniformly in the others, which is what pleased me most. The mission of San Diego is an exception. Here, since it is the poorest, and the country, because of its few villages, does not permit it, there are no common fields or even private ones, nor is *pozole* distributed there in common. There the Indians have been permitted to live in their rancherías with the obligation to come to Mass on Sundays in their turn, the same as is done in Baja California; and this is the reason why this mission is so backward, aside from the fact that its Indians are the worst of all in those new missions.

3. BLACK PIONEERS: THE SPANISH-SPEAKING AFROAMERICANS OF THE SOUTHWEST

JACK D. FORBES

The Afroamerican role in Western history has been largely overlooked by historians. In the Hispanic and Mexican periods, blacks played many and diverse roles in California. Professor Jack D. Forbes of the University of California at Davis comments upon the many positive contributions of the Afroamericans in early California. One might note that the pattern of the black man's life in the far West differed from his role elsewhere in the nation.

The story of the Negro American or Afroamerican has often been neglected in the past by historians. Recent years, however, have witnessed a proliferation of books on Negroes, especially with regard to their relationship to the Anglo-American slave system, Reconstruction, and the struggle for civil rights. Nevertheless, it is very likely that the subject of Spanish-speaking Negroes will remain shrouded in obscurity for several reasons: because it is known only to a few specialists; because it presents an image of the Afroamerican which might be disturbing to those who wish to be able to present simple generalizations about the place of Negroes in United States history; and because of a fear of publicity being given to the fact that appreciable amounts of Negro blood have seeped into the white population by means of old first families in Florida, Louisiana, Texas, California and elsewhere.

It is not yet clear when the first African Negroes arrived in the Americas, but by the 1520's mainland North America had its first African settlers, in central Mexico and the Carolinas. Thereafter, many different kinds of Africans participated in the expansion of the Spanish Empire, including olive-skinned Muslims from North Africa and darker West Africans. In addition to these persons, there were many Spaniards of part-African ancestry, a heritage of the earlier Muslim conquest of Spain, and

Jack D. Forbes, "Black Pioneers: The Spanish-Speaking Afroamericans of the Southwest," *Phylon: The Atlanta University Review of Race and Culture* (Fall 1966). Reprinted by permission of the publisher.

more recent Spanish-Negro and Indian-Negro hybrids from Haiti, Borin-quen (Puerto Rico), Cuba, and Jamaica.

Africans appeared in Mexico in the earliest days of the Spanish con-quest and soon were numerous enough to stage rebellions and to form rebel bands.[1] They also were recruited into most Spanish expeditions, as members of which they had penetrated into the Southwest by the 1530's. Perhaps the most famous Negro Southwesterner is Estevan, a Muslim who accompanied Álvar Núñez Cabeza de Vaca from Texas to Sinaloa and then became the first non-Indian known to have entered Arizona and New Mexico in 1539. Later that same year, the Vásquez de Coro-nado expedition gathered together many Negroes to travel through Ari-zona, New Mexico, Texas, and probably Oklahoma and Kansas. As a result of this enterprise, Negroes became the first non-Indian settlers in New Mexico and, possibly, Kansas.[2]

Still other early Southwestern expeditions had Negro contingents (as did the Francisco de Ibarra party in 1565), while the Alarcón group which explored the Colorado River in 1540 possessed at least one Muslim of unknown color. Further, the Bonilla de Leyva-Umaña Expedi-tion left one mulatto woman among the Indians in Kansas in the 1590's.[3] More significant, however, were the many Africans who served in Central Mexico and became the ancestors of an extensive Afro-American progeny now estimated to compose about 10 percent of the genetic heritage of the modern-day Mexican population.[4]

Very few Spaniards of European lineage were available to populate newly conquered regions and this task fell primarily to Hispanicized na-tives, mixed-bloods of all kinds, and Negroes. During the seventeenth century persons of African ancestry were present in New Mexico as colo-nists or soldiers, apparently, and mulattos or Eurafricans were fre-quently utilized as majordomos in Spanish missions.[5] Early descriptions

---

[1] In 1537, Spanish soldiers had to crush a revolt by Negro miners at the mines of Amtepeque. See George P. Winship, "The Coronado Expedition, 1540–1542" in Fourteenth Annual Report of the Bureau of American Ethnology, p. 380.

[2] *Ibid.*, p. 379; George P. Hammond and Agapito Rey, *Narratives of the Coro-nado Expedition 1540–1542* (Albuquerque, New Mexico, 1940), pp. 262, 270, 306–7; and Gerónino de Zarate Salmerón, "Relaciones de todas las cosas, que en el nuevo Méjico se han visto," Virreinato de Menco, Madrid, I, 567.

[3] Baltasar de Obregón, *Obregon's History* (tr. and ed. by George P. Hammond and Agapito Rey, Los Angeles, 1928), pp. 156, 161; Salmerón, *op. cit.*, 567; Herbert E. Belton, *Spanish Exploration in the Southwest* (New York, 1916), p. 201; and Hammond and Rey, *Coronado Narratives*, pp. 134–54.

[4] Harold E. Driver, *Indians of North America* (Chicago, 1961), p. 602.

[5] When civil war broke out in New Mexico in 1640–1643, one faction was said to be composed of *mestizos* and mulattos. Subsequently, the same general fac-tion was said to include "mestizos and sambahigos, sons of Indian men and Negroes, and mulattos." In 1680, Pueblo Indian rebels were aided by "con-fident coyotes, mestizos and mulattoes" who were able to fight on horseback and with guns as well as any Spaniard, Patronato 244, Ramo VII, Archivo General de Indias, Sevilla, Spain; Jack D. Forbes, *Apache, Navaho and Span-iard* (Norman, Oklahoma, 1960, pp. 127, 135, 138–39, 180); and Charles W. Hackett, *Revolt of the Pueblo Indians and Otermin's Attempted Reconquest, 1680–1682* (Albuquerque, New Mexico, 1942), II, 322, 329, 337–39, 355.

of the population of Spanish towns in Durango, Chihuahua, Sinaloa and elsewhere invariably mention mulattos, and here and there an individual is specifically identified, as when a mulatto traveled from the Hopi villages to southern Arizona in 1720.[6]

Many men of African ancestry were recruited into the Spanish armed forces and, in 1744, the Marquis de Altamira wrote that many garrison troops along the northern frontier and especially in Texas "are not Spaniards, but of other inferior qualities, and [are] ordinarily vicious. . . ." In 1760, Pedro de Labaquera asserted that most of the frontier soldiers were mulattos of low character and without ambition.[7] These mixed-blood soldiers, however, were absolutely essential and many of their descendants were able eventually to achieve prominence.

In 1774 a royal official asserted that the Hispano population of northern Mexico was of Negro, Indian and European ancestry and were so intermixed as to make it difficult for anyone to trace their ancestry.[8] Nevertheless, Spanish census records continued to enumerate race or color until about 1800. Some interesting trends deserve comment, however.

In general, as the status of a person improved, his race changed. He might begin life as a Negro, pure or otherwise, and end life as a mulatto or Eurafrican, *mestizo* or Eurindian, or even as *Español*. Race, therefore, was not definite by the late eighteenth century and many people were of such a mixed character that they were simply *de color quebrado*, that is to say, "all mixed up." Finally, ethnic designations came to be of little value in determining actual ancestry, since, for example, the child of a Spaniard and a *mestizo* usually was called a Spaniard and the child of a mulatto and an Indian was often called a mulatto. Thus many persons classified as *Español* in the census records were not pure-bloods and many mulattos were actually part-Indian.[9]

Some insight into the racial characteristics of the Spanish-speaking Southwest can be gained, however, from an examination of the situation in California. Mulattos serving in several capacities accompanied the first expeditions which occupied San Diego and Monterey in 1769. For example, Juan Antonio Coronel was a leather-jacket soldier (*soldado de*

[6] How the mulatto got to the Hopi villages is a mystery. See Juan Antonío Baltasar, "De nuevos progresos . . . de la Pimería Alta" in *Apostólicos Afanes* (Mexico, 1944), p. 339.

[7] Marquis de Altamira al Virrey, Biblioteca del Ministerio de Hacienda (Madrid, 1744), 975; and Charles E. Chapman, *History of California, the Spanish Period* (New York, 1921), p. 203.

[8] "Reflexiones sobre el reyno de nueva españa," virreinato de mexico, II, Biblioteca del Museo Navae, 568, Madrid.

[9] I normally prefer to use the term "eurafrican" for a Negro-Caucasian mixed-blood, but "mulatto" will be used in this paper in order to avoid implying that such mixed-bloods possessed only Negro and Caucasian ancestry. The term "mestizo" will likewise be used to refer to Indian-Spanish hybrids, although I have often used the term "eurindian" in other papers. "Eurindian" again implies a rather precise type of hybrid, while the *mestizos* of California were not always of Indian-Spanish ancestry alone.

cuero) while several other Eurafricans served as muleteers. Still other part-African soldiers came with the first expeditions, or soon afterwards.

It is not surprising that California was subdued by Spanish troops of mixed origin. Persons of Negro ancestry had participated in most or all of the early sea expeditions along the Pacific coast, and during the eighteenth century they formed a substantial part of Baja California's population. In 1790, for example, there were 844 non-Indians in that province, 243 of whom were classed as *Españoles*, 183 as mulattos, and 418 as *castas, i.e.*, miscellaneous mixed-bloods. Thus, persons of recorded African ancestry constituted 21.7 percent of the population, while other mixed-bloods composed 49.4 percent and *Españoles* equaled 28.9 percent. Altogether, 71.1 percent of the Spanish-speaking settlers were officially of mixed origin and they formed large colonies at the mines of Santa Ana (157 mulattos, 204 *castas* and 133 *Españoles*) and the provincial capital at Loreto (158 *otras castas*, 10 mulattos, and 73 *Españoles*).[10]

These figures are comparable to the combined statistics for both California and Baja California in 1794, which reveal that of 1,469 Spanish-speaking persons 23.2 percent were *de color quebrado, i.e.*, part-African, and 29.3 percent were *mestizos*. Adding these together, 52.5 percent of the Hispanos were of officially recorded mixed origin.[11] That more than one out of every five persons in Baja California in the 1790's was of part-Negro origin may come as a surprise, but, in addition, it is probable that many persons classified as Spaniards or *castas* also possessed some degree of African background. In any case, many settlers from the peninsula brought their African ancestry with them to Upper California after 1769, and still other part-Negro persons were recruited in northern Sinaloa and Sonora. For example, the Juan Bautista de Anza expedition of 1775 included seven mulattos of the twenty-nine men, or approximately one out of four.[12]

More revealing, however, are census records for individual communities and districts within California. A list of the first settlers in Los Angeles in 1781 includes the following Afro-American and part-African families.

1. Antonio Mesa, Negro, 36, from Los Alamos; married to Ana Gertrudes López, mulatto, 27; two children: Antonia María, 8; and María Paula, 10
2. Manuel Camero, mulatto, 30, from Chiametla; married to María Tomasa, mulatto, 24
3. José Nabarro (Navarro), *mestizo*, 42, from El Rosario; married to

[10] "Censo y castas . . . 1790," C-A 50, p. 64 (Bancroft Library, Berkeley). Juan Antonio Coronel was classed as a mulatto by Father Serra. See Herbert E. Bolton (tr. and ed.), *Palon's Historical Memoir of New California* (Berkeley, 1926), III, 33.
[11] "Resumen General de la Población de Ambas Californias," July 13, 1795, C-A 50, p. 148 (Bancroft Library).
[12] "Padrones y extractos . . . ," C-R 9, Carton 3 (Bancroft Library).

María Rufina Doretea, mulatto, 47; three children: José Maria, 10; José Clemente, 9; and Maria Josefa, 4

4. José Moreno, mulatto, 22, from Rosario; married to Guadalupe, mulatto, 19

5. Basilio Rosas, *indio*, 67, from Nombre de Dios, Durango; married to María Manuela Calistra, mulatto, 43; six children: José Maxino, 15; Carlos, 12; Antonio Rosalino, 7; José Marcelino, 4; Esteban, 2; and Maria Josefa, 8

6. Luís Quintero, Negro, 65, from Guadalajara; married to Petra Rubio, mulatto, 40; five children: María Gertrudes, 16; María Concepcion, 9; Thomás, 7; Rafaela, 6; and José Clemente, 3

The total population of Los Angeles in 1781 consisted of forty-six persons, of whom twenty-six were African or part-African. Thus the Afro-American percentage was 56.5.

The process of intermarriage, whereby the Negro stock was being absorbed, is revealed by the above list of settlers. Two of the adult males were classified as Negro, but their wives were mulattos and their children, therefore, also were mulattos; it should be borne in mind that the wives could have possessed Indian ancestry in addition to some Caucasian background. One of the adult males listed above was an Indian, while another was a *mestizo*. In both cases, the wives were mulattos and the nine children, or 19.5 percent of the population, were Indian-Negro-Caucasian hybrids.

An examination of all of the families in Los Angeles reveals the following marriage pattern:

Negro-Mulatto—2 families
Indian-Indian—2 families
Mulatto-Mulatto—2 families
Español-Indian—2 families
Mestizo-Mulatto—1 family
Indian-Mulatto—1 family
Indian-*Coyote**—1 family

Of the eleven Los Angeles families, seven involved some degree of intermarriage and hybridization, while two involved persons already of hybrid ancestry. Only the two all-Indian marriages failed to involve the process of race mixture.[13]

By 1790, some significant changes had occurred in Los Angeles. The total population had increased to 141, of whom 73 were classified as *Españoles*, 39 as *mestizos*, 22 as mulattos and 7 as Indians. These figures are inaccurate, however, because many of the original settlers of 1781 had experienced a change of race in the intervening years. The following list illustrates this process:

* *Coyote*—¾ Indian, ¼ Caucasian.
[13] *Ibid.*

Name	Race in 1781	Race in 1790
Pablo Rodríguez	Indian	*Coyote*
Manuel Camero	Mulatto	*Mestizo*
José Moreno	Mulatto	*Mestizo*
María Guadalupe Pérez	Mulatto	*Coyote*
Basilio Rosas	Indian	*Coyote*
José Vanegas	Indian	*Mestizo*
José Navarro	*Mestizo*	*Español*
María Rufina Navarro	Mulatto	*Mestizo* (or Indian)

The changes in racial classification were all away from Indian or mulatto and towards *Español, i.e.,* everyone acquired some fictitious Caucasian ancestry and shed Negro backgrounds—becoming, in effect, lighter as they moved up the social scale.

This process had undoubtedly taken place among the individuals who were newcomers to Los Angeles in 1790, but the census data are not at hand to ascertain their earlier classifications. In any case, by correcting those inaccuracies of which we are aware, the part-African population is increased from twenty-two to thirty-two, or 22.7 percent.

The post-1781 settlers in Los Angeles included the following part-African families.

1. José Ontiveras, *mestizo,* 47, from Real del Rosario; married to Anna María Carrasca, mulatto, 36; one child, Maria Encarnacion, mulatto, 7

2. Santiago de la Cruz Pico, *mestizo,* 60, from San Javier de Cavasón; married to Jasinta de la Bastida, mulatto, 53; two children living with them: Javier, mulatto, 23; and Patricio, mulatto, 27

3. Domingo Aruz, *Español,* 43, from Gerona, Spain; married to Gertrudis Quintero, mulatto, 26; two *mestizo* children of a previous marriage: José and Domingo; three children of present marriage: Martin, mulatto, 7; José, mulatto, 14; and Domingo, mulatto, 12

4. Francisco Reyes, mulatto, 43, from Pueblo of Spotlãn; married to María del Carmen Dominguez, *mestiza,* 23; three children: Antonio Faustin, mulatto, 4; Juana Inocencia, mulatto, 3; and José Jasinto, mulatto, 2

5. Faustino José de la Cruz, mulatto, from San Blas, age 18; not married

These families, of course, illustrate the complex process of hybridization. Significantly for an understanding of the place of the part-Africans in California society, Francisco Reyes became the *alcalde* or mayor of the community, and the descendants of Santiago Pico became prominent political leaders and wealthy ranchers.

Of the twenty-five families whose characteristics can be ascertained from the 1790 census, the following marriage pattern can be derived:

Español-Español—7 families
Español-Mestizo—4 families

Mestizo-Mulatto—4 families
Español-Coyote—3 families
Indian-Indian—2 families
Mulatto-Mulatto—2 families
Español-Indian—1 family
Español-Mulatto—1 family
Indian-Mulatto—1 family

Fourteen of the twenty-five families involved new forms of hybridization, while only nine families were composed of persons classified as nonhybrids. This latter figure must be regarded with skepticism, however, as the following census entry indicates:

> José Sinova, *Español*, 40, from Mexico City; married to María Gertrudes Bohorquez, *mestiza*, 28; *Sus hijas españolas* (their Spanish daughters): Josefa Dolores, 12; Casilda de la Cruz, 9; Maria Julia, 4; and Maria Sefernia, 1

Thus many persons classified as *Español* were actually the progeny of *Españoles* and *mestizos*, and were, therefore, at least one quarter Indian.[14] Many may also have been part-Negro, because a census summary of 1792 reduced the number of *Españoles* in Los Angeles from 73 to 59, while the mulatto class increased from 22 to 57, the total population increasing from 141 to 148. In 1792, therefore, the recorded part-Africans constituted 38.5 percent of the population of Los Angeles.[15]

The records of Santa Barbara, California, are of considerable interest also, especially in view of the contemporary romanticized interest in the Spanish heritage evident in that community. In 1785, Santa Barbara possessed the following Afro-American families and individuals:

1. José Gonzalez, mulatto, 35; married to Tomasa, mulatto, 13
2. Felipe Moreno, mulatto, 46; married to Loreta, Indian, 22
3. Josef Hores, *Español*, 33; married to Maria de la Concepción, mulatto, 14; one child
4. José Orchaga, mulatto, 29; married to María, *Española*, 21; two children
5. José Patiño, mulatto, 35; married to María Victoria, *Coyota*, 28
6. Agustín Leyva, mulatto, 45; married to María Guadalupe, *Española*, 42; five children
7. José Velarde, mulatto, 40; married to Juliana, Indian, 45
8. José Ontiveras, *mestizo*, 39; married to Ana María, mulatto, 34; two children
9. Eugenio Valdés, *Español*, 30; married to Sebastiana, mulatto, 19; two children
10. Joaquin Rodríguez, *mestizo*, 25; married to Catarina, mulatto, 20; one child

[14] "Padrón de Los Angeles," August 17, 1790, C-A 5, 159–64 (Bancroft Library.)
[15] "Estado del Censo y Castas," December 31, 1792, C-A 50, pp. 103–04 (Bancroft Library).

11. Rosalino Fernández, mulatto, 28; married to Juana, mulatto, 22; three children
12. Mariano Pina, mulatto, 25; single
13. José Cisneros, mulatto, 26; married but wife not with him
14. José Acevedo, mulatto, 30; single
15. Luciano Masauegas, mulatto, 30; widower
16. Jose Lorenzo Valdés, *lobo*, 19; single (A *lobo* was apparently an Indian-Negro mixed-blood, perhaps with some Caucasian ancestry.)

Of the 191 persons in Santa Barbara whose racial identity is given in the census, at least thirty-seven, or 19.3 percent, were part-Negro, while more than one half were officially classified as non-Spanish (Indians, *mestizos* and *Coyotes*). The marriage pattern is as follows:

Español-Español—17 families
Español-Mestizo—5 families
Español-Mulatto—4 families
Español-Indian—3 families
Mulatto-Mulatto—3 families
Mestizo-Mestizo—3 families
Indian-*Coyote*—2 families
Mestizo-Mulatto—2 families
Mulatto-Indian—2 families
Mulatto-*Coyote*—1 family
Indian-Indian—1 family
Mestizo-Coyote—1 family
Español-Coyote—1 family.

Of these forty-five families, only twenty-four failed to involve new hybridization, while only eighteen possessed unmixed lineages.

During the years from 1785 to 1792, a strong tendency existed at Santa Barbara, as elsewhere, to reclassify many mixed-bloods as *Español*. Thus, in spite of a 25 percent increase in the total population during those years, the number of non-Spaniards remained uniform.[16]

The census for San José in 1790 includes the following Afroamericans:

1. Antonio Romero, 40, *pardo,* from Guadalajara; married to Petra Acevez, 28, *parda;* one son (*Pardo* refers to an Indian-Negro-Caucasian mixed-blood, the progeny of a mulatto and a *mestizo.*)
2. Manuel Gonzalez, 70, Indian, from Valle de San Bartolo (Durango); married to Gertrudis Acevez, 20, *parda;* two sons of ages 18 and 13 (by a previous marriage, one must assume)
3. Bernardo Rosales, 46, mulatto, from Parras (Durango); married to Mónica, 28, Indian; four children
4. Manuel Amesquita, 38, mulatto, from Terrenate (Sonora); married to Graciana, 26, mulatto; four children

[16] "Padrón de la población de Santa Barbara," C-A, 50, pp. 6–10, and "Estado del Censo y Castas," December 31, 1792, C-A 50, p. 103 (Bancroft Library).

5. Antonio Acevez, 50, mulatto, from San Bartolomé (Durango); married to Feliciana Cortes, 50, *mestiza;* two children

The marriage pattern among the settlers at San José was as follows:

Español-Español—6 families
Pardo-Pardo—1 family
Coyote-Indian—1 family
Indian-*Pardo*—1 family
Mulatto-Indian—1 family
Mulatto-Mulatto—1 family
Mestizo-Español—1 family
Indian-*Español*—1 family
Mulatto-*Mestizo*—1 family
Indian-Indian—1 family

Of the fifteen families, only seven did not involve hybridization or hybrid lineages. Of the total number of settlers at San José in 1790, 24.3 percent were part-Negro and 55.5 percent were non-*Español*. Four years later the part-Negro proportion had been reclassified to form only 14.2 percent, while the non-*Español* had increased to 59.5 percent, thus indicating that some *pardos* and mulattos had become *mestizos*.[17]

Similar developments occurred at Monterey, where, in 1790, the mulattos constituted 18.5 percent of the population and the *castas* constituted an additional 50.2 percent. The latter group included part-Negroes as well as *mestizos*. The total non-*Español* proportion at Monterey was 74.2 percent of the population. Within one year, however, at least twenty-eight non-*Españoles* were reclassified as *Españoles* in the Monterey region.[18]

The 1782 census for San Francisco, listing only adult males, includes the following Afroamericans:

1. J. A. Amesquita, 43, mulatto, from Metape
2. Ignacio Linares, 37, mulatto, from Orcasitas
3. Justo R. Altamirano, 37, mulatto, from Aguage
4. Juan A. Vásquez, 47, mulatto, from Agulalco
5. Antonio Aceves, mulatto, from San Bartolomé (at San José in 1790)
6. Felipe Tapía, 37, mulatto, from Culiacán

The 1790 San Francisco census amplifies upon the above by new individuals:

1. Nicholas Galindo, 47, *mestizo*, from Real de Santa Eulalia (Durango); married to María Teresa Pinto, 34, mulatto; six children
2. José Maria Martinez, 35, *mestizo*, from Tapague (Sonora); married to María Garcia, 18, mulatto

[17] "Padrón de Vecinos de San José," October 5, 1790, C-A 50, pp. 61–64, and "Padrón del Pueblo San José," December 31, 1794, C-A 8, p. 91 (Bancroft Library).

[18] "Estado que manífiesta el número de Vasallo y habitantes," December 31, 1791, C-A 50, p. 101 (Bancroft Library).

3. José Acevez, 26, mulatto, from San Bartolomé (Durango); single
4. Pablo Acevez, 18, mulatto, from Culiacán; single

Some examples of reclassification can be noted. For example, Ignacio Linares changed his status from mulatto to Indian between 1782 and 1790. This might not seem particularly advantageous, but it made it possible for his son, Ramón Linares, and eight other children to be *mestizos*, since his wife, Gertrudis Rivas, was an *Español*. The status of *mestizo* was evidently preferable to that of mulatto.

The marriage pattern in San Francisco in 1790 was as follows:

Español-Español—11 families
Español-Mestizo—6 families
Mestizo-Mulatto—2 families
Español-Indian—1 family
Español-Mulatto—1 family
Indian-Indian—1 family
Mestizo-Indian—1 family
Mestizo-Mestizo—1 family

One half of the families, therefore, involved hybrid lineages or new hybridization. Of the total population, at least 14.7 percent possessed Negro ancestry, while 47.2 percent were classified as non-*Español*.[19]

It is very difficult to synthesize all of the various records cited above, for often the same categories are not utilized. Nevertheless, an estimate is provided here of the racial character of Spanish-speaking California in 1790, excluding San Diego:

Españoles	364	
Mestizos and *Coyotes*	127	
Mulattos	127	
Indians	60	
Pardos	16	
Castas	106	(includes *mestizo* and other mixtures)
Unknown	4	
Total	804	

It can be seen that persons of part-Negro ancestry constituted at least 17.7 percent of the population, and, in addition, the *Castas* group, or 13.1 percent, undoubtedly included many Afroamericans. Altogether, 54.8 percent of the Spanish-speaking Californians were classified as non-*Español*, although, of course, the true percentage would be much higher if it were possible to trace the various lineages back for several generations.

Conservatively, we can estimate that at least 20 percent of the Hispano-Californians were part-Negro in 1790, while probably 25 percent of the Hispano-Baja Californians possessed African ancestry.[20] Subsequent additions to the population of Spanish-Mexican California probably did

[19] "Padrón de San Francisco," August 21, 1782, C-R 9, Carton 3, and "Padrón de San Francisco," October 2, 1790, C-A 50, pp. 86–90 (Bancroft Library).
[20] See earlier summary of Baja California population.

not alter greatly the genetic heritage of the Californians, since the bulk of later immigrants were Mexicans of mixed ancestry. After about 1800, their racial character is no longer recorded but of a group of twenty-two convicts sent north in 1798, four, or 18 percent, were mulattos, six were Indians and eight were *mestizos*.[21]

The physical appearance of the Spanish-speaking Californians did not, however, remain static. From the earliest intrusion of Spanish settlers in 1769, intermarriage with native Indians was encouraged both by the Spanish government and by a dearth of Spanish-speaking women.[22] Over the years, therefore, the immigrants became more Indian, genetically speaking. In addition, the Spanish-speaking people of Caucasian, Indian and Negro ancestry steadily mixed their stocks so as to produce what amounts to a new race.

Nonetheless, the upper-class Hispano-Americans were a color-conscious people, and they were very interested in keeping track of racial ancestry. Otherwise they would not have invented so many different terms to refer to various kinds of mixtures. This race-consciousness was greatly modified in practice, however. Necessity may have forced a Spaniard to marry a mixed-blood, Negro or Indian in cases where eligible girls were rare or absent. In addition, the Crown encouraged such mixture by allowing wealthy non-Spaniards to purchase "purity of blood" certificates; for example, a pardo could become a Spaniard in 1795 for 500 *reales*.[23]

Reference has already been made to persons becoming *Español* simply by attaining sufficient status in their own community. After about 1800 the California census records no longer enumerated persons by race, perhaps because the mixtures had become so complex and because it would be impolitic to offend so many people by reminding them of their non-Spanish origins.

All of the foregoing examples of race mixture, however, should not deceive the reader into believing that California was a racial paradise. Even when a person had achieved the official status of *Español*, his color, if dark, could be a handicap. The historian, Charles E. Chapman, noted that the *gente de razón* (Spanish-speaking citizens):

> were in fact of varying shades of color. The officers and missionaries were for the most part of pure white blood, but the great majority of the rest were mestizos—part white and part Indian. In the Los Angeles district there were some mulattoes. . . . There were very marked social differences, based on rank (usually military) and

[21] "Lista de reos para poblar la Peninsula de Californias," February 12, 1798, C-A 10, p. 89 (Bancroft Library). The names of the mulattos were Juan José de la Luz Hernandez, José Leonicio Calzada, Casimiro Cornejo and José Francisco Pablo.

[22] Letter of Branciforte to Borica, June 4, 1797, C-A 8, p. 449 (Bancroft Library); and Herbert Eugene Bolton, *Anza's California Expeditions* (Berkeley, 1930), V, 104.

[23] Real Cedula, February 10, 1795, C-A 8, pp. 182–83 (Bancroft Library).

blood, and very distinctly there was a Spanish Californian aristocracy.[24]

Aside from his understating the extent of Negro ancestry, Chapman's statement is quite correct and is confirmed by R. H. Dana's observations in 1835:

Those who are of pure Spanish blood, having never intermarried with aborigines, have clear brunette complexions, and sometimes, even as fair as those of English-women. There are but few of these families in California, being mostly in official stations, or who, on the expiration of their offices, have settled here upon property, which they have acquired; and others who have been banished for state offenses. These form the aristocracy, intermarrying, keeping up an exclusive system in every respect. They can be told by their complexions, dress, manner and also by their speech; for calling themselves Castilians, they are very ambitious of speaking the pure Castilian language, which is spoken in a somewhat corrupted dialect by the lower classes. . . .

From this upper class [of pure Spaniards], they go down by regular shades, growing more and more dark and muddy, until you come to the pure Indian who runs about with nothing upon him but a small piece of cloth, kept up by a wide leather strap round his waist. Generally speaking, each person's caste is decided by the quality of the blood, which shows itself, too plainly to be concealed, at first sight. Yet the least drop of Spanish blood, if it be only of quadroon or octoroon, is sufficient to raise them from the rank of slaves and entitles them to a suit of clothes, boots, hats, cloak, spurs, long knife, all complete, and coarse and dirty as may be—and to call themselves Españoles, and to hold property, if they can get any. . . .[25]

The possession of non-Caucasian ancestry was not, of itself, enough to constitute a barrier quite as rigid as Dana would seem to indicate. An ambitious dark-skinned man might marry a light-skinned girl and produce progeny who eventually could intermarry into the "white" upper class. This latter group was not really a pure-blood caste and enough dark features appeared occasionally to allow for the acceptance of a wealthy or powerful mixed-blood.

Such indeed is the history of the Pico family, which in many ways can serve as an example of the way in which Negro genes eventually come to be dispersed widely among the "elite." The founder of the family in California, Santiago Pico, was a *mestizo*, while his wife was a mulatto. His sons, José Dolores, José María, Miguel, Patricio, and Francisco rose in stature by acquiring property and serving as soldiers. It was the next generation, however, which really acquired prominence; Pio Pico served as the last governor of Mexican California and Andrés Pico was a leader of the California resistance to the United States in 1846–47. This latter

[24] Chapman, *op. cit.*, pp. 384, 395.

[25] Richard H. Dana, *Two Years Before the Mast* (New York n.d.), pp. 72–73.

generation intermarried with many prominent *Español* families, such as
the Alvarados and Carrillos, and non-Caucasian genes were widely dispersed. José Dolores Pico produced 13 children and had over 100 descendants by 1869. Miguel Pico had 228 descendants by 1860 and the
other Picos usually could boast an average of 10 children per generation.
Many prominent "white" Californians today are descendants of the
Picos, including some who boast of the "purity" of their "Castilian" ancestry.

The change from Spanish to Mexican rule which occurred in 1822
helped to ease the situation for mixed-bloods. Many Mexicans began to
take pride in possessing vague quantities of indigenous ancestry, and
several governors were dark-complexioned. Manuel Victoria (1831–
1832) was described as a Negro, and José Figueroa (1833–1835) was
of Aztec ancestry. Nevertheless, the upper class in California had not
come to fully accept racial equality before the arrival of a contrary influence.[26]

Beginning in the 1820's, European and Anglo-American men began to
settle in California and to marry Spanish-speaking women. For various
reasons they tended to select mates from the more prosperous and
lighter-skinned California families. This had several effects: (1) it
began to lighten the color of the aristocracy still further; (2) prejudice
against darker skin color was reinforced; and (3) knowledge of Indian
or Negro ancestors was gradually suppressed. After the United States
conquest, violently racist attitudes were introduced into the region and
the Spanish-speaking Californians, quite naturally, disassociated themselves from their hybrid past. Thus commenced, incidentally, the creation of the racial mythology which is part of California's contemporary
culture.

In spite of the above, African racial characteristics soon disappeared
in California because the vast majority of the Spanish-speaking population intermarried freely. One of the last general references to Negroid
features is found in a statement by an Anglo-American visitor in 1828
who felt that a Mexican corporal "resembled a negro, rather than a
white." [27] Other pre-1848 visitors failed to note the presence of Negro
characteristics and, in fact, by the 1830's, only newcomers of Afro-
American ancestry were thought of as Negroes.[28]

Entering the state at about the same time as the Anglo-Americans and
Europeans referred to above were a number of Negroes of non-Mexican
origin. The first of these was Bob, left by a Yankee ship, the *Albatross*, in
1816. On August 16, 1819, he was baptized at Santa Barbara as Juan
Cristóbal and thereafter disappeared into the California population. A
number of other Negroes arrived in 1818—among them being Fisher or

---

[26] The color-complex was strong enough so that upper-class California women
were allegedly averse to associating with the *gobernador Negro* Victoria. This
tradition may, however, be a later invention. Hubert Howe Bancroft, *California Pastoral* (San Francisco, 1888), I, 284.

[27] James Ohio Pattie, *Personal Narrative* (Cleveland, 1905), p. 221.

[28] For example, Bancroft states that there were only two Negroes in California
in 1831. *Op. cit.*, p. 283.

Norris, who later left California, Mateo José Pascual, called a Negro or a mulatto, and a United States Negro named Francisco. In the same year, another Negro, Molina, was residing at Monterey.[29]

Subsequently, other Afroamericans came to California with Anglo-American groups and some became prominent in regional affairs; for example, Jim Beckworth's escapades as a mountain man, guide and horsethief, and Allen G. Light's service as *comisario-general* for Governor Alvarado in 1839. Occasional references also appear in regard to Spanish-speaking Negroes, as in 1831 when a female slave was brought to California from Peru and from 1838 to 1844 when Ignacio Miramontes, a Negro, served as corporal of the San Francisco garrison.[30] The bulk of these later Afro-American settlers would appear to have been absorbed into the Mexican-Californian population and they certainly experienced less discrimination than is evident in California today. It should be emphasized that there were almost no slaves of African ancestry in Hispano-Mexican California—only two are known for the entire period under discussion. The balance of the people whose names have been mentioned were soldiers or ex-soldiers, or civilian settlers, while a handful were servants or convicts.

California's Afro-American pioneers were fortunate in being able to live in a society where color was not an absolute barrier. In such civilian settlements as Los Angeles and San José especially, persons of Negro ancestry were able to rise to prominence and occupy positions of leadership. The rapid process of miscegenation allowed their children to win acceptance simply as *Californios* and their granddaughters frequently intermarried with incoming Angloamericans or Europeans. Their blood now flows in the veins of many thousands of Californians who cannot speak Spanish and who are totally unaware of their African heritage.

It is to be hoped that this survey of the importance of the Negro heritage in California and the Southwest will stimulate further research. Moreover, it is to be hoped that the story of Negroes in North America will be expanded to include those Afro-American pioneers whose descendants are not called Negroes but instead are intermixed with all of us.

[29] Hubert Howe Bancroft, *History of California* (San Francisco, 1890), II, 230–31n, 232n, 237, 248, 277, 722.

[30] *Ibid.*, IV, 91, 741; and *California Pastoral*, I, 283, 617. The rank of corporal was an important one in the Hispano-Mexican armed forces.

Chapter 2

Gold, Statehood, and the Arrival of the Immigrants, 1846–1876

The acquisition of California and the Southwest in 1846 added a new dimension to the history of minorities in the United States. With the signing of the Treaty of Guadalupe Hidalgo, which ended the war with Mexico, many thousands of Mexicans in the Southwest (including 10,000 *Californios*—descendants of the original Spanish and Mexican settlers) became American citizens. With this treaty, these new Americans were, theoretically at least, to be allowed to retain their traditional ethnic identity. Although the *Californios* constituted a majority of the population throughout much of this period, they soon were forced to accept a second-class role in political and economic affairs.

This transfer of power resulted from a number of forces during the period of 1846–1876. The decline of the *Californios* cannot be explained by the Treaty of Guadalupe Hidalgo and the first state constitution of 1850, both of which guaranteed the Mexican-Americans their property, civil rights, and religion. Instead, the rapid growth of "Anglo" power came as a result of differences in values and in life-styles and of American mastery of the political and judicial institutions of the state. The growth of Anglo power in California and the concomitant loss of power by the *Californio*, although his rights were officially guaranteed, present an interesting prelude and parallel to events in the post-Reconstruction South. It was there that the only other major national minority group experienced the same decline after the 1870s.

Two years after the Americans acquired California, the discovery of gold stimulated a world-wide migration to the American West. The experiences of minority immigrants seeking their fortunes are part of the exciting history of the mining period of the Golden State. Among these newcomers were Chinese, Japanese, Hawaiians, South Americans, and Europeans. These minorities found that the American miners used a variety of methods, both legal and extralegal, to wrest the vast mineral wealth to the advantage of the Anglos.

Perhaps the most tragic of all the minorities in California during this generation was the original American, the Indian. As was mentioned in Chapter 1, the decline of the Indian started during the Mexican period. By 1876, however, the decline had accelerated to such a degree that the Indian was virtually a vanishing race. This tragic development was a result of a number of factors. Among these were conflicts with the army, economic exploitation, governmental rapacity and mismanagement of Indian reservations, and the Indian's inability to adapt to the new competitive Anglo culture.

An often overlooked minority in California and the West at this time is the Negro. Only recently have the major sources of popular Western history—television and the motion picture—rediscovered the Negro's role in the West. Yet a study of the period indicates that black Americans participated in most of the major activities of historical interest in this era—mining, cattle ranching, and military service. Newly emerging sources such as frontier Negro newspapers indicate that the number of Negroes present was not insignificant.

The reader might consider the following questions when examining the selections in this chapter. How and why did the Americans gain dominance over the economy, the institutions, and society of the newly won West? How did the treatment of minorities in California anticipate the nativism and the abandonment of the Southern Negro in the rest of the United States after 1876? Why have minorities been overlooked in Western history?

4. ARTICLE IX, THE TREATY OF GUADALUPE HIDALGO, 1848

The Treaty of Guadalupe Hidalgo, 1848, was drafted by Nicholas Trist to settle the war claims resulting from the Mexican-American War. Accomplishing the cessation of the war, the treaty also established new boundaries for the American West and brought thousands of Mexicans into the United States as full-fledged citizens. The citizenship rights of these new and often overlooked Americans mentioned in Article IX of the Treaty included freedom of religion, property rights, and rights to partial home rule in their communities. The selection describes these rights in the Treaty's original form.

Article IX

The Mexicans who, in the territories aforesaid, shall not preserve the character of citizens of the Mexican republic conformably with what is stipulated in the preceding article, shall be incorporated into the Union of the United States, and admitted as soon as possible, according to the principles of the federal constitution, to the enjoyment of all the rights of citizens of the United States. In the mean time they shall be maintained and protected in the enjoyment of their liberty, their property, and the civil rights now vested in them according to the Mexican laws. With respect to political rights, their condition shall be on an equality with that of the inhabitants of the other territories of the United States, and at least equally good as that of the inhabitants of Louisiana and the Floridas, when these provinces, by transfer from the French republic and the crown of Spain, become territories of the United States.

The same most ample guaranty shall be enjoyed by all ecclesiastics and religious corporations or communities, as well in the discharge of the offices of their ministry, as in the enjoyment of their property of every kind, whether individual or corporate. This guaranty shall embrace all temples, houses, and edifices dedicated to the Roman catholic worship, as well as all property destined to its support, or to that of schools, hospitals, and other foundations for charitable or beneficent purposes. No property of this nature shall be considered as having become the property of the American government, or as subject to be by it disposed of, or diverted to other uses.

Finally, the relations and communication between the cat[h]olics living in the territories aforesaid, and their respective ecclesiastical authorities, shall be open, free, and exempt all hindrance whatever, even although such aut[h]orities should reside within the limits of the Mexican republic, as defined by this treaty; and this freedom shall continue, so long as a new demarkation of ecclesiastical districts shall not have been made, conformably with the laws of the Roman Catholic church.

5. HONEST AND GLORIOUS

EDWIN F. KLOTZ

Dr. Edwin F. Klotz, a Hispanic scholar, presents a traditional interpretation of the Treaty of Guadalupe Hidalgo and the rights granted to Mexican-Americans by the document. Dr. Klotz states that Mexican-Americans were not guaranteed the right to bilingual status, which contradicts the statements of the new generation of Mexican-American militants. This matter of loss of identity through the loss of one's language or inability to master the new official language, English, is a recent and heated issue in the Southwest.

It seems proper at this point to review some questions frequently posed today which refer to the Treaty of Guadalupe Hidalgo. It is sometimes said that the Treaty "guaranteed" bi-lingual conditions in those areas ceded to the United States. Yet neither the Treaty, nor any of its draft proposals ever referred directly to "language" as one of the rights to be retained by those Mexicans who chose to remain in the ceded territories. Buchanan advised Trist in his private instruction of April 15, 1847, that if the Mexicans insist upon including an article referring to personal and property rights that he should insert in the Treaty an article similar to that of Article 3 of the Louisiana Treaty of 1803:

> The inhabitants of the ceded territory shall be incorporated in the Union of the United States and admitted as soon as possible, according to the principles of the federal constitution, to the enjoyment of all the rights, advantages, and immunities of citizens of the United States; and in the meantime they shall be maintained and protected in the free enjoyment of their liberty, property and the religion which they profess.

The reader will note that the original Article IX of the Treaty dealt at length with this question. But when the American Senate ratified the Treaty they scratched this article and inserted what was essentially the same article as in the Treaty of 1803.

.   .   .

Neither did the Mexican negotiators ever mention anything as definite as "protection" of their language in the ceded areas, although Pacheco did lament in his instructions to the delegation that without some sort of understanding and protection of those citizens divested of Mexican citizenship, "they will become strangers in their own country."

The original intention of Article 3 of the Louisiana Treaty (mentioned in the *Protocol*) may throw some light on the deliberations between the

Dr. Edwin F. Klotz, "Honest and Glorious," *El Tratado de Guadalupe Hidalgo 1848 (The Treaty of Guadalupe Hidalgo)* (Sacramento, California: Telefact Foundation, 1968). Copyright 1968 Telefact Foundation, 2416 Sloat Way, Sacramento, California.

contracting parties. Barbé-Marbois, who negotiated the treaty for Napoleon, remarks that Napoleon himself prepared Article 3, so interested was the Emperor in those Louisiana Frenchmen. The following passage, says Marbois, is from "the journal of negotiations" and is evidence of Napoleon's zeal to preserve French culture in that area destined to become American.

> Let the Louisianans know that we separate ourselves from them with regret; that we stipulate in their favour every thing that they can desire, and let them hereafter, happy in their independence, recollect that they have been Frenchmen, and that France, in ceding them, has secured for them advantages which they could not have obtained from a European power, however paternal it might have been. Let them retain for us sentiments of affection; and may their common origin, descent, language, and customs perpetuate the friendship.

Moreover, when the French Commissioner Laussat officiated at the exchange of sovereign powers on November 30, 1803, he issued a proclamation which read in part: "The Treaty secures to you all the advantages and immunities of citizens of the United States. The particular government, which you will select will be adapted to your customs, usages, climate and opinions."

Since Article IX of the Treaty of Guadalupe Hidalgo is identical with that of the Treaties of 1803 with France and of 1819 with Spain, we can say that the issue of language was left up to those newly incorporated citizens under the protection of the U. S. Constitution. Since our Federal Constitution is mute on the subject of language, the issue becomes one of tradition, or of States Rights. Bilingualism followed similar paths in Louisiana, Florida and California. Article XI, Section 21, of the 1849 California Constitution gave Spanish equal importance with English. But this section was abolished 30 years later with the adoption of the Constitution of 1879. The "guarantee" of bilingualism, therefore, flows from the freedoms guaranteed by the U. S. Constitution and not from those Treaties. We should cite specifically the 9th Amendment, "The enumeration in the Constitution, of certain rights, shall not be construed to deny or disparage others retained by the people," and the 10th Amendment, "The powers not delegated to the United States by the Constitution, nor prohibited by it to the states, are reserved to the states respectively, or to the people."

Another controversial issue today concerns property claims in some parts of the West which are traced to the Treaty of 1848. The reader will note that the United States Senate suppressed Article X of the Treaty of 1848 dealing with property in Texas for the simple reason that the Congress felt they had no responsibility for property changes after 1836 and Texan independence. The *Protocol* signed by Sevier and Clifford at Querétero explaining this and other changes by the Senate assured the Mexicans that all legitimate titles would be adjudicated in the courts.

It is true that little effort was made to resolve questions of land titles in the New Mexico and Colorado areas until the late 1880's (although a claims court was established in California in 1851). At that time a delegation of prominent people, led by Governor Prince, went from New Mexico to Washington to demand action. Soon the issue became a *cause celebre*, and on July 2, 1890, President Benjamin Harrison transmitted documents relative to the claims to the U.S. Senate with the message that, "The United States owes a duty to Mexico to confirm to her citizens those valid grants that were saved by the Treaty (of Guadalupe Hidalgo) and the long delay which has attended the discharge of this duty has given just cause for complaint." [1] Bills were accordingly introduced in both Houses of Congress to establish a court of private land claims for those areas. On July 28, 1891, a legal notice appeared in the Washington Post, in both English and Spanish, that such a Court had been established by Congress. In 1897 the United States Supreme Court handed down numerous decisions relative to those very questions which some agitators are raising today by invoking the Treaty of 1848.[2]

Another question sometimes raised by those who wish to rewrite history is whether the off-shore islands north of the boundary agreed to in the Treaty still belong to Mexico! Article 5 of the Treaty specifically mentions a distance of three leagues extending off the shore into the Gulf of Mexico, yet says nothing about the Pacific side of the California coast. This apparent oversight has led some to claim that Mexico still has claims to these islands. But in fact, the absence of language only enforces the intention of the signers of the Treaty.

The documents prepared by Cabrera on this question, as well as Dr. Bowman's careful research, leave little question that the Mexicans intended to cede all lands north of the established boundary, "one marine league" south of San Diego. The real concern of the Mexican, once the American "Ultimatum" was accepted, was the need for a land corridor between the State of Sonora and Baja California. The 32nd parallel would have cut off Baja from Sonora at the Colorado River. When the boundary was established at one league south of San Diego, this protected Mexican trade routes. Nothing was said about the off-shore islands north of that point simply because it was understood that such islands would henceforth belong to the United States. Dr. Bowman notes that the maps used by the negotiating parties were detailed and clearly identified all islands belonging to Mexico at that time. . . . Lastly, the *Exposicion* of the Mexican peace commissioners make it overwhelmingly clear that it was their intention to divest themselves of those lands and islands which they were unable to defend. There is no reason to suspect,

[1] There is a bulky file in the Archives of the Mexican Ministry of Foreign Affairs which deals at length with this subject and apparently collected by the Mexican Ambassador in Washington. (Asuntos varios; ano 1890, III / o/o (73)/3 Sobre propriedad de terrenos de particulares en Nuevo Mexico, Colorado, etc.)

[2] A document on this subject, containing a list of Court Cases, has recently been published: *Guadalupe Hidalgo, Treaty of Peace, 1847,* and *the Gadsen Treaty with Mexico, 1853,* Tate Gallery, Truchas, New Mexico, P.O. Box 428 (87578).

(as Dr. Bowman also concludes) that failure to mention the islands in the Treaty was an oversight.

· · ·

Conclusion

"The historian cannot change the course of events. . . . He must judge them with a manly spirit, distinguishing what happens to be unfortunate with what is honest and glorious."

We have examined the record one hundred and twenty years after "unfortunate" circumstances led North Americans and Mexicans into bloody combat. We have seen that both warring parties, with clear consciences, signed a Treaty which proclaimed to all the world that America indeed remained honorable in victory . . . thanks to Nicolas P. Trist . . . and that Mexico remained glorious in defeat . . . thanks to the valor and pride of her race. What appeared to be "unfortunate" has perhaps turned out to be a blessing in disguise for both countries. Since 1846 America has become the world's most powerful nation; and Mexico has become stable and progressive, a model Republic to her neighbors in Hispanic America.

As our generation struggles through a period of ideological warfare and revolutionism, it seems to be more than appropriate to recall how two former "enemies" were able to pick up the pieces of history and construct a *modus vivendi* which has grown stronger with each passing decade. Some hotheads continue to spread falsehoods and rumors on both sides of the border concerning the American position vis a vis the Mexican people. But few who take the time to delve into the atmosphere of that age can deny the conciliatory attitude of the American people toward the "conquered" Mexican. Official America did not look upon the Mexicans, whether on this side of the border or on the other, as a "conquered" people. On the contrary, an examination of the records of the 10th military command in California 1846–1850, (now available on microfilm from the National Archives) will demonstrate that the Army in California was engaged in protecting the helpless Mexican and Indian from marauding American adventurers. Perhaps Walter Colton, the Alcalde of Monterey for three years, best expressed the distaste of responsible Americans for American ruffians when he compared their bad behavior with that of the easy-going Mexican, exclaiming: "You are shut up to the shrewdness and sharpness of the Yankee on the one hand, and the liberality of the Californians on the other. Your choice lies between the two, and I have no hesitation in saying, give me the Californian!"

Again, there was much spirit of harmony and accord as Californians met in Convention in Monterey in 1849 to draft their bilingual Constitution. A demonstration of that harmony was the proclamation of acting Governor Colonel Robert Mason upon hearing of the signing of the Treaty of Querétero: "From this new order of things," he proclaimed, "there will result to California a new destiny . . . Americans and Californians will now be one and the same people, subject to the same laws, and enjoying the same rights and privileges. They should therefore become a band of brothers, emulating each other in their exertions to develop the wealth and resources, and to secure the peace, happiness, and permanent prosperity of their common country." A year after this proclamation was issued, eight native Californians joined with their North American companions as free men to produce a bilingual constitution for the 32nd State of the Union.

This spirit of '49 is still the spirit of Californians and of all Americans. Today the population of California nearly equals that of the sovereign state of Mexico. Today's Californians are increasingly conscious of their links to Mexico and to its Hispanic tradition. Indeed, the steady stream of Mexican immigrants who seek opportunity for a better life this side of the border is reassurance that the U. S. Constitution continues to provide these newcomers with "the same rights and privileges" shared by all Americans. Since 1848 Americans and Mexicans have lived in relative peace and without the need for fortifying their frontiers. They live in peace and harmony because they have learned to respect and understand each other's values and traditions. They have learned to judge each other with "a manly spirit." They have agreed on what is honest and what is glorious.

6. A *CHICANO* VIEW OF THE TREATY OF GUADALUPE HIDALGO

FELICIANO RIVERA

Professor Feliciano Rivera of San Jose State College discusses the plight of the Mexican-American today as a result of the Mexican-American War. Rivera, in a revisionist interpretation of American history, concludes that the history of Mexican-Americans, or Chicanos, in the Southwest is one of a conquered people who have been exploited and denied their history and identity.

An important question to pose is the legal status of the Mexican American, and on what date did he become a citizen of this republic. Although the Mexican Americans were indigenous to California, it was not until the terms of the Treaty of Guadalupe Hidalgo in 1848 that the status of the Mexican Americans north of the Rio Grande was determined. . . .

As the present states of the Southwest entered statehood . . . citizens of Mexican parentage became American citizens with all the rights, privileges, and responsibilities thereof. However, I believe the United States has breached its promise. There have been many violations by the Departments of Education throughout the Southwest, direct violations of the Treaty of Guadalupe Hidalgo. The different Departments of Education have tried to make every Mexican American, or *Chicano*, in the

Excerpt from a speech given at the NDEA Conference on the Role of Minorities in American History, Monterey Peninsula College, March 1, 1969. Reprinted by permission of Feliciano Rivera.

image of their Anglo American counterpart. . . . Mexican American traditions are denied and ridiculed in the schools.

With the exception of the Indian, outside the Mexican American group, there is no other group that has a contract that could be brought up before the United Nations specifying their rights and privileges. The Mexican Americans are a conquered group. They started out as a conquered group and because of this their problems are unique, having their roots in these earlier problems. This treaty has not been studied as it should be; however, there is a new group, the Chicano militants, studying it now as it relates to the Mexican American.

In the eyes of most Anglo Americans, Mexican Americans are identified as a foreign group with some kind of foreign loyalty. Yet the base of Western history, American history, and California history should be Spanish colonial because the Mexican American has been in the Southwest for over 370 years. It was not until 1848 that the Mexican American became part of the United States. The Americans who conquered the Mexicans were the beneficiaries of their 300 years of labor.

The Mexican American War was merely an incident in a chain of events that started some years before and survived long after the Treaty of Guadalupe Hidalgo. Historians and administrators perpetuate the prevalent societal point of view. The roots of the poison can be found in three paragraphs taken from an article by William Perkins in an 1851 issue of the *Sonora Herald:*

> The streets of the town are full of lazy, lounging greasers as the Mexicans are commonly denominated. They are a singular people, it is difficult to say which race they assimilate with—their Spanish fathers or their Indian mothers. They are all *mestizos* except for the southern part of Mexico where the Negro blood has come from the West Indies which has degraded the race still lower.
>
> The greaser has all the characteristic vices of the Spaniards, jealous, revengeful, and passionate with a passion for gambling; with a still greater likeness for the inferior tribes of Indians. The same apathetic indolence and the same propensity for thievery. . . .
>
> Never caring for tomorrow or the past. Strictly believing the power of the church to remove all sins without the disagreeable necessity for repentance. . . . They are ready at any moment to rob and murder and do so without fear of detection. They are cowardly to the point of degradation. Their principal and in fact only delights are gambling, sitting on their haunches all day, and dancing all night to the music . . . of cracked voices.

7. THE DESTRUCTION OF THE CALIFORNIA INDIAN

SHERBURNE F. COOK

Dr. Sherburne F. Cook, Professor Emeritus of the University of California, examines the tragic decline of the California Indians. Greed, racism, disease, and land hunger were the combined reasons for the destruction of the forgotten original American.

On January 7, 1858, the San Francisco *Bulletin* quoted the Red Bluffs *Beacon* concerning the recent demise of one Bill Farr: ". . . Bill was a terror to the Indians, having killed a great many in his time; some of whom, as he said himself, he shot to see them fall."

On August 28, 1855, Captain H. M. Judah, at Fort Jones, reported to his commanding general: "Since the recent disturbances on the Klamath, it appears to be the unanimous decision of the miners in this section of the state that no male Indian will hereafter be permitted to reside among them or frequent their vicinity under the penalty of being shot down. . . ."

D. N. Cooley, agent at the Tule River Farm, wrote in his annual report, August 17, 1866: "A cruel, cowardly vagabond, given to thieving, gambling, drunkenness, and all that is vicious, without one redeeming trait, is a true picture of the California Digger. . . ."

There must be some explanation for these statements, which may be regarded as commonplace for their time. As a starting point it is worthwhile to consider the philosophy of the people who migrated from the United States to California after the acquisition of the territory and the discovery of gold. Prior to their advent, Upper California had been under the control of Ibero-Americans who brought the tradition of the missions and a racial tolerance sufficiently broad to encompass free intermarriage. It is true that they based their material culture upon the ruthless economic exploitation of the native, but they never even remotely contemplated his physical destruction.

The Anglo-Americans, in contrast to those of Spanish and Mexican derivation, had been engaged for 200 years in a murderous struggle with the indigenous peoples of North America, first for survival, then for occupation and conquest. Armed hostility rapidly crystallized a fundamental cultural disparity so as to produce an implacable hatred of the red race. This hatred was inflamed by the prolonged and competent resistance offered by the warlike tribes who inhabited the Mississippi basin. To those who crossed the plains in covered wagons, every Indian was a deadly enemy. When these pioneers reached the Pacific, they did not recognize the generally peaceable nature of the aboriginal Californians,

Sherburne F. Cook, "The Destruction of the California Indian," *California Monthly* (December 1968). Reprinted by permission of author and publisher.

but carried over against them the fury generated by decades of bitter warfare on the frontier. This hostility was quite misdirected.

We need only consider that scarcely 100 men in the Portola-Serra expedition of 1789 had occupied and consolidated an area held by 50 to 100,000 natives, and had brought the latter into a religious system operated by only a few score priests and soldiers. Indeed, by 1845 there were still less than 10,000 white people in the entire state. Hence we may imagine the impact of the 100,000 gold seekers and adventurers who swarmed through the Golden Gate within the interval of a year or two. This horde was reinforced by other immigrants, and so by the early fifties close to a quarter of a million persons, mostly Americans, had settled in California.

Some idea of what happened to the natives may be obtained merely by following their number through the mid-nineteenth century. A reasonable estimate of the Indian population within the state in 1769 would be a quarter of a million. During the Spanish and Mexican period up to 1845 there was steady attrition among the inhabitants of the central coast, the San Joaquin Valley, and southern California. Most of the casualties were referable to disturbance of native society, minor warfare in the interior, and a high mortality caused by disease both among the wild tribes of the Central Valley, and within the mission establishments. Just prior to the Gold Rush there probably were fully 175,000 Indians left, 40 to 50,000 of whom lived in the coastal regions south from San Francisco Bay to the Mexican border. Of the remainder, some lived in the San Joaquin basin, but most still existed relatively undisturbed in the northern Coast Ranges, across the mountains to the Shasta area, and down the Sierra foothills all the way to the Tehachapi. In 1849 it was precisely these regions which were overrun by gold seekers. Population estimates for the next few years are unsatisfactory, but the best evidence indicates that there were 75 to 100,000 Indians still to be found in 1850–51. By 1880 conditions had sufficiently stabilized to permit a fairly good count, and at that time there can have been no more than 20,000.

The period since 1880 has seen a trend toward an increase, and there may now be 30 or 40,000 persons who possess Indian blood. However, the augmentation has occurred primarily through mixture with other races, so there are extremely few individuals alive who are of pure California Indian stock.

Apart from a probable fall in birth rate, concerning which we have very little factual knowledge, the immediate causes of decline in numbers were disease, homicide, and starvation.

As far back as the 1830s, withering epidemics of smallpox and malaria swept through the Central Valley and the Coast Ranges, killing several thousand. Moreover, even at the missions, where living conditions otherwise were quite good, the extremely high mortality rate can be attributed in large part to such infections as measles, typhoid, and tuberculosis, and to venereal disease. Among the non-missionized tribes these maladies quickly became endemic, particularly after the massive immigration of 1849 distributed all the pathogens known to man amid a scene of universal bad sanitation, water pollution, and complete lack of social control.

Actual physical conflict between the races accounted directly for much mortality. It must be understood that an Indian's life counted as nothing. No non-Indian, of whatever ethnic origin, could be held responsible for the death of a native, nor could any legal action be taken against him. Specifically, we ought to distinguish between two types of killing, military and social homicide.

Military activity began in conjunction with the occupation of California during the Mexican War of 1845–48. It followed entirely conventional lines. Small bodies of troops established "forts" throughout the territory, the primary purpose of which was to hold in check and pacify the Indians, who, according to all previous experience, would soon initiate strong physical resistance. As one might expect, the least sign of armed hostility was countered by a crushing military expedition, in the course of which it was standard practice to burn the native villages and destroy all stored food. Occasionally these operations went so far as to offend the conscience of even the contemporary society. Here might be mentioned the infamous Clear Lake Massacre of 1850 and the Humboldt Bay Massacre of 1860, on both of which occasions armed white men, military and civilian alike, slaughtered dozens of helpless women and children.

Social homicide was the result of the ordinary, day-to-day quarrelling, fighting, and shooting, with or without benefit of liquor, which characterized the culture of the 1850s in California. That many Indians should be the victims is easily appreciated, particularly since no retribution whatever could be visited upon the guilty parties. I once made a count of the deaths incurred by Indians from 1852 to 1865 which were reported in four prominent newspapers, two in San Francisco, one each in Sacramento and Marysville. My total was 289, of which 73 were executions or lynchings during or after the commission of a crime or misdemeanor. The number is not very great, but it is indicative of the brutal atmosphere in which the native population carried on its existence. In this context it might be appropriate to quote an item from the *Alta California* (San Francisco) for August 8, 1854: "Two Indians were found murdered in our streets the past week, by persons unknown, and dumped into the common receptacle made and provided for such cases."

The third factor in the destruction of the red man in our state was economic. Everyone must eat. When the aboriginal sources of subsistence were denied to the Indian, and when no substitute means of support were permitted him, he had no recourse but to fight and be killed quickly, or to starve and die slowly.

The native food supply was copious, but there were two commodities which surpassed all others in importance: fish from the rivers and acorns from the oak forests. [Placer mining] of every water course in the Sierra foothills and the northern Coast Ranges so muddied the water as to damage seriously the runs of salmon and steelhead. Farming operations in the flat country destroyed much of the acorn reserve. But the most destructive effect was produced by the simple occupation of the land. Since the Indian had no property rights, he was dispossessed and driven out wherever a farmer wished to settle, or a miner wanted to pan gold. The situation is epitomized in a single brief sign, two words: "No trespassing." If, at the present day, I violate such an order, and enter private property, I may perhaps be arrested, go to court, and be fined a few dollars. The Indian did not go to court; he was shot.

The effects of this mass eviction were manifold. On the one hand, the Indian might resort to stealing cattle for food, and precipitate a local "war." On the other hand, he might move into a settlement or town and try to exist by scavenging and beggary. Living thus in utter squalor and poverty, he became a serious social problem.

One might properly ask why this horde of mendicants were not absorbed by the labor market, which, in a pioneer community always finds room for workers. The answer is complex. One fundamental difference between the Hispanic and the Anglo-American cultures has always been the fact that the former utilized the native as its primary source of labor whereas the latter never did. There simply was no place in the American cosmos for the Indian. Such a condition is remarkable in view of the extensive reliance placed upon the Negro, both slave and free. Certain psychological factors are also involved, among them the bitter animosity previously mentioned. In addition, there was a deep-rooted feeling among settlers and pioneers that the Indian was mentally and morally incapable of productive effort. He was lazy, shiftless, dirty, and incompetent.

It is true that the American native had never encountered labor of the type favored by white men; long, tedious, exhausting hours and days spent at physical tasks on the farm and in the factory. From the standpoint of his own experience there was no reason for such effort, and, at least in California, he found adaptive transition too difficult to accomplish in the face of an intolerant, hostile, social environment.

The personal violence and economic suffering to which the California Indian was subjected was accompanied by a moral degradation such as has been the lot of few minority groups in the New World. Civil liberty as we understand the term, and as, even in 1850, it was embodied in the Constitution, simply did not apply to the aborigine. He did not vote; he did not hold office; he had no police protection; he was not permitted to testify in court; he could not accuse a white man of any legal infraction, nor could he bring suit for any damages. He could be picked up without a warrant and could be held in jail without bail and upon no charge. If he were arrested, the then prevailing indenture system permitted any white man to secure his services for a period of days or weeks without pay. In theory the white man furnished food and lodging. If the Indian absconded he could be brought back by force.

One of the worst manifestations of oppression was in the area of sex. Particularly in the gold mining regions there existed thousands of unattached white men, frequently of the lowest character. It was quite customary for these individuals to make such use as they wished of the native women. If the latter, or their men-folk objected, force was applied without hesitation. These relationships were often more than casual. Many whites took Indian women as concubines and lived with them for extended periods, thus earning for themselves as a class the name of "squaw men." Furthermore, prostitution was common, and the local press gives accounts of Indian women selling themselves for a mouthful of food.

Of all the indignities to which the California natives were exposed, probably the most vicious was the kidnapping of small children in the mountains for sale to white citizens in the towns. The practice began before the American occupation of California, when the Spanish-speaking ranchers raided local tribes to capture transient labor. But by 1860 the kidnapping of children had reached the dimensions of an industry. In an editorial on July 19, 1862, the *Sacramento Union* stated that a class of "pestilent" whites were actually killing adults to get the children to sell. The latter brought from $30 to $200 apiece, and might be seen in every fourth white man's house. It may be estimated that fully 3,000 children were thus stolen during the fifteen years from 1852 to 1867. Several attempts were made to prosecute known operators in this business, but legal technicalities and outright acquittals prevented any from being brought to punishment.

After 1849, as California began to fill up with sober and responsible immigrants from the East, who came to establish homes, not to mine gold, the atrocities which were being inflicted upon the native population began to arouse public indignation. At first, efforts to bring relief were sporadic and ineffective. A few important landowners in the Central Valley "treated their Indians well." Groups of ladies in San Francisco and elsewhere made collections of food and clothing for the benefit of small numbers of indigents. It was very clear that private good will and charity could not touch the problem. But the Federal Government was at the time beginning to develop the Reservation System.

There is an opinion current that the Reservations were nothing more than concentration camps, and it must be admitted that at their worst there was a certain degree of resemblance. However, the theory on which they were based was relatively altruistic, even though the practice often fell far short of the theory.

In the middle of the nineteenth century, especially in the eastern part of the United States, where no one had seen a wild Indian for decades, there grew up a fairly strong humanitarian sentiment directed against the white people in the West who were seeing wild Indians all the time. This feeling undoubtedly went hand in hand with the rising abolition movement. It was argued quite cogently that if the Negroes were to be liberated from slavery, at least some of the Indians should be liberated from conditions which could be regarded as worse than slavery.

Out of this sentiment, and out of the many hit-or-miss, helter-skelter schemes for "doing something," emerged the Reservations. Moreover, behind their inception, lay an official, legalistic theory not unlike what we see today in urban redevelopment. The argument ran with the Indians, as it runs today with owners of condemned property, that society had dispossessed them of valuable lands and homes which, in all equity, should be replaced by something just as good.

It is true that, a century or more ago, there were great areas of vacant land in the plains and Great Basin regions to which the remnants of the eastern and middle western tribes could be moved. The fact was recognized that these forced migrants would have to be given help in order to get established and make a living under the American economic system. Hence they were to be supplied with tools, with seed, and with building materials, as well as with land itself. On the whole, the system probably was as good as could have been devised at the time, and under the existing circumstances.

Nevertheless, as applied to California, and as there administered, it was a failure. The reason lay basically in the peculiar political organization of the local natives and the complete disregard by white society of the ancient habitats and cultural values. California was unique in the United States in that instead of a few large tribes such as the Iroquois, Sioux or Apache, it contained dozens of little ones. Each one had its own clearly defined home with surrounding territory for foraging not more than a few miles. Each one had lived in that home for generations. To uproot such a tribe forcibly and transport it to a far place under strange conditions inflicted a profound emotional and psychic injury.

The dislocations to which the California native groups were subjected were carried out in a most callous and brutal manner. People from the upper Sacramento Valley were thrown together with others from the coast in localities which neither one had ever seen before. Some of these were in heavily forested northern areas where little natural food existed, and where cultivation was difficult for experienced white farmers, to say nothing of utterly unsophisticated aborigines. Moreover, the Reservation Indians for many years were systematically attacked and plundered by neighboring whites and their most desirable land was preempted without ceremony.

It was anticipated that such abuses would be abated by the resident agents, who, under federal law, were vested with broad discretionary powers over both the Reservation inhabitants and the surrounding white community. However, these functionaries, as a class, have always enjoyed a very low reputation for both integrity and competence. A sweeping indictment may contain some element of injustice, because a perusal of their annual reports leaves the impression that many agents honestly tried to make the system succeed. On the other hand, there unquestionably were many who were corrupt, or at least indifferent, and who shared the universal public antipathy toward their charges. Under such conditions of chaotic administration, and in the face of solid local hostility, the entire Reservation organization fell into a state of collapse, and had to be completely renovated in the late 1860s.

By that time the Indian population had shrunk to insignificance. This alone brought some relief. When California civil society finally settled down after the confusion and uproar of the Mexican War, the gold stampede, and the Civil War, it was found that there really were not enough Indians left to cause much trouble, perhaps 20,000 in all. Of these, many were uneasily established on Reservations such as Hupa, Round Valley, and Palm Springs, where the government took care of them as a rule by outright subventions. The others had retreated into the obscurity of the remote valleys of the Coast Ranges, the Sierra Nevada, or little oases in the southern desert, supporting themselves by subsistence farming reinforced by frequent federal aid. Here they have slowly gathered themselves together and are now beginning to ask why they may not be regarded as full American citizens.

8. THE NEGRO COWBOY

PHILIP DURHAM AND EVERETT L. JONES

Professors Philip Durham and Everett L. Jones vividly describe part of the forgotten history of the American West. In their book The Negro Cowboys *the authors present an image of a rugged black frontiersman that is at variance with an earlier stereotype of the ineffectual Negro male.*

Among the cowboys who went up the trails from Texas during the years following the Civil War, more than five thousand Negroes played a part and did a job—doing no more and no less than cowboys of other races and nationalities. The real story is not about one group alone, but about all the men who conquered the grassland of the "Great American Desert," a vast area which suddenly became the Western cattle empire. In perspective, that achievement must be seen as the work of many men engaged in a common enterprise. It is best understood as a movement of people driven by economic forces, excited by new challenges and eager for adventure.

An observer standing on a rise and watching a herd of cattle being driven up a trail could not differentiate one cowboy from another. He saw only a group of men doing a job in a cloud of dust. Unless he rode down and met them individually, he could not tell whether they were Texans or Mexicans, whites or Negroes. Yet as he watched the cattle pushing north, he was viewing the making of history.

This history was made primarily by white Southerners who had worn the uniform of the Confederacy. With them rode men who had fought for the Union. With them, too, were a number of Mexican vaqueros, as well as an occasional German, Irishman, Englishman or Swede. But more numerous than Northerners or foreigners, frequently among the most capable men in the crew, were the Negro cowboys.

There had always been Negroes in the West. They had, indeed, been

scattered throughout the Western Hemisphere since their first importation as slaves at the beginning of the sixteenth century. Estevánico, a
Spanish slave from the west coast of Morocco, was a member of an unfortunate party of four hundred explorers who landed near Tampa Bay
in 1528. After a series of disasters, all of the party were lost except
Estevánico, his master and two companions, who were marooned on the
Texas coast. They were enslaved by Indians and spent seven years freeing themselves and making their way across Texas and Mexico to the
frontiers of New Spain. Once there, they told stories they had heard of
the Seven Cities of Cíbola, and their reports were directly responsible for
the Coronado expedition. Estevánico continued his explorations, discovered the pueblos of New Mexico, and was killed by the Zuñis in 1539.

More than two hundred years later, Negroes and Negro-Indian families helped to found what is now the largest city in the West. Their settlement was established to grow food for the military, and it was called
El Pueblo de Nuestra Señora La Reina de Los Angeles. Negroes and descendants of Negroes were literally among the first families of Los Angeles just as they were among the first settlers in the Spanish colonies of
New Mexico.

Negroes also took part in American exploration of the West. When
Lewis and Clark commanded the first official attempt to extend the "geographical knowledge of our continent," a Negro went with them. Clark's
slave, a man named York, accompanied the expedition from the time it
hoisted sail near the mouth of the Missouri River in 1804 until it returned in 1806 after having crossed the Rocky and Bitterroot Mountains
and pushed to the mouth of the Columbia River. Nearly forty years later
a free Negro, Jacob Dodson, accompanied John C. Frémont on his 1843
expedition to search for a new pass through the High Sierra. Another
free Negro, Saunders Jackson, joined Frémont's fourth expedition in
1848.

Several Negroes ranged through the Rocky Mountains searching for
beaver. One was James P. Beckwith (sometimes Beckwourth), the son of
a white father and a Negro slave, who in 1823 was the blacksmith for
General William Ashley's fur brigade. In time, he became one of the
most famous of the mountain men (as well as a famous storyteller), his
exploits rivaling those of Kit Carson and Jim Bridger, with both of whom
he associated. During the last years of his life he was a chief among the
Crows, earning new fame as a warrior and horse thief. Even his early
death before the middle of the century was a subject of legend: it was
said that his own tribe poisoned him, using a poison so deadly that not
even his own powerful medicine (a bag containing a hollow bullet and
two oblong beads) could save his life. Edward Rose was another such
mountain man, "a morose, moody misfit of mixed blood and lawless disposition," who "eventually joined the Crow tribe and abandoned civilization entirely."

The explorations of Lewis and Clark, Frémont and the mountain men
helped open the way to Oregon. Ironically, although Negroes participated in these expeditions, they were early barred from the Oregon frontier settlements. Many of the first settlers of the Williamette Valley were

Southerners, and while they could not change the ruling of the 1843 provisional constitution that prohibited slavery, they added a provision in 1844 which expelled all the Negroes and mulattoes. So in that same year, when George W. Bush, a free Negro, joined an expedition to Oregon, he was refused settlement there. He moved north to Puget Sound and took up a homestead, where he lived the rest of his life. One of the earliest settlers, he helped later arrivals with interest-free loans of grain and other foodstuffs, assisting hundreds of white newcomers to survive their first months on the new frontier.

Another free Negro worked at the start of the Oregon Trail in Independence, Missouri. There Hiram Young operated wagon factories and engaged in a general blacksmithing business, at one time employing more than fifty men on twenty-five forges. He also owned and employed slaves.

After 1848 many travelers of the Oregon Trail turned south to California, where gold had been discovered. Among them were Negroes, both slave and free, who staked claims and formed mining companies. Negro prospectors and miners also joined in later developments in Nevada, Idaho and Montana, and they were among those who headed for Colorado to become part of the Pike's Peak gold rush of 1858. Other Negroes appeared in the West as muleskinners, hostlers, hotelkeepers and unskilled laborers. Some worked for Russell, Majors and Waddell and their Pony Express. Negro women cooked for hungry trappers in isolated mountain forts and for travelers on the Butterfield stages that rolled through Texas and Arizona.

Negroes, even as slaves, were usually more fortunate than the American Indians. During slavery days, Negroes were valuable property, and after the Civil War they rarely challenged the ambition and greed of Western pioneers. But the Indians were always despised, fair game for treachery and murder. In the West, as in the East, Americans dishonored treaty after treaty, driving Indians from one area to another, systematically attempting to exterminate whole tribes. The Indians fought back, and as they fought they were sometimes opposed, sometimes aided, by Negroes.

In the Indian Nations (now Oklahoma) some wealthy Indians of the Five Civilized Tribes owned large plantations and hundreds of slaves. Others became slavers, kidnapping and selling Negroes "down the river." Still others lived with Negro friends and relatives, learning together to make a new life in the West after their violent removal from ancestral lands in Florida, Georgia, Alabama and Mississippi. Some of the Seminole Indians, for example, rode with Negroes all the way through Texas to take up land in Coahuila province in Mexico. There, under the command of John Horse, the son of an Indian father and a Negro mother, a band of about a hundred Negroes joined with Seminole and Kickapoo Indians in campaigns against Mescalero and Comanche Indians.

In Texas, as white settlers occupied new lands, both they and their slaves suffered from Indian reprisals. As early as 1839, Indians killed a Negro hauling lumber between Bastrop and Austin. Another died in the same year when his surveying party was raided. Comanche raiders killed eleven more Negroes the next year and carried off several as prisoners. From 1839 until long after the Civil War, Texas Negroes fought against Indians.

But some became renegades, riding with Comanches, sometimes leading attacks on white settlements. One Negro was with an Indian raiding party that attacked the Hoover family in 1861; another was with the Indians who raided the Friend home in Llano County, Texas, in 1866. A "big Negro" led a party of thirty-five Indians that killed rancher George Hazelwood and fought against Hazelwood's cowboys in 1868. He was perhaps the same one who in 1868 led an Indian attack on the Ledbetter Saltworks in Shackelford County. Still another Negro led a band of more than forty Indians in surrounding a dozen cattlemen and cowboys "near the borders of Young and Palo Pinto counties, not far from Fort Belknap, on May 16, 1869." He sat on a large rock, well out of gun range, and commanded his forces in their attack. He and his Indians hurt the cattlemen badly, killing three and seriously wounding five, but they were forced to retreat when the besieged group was relieved by a rescue party summoned and led by a Negro cowboy.

References to Negro renegades are not uncommon in accounts of Indian fights in the West and Southwest. Some of these renegades were themselves part Indian—usually Seminole or Creek, but occasionally part Comanche or Sioux. Some had been captured as children and raised in the tribes. Others deserted from the Army: fled courts-martial or merely went over the hill. Such men, particularly if they had long Army experience, made invaluable allies for the Indians. Probably one such man was the Negro bugler who accompanied the Indians in a famous attack on a group of buffalo hunters at Adobe Walls in the Texas Panhandle in 1874.

But for every Negro renegade who joined against the white men, a company of Negro soldiers fought Indians. No story of the seizure and settlement of the West would be complete without including an account of the Negro soldiers in the 24th and 25th Infantry Regiments and the Negro troopers in the 9th and 10th Cavalry Regiments. Organization of Negro regiments in the Regular Army was first authorized in 1866. During the Civil War, 178,975 Negro soldiers wore the blue uniforms of the Union Armies, and Negroes took part in 449 engagements. More than 38,000 were listed as killed, wounded or missing in action. With such a record, Negroes proved their effectiveness as soldiers, and the federal government prepared to use them.

The Congressional Act of July 28, 1866 (later modified by supplementary legislation in 1869), established two Negro infantry regiments and two Negro cavalry regiments. All four saw continuous service in the West during the three decades following the Civil War. Negro infantry served in both Texas and the Dakota Territory, and Negro cavalry fought in almost every part of the West from Mexico to Montana. Both General Miles and General Merritt, as well as other officers who commanded Negro troops during the Indian campaigns, praised their courage and skill: "I have always," wrote General Merritt, "found the colored race represented in the army obedient, intelligent and zealous in the discharge of duty, brave in battle, easily disciplined, and most efficient in the care of their horses, arms and equipment."

The story of either cavalry regiment alone would be an exciting history. The men were carefully picked, held to high standards of physical fitness and mental alertness, and were commanded by some of the Army's best white officers. (Three Negroes graduated from West Point in the years before 1900, and a few Negroes were commissioned as chaplains, but all other officers were white.)

The men took quickly to the routine of fort and camp, maintained excellent morale and proved to be excellent soldiers. Because few of them had received more than a smattering of education, a company commander's biggest problem was training men for the inevitable War Department paper work. The men believed that wearing the Army uniform was a privilege and an honor, and they equaled and sometimes surpassed white troops in the field. "Their desertion rate was lower, court-martial record better, and general physical fitness superior."

During the years before the Spanish-American War, troops of the 9th Cavalry served in Texas, New Mexico, Kansas, Oklahoma, Nebraska, Utah and Montana. The 10th Cavalry served in Kansas, Oklahoma, Texas, New Mexico and Arizona. Negro troopers fought against Comanches, Apaches and Sioux. They fought against Crazy Horse and his warriors, and they captured Geronimo.

The Indians called the Negro troopers Buffalo Soldiers because of the similarity between their tightly curled hair, generally short, and that of the buffalo. The white soldiers called them the Brunettes. The War Department knew they were efficient.

Frederic Remington posed a rhetorical question: "Will they fight?" And he answered it himself: "They have fought many, many times. The old sergeant sitting near me, as calm of feature as a bronze statue, once deliberately walked over a Cheyenne rifle pit and killed his man. One little fellow near him once took charge of a lot of stampeded cavalry horses when Apache bullets were flying loose and no one knew from what point to expect them next. These little episodes prove the sometimes doubted self-reliance of the Negro."

Negro soldiers and troopers were also called to keep the peace among white cattlemen and settlers. When Billy the Kid was trapped in a burning building in Lincoln, New Mexico, Negro troops surrounded him. When settlers tried to preempt lands in the Indian Nations, and when Sooners tried to sneak into Oklahoma Indian lands before they were officially opened for settlement, Negro cavalry stopped them. When Wyoming cattlemen started the Johnson County War, only to find themselves outnumbered and pinned down by angry settlers, Negro cavalry rescued them.

The soldiers helped to make the expansion of the cattle empire possible. Sometimes with their help and sometimes without it, cattlemen drove through Kansas and Nebraska to the Dakota Territory or through New Mexico and Colorado to Wyoming and Montana. And with the Texas cattlemen came the Negro cowboys.

These cowboys crossed the Red River and the Cimarron to ride the streets of all the early cowtowns. They stood in the saloons and slept in the jails. They fought Indians and other cowboys, and some of them were buried on Boot Hill or in unmarked graves along the trail. At the end of the long drives, a few remained on northern ranges to become horsebreakers, ranch hands or even outlaws, but most of them drew their pay and rode back to Texas.

While the trail drives lasted, Negroes had a conspicuous place in the life of the cattleman's West. They fought with guns and bullwhips on the streets of Dodge City, and they roamed the streets of Cheyenne. They carried gold through outlaw country, and they took part in bloody range wars. If one got drunk, he could crash through a plate glass window, shoot up a saloon or land in jail. If he turned outlaw, he usually died young.

Negro cowboys hunched in their saddles during blizzards and thunderstorms, fought grass fires and turned stampedes, hunted wild mustangs and rode wild horses. Wolves threatened their cattle, and rattlesnakes crawled into their camps. Their lives were like those of all other cowboys—hard and dangerous.

The point of their history is not that they were different from their companions but that they were similar. They had neither peculiar virtues nor vices to be glorified or condemned. But they should be remembered.

Chapter 3

The Turn of
the Century,

1876–1920

There were several important changes in California during the period from 1876 to 1920. The completion of the transcontinental railroads brought large numbers of Anglos to the Pacific coast. This "land boom" of the 1880s reduced the percentage of *Californios* to an even smaller minority. The ascent of the Anglo could be seen in a number of ways. The bilingual legal provision of the original state constitution was deleted in 1879 when the second state constitution was adopted. *Californios* also continued to lose control and ownership of their land. A series of lengthy court decisions concerning the old Mexican land grants usually resulted in Anglos gaining ownership of the disputed lands.

Another minority, the Orientals, grew in numbers as the *Californios* declined. Chinese immigrants added to the Asians who earlier had come to the Golden State to work in the mines and railroads. Many of the immigrants were agricultural workers from southern China whose ambition was to earn a fortune and return to their homeland. Unlike other migrants to California, they did not consider themselves permanent residents. Consequently, they never really made an attempt to assimilate or to enter the general society. Isolated by language, customs, and the leaders of their fraternal societies, these Chinese sojourners banded together in small rural communities and in rapidly growing "Chinatown" sections of the larger cities.

White reactions to the large influx of Chinese were mixed. Some Americans felt genuine sympathy for their wretched living conditions. Californians with Victorian social attitudes, on the other hand, were shocked by Chinese social mores. The tong wars, opium dens, gambling, and prostitution rings horrified members of proper California society. And yet the basic cause of concern was economic. Such issues as the lowering of the established wage scale and the intrusion of the Oriental into California agriculture inflamed the political scene in the years before World War I. The result of this white fear and distrust of the Chinese can be seen in the Oriental land laws, Oriental school segregation, and frequent use of extralegal force.

The second large Oriental minority, the Japanese, came to stay. They first arrived in 1869, but the largest influx of Japanese was at the turn of the century. Japanese immigrants were farmers, but by the first decade of the twentieth century many were forced off the land, innocent victims of an increasing xenophobia. Growing national concern over the "Yellow Peril" was stimulated in California by the famed newspaper publisher William Randolph Hearst. As was the case with the Chinese, the industriousness and ability of the Japanese contributed to the fears of the white working class.

In 1910 a new wave of Mexican immigrants entered California. Refugees from the violence of the Revolution in Mexico, these people sought peace and economic opportunity in the American Southwest. Because of their numbers and the previous patterns of Anglo prejudice toward Spanish-speaking persons, most Mexican immigrants were reduced to accepting employment with low pay. They worked in railroad construction, farm labor, and unskilled factory jobs, regardless of their skills or abilities. The irony of this situation was that as the Mexicans arrived and worked at the edge of poverty, Anglo-Californians were rediscovering the Hispanic mission period. The Anglos recreated in yearly fiestas the glories of the "Spanish period" while the immigrants from Mexico were ignored.

Thus, the era from 1876 to World War I was a period when the racial and ethnic composition of California changed. The following questions might be posed as the selections of this chapter are considered. Were all newcomers to California accorded the same welcome? How are attitudes in California a reflection of the rise of American imperialism at the turn of the century?

9. SOUTHERN CALIFORNIA: ERSATZ MYTHOLOGY

CAREY MCWILLIAMS

To many Californians the Indian is a stereotype that only appears in motion pictures or is represented in one of the many Southern California pageants or parades. The noted author, editor, and historian Carey McWilliams examines both the myth and reality of the Indian in California history. The myth continues to be accepted by many Californians.

Clear ring the silvery Mission bells
   Their calls to vesper and to mass;
O'er vineyard slopes, thro' fruited dells,
   The long processions pass.

The pale Franciscan lifts in air
   The cross above the kneeling throng;
Their simple world how sweet with prayer,
    With chant and matin song!
              —Ina Coolbrith

Considering the long dark record of Indian mistreatment in Southern California, it is difficult to account for the curious legend that has developed in the region about the well-being of the natives under Mission rule. According to this legend, the Missions were havens of happiness and contentment for the Indians: places of song, laughter, good food, beautiful languor, and mystical adoration of the Christ. What is still more astonishing is the presence in the legend of an element of masochism, with the Americans, who manufactured the legend, taking upon themselves full responsibility for the criminal mistreatment of the Indian and completely exonerating the Franciscans. "In the old and happy days of Church domination and priestly rule," writes one Protestant historian, "there had been no 'Indian question.' That came only after American 'civilization' took from the red men their lands and gave them nothing in return."

Equally baffling, at first blush, is the intense preoccupation of Southern California with its Mission-Spanish past. Actually one of the principal charms of Southern California, as Farnsworth Crowder has pointed out, is that it is not overburdened with historical distractions. "As against any European country, certain parts of the United States and even neighboring Mexico," writes Mr. Crowder, "human culture has left relatively few marks, monuments and haunts over the vast virginal face of the state. Almost any square block of London is more drenched with flavors of the past than the whole of Los Angeles. The desert areas and valleys cannot evoke any such awareness of human antiquity and the

FROM Carey McWilliams, "Southern California: Ersatz Mythology," *Common Ground* (Winter 1946). Reprinted by permission of the author and the American Council for Nationalities Service.

genesis of great religions and civilizations as can the borderlands of the
Mediterranean. No Wordsworths, no Caesars, no Pharaohs have made
their homes here. The Californian simply cannot feed upon the fruits
and signs of yesterday as can a Roman, a Parisian, an Oxonian." And yet
this is precisely what he attempts to do. The newness of the land itself
seems, in fact, to have compelled, to have demanded, the evocation of a
mythology which could give people a sense of continuity in a region long
characterized by rapid social dislocations. And of course it would be a
tourist, a goggle-eyed umbrella-packing tourist, who first discovered the
past of Southern California and peopled it with curious creatures of her
own invention.

II

Some day the Los Angeles Chamber of Commerce should erect a great
bronze statue of Helen Hunt Jackson at the entrance to Cajon Pass. Be-
neath the statue should be inscribed no flowery dedication but the simple
inscription: "H. H.—In Gratitude." For little, plump, fair-skinned, blue-
eyed Helen Hunt Jackson—"H.H." as she was known to every resident of
Southern California—was almost solely responsible for the evocation of
its Mission past, and it was she who catapulted the lowly Digger Indian
of Southern California into the empyrean.

Born in Amherst, Massachusetts, on October 15, 1830, Helen Maria
Fiske became a successful writer of trite romances and sentimental
poems quite unlike those written by her friend and neighbor, Emily
Dickinson. She was married in 1852 to Lieutenant Edward Bissell Hunt,
of the Coast Survey, who died a few years after the marriage. In later
years, she married William Sharpless Jackson, a wealthy banker and
railroad executive of Colorado Springs. It is rather ironic to note that
Mrs. Jackson, who became one of the most ardent freelance apologists
for the Catholic Church in America, was a confirmed anti-Papist until
she visited California. As might have been expected, she first became
interested in Indians while attending a tea party in Boston. At this tea,
she met Standing Bear and Bright Eyes, who were lecturing on the griev-
ous wrongs suffered by the Poncas tribe. At the time of this meeting,
Mrs. Jackson was forty-nine years of age, bubbling with enthusiasm, full
of rhymes. Quick to catch the "aboriginal contagion," which had begun
to spread among the writers of American romances, she immediately
usurped the position of defender of the Poncas tribe, and thereafter no
more was heard of Standing Bear and Bright Eyes. In 1881 Harper's
published her well-known work, *A Century of Dishonor*, which did
much to arouse a new, although essentially spurious, interest in the
American Indian.

In the spring of 1872, Mrs. Jackson had made a brief visit, as a tourist, to the northern part of California. Later she made three trips, as a
tourist, to Southern California: in the winter of 1881–1882; the spring
of 1883; and the winter, spring, and summer of 1884–1885. It scarcely
needs to be emphasized that her knowledge of California, and of the
Mission Indians, was essentially that of the tourist and casual visitor.

Although she did prepare a valuable report on the Mission Indians, based on a field trip she made with Abbot Kinney of Los Angeles, most of her material about Indians was second-hand and consisted, for the greater part, of odds-and-ends of gossip, folk tales, and Mission-inspired allegories of one kind or another.

She had originally been sent to Southern California by Century magazine to write some stories about the Missions, which, according to the illustrator who accompanied her, were to be "enveloped in the mystery and poetry of romance." In Southern California she became deliriously enamored of the Missions, then in a state of general disrepair and neglect, infested with countless swallows and pigeons, overrun by sheep and goats, and occasionally inhabited by stray dogs and wandering Indians. "In the sunny, delicious, winterless California air," these crumbling ruins, with their walled gardens and broken bells, their vast cemeteries and caved-in wells, exerted a potent romantic influence on Mrs. Jackson's highly susceptible nature. Out of these brief visits to Southern California came *Ramona*, the first novel written about the region, which became, after its publication in 1884, one of the most widely read American novels of the time. It was this novel which firmly established the Mission legend in Southern California.

When the book was first published, it provoked a storm of protest in the Southland. Egged on by various civic groups, the local critics denounced it as a tissue of falsehoods; a travesty on history; a damnable libel on Southern California. But the book was perfectly timed—providentially timed—to coincide with the great invasion of home-seekers and tourists to the region. As these hordes of winter tourists began to express a lively interest in visiting "Ramona's land," Southern California experienced an immediate change of attitude and, overnight, became passionately Ramona-conscious. Beginning about 1887, a Ramona promotion of fantastic proportions began to be organized in the region.

Picture postcards by the tens of thousands were published showing "the school attended by Ramona," "the original of Ramona," "the place where Ramona was married," and various shots of the "Ramona country." Since the local chambers of commerce could not, or would not, agree upon the locale of the novel—one school of thought insisted the Camulos rancho was the scene of the more poignant passages, while still another insisted that the Hacienda Guajome was the authentic locale—it was not long before the scenic postcards depicting the Ramona Country had come to embrace all of Southern California. In the '80s, the Southern Pacific tourist and excursion trains stopped regularly at Camulos, so that the wide-eyed Bostonians, guidebooks in hand, might detrain, visit the rancho, and bounce up and down on "the bed in which Ramona slept." Thousands of Ramona baskets, plaques, pincushions, pillows, and souvenirs of all sorts were sold in every curio shop in California. Few tourists left the region without having purchased a little replica of the "bells that rang when Ramona was married." To keep the tourist interest alive, local press agents for fifty years engaged in a synthetic controversy over the identities of the "originals" for the universally known characters in the novel. Some misguided Indian women began to take the promotion seriously and had themselves photographed—copyright reserved—as "the original Ramona." A bibliography of the newspaper stories, magazine articles, and pamphlets written about some aspect of the Ramona legend would fill a volume. Four husky volumes of Ramonana appeared in Southern California: *The Real Ramona* (1900), by D. A. Hufford; *Through Ramona's Country* (1908)—the official, classic document—by George Wharton James; *Ramona's Homeland* (1914), by Margaret V. Allen; and *The True Story of Ramona* (1914), by C. C. Davis and W. A. Anderson.

From 1884 to date, the Los Angeles Public Library has purchased over a thousand copies of *Ramona*. Thirty years after publication, the same library had a constant waiting list for 105 circulating copies of the book. The sales to date total 601,636 copies, with a Regular Edition, a Monterey Edition (in two volumes), a Deluxe Edition, a Pasadena Edition, a Tourist Edition, a Holiday Art Edition, and a Gift Edition. Hundreds of unoffending Southern California babies have been named Ramona. A town site was named Ramona. And, in San Diego, thousands of people make a regular pilgrimage to "Ramona's Marriage Place," where the True Vow Keepers Clubs—made up of couples who have been married fifty years or longer—hold their annual picnics. The Native Daughters of the Golden West have named one of their "parlors," or lodges, after Ramona. The name Ramona appears in the corporate title of fifty or more businesses currently operating in Los Angeles. Two of Mrs. Jackson's articles for Century—"Father Junipero and His Work," and "The Present Condition of the Mission Indians of Southern California"—were for years required reading in the public schools of California. Reprints of Henry Sandham's illustrations for *Ramona* are familiar items in Southern California homes, hotels, restaurants, and places of business. In 1914 one of the Ramona historians truthfully said that "Mrs. Jackson's name is familiar to almost every human being in Southern California, from the little three-year-old tot, who has her choice juvenile stories read to him, to the aged grandmother who sheds tears of sympathy for Ramona." Two generations of Southern California children could recite from memory the stanzas from Ina Coolbrith's verses to Helen Hunt Jackson, often ornately framed on the walls of Southern California homes:

> There, with her dimpled, lifted hands,
>   Parting the mustard's golden plumes,
> The dusky maid, Ramona, stands,
>   Amid the sea of blooms.
>
> And Alessandro, type of all
>   His broken tribe, for evermore
> An exile, hears the stranger call
>   Within his father's door.

Translated into all known languages, *Ramona* has also been dramatized. The play based on the novel was first presented at the Mason Opera House in Los Angeles on February 27, 1905, the dramatization having been written by Virginia Calhoun and General Johnstone Jones.

Commenting upon Miss Calhoun's performance in the role of Ramona, the Los Angeles Times reported: "In the lighter parts she held a fascination that was tempered with gentleness and playfulness. Her slender figure, graceful and pliant as a willow, swayed with every light touch of feeling, and the deeper tragic climaxes she met in a way to win tears from the eyes of many." Over the years, three motion picture versions of the novel have appeared. In 1887, George Wharton James, who did much to keep the Ramona promotion moving along, "tramped every foot of the territory covered by Mrs. Jackson," interviewing the people she had interviewed, photographing the scenes she had photographed, and "sifting the evidence" she had collected. His thick tome on the Ramona country is still a standard item in all Southern California libraries. For twenty-five years, the chambers of commerce of the southland kept this fantastic promotion alive and flourishing. When interest seemed to be lagging, new stories were concocted. Thus on March 7, 1907, the Los Angeles Times featured, as a major news item, a story about "Condino, the newly discovered and only child of Ramona." In 1921, the enterprising Chamber of Commerce of Hemet, California, commissioned Garnet Holme to write a pageant about Ramona. Each year since 1921 the pageant has been produced in late April or early May in the heart of the Ramona country by the Chamber of Commerce. At the last count, 200,000 people had witnessed it.

The legendary quality of Mrs. Jackson's famous novel came about through the amazing way in which she made elegant pre-Raphaelite characters out of Ramona and "the half-breed Alessandro." Such Indians were surely never seen upon this earth. Furthermore, the story extolled the Franciscans in the most fulsome manner and placed the entire onus of the mistreatment of the Indians upon the noisy and vulgar Gringoes. At the same time, the sad plight of Ramona and Alessandro got curiously mixed up, in the telling, with the plight of the "fine old Spanish families." These fine old Spanish families, who were among the most flagrant exploiters of the Indian in Southern California, appeared in the novel as only slightly less considerate of his welfare than the Franciscans. Despite its legendary aspects, however, the Ramona version of the Indians of Southern California is now firmly implanted in the mythology of the region. It is this legend which largely accounts for the "sacred" as distinguished from the "profane" history of the Indian in Southern California.

It should be said to Mrs. Jackson's credit, however, that she did arouse a momentary flurry of interest in the Mission Indians. Her report on these Indians, which appeared in all editions of *A Century of Dishonor* after 1883, is still a valuable document. As a result of her work, Charles Fletcher Lummis founded the Sequoya League in Los Angeles in 1902, "to make better Indians," and, through the activities of the League, the three hundred Indians who were evicted from the Warner Ranch in 1901 were eventually relocated on lands purchased by the government. Aside from the relocation of these Indians, however, nothing much came of Mrs. Jackson's work in Southern California, for the region accepted the charming Ramona as a folk figure, but completely rejected the Indians still living in the area. A government report of 1920 indicated that 90 per cent of the residents of the sections in which Indians still live in Southern California were wholly ignorant about their Indian neighbors and that deep local prejudice against them still prevailed.

At the sacred level, it is the half-breed Alessandro who best symbolizes the Indian heritage of Southern California. At the secular level, however, one must turn to the local annals to select more appropriate symbols. There is, for example, the character Polonia, an Indian of great stature and strength, whose eyes had been burned out of their sockets. Clad in a tattered blanket, this blind Indian was a familiar figure on the dusty streets of Los Angeles in the '50s and '60s. And there was Viejo Cholo, or Old Half Breed, who wore a pair of linen pantaloons and used a sheet for a mantle. His cane was a broom-handle; his lunchcounter, the swill basket. Viejo Cholo was succeeded as the principal Indian eccentric of Los Angeles by another halfbreed, Pinikahti. A tiny man, Pinikahti was only four feet in height. Badly pockmarked, he had a flat nose and stubby beard. He was generally attired, notes Harris Newmark, "in a well-worn straw hat, the top of which was missing, and his long, straight hair stuck out in clumps and snarls. A woolen undershirt and a pair of overalls completed his costume, while his toes, as a rule, protruded from his enormous boots." Playing Indian tunes on a flute made out of reeds from the bed of the Los Angeles River, Pinikahti used to dance in the streets of the town for pennies, nickels, and dimes, or a glass of aguardiente. Polonia, Viejo Cholo and Pinikahti—these are the real symbols of the Indian heritage of Southern California.

10. THE GREAT INVASION

CAREY MCWILLIAMS

Beginning with the Mexican Revolution in 1910, there was a large migration of Mexicans to California. Carey McWilliams comments on the impact of the Great Migration upon the immigrants and their contribution to the American Southwest. The author suggests that their contributions were accompanied by a painful introduction to American society.

By the 1890's Mexicans had become merely a "picturesque element" in the life of the Southwest. They carried on, but in minor roles and occupations, "colorful" representatives of a subculture that was rapidly disappearing—or so everyone thought. Ironically it was at this junction that the newcomers to the Southwest suddenly discovered, in a most romantic way, the "Spanish heritage" of the region. The event which more than any other signaled the inception of this sentimental "rediscovery" of the Hispanic heritage was the publication in 1884 of Helen Hunt Jackson's novel *Ramona*, which glamorized the "old days," made much of the missions, and idealized the Indians. Mrs. Jackson, a newcomer to the region, was a Protestant, but she did more, perhaps, "to save the missions" than

Reprinted with the permission of the publisher from Carey McWilliams' *The Mexicans in America* (New York: Teachers College Press), 1968.

any Catholic before or since. Her novel was a best seller for years. It was produced as a play in 1905, and in 1921, the Ramona Pageant, which has continued ever since, was initiated. Shortly after *Ramona* was published, the Association for the Preservation of the Missions was formed, marking the beginning of a period in which "mission" architecture, furnishings and craft products enjoyed an enormous vogue. In 1902, the Mission Inn was opened in Riverside, California. Somewhat later John Steven McGroarty, California's poet laureate, wrote the *Mission Play.* First performed in 1912, it has since been seen by literally millions of tourists. The rise of this romantic, largely mythical pseudo-tradition occurred in the Southwest at the very moment when the real tradition seemed to be in danger of being totally eclipsed. Charles Gibson has described the "idealization" of the Mexican-Spanish past in these terms: "What Washington Irving had felt at the Alhambra, others felt at Santa Fe and Capistrano . . . In prose and poetry the borderlands were Alhambraized." For the most part, this "idealization" of the Spanish background—so unrelated to the existing social scene—did little to improve the lot of the Spanish-speaking. But at about the same time that the missions were being popularized, Charles Fletcher Lummis, the first of a number of fine regional historians, began a somewhat more realistic resurrection of the past which has continued down to the present time.

It is also ironic that the land boom of the late 1880's in Southern California, which engulfed the Mexicans and at the same time gave rise to a booster-inspired legend of the past, also set in motion the invasion of the Southwest by thousands of Spanish-speaking Mexicans who returned to the land of their fathers in response to the demand for labor. As a matter of fact, there had been a slow but steady influx of Mexican immigrants prior to 1900. In that year, the Mexican immigrant population of Texas was estimated at 71,061, of Arizona at 14,172, of California at 8,096, and of New Mexico at 6,649. But between 1900 and 1964, 1.3 million Mexicans entered the regions in two great waves; the first from 1900 to 1920, the second from 1920 to 1930. It has been estimated that the number of Mexicans entering the United States between 1900 and 1920 was roughly the equivalent of one-tenth of the population of Mexico.

Mexican Immigration

The details of Mexican immigration to the United States are quite complex and only the essential facts can be summarized here. In all mass migration movements, two sets of factors are at work: "push" factors—those that set people in motion—and "pull" factors—those that pull them to a particular place. There were many "push" factors operating in the period from 1900 to 1964. In the first place, the portion of the old "borderlands" immediately south of the U.S.–Mexican border offered no very great inducements for people to stay there. Population was expanding but economic opportunities were not. From this region Mexicans could be easily induced to cross the border in search of work, the more so since crossing the border involved no great problems and the trip was not expensive. Then, too, in the period from 1880 to 1910, rail-road lines were constructed in northern Mexico which made it possible for those seeking employment to travel "by coach" from such cities as Durango, Zacatecas, Chihuahua and Sonora, to one or another of the communities on the American side. Another powerful "push" factor was, of course, the Mexican Revolution which, in the period from 1910 to 1920, resulted in a great deal of confusion, border troubles, and internal upheaval in Mexico. It was not so much that people fled to the States to avoid involvement in the revolution, as that they were driven to the States in search of work and some means of earning a livelihood. Then, when some of the great objectives of the Mexican Revolution, such as land redistribution, were not fully realized, many Mexicans left for the States out of a sense of frustration and disappointment.

The major "pull" factors, on the other hand, had to do with the rise of the Southwest as an economic empire. Originally it had been regarded as a largely arid region of little economic importance, but it was not long before its potentialities were perceived. Before its resources could be un-locked, rail lines had to be constructed. Mexicans, of course, had estab-lished the first trails which connected one Spanish outpost with another; they had also operated the packtrains that connected these outposts with points of settlement in Mexico. So it was quite appropriate, symbolically, that Mexican immigrants should have been imported to construct the new rail lines that ended the isolation of the region. It was no easy feat to push rail lines through the rugged, semi-desert, mountainous terrain. There were few points at which materials could be assembled; the isola-tion of the region impeded construction. But fortunately, cheap Mexican labor, both resident and immigrant, was available in large quantities. Long after the major lines were completed, Mexicans continued to con-stitute 70 per cent or more of the section crews and 90 per cent of the extra gangs used in maintenance. Other lines, operating outside the re-gion, also began to use Mexican labor. Once imported for this purpose, Mexican immigrants drifted into other types of work and their places were taken by new recruits from Mexico. Along the major rail lines of the Southwest, Mexican settlements sprang up, usually in the form of "boxcar" housing or, later, of rows of company housing. In the sparsely settled Southwest, rail lines were constructed well in advance of actual need and as a means of inducing newcomers to visit the region and, hopefully, to settle there. Construction of these lines would have taken much longer and would have cost much more, if cheap Mexican labor had not been available in the desired volume. It was a type of labor, also, which was well adapted for work in the hot, rugged terrain.

Hispanos and Industrial Employment

Although the Spanish-Mexican settlers did not find the "mines" they had originally sought in the Southwest, they did make some discoveries there that were of great importance to the mining industry. Spain had, of course, an ancient mining tradition, which the original colonists brought to Mexico. This tradition included, in addition to that great technical lore about mines and mining methods, a highly developed law of mines and minerals. A large part of this traditional lore was transported, so to speak, to the Southwest. It is well known, for example, that the mining law of California was largely based on the mining law of Spain and Mexico. As early as 1557, a Mexican miner at Pachuca, Mexico, revolutionized mining technique by the invention of the *patio* process for separating silver from ore by the use of quicksilver. And it was the Mexicans who discovered the famous New Almaden quicksilver mine near San Jose, California, named after the original Almaden mine in Spain. The quicksilver produced at this mine played a key role in unlocking the gold and silver resources of California and the West. Not only was the mine discovered by a Mexican but, for many years, it was operated almost entirely by Mexican labor. And in 1800 a Spanish colonel, guided by an Apache Indian, discovered the famous Santa Rita silver and copper mine in New Mexico. The Santa Rita was one of the most famous mines in the West; it was here that the techniques of copper mining were first developed. Copper mining, on a large scale, did not get under way in the Southwest until much later, after the final "pacification" of the Apaches in 1875. But once large-scale mining operations began, Mexicans played a key role in the industry, not only in Arizona but in Utah and Nevada. The census of 1930 listed 16,668 Mexicans engaged in mining in this country.

Mexicans also played enormously important roles in the sheep and cattle industries. The initial colonists brought herds with them on the long overland marches from points in Mexico. In New Mexico, sheep fed, clothed, and, in a sense, supported the initial colonists. Spain had, of course, a traditional sheep culture which was transplanted to the Southwest. Historians of the industry state that there is no doubt whatever that sheep husbandry in the United States owes more to Spain than to any other nation. One could make the same statement, of course, about the range cattle industry. "The range cattle industry," wrote J. Frank Dobie, "began in the mesquitals along the Rio Bravo." Much of the lore of the sheep and cattle industries is unmistakably Mexican in origin. From the Mexican *vaquero*, the American cowboy took over, and adapted in his own way, the Spanish horned saddle, bridle, bit and spurs, not to mention his lasso or lariat, cinch, halter, *mecate* or horsehair rope, "chaps" or *chaparejos*, "taps" or stirrup tips (*tapaderas*), the chin-strap for his hat (*barboquejo*), the feed-bag for his horse (*morral*), and his rope halter or *bosal*. Most of the lore of brands and branding is Mexican-Spanish in origin. The powerful cattlemen's associations in the West are based upon the Spanish institution of the *alcaldes de la mesta*.

[margin note: Cowboys branding association]

In all these industries—railroads, mines, sheep and cattle—Mexicans played a key role. But it was the emergence of the Southwest as an agricultural empire that brought the first waves of Mexican immigrants to the States. From the 1890's to 1910, the cattle industry began to give way to large-scale cotton farming, first in middle Texas and later in west Texas. As cotton pushed its way into the Southwest, Mexican labor came north to meet it. It so happened that the expansion of cotton farming coincided, roughly, with the inception of a period of revolutionary ferment in Mexico, which predisposed many Mexicans to "flee the revolution" and seek jobs in the States. Later, World War I greatly stimulated the expansion of the cotton industry in the Southwest by creating an active demand for long-staple cotton which is best grown on the irrigated cotton farms in Arizona and California. In 1910, the year which marked the inception of the Mexican Revolution, cotton was first planted in the Imperial Valley in California. Much of the new land that was devoted to cotton raising was brought into production through the use of large quantities of Mexican labor. By 1940, nearly 400,000 migratory workers, two-thirds of whom were Mexicans, were following the cotton crop in Texas alone. A lot of this labor was of the contract variety; that is, growers would contract with a labor contractor, usually a Mexican, who would in turn recruit, supervise and pay the workers. The contract system made for bad labor relations and for deplorable working conditions. Cotton, of course, is a cash crop; that is, it is produced to sell, not to consume or feed to livestock. As such, cotton provided a tremendous source of wealth and income to the rapidly expanding economy of the Southwest.

One of the keys which unlocked the resources of the Southwest was irrigation. The passage of the Reclamation Act in 1902 was a significant event in the history of the region. Irrigation farming is intensive farming; it means high yields per acre, it involves (or did originally) heavy labor requirements. In some areas, as in Imperial Valley, and other "winter gardens" of the Southwest, it means that two and three crops can be produced from the same acreage in the same year. Produce farming is carried on in these areas on a year-round basis. It has been, and is, an enormously profitable industry in the Southwest.

A number of factors account for the rapid development of produce farming in the Southwest after 1900: the development of refrigerator cars which made it possible to ship produce long distances; changes in the eating habits of the American people; the development of the canning industry; the shift of an increasing percentage of the population from small towns and farms, where every family had a garden, to large urban areas; and, of course, the development of irrigation projects. Today the "winter gardens" of the Southwest produce an amazing variety and volume of table crops: tomatoes, carrots, broccoli, spinach, turnips, peppers, lettuce, etc. Citrus crops which increased five fold in size between 1900 and 1950 also brought new sources of wealth to the region. Most of these crops are planted, cultivated and harvested by Mexican labor. Mexican labor was used to bring most of the "winter gardens" into production—to clear and prepare the land and construct the irrigation lines. It should be emphasized also that the "cheapness" of Mexican labor played a vital part in the development of these industries. Originally agricultural production in the Southwest suffered from certain cost handicaps, such as the cost of irrigation, the cost of refrigeration, the cost of shipping (often over great distances), the high capital costs of bringing land into production, and, finally, the large amount of hand labor many of these crops originally required (mechanization is, of course, reducing the demand for hand labor). To grow and harvest an acre of lettuce required, until quite recently, 126 man-hours of labor, an acre of strawberries 500 man-hours of labor, by comparison with only 13 man-hours of labor needed to produce an acre of wheat. Cotton, citrus, and produce farming would never have developed so rapidly in the Southwest, or been as profitable, had it not been for the availability of "cheap" Mexican labor—cheap, that is, by comparison with labor costs elsewhere. And it should be stressed also that Mexican labor was acclimatized; the Mexican was familiar with the environment. By 1940, the produce crops alone contributed more than a billion dollars annually in cash farm income. In the growth of commercial fruit, vegetable and cotton farming in the Southwest, Mexicans have played a major role.

Outside the Southwest, Mexicans were widely used in the sugar beet industry which began to expand after 1897, when a heavy tax was imposed on imported sugar. Today the crop is largely mechanized but, in the past, thousands of migratory Mexican workers journeyed north from south Texas communities to work in sugar beet fields in Montana, Colorado, the Dakotas, Michigan and Ohio. In 1927, it was estimated that of 58,000 sugar beet workers, 30,000 were Mexicans. Over the years some of these Mexican beet workers were either left stranded in the sugar beet areas after the crop was harvested or decided to stay on and, in this way, small colonies of Mexican settlement sprang up. But, by and large, Mexican immigration has been confined to the original fan of settlement and, as a consequence, the Spanish-Mexican influence has been massively re-enforced. In 1890 it seemed as though Mexicans were a vanishing element in the Southwest, but they are a large and expanding element there today.

Waves of Immigration

Unlike European immigration, there has been an ebb-and-flow to Mexican immigration. To repeat a figure previously cited, between 1900 and 1964, 1.3 million Mexicans immigrated to the United States, but they have come in waves and, at different periods, many have returned. The first great wave, of 224,706, crossed the border between 1910 and 1920. The next large wave, of roughly 436,733, swept north between 1920 and 1930. Still a third wave, of 293,000, was recorded in the period from 1950 to 1960. But in the 1930–1940 decade, only 27,937 immigrants crossed the border and from 1940 to 1950 the number was 54,290. There is, of course, an explanation for the relative decline registered in these decades. The 1930's marked a period of depression. It was in this period, also, that tens of thousands of dust bowl migrants, the so-called Okies and Arkies, came to Arizona and California and, to some extent, displaced the Mexicans in certain types of work. In the period from 1940 to 1950, with the demand for labor soaring, the number of Mexican "wetbacks," or illegal entrants, greatly increased, and this increase was not included in the immigration totals. In fact, the demand for labor during World War II and the Korean War became so great that the governments of the United States and Mexico entered into an agreement under which Mexican labor was imported, known as the *bracero* program. The *braceros*, or imported workers, were not included in the immigration total. They were imported, under contract, to work in certain crops and returned to Mexico once the crops were harvested. Generally speaking, when the demand for labor in the Southwest has increased, the volume of Mexican immigration has increased, but in depression years immigration has tapered off and, in some years, many immigrants have returned to Mexico. For example, during the depression years welfare agencies in California deported thousands of Mexican aliens.

The "wetback" situation requires a word of comment. There have always been wetbacks in the border states and, in some periods, very large numbers indeed. During World War II, with the dust bowl migrants being drawn into the shipyards and industrial plants, and with the Japanese-Americans being removed from the West Coast, the number of "wetbacks" zoomed. At the same time, thousands of *braceros* were imported (the first contingent arrived in Stockton, California, in September, 1942). The demand for labor was so great that the wetback situation soon got out of control; the Border Patrol was not in a position to stop the influx even if it had wanted to stop it. For every Mexican legally imported under the *bracero* program, at least four alien Mexicans or "wetbacks" were apprehended by the Border Patrol. Of the 875,000 apprehended in 1953, thousands were found to hold non-agricultural jobs. In fact, the wetback influx had such a demoralizing effect on wages and labor standards, and drained off so much purchasing power from local communities in the form of remittances sent to relatives in Mexico, that a determined effort was finally made to stop it. In 1953, the number of wetbacks rose to 1,035,282, but the next year the Border Patrol reported that the influx had been greatly reduced. Since then the border has been under fairly tight control. The *bracero* program continued, in one form or another, until it was permitted to lapse in December, 1964. The number of workers imported under this program varied from year to year; 447,000 were imported in 1959, only 183,000 in 1964. The wetback problem, so troublesome and complex, is merely one of numerous aspects of Mexican immigration not to be found in the pattern of European immigration.

The years of heaviest Mexican immigration occurred *after* the peak of European immigration. Mexican immigration, in a word, has been a late chapter in the saga of immigration. The first restrictive immigration acts in the 1920's made an exception for immigration from the Western Hemisphere, so that Mexican immigration continued long after European immigration had, for all practical purposes, ceased to be important. Legislation adopted in 1965 for the first time fixed a quota of 120,000 per year for Mexican immigration. Mexican immigration, of course, continues. In 1965 it was estimated that in five of the eleven years since 1954, permanent visas issued to immigrants born in Mexico exceeded the number of immigrants from any other country. In the fiscal year ending June 30, 1965, 55,253 immigrants born in Mexico entered the United States under permanent immigrant visas. There is also a high and steadily mounting movement of peoples back and forth across the border; more Mexicans visit the United States, more Americans visit Mexico. And since the Southwest is still expanding, it is reasonable to assume that Mexican immigration, in substantial volume, will continue for a long time.

11. EUROPEAN IMMIGRANT AND ORIENTAL ALIEN: ACCEPTANCE AND REJECTION BY THE CALIFORNIA LEGISLATURE OF 1913

SPENCER C. OLIN, JR.

One of the apparent paradoxes of California and American history is that reform and racial discrimination went hand in hand during the Progressive era. The Oriental in California had been the target of prejudice before the twentieth century, but as Asians entered the West in larger numbers, many Californians began to consider them a threat and acted. Professor Spencer C. Olin of the University of California at Irvine describes the Progressive politicians' response to the Oriental problem.

After the political catharsis of the Bull Moose campaign of 1912, many California progressives had had enough of reform. Their original reform goals had been three: "turn out the railroad villains," "purify" the administration of governmental affairs, and "democratize" the political system. Such a general program had offended few people and had received enthusiastic endorsement by a large majority of the state's citizens. In fact, the great strength of the California reform movement of 1910–1911 was due to the relatively uncontroversial nature of its "ideology" and to its consequent broad appeal. But by 1913 the pledges of the 1910 campaign had been fulfilled. The Southern Pacific Railroad Company had been kicked out of politics, state agencies had been fumigated by a newly created Board of Control, and the people had been given additional political power through direct legislation measures. Was there more to be done? Could more be asked of them?

Before the legislature of 1913 convened, it had become quite apparent that the basic unity which characterized the California progressive movement in the earlier years no longer existed. Conflict was inevitable between those legislators who felt that reform had gone far enough and those who recognized the necessity for additional legislation. Governor Hiram Johnson's opening address to the session seemed designed to pacify the former element, as he asked only for two specific measures: higher corporate taxes and the creation of a state administrative board to manage all state institutions and to have powers commensurate with the financial jurisdiction of the Board of Control. But if Johnson did not publicly urge the 1913 legislature to enact sweeping reforms, and if he had no well-formulated legislative program of his own, it is to his credit that he supported and helped push through the legislature several pro-

Spencer C. Olin, Jr., "European Immigrant and Oriental Alien: Acceptance and Rejection by the California Legislature of 1913," *Pacific Historical Review*, Vol. 35 (August 1966). Reprinted by permission.

gressive measures advocated by various pressure groups and influential citizens.

The session of 1913, though less memorable than that of 1911, considered and passed a significant body of legislation. Among the most important was the establishment of three new state agencies—an Industrial Welfare Commission, an Industrial Accident Commission, and a Commission of Immigration and Housing—and the passage of an Alien Land Law. Neither the Industrial Welfare Commission nor the Industrial Accident Commission will be discussed here. Rather, discussion centers on the concern for the plight of the European immigrant, expressed in the creation of a Commission of Immigration and Housing, and on the simultaneous disregard for the rights of the Oriental alien, expressed in the passage of an Alien Land Law.

It is true that the living conditions of Japanese workers engaged in agricultural labor were also improved by accomplishments of the Commission of Immigration and Housing. Yet when these same Orientals began to buy their own land, and to monopolize cheap farm labor, they presented an economic threat to American farm owners which could not be ignored.

California agriculture has always been dependent upon a large, mobile supply of cheap labor. As Henry George pointed out in *Progress and Poverty*, published in 1879, the early agricultural development of the state resulted in large-scale farming units worked by wage laborers, and not in extensive farm tenancy.[1] Such an agricultural system attracted thousands of unskilled aliens to California and dictated the substandard living conditions of a large portion of this population. Chinese, Japanese, Mexicans, Filipinos, and native migrants followed the harvests, living in camps or "jungles." Inadequate housing conditions and poor sanitary facilities resulted in sporadic uprisings in California's "factories in the fields," such as the famous Wheatland hop fields riot of 1913.[2]

In addition, thousands of immigrants from southern and eastern Europe flocked to California, lured by the advertised promise of wealth, health, and happiness. Once here, however, they often found that the Golden State for the immigrant was a kind of Hell. For them life was dismal; they were underfed, underpaid, exploited, and ignorant of the language and of their rights under American law. Many returned to their native lands, but many stayed, hoping for a better future.

These aliens, whether living with their families in rural labor camps or in urban slums, constituted a serious challenge to an administration concerned with social amelioration. The Johnson administration accepted the challenge, and a liberal reformer named Simon Lubin provided the main thrust. The result was the creation of perhaps the most important of the three social welfare agencies established in 1913—the

[1] Charles A. Barker, "Henry George and the California Background of *Progress and Poverty*," *California Historical Society Quarterly*, XXIV (1945), 109.

[2] Charleton H. Parker's report to Governor Hiram Johnson on the causes of the Wheatland riot, reprinted in his *The Casual Laborer and Other Essays* (New York, 1920), 171–199. His account of the Wheatland episode in Chapter II is most informative. Parker was executive secretary of the Commission of Immigration and Housing.

Commission of Immigration and Housing. Launching a program of immigrant assimilation unparalleled in the United States at that time, this agency was a pioneer not only in immigrant housing, but in education and labor camp inspection.

"To Simon Lubin more than any man," writes Samuel E. Wood, a specialist on problems created by immigration, "must be credited the creation of the Commission of Immigration and Housing. He insisted upon an independent agency, invested with powers adequate to cope with the complexity of the immigration problem in this state." [3] Lubin selected the personnel of the commission and as its president was instrumental in determining the policy and charting the activities of the agency for ten years.

Simon Lubin, born in Sacramento in 1876, was the son of David Lubin and the nephew of Harris Weinstock, both prosperous Sacramento merchants and crusaders for industrial and agrarian reform.[4] Educated at Harvard, Simon Lubin spent his college vacations working in the lower East Side of New York. From 1903 to 1904 he was a resident of South End House, a Boston social settlement. During his last two years at Harvard he made special investigations of immigrant problems in New York and Boston. In 1906 he returned to California. From then until his death in 1936 he was secretary and manager of Weinstock, Lubin, and Company of Sacramento. The employee-employer relationships of this company were characterized by advanced schemes of management—employee representation, credit unions, and retirement systems. Much of California's social legislation during this period was drafted by Lubin at his desk in the company offices.[5]

Lubin's first conversation with Government Johnson regarding a state program directed at the immigrant problem was just prior to the Bull Moose convention in 1912. Johnson discussed Lubin's suggestions with "some of those in whom I have confidence" during the convention and after his return of California.[6] The social worker-businessman continued to urge immediate action and finally prevailed upon Johnson to appoint a special committee which would submit a report to the next session of the legislature. On August 21, 1912, Lubin received his appointment to this committee. At the same time, Johnson wrote Lubin his

[3] See the excellent and neglected work by Samuel E. Wood, "The California State Commission of Immigration and Housing: A Study of Administrative Organization and the Growth of Function" (unpublished Ph.D. dissertation, University of California, Berkeley, 1942), p. 82.

[4] For a biography of David Lubin see Olivia Rossetti Agresti, *David Lubin: A Study in Practical Idealism* (Berkeley, 1941). Lubin and his stepbrother, Harris Weinstock, opened a dry goods store in Sacramento in 1874. Within ten years it was the largest department store and mail order house on the Pacific coast. Lubin was also a founder of the International Institute of Agriculture in Rome and devoted much of his life after 1885 to agricultural matters.

[5] Wood, "The California State Commission of Immigration and Housing," 83–85. All Lubin letters mentioned hereafter are cited in this dissertation. The Lubin Papers are housed in the Bancroft Library, but certain sections are restricted.

[6] Johnson to Simon Lubin, Aug. 15, 1912, Lubin Papers.

own personal thoughts on planning for the future. "My hope," explained the governor, "is that by timely action on our part, even if the immigration diverted to us by the opening of the Panama Canal shall be as great as that which in recent years has come to the Atlantic Coast, we may prevent the dreadful conditions of poverty that prevail in the great cities there." [7]

The temporary agency recommended legislation to create a permanent commission rather than attempting to strengthen existing state agencies. Lubin prepared a rough draft of an act creating an unpaid Commission of Industries and Labor, consisting of five members appointed by the governor. This commission was to direct and supervise a Bureau of Industry and Immigration and appoint all its employees.[8]

Lubin met with Johnson in late November, 1912, after which he reported to a fellow committeeman that he was sure the governor had "caught the spirit of the act." Johnson liked the idea of an unpaid commission which would determine policy and hire paid experts to administer the program. He advised Lubin to prepare a memorandum for the Board of Control, explaining the organization and proposed expenditures of the commission. In this memorandum Lubin recommended an appropriation of $50,000.00 a year to support the commission.[9]

While Johnson officially sponsored the measure and chose specific legislators to lead the fight in the Senate and assembly, he left the mobilization of pressure and the handling of the opposition to Lubin and his fellow committeemen. During the spring of 1913 Lubin remained in Sacramento to press for the passage of his bill. He arranged for witnesses to appear at committee hearings. He convinced C. K. McClatchy to wage an editorial battle for the bill in the Sacramento *Bee*. He prepared articles for newspapers and saw to it that letters were written to key legislators.[10] The legislature, responding favorably, passed the measure (which included a $50,000.00 appropriation for the gathering of information and data), and sent it to the governor in June.[11]

Members of the new commission were well aware of the general conditions under which aliens lived in California. But they lacked factual data upon which to base a specific remedial program. The first order of business, therefore, was to employ housing experts and special investigators to make field surveys. Between April 1 and August 11, 1914, 641 labor camps in every county of the state, housing over 41,000 laborers, were inspected. Of the total number, 188 were found to be in dangerous sanitary condition, and only 195 met the modest minimum sanitation

[7] Johnson to Simon Lubin, Aug. 20, 1912, Lubin Papers. Other appointees included Robert Watchorn and Reverend Dana W. Bartlett of Los Angeles and Katherine Felton and Robert N. Lynch of San Francisco. Also see Franklin Hichborn's article in the Sacramento *Bee*, March 8, 1913.

[8] Lubin to commissioners, Nov. 2, 1912, Lubin Papers.

[9] Lubin to Robert Lynch, Nov. 23, 1912, Lubin Papers. Also see Wood, "The California State Commission of Immigration and Housing," 95.

[10] Wood, *op. cit.*, 102.

[11] By September, Johnson had announced his appointments to the new commission: Simon Lubin as Chairman, Reverend Edward J. Hanna, Paul Scharrenberg, Mrs. Frank A. Gibson, and Arthur J. Fleming.

standards established by the commission. In addition to labor camps, the commission's experts investigated lodging houses and tenements in the larger cities, into which newly arrived Spanish, Mexican, Portuguese, and Italian families were packed like sardines.[12] These various surveys resulted in thirty-five special reports, three of which were eventually published.[13]

The commission's *Report on Unemployment,* published in December, 1914, called for the creation of a state bureau of labor exchanges with branch offices in major cities. It urged the passage of adequate camp sanitation laws and a complete revision of the state's housing laws. It also recommended legislation to prevent and punish fraud and misrepresentation in the sale of agricultural land. Governor Johnson was very enthusiastic about this report, and Lubin described his reaction in a letter to Mrs. Frank Gibson, a fellow commissioner:

> In all my contact with the Governor I never saw him so enthusiastic. He asked a great many questions, and then began to give again his opinion of the value of our work in the state, saying that he thought the real fruits of our efforts would not be seen until most of us had passed away. . . . He said that we could expect his cooperation at every stage of the game, and that he wants us to know that he is in entire sympathy with all we are trying to do.[14]

It was not until 1915 that the legislature authorized the Bureau of Labor Statistics to establish free employment bureaus in specific cities, passed a Labor Camp Act which required proper bedding, bathing, and eating facilities in all labor camps, and created a State Colonization and Rural Credits Committee.[15] But a substantial beginning was made during 1913 and 1914 to ameliorate the conditions under which immigrants in California were forced to live. Californians had invited the world to share the blessings of their state. The least the legislature could do was to insure that those blessings could be enjoyed by all who accepted that invitation.

[12] Charleton H. Parker, "State Commission of Immigration and Housing," *Labor Clarion,* XIII (Sept. 4, 1914), 56–57. For a thorough discussion of the commission's remarkable activities with respect to labor camp inspection, immigrant education, and housing see the *Second Annual Report of the Commission of Immigration and Housing, January 2, 1916* (Sacramento, 1916), *passim.*

[13] Wood cites the *Report on Unemployment to His Excellency, Governor Hiram Johnson* (Sacramento, 1914), which includes two studies: "Life-History Statistics" and "Employment Agency Situation in California." The third published report was "The Wheatland Hop Field Riot," which may be found in U. S. Senate, Subcommittee of the Commission on Education and Labor, *Hearings, Agricultural Labor in California,* 76th Cong. 3rd sess., Part 54, 20069–20072. Summaries of all the surveys are found in the Annual Reports of the Commission of Immigration and Housing for 1915 and 1916.

[14] Lubin to Mrs. Frank Gibson (undated), 1915, Commission File, cited in Wood, "The California State Commission of Immigration and Housing," 258n.

[15] See Earl C. Crockett, "The History of California Labor Legislation, 1910–1930" (unpublished Ph.D. dissertation, 1931), 240 and Wood, *op. cit.,* 188–189. For the early activities of the free employment bureaus see the *Labor Clarion,* Sept. 1, 1916, 8–10.

It may seem strange that an administration so concerned about the plight of the immigrant would at the same time support legislation designed to restrict the activities of a large portion of the state's alien population, the Orientals. Yet twice within a period of seven years, Californians, by their actions against the Japanese, embarrassed the national government and involved it in international difficulties.

There had been no significant anti-Japanese legislation passed in California prior to 1913, but there had been a long struggle for Japanese exclusion.[16] This struggle was highlighted, in 1905, by the formation of the Asiatic Exclusion League in San Francisco, and, in 1906, by the San Francisco school board's segregation of Japanese and Korean students from American. The Gentlemen's Agreement of 1907 temporarily decreased Japanese immigration, but California exclusionists were not completely satisfied.

So long as the Japanese remained wage laborers, agitation against them came largely from nonfarm groups which feared competition from "cheap labor." Farmer-employers, on the other hand, welcomed this source of mobile, cheap labor. As one Fresno fruit grower explained in January, 1907: ". . . we are wholly dependent upon [Japanese] labor. If they are excluded, we shall have to give up our farms and go out of business." [17]

However, a shift of Japanese population from urban to rural areas after 1908 increased anti-Japanese feeling in those districts, especially in the Central Valley. The Japanese began to acquire land and to employ as workers members of their own race exclusively, thereby reducing the farm labor pool. As Japanese land owners began to monopolize such cheap farm labor, they incurred the animus of both large and small growers. The Japanese were no longer merely a convenient source of manpower, but had gradually become active competitors for farm labor, farm land, and agricultural markets. "The real prejudice against the Japanese," writes Carey McWilliams, "dates from the time when they began to be small owners, rather than farm laborers." [18]

Yet in 1909 there were still approximately 30,000 Japanese occupied in agricultural labor in California. They were employed chiefly during cultivation and harvest, but were far more difficult to manage than the Chinese had been. Their characteristic independence was bemoaned by large growers, one of whom expressed his dismay in this manner:

> The Chinese when they were here were ideal. They were patient, plodding, and uncomplaining in the performance of the most menial service. They submitted to anything, never violating a contract. The

[16] For a good account of anti-Orientalism during the Johnson administration see Roger Daniels' *The Politics of Prejudice: The Anti-Japanese Movement in California and the Struggle for Japanese Exclusion* (Berkeley, 1962), particularly pp. 16–64.

[17] See Herbert B. Johnson, *Discrimination against Japanese in California* (Berkeley, 1907), 42, quoting from the San Francisco *Chronicle*, Jan. 2, 1907.

[18] Carey McWilliams, *Factories in the Field* (Boston, 1939), 111. Also see Fred H. Matthews, "White Community and 'Yellow Peril,'" *Mississippi Valley Historical Review*, (1964), 618.

exclusion acts drove them out. The Japanese now coming are a tricky and cunning lot, who break contracts and become quite independent.[19]

These feelings of irritation at the continued threat to the existence of large units of production and dismay at the decrease in the supply of cheap, manageable labor were manifested in increased anti-Japanese activity in the California legislature. When such economic pressures were merged with latent social and racial hostility, the issue was sure to become of prime political importance.

During the 1910 campaign, Democrats monopolized the anti-Oriental issue. Hiram Johnson decided not to take a public stand on the question and turned down invitations to address the Asiatic Exclusion League. But he did assure A. E. Yoell, the League's secretary, that he favored exclusion.[20] Once elected, however, Johnson informed Philander Knox, President Taft's secretary of state, that he would do everything he could to prevent the passage of anti-Oriental legislation in 1911. Johnson successfully bottled up such legislation in committee and no measures passed.[21]

In 1913, California business leaders in charge of organizing the Panama-Pacific International Exposition worked to quash further discriminatory legislation for fear it might impair trade relations with Japan and China. Chester Rowell, a member of the exposition's Advisory Council and a close friend of Johnson, explained to him in January, 1913, that the Japanese Diet was about to convene and would be debating its proposed budget. Included in that budget was an appropriation of some $1,500,000.00 for the exposition. Rowell and his fellow commissioners feared that if that item were defeated or slashed, it might seriously harm the exposition. Johnson was urged to press for postponement of anti-Oriental legislation. "There is no immediate urgency in passing the bill at all," Rowell declared. "The law must be passed ultimately, if California is not to be Hawaiianized, but there is no emergency so long as Japan continues in good faith to carry out the present arrangement." [22]

Johnson, in turn, suggested that a committee from the exposition come to Sacramento and address a conference of legislators. The commissioners were reluctant initially, fearing that such action might overdramatize the issue and provoke adverse reaction.[23] Eventually they agreed to accept the governor's suggestion and met with him prior to the

[19] California Fruit Growers' Convention *Proceedings,* 1907, p. 69, as quoted in the California State Relief Administration's study, *Migratory Labor in California* (Sacramento, 1936), 22. Chester Rowell repeated this charge in 1909: "The one overshadowing contrast is this: The Chinese will keep a contract; the Japanese will not." See "Chinese and Japanese in America," *The Annals of the American Academy of Political and Social Science,* XXXIV (1909), 5.

[20] Johnson to A. E. Yoell, May 18 and July 29, 1910, Johnson Papers.

[21] Johnson to Knox, Jan. 6, 1911, Johnson Papers.

[22] Rowell to Johnson, Jan. 6, 1913, Rowell Papers.

[23] Rowell to Johnson, March 16, 1913, Rowell Papers.

opening of the legislative session. Johnson assured the nine-man delegation that he would support their efforts to head off an alien land act. The delegation then met individually with nearly every senator and assemblyman in an effort to quash any legislation dealing with aliens.

Their efforts were in vain, for when the session opened anti-Japanese measures were submitted by Democrats and Republicans in both houses. Johnson later explained to Theodore Roosevelt that the exposition officials might have succeeded in their task had not many legislators, up to that time uncommitted, been persuaded by the impressive testimony of farmers from various communities in the state. "These farmers insisted that an alien land bill was absolutely essential for their protection, and necessary for the future welfare of California," Johnson reported.[24]

Perhaps equally important was the challenge presented to Johnson and California politicians by the federal government's intervention in April, 1913. For Johnson, this intervention was a major event, marking "the breaking down of the barrier that has heretofore existed between the national government and legislation in the states." [25]

After Woodrow Wilson had taken office, Johnson had informed Rowell of his suspicions that such pressures would be exerted to block discriminatory legislation.[26] Much to Johnson's surprise, however, Wilson did not immediately intervene to thwart anti-Oriental measures. In fact, the President even encouraged Democratic politicians in California to continue their course: "I have never been inclined to criticize," Wilson wrote James D. Phelan. "I have only hoped that the doing of the thing might be so modulated and managed as to offend the susceptibilities of a friendly nation as little as possible." [27]

Rather than intervene directly in California's affairs, Wilson chose to express his point of view to Representative William Kent, a progressive from northern California. During an interview held the first week of April, 1913, Wilson suggested to Kent that California legislators might frame their bill in less offensive form by excluding from land ownership those persons who had not applied for American citizenship, without singling out the Japanese. Kent relayed this suggestion to Hiram Johnson, and the doughty governor replied that Wilson should communicate with him directly if he had anything to propose.[28]

[24] Johnson to Roosevelt, June 21, 1913, Johnson Papers. As Robert Kelley points out in a recent article, V. S. McClatchy, president of the Sacramento Bee and owner of 1,200 acres of land in the Sutter Basin, was an avid opponent of Japanese immigration: "If he was creating a farm empire for the purpose of preserving what agrarians always regarded as the bedrock of American society, the family farm, the families on them had also to be traditionally American, not Japanese." Pacific Historical Review, XXXIV (1965), 46–47.

[25] Johnson to Roosevelt, June 21, 1913, Johnson Papers.

[26] Johnson to Rowell, March 17, 1913, Rowell Papers.

[27] Wilson to Phelan, April 9, 1913, Wilson Papers, as quoted in Arthur S. Link, Wilson: The New Freedom (Princeton, 1956), 290.

[28] See William Kent, "Some Reminiscences of Hiram Johnson," manuscript in the Kent Papers, Yale University; Kent to Johnson, April 7, 1913, Wilson Papers, Library of Congress; and Johnson to Kent, April 8, 1913, Kent Papers — all cited in Link, op. cit., 290–291.

The President's dilemma was temporarily resolved when Johnson agreed to his request that Secretary of State William Jennings Bryan consult with the California governor. But Bryan's mission was hopeless from the beginning, for the legislature was more than ever determined to pass an anti-alien measure. By the time Bryan arrived in Sacramento, substantial progress had been made preparing a bill for passage.

During a period of one week Bryan summoned various senators and assemblymen for personal interviews, discussing with them the diplomatic consequences of anti-Oriental legislation and urging them to reconsider their views. His overtures were completely disregarded. In early May the Alien Land Bill passed the Senate by a vote of 35 to 2 and the Assembly 72 to 5.[29] Limiting leases of agricultural land to Japanese to maximum terms of three years, the law barred further land purchases by Japanese aliens. Aliens eligible for citizenship, on the other hand, could own property without limitation.

Johnson promised Bryan that he would not sign the bill until the secretary had conferred with President Wilson. On May 11, 1913, Bryan sent Johnson a telegram suggesting that the bill be vetoed. In his lengthy reply, Johnson clearly stated California's position, stressing the fact that, in his opinion, the federal government had established the precedent for Oriental discrimination. It was California, not the Oriental, which was being discriminated against. Accordingly, on May 19, 1913, Johnson signed the bill.[30]

The Asiatic Exclusion League immediately announced that it intended to invoke direct legislation against the Alien Land Act and to substitute a law prohibiting Japanese from either owning or leasing any land in California. Despite some dissatisfaction with the bill, however, most Californians seemed to feel that the problem of Orientals had been laid to rest. As a result, there was very little anti-Japanese agitation for the remainder of Johnson's tenure in office.

What role did Johnson play in the passage of the Alien Land Act of 1913? What beliefs and political calculations motivated him? In late March of 1913 he had assured the Panama-Pacific Exposition delegation that he would support their efforts to head off the alien land bill. Yet Roger Daniels, author of a detailed study of the movement for Japanese exclusion in California, reports: "it is now quite clear that from the middle of March Johnson was the behind-the-scenes manager of the alien land bill." [31] In support of this statement Daniels cites a telegram of March 23 from Johnson to Rowell: "HAVE INFORMED [Assemblyman E. S.] BIRDSALL [sponsor of a general anti-alien bill] THAT HE MAY

[29] *Journal of the Senate, 1913*, p. 2324; *Journal of the Assembly, 1913*, p. 2495.
[30] See Johnson's reply to Bryan of May 14, 1913, Johnson Papers. Also see Thomas A. Bailey, "California, Japan, and the Alien Land Legislation of 1913." *Pacific Historical Review*, (1932), 40.
The Naturalization Act of 1906 restricted naturalization to white persons and persons of African descent, and by a special Act of Congress Chinese were specifically barred. There was no direct provision relating to Japanese, but, West Coast exclusionists assumed that the Japanese, being neither white nor of African descent, were not entitled to naturalization.
[31] Daniels, *The Politics of Prejudice,* 59.

ACT IF HE DESIRES." [32] What caused Johnson to so instruct Birdsall? What prompted him to renege on his promise to the Panama-Pacific Exposition delegation? Daniels does not discuss the reason for Johnson's switch from opposition to support of the bill, but several may be advanced.

Johnson obviously enjoyed his skirmish with the federal government, although he admitted afterwards that he had never "skated on thinner ice than . . . in the contest with Mr. Bryan." [33] Writing to Theodore Roosevelt, Johnson exulted: "We have shown the Democratic doctrine of 'State's rights' to be sham and pretense, insisted upon when it is their state that is affected but denied when they represent the federal government and our State is affected." [34] In waging a victorious battle against the federal government on behalf of "states rights," Johnson not only succeeded in embarrassing the Wilson administration but also in attracting national publicity.

It is also probable that Johnson saw the handwriting on the wall: if the legislature were bound and determined to pass the Alien Land Law, why should he risk his political neck to fight for its defeat? What must be stressed is Johnson's belief that the passage of the bill was essential for his own political survival. In a particularly revealing letter to Meyer Lissner, Johnson commented on recent progressive defections:

> You can not make people be good faster than they want to be good. . . . Communities will stand just so much reform legislation at one time, and wise is the man who intuitively has some conception of just how far he can go. . . . Indeed, our legislation had brought us to the very verge of disaster. . . . The alien land bill rehabilitated us north of Tehachapi; but aside from the right of the alien land bill, its necessity etc., it was the most fortunate thing that ever occurred from a political standpoint.[35]

Anti-Oriental legislation thus became the means by which Johnson could regain the esteem which he felt had been lost by his support of "excessively radical" legislation. Such demagoguery was not uncharacteristic of Johnson, but the fact that he was willing to involve the United States government in international difficulties mainly to enhance his own political position makes his actions seem quite irresponsible.

Daniels has pointed out that Johnson's support of the alien land bill was particularly wanton because he "knew well that Japanese land tenure in California would not be seriously affected by it." [36] As Californians quickly discovered, the Alien Land Law was rendered ineffective when the Japanese continued to buy and lease land in the names of their children who were American citizens. Orientals also formed corporations and bought or leased land in the corporate name, after issuing a majority

[32] *Ibid.*, 135, note 66.
[33] Johnson to Lissner, May 7, 1913, Johnson Papers.
[34] Johnson to Roosevelt, June 21, 1913, Johnson Papers.
[35] Johnson to Lissner, June 9, 1913, Johnson Papers.
[36] Daniels, *The Politics of Prejudice,* 63.

of the capital stock to American citizens, who served as trustees. In 1920 a new land law remedied these "defects": Japanese were thereafter prohibited from buying or selling land in the names of their children or through the medium of corporations.[37]

While it was possible to evade the law, it must not be assumed that Japanese farmers were not seriously affected by the Alien Land Law. Often the Japanese would win their court cases and be impoverished in the process. The anti-alien laws made land ownership uncertain and subject to the whims of politicians and district attorneys.[38] Progressives of both parties were responsible for this unfortunate affront to the dignity of the Japanese people. Ostensibly dedicated to the principles of democracy, yet blinded by racial prejudice, these "reformers" were so influenced by unfounded fears of Oriental inundation that they participated in an essentially undemocratic act.

Despite the reluctance of many progressive legislators to proceed farther along the reform path, the 1913 legislature established an impressive record, marred only by the Alien Land Law. Social welfare legislation set the pattern for the session, and individuals such as Simon Lubin provided the main impetus for the passage of these measures. Characteristic of the California progressives' "scientific" approach to social and economic problems was the creation of numerous commissions—the Industrial Welfare Commission, the Industrial Accident Commission, and the Commission of Immigration and Housing. Yet it was the Johnson Administration's commitment to the immigrant, in the form of a special commission, which was most unique and significant. The activities and accomplishments of Simon Lubin's Commission of Immigration and Housing expressed a deep concern for the plight of the immigrant, especially the immigrant of European stock. It is unfortunate, though typically in character, that the progressives' concern was not coupled with an understanding of the aspirations of nonwhite aliens.

[37] *Ibid.* Also see the State Board of Control report, *California and the Oriental* (Sacramento, 1920), 135; U.S., H.R., Committee on Immigration and Naturalization, *Hearings on Japanese Immigration 1920*, 66th Cong. 2d sess., pp. 98–99; and T. Iyenaga and Kenoske Sato, *Japan and the California Problem* (New York, 1921), 139–140. The 1913 Alien Land Law is reprinted in its entirety on pp. 204–206 of the latter work; the 1920 law on pp. 207–215.

[38] See T. Scott Miyakawa's review of *The Politics of Prejudice* in the *Southern California Quarterly*, XLVI (1964), 107–108.

Chapter 4

The Impact of Boom, Depression, and War upon the Minorities, 1920-1945

The quarter of a century that preceded the end of World War II was a time of rapid change in California. This generation started with a "boom" in the 1920s that was unprecedented in previous California history. Americans from throughout the nation flocked to California seeking economic opportunities. Motion pictures attracted the talented and the not so talented to California and provided a new celluloid glamour to the Pacific coast.

Among those who came West were the minorities. The immigrants from Mexico continued to come in large numbers. By the 1920s a few Negroes began to come to the Golden State. Many settled in the older sections of the rapidly growing cities, and a pattern of residential segregation began to develop. The new, expanding suburbs were all white; the central cities were gradually becoming the dwelling place for Mexican-Americans, Orientals, and the new black Californians.

These enclaves of Orientals, blacks, and Mexicans had greater significance in the decades that followed. Urban communities such as the Watts district of Los Angeles and central parts of Oakland became the "ports of entry" for Negroes from Southern states. Mexicans located in different but nearby central-city *barrios*. These minorities came in ever-increasing numbers in the 1930s and especially during World War II.

During the 1930s the Oriental expulsion and the rapid growth of California's economy had an impact upon the Asian-Americans. Many second-generation Japanese (Nisei) and Chinese decided that they were in America to stay. They began the process of outward assimilation to the prevailing white, middle-class values. Perhaps because of the close-knit Oriental family structure and the emphasis among Orientals upon education, second and third generation Japanese-Americans (Sansei) in the years before World War II had the training to resume their place in society and to overcome the personal trauma of their exile to relocation camps during the war years.

In the 1930s the majority and minority suffered alike. Although California felt the impact of the Great Depression somewhat later than the rest of the country, by 1933 America's problems became California's problems. Thousands of poor, frightened Americans drove their rickety automobiles to find that the golden land they saw in Hollywood films was a mirage. For the first time in decades, thousands of Anglo migrants felt the same pinch of hunger and feelings of privation that minorities had known so well.

The film industry suffered relatively little during the Depression. In this period hundreds of Hollywood films were produced each year. Although these pictures did not dwell upon problems concerning minorities, they nonetheless had parts for minority actors who had a profound influence upon the general audience. The images that the film makers created in the 1920s and 1930s still persist. The lazy Mexican, the predatory Indian, the obsequious Negro all became part of the popular history created by Hollywood.

World War II was a significant turning point for minorities in California. Thousands of Negroes came to work in the new defense industries. The shortage of domestic and agricultural labor that accompanied the war caused farmers and other employers to look for a new source of inexpensive manpower. Recalling the hard work done by earlier Mexican immigrants and the low wages paid them, Southwestern employers again turned to labor sources south of the border. The result of their search was the *bracero* program of imported contract laborers. This program lasted to the mid-1960s. The *braceros* worked diligently, forcing down the wages of Mexican-American and other domestic farm laborers. The impact of the *bracero* was felt for years in California agriculture. A different problem was present for urban Mexican-American youth. In the cities during the war years, groups of these youths, called *Pachucos*, encountered the antipathy of many whites because of their different way of life.

The generation that ended in 1945 underwent a number of changes. The reader should consider what changes occurred in the racial and ethnic population of the state during these years. How did World War II drastically alter the situation for a number of minorities? In considering these questions the reader should try to relate what was happening in California to national trends and attitudes during the same period.

12. FROM *THE GRAPES OF WRATH*

JOHN STEINBECK

*The Great Depression of the 1930s brought large numbers of migrants
from the Southwest and Midwest. These farmers sought a fresh start
and economic prosperity in the Golden State. John Steinbeck, a Nobel
prizewinning novelist, at one time lived and worked among
California's "grapes of wrath." The following is an excerpt from his
well-known novel.*

Once California belonged to Mexico and its land to Mexicans; and a
horde of tattered feverish Americans poured in. And such was their
hunger for land that they took the land—stole Sutter's land, Guerrero's
land, took the grants and broke them up and growled and quarreled over
them, those frantic hungry men; and they guarded with guns the land
they had stolen. They put up houses and barns, they turned the earth
and planted crops. And these things were possession, and possession
was ownership.

The Mexicans were weak and fed. They could not resist, because they
wanted nothing in the world as frantically as the Americans wanted
land.

Then, with time, the squatters were no longer squatters, but owners;
and their children grew up and had children on the land. And the hunger
was gone from them, the feral hunger, the gnawing, tearing hunger for
land, for water and earth and the good sky over it, for the green thrust-
ing grass, for the swelling roots. They had these things so completely
that they did not know about them any more. They had no more the
stomach-tearing lust for a rich acre and a shining blade to plow it, for
seed and a windmill beating its wings in the air. They arose in the dark
no more to hear the sleepy birds' first chittering, and the morning wind
around the house while they waited for the first light to go out to the dear
acres. These things were lost, and crops were reckoned in dollars, and
land was valued by principal plus interest, and crops were bought and
sold before they were planted. Then crop failure, drought, and flood were
no longer little deaths within life, but simple losses of money. And all
their love was thinned with money, and all their fierceness dribbled
away in interest until they were no longer farmers at all, but little shopkeepers of crops, little manufacturers who must sell before they can
make. Then those farmers who were not good shopkeepers lost their land
to good shopkeepers. No matter how clever, how loving a man might be
with earth and growing things, he could not survive if he were not also a
good shopkeeper. And as time went on, the business men had the farms,
and the farms grew larger, but there were fewer of them.

Now farming became industry, and the owners followed Rome, although they did not know it. They imported slaves, although they did not

call them slaves: Chinese, Japanese, Mexicans, Filipinos. They live on rice and beans, the business men said. They don't need much. They wouldn't know what to do with good wages. Why, look how they live. Why, look what they eat. And if they get funny—deport them.

And all the time the farms grew larger and the owners fewer. And there were pitifully few farmers on the land any more. And the imported serfs were beaten and frightened and starved until some went home again, and some grew fierce and were killed or driven from the country. And the farms grew larger and the owners fewer.

And the crops changed. Fruit trees took the place of grain fields, and vegetables to feed the world spread out on the bottoms: lettuce, cauliflower, artichokes, potatoes—stoop crops. A man may stand to use a scythe, a plow, a pitchfork; but he must crawl like a bug between the rows of lettuce, he must bend his back and pull his long bag between the cotton rows, he must go on his knees like a penitent across a cauliflower patch.

And it came about that owners no longer worked on their farms. They farmed on paper; and they forgot the land, the smell, the feel of it, and remembered only that they owned it, remembered only what they gained and lost by it. And some of the farms grew so large that one man could not even conceive of them any more, so large that it took batteries of bookkeepers to keep track of interest and gain and loss; chemists to test the soil, to replenish; straw bosses to see that the stooping men were moving along the rows as swiftly as the material of their bodies could stand. Then such a farmer really became a storekeeper, and kept a store. He paid the men, and sold them food, and took the money back. And after a while he did not pay the men at all, and saved bookkeeping. These farms gave food on credit. A man might work and feed himself; and when the work was done, he might find that he owed money to the company. And the owners not only did not work the farms any more, many of them had never seen the farms they owned.

And then the dispossessed were drawn west—from Kansas, Oklahoma, Texas, New Mexico; from Nevada and Arkansas families, tribes, dusted out, tractored out. Carloads, caravans, homeless and hungry; twenty thousand and fifty thousand and a hundred thousand and two hundred thousand. They streamed over the mountains, hungry and restless—restless as ants, scurrying to find work to do—to lift, to push, to pull, to pick, to cut—anything, any burden to bear, for food. The kids are hungry. We got no place to live. Like ants scurrying for work, for food, and most of all for land.

We ain't foreign. Seven generations back Americans, and beyond that Irish, Scotch, English, German. One of our folks in the Revolution, an' they was lots of our folks in the Civil War—both sides. Americans.

They were hungry, and they were fierce. And they had hoped to find a home, and they found only hatred. Okies—the owners hated them because the owners knew they were soft and the Okies strong, that they were fed and the Okies hungry; and perhaps the owners had heard from their grandfathers how easy it is to steal land from a soft man if you are fierce and hungry and armed. The owners hated them. And in the towns, the storekeepers hated them because they had no money to spend. There is no shorter path to a storekeeper's contempt, and all his admirations are exactly opposite. The town men, little bankers, hated Okies because there was nothing to gain from them. They had nothing. And the laboring people hated Okies because a hungry man must work, and if he must work, if he has to work, the wage payer automatically gives him less for his work; and then no one can get more.

And the dispossessed, the migrants, flowed into California, two hundred and fifty thousand, and three hundred thousand. Behind them new tractors were going on the land and the tenants were being forced off. And new waves were on the way, new waves of the dispossessed and the homeless, hardened, intent, and dangerous.

And while the Californians wanted many things, accumulation, social success, amusement, luxury, and a curious banking security, the new barbarians wanted only two things—land and food; and to them the two were one. And whereas the wants of the Californians were nebulous and undefined, the wants of the Okies were beside the roads, lying there to be seen and coveted: the good fields with water to be dug for, the good green fields, earth to crumble experimentally in the hand, grass to smell, oaten stalks to chew until the sharp sweetness was in the throat. A man might look at a fallow field and know, and see in his mind that his own bending back and his own straining arms would bring the cabbages into the light, and the golden eating corn, the turnips and carrots.

And a homeless hungry man, driving the roads with his wife beside him and his thin children in the back seat, could look at the fallow fields which might produce food but not profit, and that man could know how a fallow field is a sin and the unused land a crime against the thin children. And such a man drove along the roads and knew temptation at every field, and knew the lust to take these fields and make them grow strength for his children and a little comfort for his wife. The temptation was before him always. The fields goaded him, and the company ditches with good water flowing were a goad to him.

And in the south he saw the golden oranges hanging on the trees, the little golden oranges on the dark green trees; and guards with shotguns patrolling the lines so a man might not pick an orange for a thin child, oranges to be dumped if the price was low.

He drove his old car into a town. He scoured the farms for work. Where can we sleep the night?

Well, there's Hooverville on the edge of the river. There's a whole raft of Okies there.

He drove his old car to Hooverville. He never asked again, for there was a Hooverville on the edge of every town.

The rag town lay close to water; and the houses were tents, and weed-thatched enclosures, paper houses, a great junk pile. The man drove his family in and became a citizen of Hooverville—always they were called Hooverville. The man put up his own tent as near to water as he could get; or if he had no tent, he went to the city dump and brought back cartons and built a house of corrugated paper. And when the rains came the house melted and washed away. He settled in Hooverville and he scoured the countryside for work, and the little money he had went for gasoline to look for work. In the evening the men gathered and talked together. Squatting on their hams they talked of the land they had seen.

There's thirty thousan' acres, out west of here. Layin' there. Jesus, what I could do with that, with five acres of that! Why, hell, I'd have ever'thing to eat.

Notice one thing? They ain't no vegetables nor chickens nor pigs at the farms. They raise one thing—cotton, say, or peaches, or lettuce. 'Nother place'll be all chickens. They buy the stuff they could raise in the dooryard.

Jesus, what I could do with a couple pigs!

Well, it ain't yourn, an' it ain't gonna be yourn.

What we gonna do? The kids can't grow up this way.

In the camps the word would come whispering, There's work at Shafter. And the cars would be loaded in the night, the highways crowded—a gold rush for work. At Shafter the people would pile up, five times too many to do the work. A gold rush for work. They stole away in the night, frantic for work. And along the roads lay the temptations, the fields that could bear food.

That's owned. That ain't our'n.

Well, maybe we could get a little piece of her. Maybe—a little piece. Right down there—a patch. Jimson weed now. Christ, I could git enough potatoes off'n that little patch to feed my whole family!

It ain't our'n. It got to have Jimson weeds.

Now and then a man tried; crept on the land and cleared a piece, trying like a thief to steal a little richness from the earth. Secret gardens hidden in the weeds. A package of carrot seeds and a few turnips. Planted potato skins, crept out in the evening secretly to hoe in the stolen earth.

Leave the weeds around the edge—then nobody can see what we're a-doin'. Leave some weeds, big tall ones, in the middle.

Secret gardening in the evenings, and water carried in a rusty can.

And then one day a deputy sheriff: Well, what you think you're doin'?

I ain't doin' no harm.

I had my eye on you. This ain't your land. You're trespassing.

The land ain't plowed, an' I ain't hurtin' it none.

You goddamned squatters. Pretty soon you'd think you owned it. You'd be sore as hell. Think you owned it. Get off now.

And the little green carrot tops were kicked off and the turnip greens trampled. And then the Jimson weed moved back in. But the cop was right. A crop raised—why, that makes ownership. Land hoed and the carrots eaten—a man might fight for land he's taken food from. Get him off quick! He'll think he owns it. He might even die fighting for the little plot among the Jimson weeds.

Did ya see his face when we kicked them turnips out? Why, he'd kill a fella soon's he'd look at him. We got to keep these here people down or they'll take the country. They'll take the country.

Outlanders, foreigners.

Sure, they talk the same language, but they ain't the same. Look how they live. Think any of us folks'd live like that? Hell, no!

In the evenings, squatting and talking. And an excited man: Whyn't twenty of us take a piece of lan'? We got guns. Take it an' say, "Put us off if you can." Whyn't we do that?

They'd jus' shoot us like rats.

Well, which'd you ruther be, dead or here? Under groun' or in a house all made of gunny sacks? Which'd you ruther for your kids, dead now or dead in two years with what they call malnutrition? Know what we et all week? Biled nettles an' fried dough! Know where we got the flour for the dough? Swep' the floor of a boxcar.

Talking in the camps, and the deputies, fat-assed men with guns slung on fat hips, swaggering through the camps: Give 'em somepin to think about. Got to keep 'em in line or Christ only knows what they'll do! Why, Jesus, they're as dangerous as niggers in the South! If they ever get together there ain't nothin' that'll stop 'em.

> Quote: In Lawrenceville a deputy sheriff evicted a squatter, and the squatter resisted, making it necessary for the officer to use force. The eleven-year-old son of the squatter shot and killed the deputy with a .22 rifle.

Rattlesnakes! Don't take chances with 'em, an' if they argue, shoot first. If a kid'll kill a cop, what'll the men do? Thing is, get tougher'n they are. Treat 'em rough. Scare 'em.

What if they won't scare? What if they stand up and take it and shoot back? These men were armed when they were children. A gun is an extension of themselves. What if they won't scare? What if some time an army of them marches on the land as the Lombards did in Italy, as the Germans did on Gaul and the Turks did on Byzantium? They were land-hungry, ill-armed hordes too, and the legions could not stop them. Slaughter and terror did not stop them. How can you frighten a man whose hunger is not only in his own cramped stomach but in the wretched bellies of his children? You can't scare him—he has known a fear beyond every other.

In Hooverville the men talking: Grampa took his lan' from the Injuns.

Now, this ain't right. We're a-talkin' here. This here you're talkin' about is stealin'. I ain't no thief.

No? You stole a bottle of milk from a porch night before last. An' you stole some copper wire and sold it for a piece of meat.

Yeah, but the kids was hungry.

It's stealin', though.

Know how the Fairfiel' ranch was got? I'll tell ya. It was all gov'ment lan', an' could be took up. Ol' Fairfiel', he went into San Francisco to the bars, an' he got him three hunderd stew bums. Them bums took up the lan'. Fairfiel' kep' 'em in food an' whisky, an' then when they'd proved the lan', ol' Fairfiel' took it from 'em. He used to say the lan' cost him a pint of rotgut an acre. Would you say that was stealin'?

Well, it wasn't right, but he never went to jail for it.

No, he never went to jail for it. An' the fella that put a boat in a wagon an' made his report like it was all under water 'cause he went in a boat— he never went to jail neither. An' the fellas that bribed congressmen and the legislatures never went to jail neither.

All over the State, jabbering in the Hoovervilles.

And then the raids—the swoop of armed deputies on the squatters' camps. Get out. Department of Health orders. This camp is a menace to health.

Where we gonna go?

That's none of our business. We got orders to get you out of here. In half an hour we set fire to the camp.

They's typhoid down the line. You want ta spread it all over?

We got orders to get you out of here. Now get! In half an hour we burn the camp.

In half an hour the smoke of paper houses, of weed-thatched huts, rising to the sky, and the people in their cars rolling over the highways, looking for another Hooverville.

And in Kansas and Arkansas, in Oklahoma and Texas and New Mexico, the tractors moved in and pushed the tenants out.

Three hundred thousand in California and more coming. And in California the roads full of frantic people running like ants to pull, to push, to lift, to work. For every manload to lift, five pairs of arms extended to lift it; for every stomachful of food available, five mouths open.

And the great owners, who must lose their land in an upheaval, the great owners with access to history, with eyes to read history and to know the great fact: when property accumulates in too few hands it is taken away. And that companion fact: when a majority of the people are hungry and cold they will take by force what they need. And the little screaming fact that sounds through all history: repression works only to strengthen and knit the repressed. The great owners ignored the three cries of history. The land fell into fewer hands, the number of the dispossessed increased, and every effort of the great owners was directed at repression. The money was spent for arms, for gas to protect the great holdings, and spies were sent to catch the murmuring of revolt so that it might be stamped out. The changing economy was ignored, plans for the change ignored; and only means to destroy revolt were considered, while the causes of revolt went on.

The tractors which throw men out of work, the belt lines which carry loads, the machines which produce, all were increased; and more and more families scampered on the highways, looking for crumbs from the great holdings, lusting after the land beside the roads. The great owners formed associations for protection and they met to discuss ways to intimidate, to kill, to gas. And always they were in fear of a principle—three hundred thousand—if they ever move under a leader—the end. Three hundred thousand, hungry and miserable; if they ever know themselves, the land will be theirs and all the gas, all the rifles in the world won't stop them. And the great owners, who had become through their holdings both more and less than men, ran to their destruction, and used every means that in the long run would destroy them. Every little means, every violence, every raid on a Hooverville, every deputy swaggering through a ragged camp put off the day a little and cemented the inevitability of the day.

The men squatted on their hams, sharp-faced men, lean from hunger and hard from resisting it, sullen eyes and hard jaws. And the rich land was around them.

D'ja hear about the kid in that fourth tent down?

No, I jus' come in.

Well, that kid's been a-cryin' in his sleep an' a-rollin' in his sleep. Them folks thought he got worms. So they give him a blaster, an' he died. It was what they call black-tongue the kid had. Comes from not gettin' good things to eat.

Poor little fella.

Yeah, but them folks can't bury him. Got to go to the county stone orchard.

Well, hell.

And hands went into pockets and little coins came out. In front of the tent a little heap of silver grew. And the family found it there.

Our people are good people; our people are kind people. Pray God some day kind people won't all be poor. Pray God some day a kid can eat.

And the associations of owners knew that some day the praying would stop.

And there's the end.

13. WORLD WAR II AND THE NISEI

The internment of Japanese-Americans during World War II is one of the unpleasant pages in American history. With little regard shown for their freedom and property, the Nisei were deported to camps throughout the nation. These citizens were victims of wartime hatreds and profiteering. It also appears that they were victims of racial prejudice, because virtually no Italian-Americans or German-Americans experienced the same loss of freedom. Twenty-five years later, in a pamphlet sponsored by the Japanese-American Citizens League, the Nisei leaders comment upon their experience.

Like the Chinese before us, we Issei were easy to single out as objects of ridicule and scorn. Appearance and language set us apart. It was supreme irony. The very pioneer virtues of industry and thrift so much admired in others became symbols of hatred and fear.

"Yellow peril!" they cried.

Read the headlines in the San Francisco Chronicle's hate campaign of 1905: "The Japanese Invasion" . . . "Japanese, a Menace to American

FROM *100 Years of Japanese in America; Wakamatsu Colony Centennial, 1869–1969* (San Francisco: Japanese American Citizens League, 1969). Reprinted by permission of the Japanese American Citizens League.

Women" . . . "Brown Men an Evil in the Public Schools" . . . "Crime and Poverty Go Hand in Hand With Asiatic Labor."

In the wake of such campaigns, hundreds of anti-Japanese laws were adopted by the states which once had welcomed us. Our lives became circumscribed, thwarted.

Where was the freedom which had beckoned?

It was still there, glimmering through the legal/social barriers like the *unuhana* which welcomes the springtime. From within our ethnic ghetto, barred from many jobs for which we were educated and superbly fitted, we could still see *outside* the thing which had brought us to this land.

"*Yoshi,*" we said. "All right." We had a heritage of determination, of faith and patience.

By the late 1930s, Nisei voices grew louder, more eloquent.

.   .   .

Sunday, December 7, 1941.

We recall that date in a way other Americans cannot. It was the beginning of a nightmare. They call it public hysteria, vigilantism, "the blackest chapter in the history of American democracy." It was a bloodless pogrom but there were acts of brutality, of hostile violence.

What are these words, these labels, in the face of the reality? Racism, political opportunism, greed—all operated behind the mask of "military necessity." There was no *due process of law,* no charges filed, no hearings held.

On March 2, 1942, the madness reached its climax in a Presidential Executive Order. By that order, some 120,000 of our people, two-thirds of them American by birth, were herded out of the coastal states and into ten concentration camps.

The evacuation was completed in 137 days with a terrifying affront to human values and democratic ideals. Businesses were closed, farms abandoned, homes boarded up, furnishings sold for pennies on the dollar.

What a bitter experience this loss of freedom was in the *Land of the Free*. Repudiated by our government, knowing that a basic American principle was being violated, we were imprisoned for having "the wrong ancestors."

And not a single act of disloyalty was reported against us by responsible authorities, then or later.

Our concentration camps were hastily converted from fairgrounds, racetracks, parks, pavilions. We found ourselves behind barbed wire fences guarded by sentries in watchtowers complete with mounted machineguns and searchlights in the name of "military necessity." The average time we had been permitted to uproot our lives—15 days.

Well . . . we hadn't even had that much time at Aizu, but the "military necessity" had been a bit more obvious.

The Federal Reserve Bank of San Francisco estimated our loss at $400 million. With what system of values do you measure the loss for our Issei and their Nisei children? How can you put a sum of money as balance against the work of a lifetime obliterated by a single stroke of the Presidential pen?

.   .   .

Something profound had happened to us in this new land, though. Our dream refused to die.

> 'Left all untended,
> Still it flourished—this
> Flower we planted.'

Individually and together through the Japanese American Citizens League, the Niseis demanded the right to exercise their duties and obligations as Americans.

This is how histories are written, you see:

On February 1, 1943, the U.S. Army formed the 442nd Regimental Combat Team composed of volunteers from Hawaii and the continental United States, most of the latter coming from the concentration camps.

Their motto: "Go For Broke."

Behind that motto, the 442nd became the most decorated unit of its size and length of service in American military history. The 442nd was to be merged later with that other band of heroes whose ancestors came from Japan, the 100th Infantry Battalion. The 100th, organized in Hawaii, trained on the mainland, was committed to action at Salerno, Volturno, Cassino, Anzio Beachhead, the Rapido River, the breakthrough to Rome . . .

.   .   .

What length of time did it take before the European-American became simply American? What price did he pay? Do the survivors of the 100th and the 442nd know?

Are there others who can answer these questions?

The War Department recruited volunteers from the concentration camps to serve in Military Intelligence. Although few knew it, Nisei linguists had been engaged in this highly sensitive work long before *Senso* dispatched his lightning bolts in World War II.

More than 6,000 Nisei served in virtual anonymity in the Pacific War against the land of their ancestors. A select few were engaged in intelligence work in the Philippines, later escaped to Bataan and Corregidor and finally were ordered to Australia by General MacArthur. Others were assigned to the Pacific Islands and Alaska, were loaned to our allies and attached to the Joint Intelligence Center at Hawaii. They served from New Delhi to China and saw battle with Merrill's Marauders.

Much of this was doubly dangerous front line duty where a Nisei linguist faced the guns of his American comrades who, seeing an oriental face, might shoot without warning. A classic and tragic example of this involved Sgt. Frank Hachiya, mortally wounded by invading American troops at Leyte as he attempted to return to his own lines with valuable information about enemy defenses. He accomplished his mission as he was dying. Sgt. Hachiya posthumously received the Distinguished Service Cross. Ironically, this happened as his name was being stricken from the honor roll in his Oregon hometown because he was of Japanese ancestry.

Of such heroism is the Nisei legend woven. These are landmarks of the transformation from Japanese-American to simply American. There are other landmarks, as well—

Manjiro Nakahama, a castaway in 1841, was rescued by a whaler and taken to Boston, Mass. He became the first Japanese to learn English. Hizoko Hamada recorded his name as Joseph Heco when he became the first naturalized Issei on June 30, 1858. (This door to citizenship was closed later, not being restored until the 1952 Act which restored naturalization privileges to immigrants from Japan.) There are the Nisei casualties of World War II—9,468 (600 killed in action). . . .

Landmarks of the transformation.

What lies ahead?

.   .   .

The Nisei made an American dream come true for their aging parents, and secured for themselves and their children the right to walk in peace and dignity among their fellow Americans, a remarkable record of achievement which grew out of a people subjected to extreme hostility and a constant atmosphere of discrimination.

Perhaps we are all like the few who braved defeat at Gold Hill [the first Japanese settlement in the United States]—farmers all. And what we nurture is the seed of eventual justice for every human.

"History shows us how much we owe to the past sacrifices of others. It kindles within us a quiet pride in the accomplishments of our forebears, and makes us determined to put the future in debt to us."

14. BLOOD ON THE PAVEMENT

CAREY MCWILLIAMS

In the 1940s the relationship between some Mexican-American barrio youths and the dominant elements of California society was one of mutual distrust. Particularly violent results of this antipathy were the "Pachuco Riots" of 1943. The term "pachuco" described a segment of young, urban Mexican-Americans whose garb reflected their search for a separate identity. Their long, slick hair, their tightly cut trousers, and their zoot suits made them stand out in a wartime nation of crewcut soldiers. Carey McWilliams discusses the impact of a hostile Anglo world upon the pachucos in Los Angeles.

On Thursday evening, June 3, 1943, the Alpine Club—made up of youngsters of Mexican descent—held a meeting in a police substation in Los Angeles. Usually these meetings were held in a nearby public school

FROM Carey McWilliams, *North from Mexico* (Westport, Conn.: Greenwood Press, 1968). Reprinted by permission.

but, since the school was closed, the boys had accepted the invitation of a police captain to meet in the substation. The principal business of the meeting, conducted in the presence of the police captain, consisted in a discussion of how gang-strife could best be avoided in the neighborhood. After the meeting had adjourned, the boys were taken in squad cars to the street corner nearest the neighborhood in which most of them lived. The squad cars were scarcely out of sight, when the boys were assaulted, not by a rival "gang" or "club," but by hoodlum elements in the neighborhood. Of one thing the boys were sure: their assailants were not of Mexican descent.

Earlier the same evening a group of eleven sailors, on leave from their station in Los Angeles, were walking along the 1700 block on North Main Street in the center of one of the city's worst slum areas. The surrounding neighborhood is predominantly Mexican. On one side of the street the dirty brick front of a large brewery hides from view a collection of ramshackle Mexican homes. The other side of the street consists of a series of small bars, boarded-up store fronts, and small shops. The area is well off the beaten paths and few servicemen found their way this far north on Main Street. As they were walking along the street, so they later stated, the sailors were set upon by a gang of Mexican boys. One of the sailors was badly hurt; the others suffered minor cuts and bruises. According to their story, the sailors were outnumbered about three to one.

When the attack was reported to the nearest substation, the police adopted a curious attitude. Instead of attempting to find and arrest the assailants, fourteen policemen remained at the station after their regular duty was over for the night. Then, under the command of a detective lieutenant, the "Vengeance Squad," as they called themselves, set out "to clean up" the gang that had attacked the sailors. But—miracle of miracles!—when they arrived at the scene of the attack they could find no one to arrest—not a single Mexican—on their favorite charge of "suspicion of assault." In itself this curious inability to find anyone to arrest— so strikingly at variance with what usually happened on raids of this sort—raises an inference that a larger strategy was involved. For the raid accomplished nothing except to get the names of the raiding officers in the newspapers and to whip up the anger of the community against the Mexican population, which may, perhaps, have been the reason for the raid. . . .

Thus began the so-called "Zoot-Suit Race Riots" which were to last, in one form or another, for a week in Los Angeles.

1. The Taxicab Brigade

Taking the police raid as an official cue,—a signal for action,—about two hundred sailors decided to take the law into their own hands on the following night. Coming down into the center of Los Angeles from the Naval Armory in Chavez Ravine (near the "Chinatown" area), they hired a fleet of twenty taxicabs. Once assembled, the "task force" proceeded to cruise straight through the center of town en route to the east side of Los Angeles where the bulk of the Mexicans reside. Soon the sailors in the lead-car sighted a Mexican boy in a zoot-suit walking along the street. The "task force" immediately stopped and, in a few moments, the boy was lying on the pavement, badly beaten and bleeding. The sailors then piled back into the cabs and the caravan resumed its way until the next zoot-suiter was sighted, whereupon the same procedure was repeated. In these attacks, of course, the odds were pretty uneven: two hundred sailors to one Mexican boy. Four times this same treatment was meted out and four "gangsters,"—two seventeen-year-old youngsters, one nineteen, and one twenty-three,—were left lying on the pavements for the ambulances to pick up.

It is indeed curious that in a city like Los Angeles, which boasts that it has more police cars equipped with two-way radio than any other city in the world (Los Angeles *Times*, September 2, 1947), the police were apparently unable to intercept a caravan of twenty taxicabs, loaded with two hundred uniformed, yelling, bawdy sailors, as it cruised through the downtown and east-side sections of the city. At one point the police did happen to cross the trail of the caravan and the officers were apparently somewhat embarrassed over the meeting. For only nine of the sailors were taken into custody and the rest were permitted to continue on their merry way. No charges, however, were ever preferred against the nine.

Their evening's entertainment over, the sailors returned to the foot of Chavez Ravine. There they were met by the police and the Shore Patrol. The Shore Patrol took seventeen of the sailors into custody and sent the rest up to the ravine to the Naval Armory. The petty officer who had led the expedition, and who was not among those arrested, gave the police a frank statement of things to come. "We're out to do what the police have failed to do," he said; "we're going to clean up this situation. . . . Tonight [by then it was the morning of June fifth] the sailors may have the marines along."

The next day the Los Angeles press pushed the war news from the front page as it proceeded to play up the pavement war in Los Angeles in screaming headlines. "Wild Night in L.A.—Sailor Zooter Clash" was the headline in the *Daily News*. "Sailor Task Force Hits L.A. Zooters" bellowed the *Herald-Express*. A suburban newspaper gleefully reported that "zoot-suited roughnecks fled to cover before a task force of twenty taxicabs." None of these stories, however, reported the slightest resistance, up to this point, on the part of the Mexicans.

True to their promise, the sailors were joined that night, June fifth, by scores of soldiers and marines. Squads of servicemen, arms linked, paraded through downtown Los Angeles four abreast, stopping anyone wearing zoot-suits and ordering these individuals to put away their "drapes" by the following night or suffer the consequences. Aside from a few half-hearted admonitions, the police made no effort whatever to interfere with these heralds of disorder. However, twenty-seven Mexican boys, gathered on a street corner, were arrested and jailed that evening. While these boys were being booked "on suspicion" of various offenses, a mob of several hundred servicemen roamed the downtown section of a great city threatening members of the Mexican minority without hindrance or interference from the police, the Shore Patrol, or the Military Police.

On this same evening, a squad of sailors invaded a bar on the east side and carefully examined the clothes of the patrons. Two zoot-suit customers, drinking beer at a table, were peremptorily ordered to remove their clothes. One of them was beaten and his clothes were torn from his back when he refused to comply with the order. The other—they were both Mexicans—doffed his "drapes" which were promptly ripped to shreds. Similar occurrences in several parts of the city that evening were sufficiently alarming to have warranted some precautionary measures or to have justified an "out-of-bounds" order. All that the police officials did, however, was to call up some additional reserves and announce that any Mexicans involved in the rioting would be promptly arrested. That there had been no counterattacks by the Mexicans up to this point apparently did not enter into the police officers' appraisal of the situation. One thing must be said for the Los Angeles police: it is above all consistent. When it is wrong, it is consistently wrong; when it makes a mistake, it will be repeated.

By the night of June sixth the police had worked out a simple formula for action. Knowing that wherever the sailors went there would be trouble, the police simply followed the sailors at a conveniently spaced interval. Six carloads of sailors cruised down Brooklyn Avenue that evening. At Ramona Boulevard, they stopped and beat up eight teen-age Mexicans. Failing to find any Mexican zoot-suiters in a bar on Indiana Street, they were so annoyed that they proceeded to wreck the establishment. In due course, the police made a leisurely appearance at the scene of the wreckage but could find no one to arrest. Carefully following the sailors, the police arrested eleven boys who had been beaten up on Carmelita Street; six more victims were arrested a few blocks further on, seven at Ford Boulevard, six at Gifford Street—and so on straight through the Mexican east-side settlements. Behind them came the police, stopping at the same street corners "to mop up" by arresting the injured victims of the mob. By morning, some forty-four Mexican boys, all severely beaten, were under arrest.

2. Operation "Dixie"

The stage was now set for the really serious rioting of June seventh and eighth. Having featured the preliminary rioting as an offensive launched by sailors, soldiers, and marines, the press now whipped public opinion into a frenzy by dire warnings that Mexican zoot-suiters planned mass retaliations. To insure a riot, the precise street corners were named at which retaliatory action was expected and the time of the anticipated action was carefully specified. In effect these stories announced a riot and invited public participation. "Zooters Planning to Attack More Servicemen," headlined the *Daily News;* "Would jab broken bottlenecks in the faces of their victims. . . . Beating sailors' brains out with hammers also on the program." Concerned for the safety of the Army, the

Navy, and the Marine Corps, the *Herald-Express* warned that "Zooters
. . . would mass 500 strong."

By way of explaining the action of the police throughout the subsequent rioting, it should be pointed out that, in June, 1943, the police
were on a bad spot. A man by the name of Beebe, arrested on a drunk
charge, had been kicked to death in the Central Jail by police officers.
Through the excellent work of an alert police commissioner, the case
had finally been broken and, at the time of the riots, a police officer by
the name of Compton Dixon was on trial in the courts. While charges of
police brutality had been bandied about for years, this was the first time
that a seemingly airtight case had been prepared. Shortly after the riots,
a Hollywood police captain told a motion picture director that the police
had touched off the riots "in order to give Dixie (Dixon) a break." By
staging a fake demonstration of the alleged necessity for harsh police
methods, it was hoped that the jury would acquit Dixon. As a matter of
fact, the jury did disagree and on July 2, 1943, the charges against
Dixon were dismissed.

On Monday evening, June seventh, thousands of *Angelenos*, in response to twelve hours' advance notice in the press, turned out for a
mass lynching. Marching through the streets of downtown Los Angeles,
a mob of several thousand soldiers, sailors, and civilians, proceeded to
beat up every zoot-suiter they could find. Pushing its way into the important motion picture theaters, the mob ordered the management to turn
on the house lights and then ranged up and down the aisles dragging
Mexicans out of their seats. Street cars were halted while Mexicans, and
some Filipinos and Negroes, were jerked out of their seats, pushed into
the streets, and beaten with sadistic frenzy. If the victims wore zoot-
suits, they were stripped of their clothing and left naked or half-naked
on the streets, bleeding and bruised. Proceeding down Main Street from
First to Twelfth, the mob stopped on the edge of the Negro district.
Learning that the Negroes planned a warm reception for them, the mob-
sters turned back and marched through the Mexican east side spreading
panic and terror.

Here is one of numerous eye-witness accounts written by Al Waxman,
editor of *The Eastside Journal:*

> At Twelfth and Central I came upon a scene that will long live in my
> memory. Police were swinging clubs and servicemen were fighting
> with civilians. Wholesale arrests were being made by the officers.
> Four boys came out of a pool hall. They were wearing the zoot-
> suits that have become the symbol of a fighting flag. Police ordered
> them into arrest cars. One refused. He asked: "Why am I being
> arrested?" The police officer answered with three swift blows of the
> night-stick across the boy's head and he went down. As he sprawled,
> he was kicked in the face. Police had difficulty loading his body into
> the vehicle because he was one-legged and wore a wooden limb.
> Maybe the officer didn't know he was attacking a cripple.
> At the next corner a Mexican mother cried out, "Don't take my
> boy, he did nothing. He's only fifteen years old. Don't take him." She

was struck across the jaw with a night-stick and almost dropped the
two and a half year old baby that was clinging in her arms. . . .

Rushing back to the east side to make sure that things were quiet
here, I came upon a band of servicemen making a systematic tour of
East First Street. They had just come out of a cocktail bar where
four men were nursing bruises. Three autos loaded with Los Angeles
policemen were on the scene but the soldiers were not molested. Farther down the street the men stopped a streetcar, forcing the motor-
man to open the door and proceeded to inspect the clothing of the
male passengers. "We're looking for zoot-suits to burn," they
shouted. Again the police did not interfere. . . . Half a block away
. . . I pleaded with the men of the local police substation to put a
stop to these activities. "It is a matter for the military police," they
said.

Throughout the night the Mexican communities were in the wildest
possible turmoil. Scores of Mexican mothers were trying to locate their
youngsters and several hundred Mexicans milled around each of the police substations and the Central Jail trying to get word of missing members of their families. Boys came into the police stations saying: "Charge
me with vagrancy or anything, but don't send me out there!" pointing to
the streets where other boys, as young as twelve and thirteen years of
age, were being beaten and stripped of their clothes. From affidavits
which I helped prepare at the time, I should say that not more than half
of the victims were actually wearing zoot-suits. A Negro defense worker,
wearing a defense-plant identification badge on his workclothes, was
taken from a street car and one of his eyes was gouged out with a knife.
Huge half-page photographs, showing Mexican boys stripped of their
clothes, cowering on the pavements, often bleeding profusely, surrounded by jeering mobs of men and women, appeared in all the Los
Angeles newspapers. As Al Waxman most truthfully reported, blood had
been "spilled on the streets of the city."

At midnight on June seventh, the military authorities decided that the
local police were completely unable or unwilling to handle the situation,
despite the fact that a thousand reserve officers had been called up. The
entire downtown area of Los Angeles was then declared "out of bounds"
for military personnel. This order immediately slowed down the pace of
the rioting. The moment the Military Police and Shore Patrol went into
action, the rioting quieted down. On June eighth the city officials brought
their heads up out of the sand, took a look around, and began issuing
statements. The district attorney, Fred N. Howser, announced that the
"situation is getting entirely out of hand," while Mayor Fletcher Bowron
thought that "sooner or later it will blow over." The chief of police, taking a count of the Mexicans in jail, cheerfully proclaimed that "the situation has now cleared up." All agreed, however, that it was quite "a
situation."

Unfortunately "the situation" had not cleared up; nor did it blow over.
It began to spread to the suburbs where the rioting continued for two
more days. When it finally stopped, the Eagle Rock *Advertiser* mourn-
fully editorialized: "It is too bad the servicemen were called off before

they were able to complete the job. . . . Most of the citizens of the city
have been delighted with what has been going on." County Supervisor
Roger Jessup told the newsmen: "All that is needed to end lawlessness is
more of the same action as is being exercised by the servicemen!" While
the district attorney of Ventura, an outlying county, jumped on the
bandwagon with a statement to the effect that "zoot suits are an open
indication of subversive character." This was also the opinion of the Los
Angeles City Council which adopted a resolution making the wearing of
zoot-suits a misdemeanor! On June eleventh, hundreds of handbills were
distributed to students and posted on bulletin boards in a high school
attended by many Negroes and Mexicans which read: "Big Sale. Second-
Hand Zoot Suits. Slightly Damaged. Apply at Nearest U.S. Naval Station.
While they last we have your Size."

PART TWO

Current
Minority Problems
in California

Chapter 5

The Quest
for Identity:
The Negro

Americans first became aware of the term "black power" during the summer of 1966, when twenty-three-year-old Stokely Carmichael came to the fore as a black militant leader. This new concept emerged from the civil rights movement of the early 1960s. Of course, "black power" can be interpreted in a variety of ways. Carmichael and other advocates of black power began employing a rhetoric that had a dissonant ring to Americans who were accustomed to the more moderate appeals of older, established Negro spokesmen and white liberals.

This modern generation of black militants, it should be noted, is not without historical antecedents. Throughout America's past there have been numerous efforts by the black to assert himself as a man. These attempts to gain freedom assumed various forms—including physical force, as in the instance of the revolt led by Nat Turner in the 1830s, and economic power, as exerted by the followers of Marcus Garvey almost a century later. Similarly, the black power program today should not be seen as a homogeneous one, but, rather, as a loosely knit movement that contains many diverse factions.

Despite this diversity, there is among these groups that profess to be speaking for their race a commonality that binds them together. Perhaps the basic tenet that many young Negroes share today is the belief that "black is beautiful." Whether we consider their garb patterned after African motifs, the "natural" hairdo that makes no effort to conceal their kinky hair, or their new zeal for learning about the Negro past, it is apparent that there is now a growing pride in having black skin.

Moreover, pervading much black militant thought today is the rejection of the white middle-class value system, which is seen as essentially materialistic and antihumanist. In its place, many young Negroes want to establish a society in which "soul," or the capacity for human relationships, would be central.

Another common denominator among the black militants, who are influential beyond their numbers, is their search for the power to control their own lives. Not only are they demanding a stronger voice in the education of their children, but they are also requiring real opportunities in the schools and in the spheres of housing and employment. Finally, in their judgment, nowhere is their powerlessness more apparent than in the area of law enforcement, where they see themselves as a colonial people at the mercy of an alien, callous police force that has little awareness of or sympathy for their problems.

It is perhaps in these terms that the riots in the ghettos of our large urban centers in recent summers can be best understood. The large-scale violence, destruction, and lawlessness that began in August 1965 convey the rage of black people no longer willing to submit peaceably to a societal structure in which they feel that they are allowed no power. Barraged by information from the media, government reports, and other sources, many blacks have become convinced that the promise of "progress" is a chimera, that the old technique of gradualism and the traditional reliance upon white liberalism are not enough to achieve equality and social justice for their people.

Thus, among the ranks of the black militants today, there is a rejection of the virtues of integration implicit in the white liberal credo and a demand that new directions be pursued. If integration is not to be the ideal in American society, must the goal be separatism, as some blacks seem to be indicating? Or is the matter a more subtle one than the above options suggest? And how does the vague, almost mystical concept of "identity" figure in this problem of integration versus separatism? Finally, how relevant are the following readings, which deal with the quest for black identity in California, to the problems of blacks elsewhere in America?

15. FEAR AND DOUBT

HUEY P. NEWTON

The need for self-identity is widely recognized by the black community today. Huey P. Newton, the national Minister of Defense of the supermilitant Black Panther party and a member of the Oakland, California, chapter, asserts that white society, in its efforts to impose its values on the Negro, has created a schizophrenic, self-hating object of pity. The following selection is taken from Newton's Essays from the Minister of Defense.

The lower socio-economic Black male is a man of confusion. He faces a hostile environment and is not sure that it is not his own sins that have attracted the hostilities of society. All his life he has been taught (explicitly and implicitly) that he is an inferior approximation of humanity. As a man, he finds himself void of those things that bring respect and a feeling of worthiness. He looks around for something to blame for his situation, but because he is not sophisticated regarding the socio-economic milieu and because of negativistic parental and institutional teachings, he ultimately blames himself.

When he was a child, his parents told him that they were not affluent because "we didn't have the opportunity to become educated," or "we did not take advantage of the educational opportunities that were offered to us." They tell their children that things will be different for them if they are educated and skilled, but there is absolutely nothing other than this occasional warning (and often not even this) to stimulate education. Black people are great worshippers of education, even the lower socio-economic Black person, but at the same time, they are afraid of exposing themselves to it. They are afraid because they are vulnerable to having their fears verified; perhaps they will find that they can't compete with white students. The Black person tells himself that he could have done much more if he had really wanted to. The fact is, of course, that the assumed educational opportunities were never available to the lower socio-economic Black person due to the unique position assigned him in life.

It is a two-headed monster that haunts this man. First, his attitude is that he lacks innate ability to cope with the socio-economic problems confronting him, and second, he tells himself that he has the ability but he simply has not felt strongly enough to try to acquire the skills needed to manipulate his environment. In a desperate effort to assume self-respect, he rationalizes that he is lethargic; in this way, he denies a possible lack of innate ability. If he openly attempts to discover his abilities, he and others may see him for what he is—or is not, and this is the real fear. He then withdraws into the world of the invisible, but not without a struggle. He may attempt to make himself visible by processing his hair,

Huey P. Newton, "Fear and Doubt," May 15, 1967, *Essays from the Minister of Defense* (Black Panther Party, San Francisco). Reprinted by permission of the author.

acquiring a "boss mop," or driving a long car, even though he can't afford it. He may father several illegitimate children by several different women in order to display his masculinity. But in the end, he realizes that he is ineffectual in his efforts.

Society responds to him as a thing, a beast, a non-entity, something to be ignored or stepped on. He is asked to respect laws that do not respect him. He is asked to digest a code of ethics that acts upon him but not for him. He is confused and in a constant state of rage, of shame and doubt. This psychological set permeates all his interpersonal relationships. It determines his view of the social system. His psychological development has been prematurely arrested. This doubt begins at a very early age and continues through his life. The parents pass it on to the child and the social system reinforces the fear, the shame, and the doubt. In the third or fourth grade, he may find that he shares the classroom with white students, but when the class is engaged in reading exercises, all the Black students find themselves in a group at a table reserved for slow readers. This may be quite an innocent effort on the part of the school system. The teacher may not realize that the Black students feared (in fact, feel certain) that Black means dumb and white means smart. The children do not realize that the head start the children got at home is what accounts for the situation. It is generally accepted that the child is the father of the man; this holds true for the lower socio-economic Black people.

With whom, with what can he, a man, identify? As a child he had no permanent male figure with whom to identify; as a man, he sees nothing in society with which he can identify as an extension of himself. His life is built on mistrust, shame, doubt, guilt, inferiority, role confusion, isolation and despair. He feels that he is something less than a man, and it is evident in his conversation: "the white man is 'THE MAN,' he got everything, and he knows everything, and a nigger ain't nothing." In a society where a man is valued according to occupation and material possessions, he is without possessions. He is unskilled and more often than not, either marginally employed or unemployed. Often his wife (who is able to secure a job as a maid cleaning for white people) is the breadwinner. He is, therefore, viewed as quite worthless by his wife and children. He is ineffectual both in and out of the home. He cannot provide for or protect his family. He is invisible, a non-entity. Society will not acknowledge him as a man. He is a consumer and not a producer. He is dependent upon the white man ('THE MAN') to feed his family, to give him a job, educate his children, serve as the model that he tries to emulate. He is dependent and he hates 'THE MAN' and he hates himself. Who is he? Is he a very old adolescent or is he the slave he used to be?

What did he do to be so BLACK and blue?

16. THE "MARGINAL MAN" IN A COLONIAL SOCIETY

STOKELY CARMICHAEL AND CHARLES V. HAMILTON

In this stinging excerpt from their book Black Power, *the young black militant Stokely Carmichael and Professor Charles V. Hamilton of Roosevelt University tell what it means to be black in a society where "whiteness" is a primary prerequisite for success and acceptance. Their perspective is one larger than Huey P. Newton's in the preceding selection, as they draw a parallel between the techniques used in Africa and in the United States to deny the black man his humanity.*

The social and psychological effects on black people of all their degrading experiences are also very clear. From the time black people were introduced into this country, their condition has fostered human indignity and the denial of respect. Born into this society today, black people begin to doubt themselves, their worth as human beings. Self-respect becomes almost impossible. Kenneth Clark describes the process in *Dark Ghetto:*

> Human beings who are forced to live under ghetto conditions and whose daily experience tells them that almost nowhere in society are they respected and granted the ordinary dignity and courtesy accorded to others will, as a matter of course, begin to doubt their own worth. Since every human being depends upon his cumulative experiences with others for clues as to how he should view and value himself, children who are consistently rejected understandably begin to question and doubt whether they, their family, and their group really deserve no more respect from the larger society than they receive. These doubts become the seeds of a pernicious self- and group-hatred, the Negro's complex and debilitating prejudice against himself.
>
> The preoccupation of many Negroes with hair straighteners, skin bleachers, and the like illustrates this tragic aspect of American racial prejudice—Negroes have come to believe in their own inferiority [pp. 63–64].

There was the same result in Africa. And some European colonial powers—notably France and Portugal—provided the black man "a way out" of the degrading status: to become "white," or assimilated. France pursued a colonial policy aimed at producing a black French elite class, a group exposed and acculturated to French "civilization." In its African colonies of Mozambique and Angola, Portugal has attempted a colonial policy of assimilation which goes even further. There is no pretense—as in the British colonies and in American rhetoric—of black people mov-

FROM *Black Power*, by Stokely Carmichael and Charles V. Hamilton, pp. 29–32. Copyright © 1967 by Stokely Carmichael and Charles V. Hamilton. Reprinted by permission of Random House, Inc., and Jonathan Cape Ltd.

ing toward self-government and freedom. All Independence groups have been suppressed. There prevails in these Portuguese colonies a legal process whereby an African may become, in effect, a "white" man if he measures up to certain Western standards. The *assimilado* is one who has adopted Portuguese customs, dress, language, and has achieved at least a high school education. He is, of course, favored with special jobs and better housing. This status likewise qualifies him to receive a passport to travel abroad, mainly to Portugal and Brazil. Otherwise, such freedom of movement is denied. The *assimilado* is accepted socially by the whites in the restaurants and night clubs. In fact, the Portuguese officials will even import a white Portuguese woman to Mozambique to marry an *assimilado* man. (American colonialism has not gone this far.) But to submit to all of this, the *assimilado* must reject as intrinsically inferior his entire African heritage and association.

In a manner similar to that of the colonial powers in Africa, American society indicates avenues of escape from the ghetto for those individuals who adapt to the "mainstream." This adaptation means to disassociate oneself from the black race, its culture, community and heritage, and become immersed (dispersed is another term) in the white world. What actually happens, as Professor E. Franklin Frazier pointed out in his book, *Black Bourgeoisie*, is that the black person ceases to identify himself with black people yet is obviously unable to assimilate with whites. He becomes a "marginal man," living on the fringes of both societies in a world largely of "make believe." This black person is urged to adopt American middle-class standards and values. As with the black African who had to become a "Frenchman" in order to be accepted, so to be an American, the black man must strive to become "white." To the extent that he does, he is considered "well adjusted"—one who has "risen above the race question." These people are frequently held up by the white Establishment as living examples of the progress being made by the society in solving the race problem. Suffice it to say that precisely because they are required to denounce—overtly or covertly—their black race, *they are reinforcing racism in this country*.

In the United States, as in Africa, their "adaptation" operated to deprive the black community of its potential skills and brain power. All too frequently, these "integrated" people are used to blunt the true feelings and goals of the black masses. They are picked as "Negro leaders," and the white power structure proceeds to talk to and deal only with them. Needless to say, no fruitful, meaningful dialogue can take place under such circumstances. Those hand-picked "leaders" have no viable constituency for which they can speak and act. All this is a classic formula of colonial co-optation.

At all times, then, the social effects of colonialism are to degrade and to dehumanize the subjected black man. White America's School of Slavery and Segregation, like the School of Colonialism, has taught the subject to hate himself and to deny his own humanity. The white society maintains an attitude of superiority and the black community has too often succumbed to it, thereby permitting the whites to believe in the correctness of their position. Racist assumptions of white superiority have been so deeply engrained into the fiber of the society that they infuse the entire functioning of the national subconscious. They are taken for granted and frequently not even recognized. As Professors Lewis Killian and Charles Grigg express it in their book, *Racial Crisis in America:*

> At the present time, integration as a solution of the race problem demands that the Negro foreswear his identity as a Negro. But for a last solution, the meaning of "American" must lose its implicit racial modifier, "white." Even without biological amalgamation, integration requires a sincere acceptance by all Americans that it is just as good to be a black American as to be a white American. Here is the crux of the problem of race relations—the redefinition of the sense of group position so that the status advantage of the white man is no longer an advantage, so that an American may acknowledge his Negro ancestry without apologizing for it. . . . They [black people] live in a society in which to be unconditionally "American" is to be white, and to be black is a misfortune [pp. 108–9].

The time is long overdue for the black community to redefine itself, set forth new values and goals, and organize around them.

17. BLACK LIBERATION: THE FIRST STEP

FRANK GREENWOOD

A Negro journalist suggests that black Americans have never enjoyed true citizenship because, historically, they have suffered from a feeling of powerlessness. Writing in an underground newspaper, the Los Angeles Free Press, Frank Greenwood explains the difference between whites, who came to America voluntarily and soon became full participants in their society, and Negroes, who have never enjoyed the right of self-determination. The solution, he feels, lies in black power.

What is the true status of the Black man in America? We have often been referred to as "second class" citizens, whatever that is. I don't know what it is because after a close scrutiny of both the Declaration of Independence and the Constitution I have neither found the definition of a so-called second class citizen or even seen it mentioned. There ain't no such animal. One is either a citizen or one is not.

The mere fact that a civil rights movement for Blacks still exists to get the right of Blacks to sit on toilets next to whites disproves the false idea that we are citizens.

How, then, does one become a citizen? If my civic lessons still hold true there are only two ways: Through a birth or naturalization. We are all aware of the racist immigration quotas dealing with restrictions on Blacks entering this dangerous land so we won't even discuss naturaliza-

Frank Greenwood, "Black Liberation: The First Step," *Los Angeles Free Press,* Vol. 5 (May 24, 1968). Reprinted by permission of Frank Greenwood.

tion. The overwhelming mass of Blacks in this country were born here. We are so-called citizens because our parents and foreparents were also citizens.

The whites in this country achieved their citizenship because they determined for themselves that they wanted to become a citizen. They were not forced to by the penalty of birth to become citizens. They made an agreement or contract with the rulers of this country to help build and serve it in exchange for certain rights and privileges. The new white citizen not only agreed to serve the new government but he had the right to even become the government. He elected representatives to serve and look out for his interests. The white newcomer could help determine the new laws that he agreed to obey and enforce. In short he exercised self determination from the moment he stepped upon these racist shores.

Blacks were captured from their native land of Africa and forced to come to these shores. Our language, culture, history, names, etc. were stripped from us. We ceased to be Africans and immediately became "negroes." We had no rights a white man was bound to respect. We ceased to be human beings and became chattel property. We were on the same level as a horse or cow or mule to be used, abused and worked as a beast of burden for the pleasure and enrichment of the master. To help complete the dehumanization process the areas we were forced to exist in were called "slave pens." And the U.S. Constitution to this day still refers to us as three-fifths of a human being.

Needless to say, Blacks were not asked to come to America. We had no self determination in that decision. Even when this country went to war against the British in 1776, George Washington made it clear that he didn't even want Blacks to serve in the lily white colonial army because he was engaged in a white man's war. The British, however, being hard pressed for manpower, promised the Blacks freedom if they would fight on the side of the crown. Thousands of slaves flocked to the British colors so George had to reverse his decision to keep Blacks out of his army. Slaves and Free Blacks then fought on the side of the colonists.

Later Washington confided to a friend the vital role Blacks played in helping to defeat the British when he told him that "the side who armed the slaves first would win the war."

Not even after our contributions here did Blacks become citizens. Oh, yes, some became "freedmen" but not citizens. It's also true that Blacks have fought in every war this country has engaged in but still we are not citizens. Even the so-called "free" Blacks who existed during the time of chattel slavery were not citizens but mere "free" slaves with no rights white man was bound to respect.

After Lincoln issued the Emancipation Proclamation we were said to be free. But if that was true why was it necessary to issue the 13th, 14th and 15th amendments to the Constitution? Obviously it was because we were still [not] free. If we had really achieved freedom Blacks would have had self-determination. They could have decided for themselves what status they would seek in the land that had robbed them of 246 years of free labor, labor they never received a dime for. They would have had the right to determine for themselves where they wanted to stay in this racist land, whether they wanted to emigrate to Africa, the land of their forefathers, or elsewhere. This right of self-determination was never considered by the white lawmakers. No referendum was presented to Blacks. No Black leaders were sought from the Black masses to come forward and express the will of the Blacks. No indeed. All decisions and laws and proposals were made by the whites. Not a single Black lawmaker represented the interests of Blacks.

Now any court of law will tell you that no contract or agreement is binding unless both involved parties agree to the terms. Blacks never had a say in the Constitution of the United States. None of their representatives had a say. Therefore the Law of the Land applies only to the Whites, not Blacks. Blacks were still forced to be slaves without a voice in their own destiny. It's true that we no longer are on the plantation. The white master no longer owns slaves, now he just rents them!

Blacks are not citizens of this country because this country was not set up for us to be citizens in it and because the laws the man made just for us are not enforced and have no intention of being enforced by the master.

Blacks are not citizens in this country because we have never made any agreement or contract with the state to become citizens. "Citizenship" has been imposed upon us.

What then is our true status in America? We are descendents of slaves. We are not citizens but a colonized people whose land is controlled by outsiders for the outsiders' profit. Blacks do not control the government, politics, or economy of communities. The white cops who brutalize us or shoot us down for being Black do not live in the Black community but are the occupying army of the power elite that fattens off our blood and misery.

The sooner the so-called middle-class Negroes realize this fact of life and stop trying to integrate (moving from Black communities to white) the sooner they will bring their education and skills back to the Black masses and help us all attain the first thing on the agenda towards recognition of us as human being[s]—Black Liberation.

18. THE NEED AND SUBSTANCE OF
BLACK POWER

STOKELY CARMICHAEL AND CHARLES V. HAMILTON

*For many Americans the phrase "black power" seems to defy
understanding. An effort to explain the need and substance of black
power is made by Stokely Carmichael and Professor Charles V.
Hamilton in their book* Black Power. *Stripping the term of the anxiety
and fears that it often evokes, the authors suggest that black power is
in the mainstream of the American tradition of self-help and ethnic
solidarity.*

The adoption of the concept of Black Power is one of the most legitimate
and healthy developments in American politics and race relations in our
time. The concept of Black Power speaks to all the needs mentioned in
this chapter. It is a call for black people in this country to unite, to recognize their heritage, to build a sense of community. It is a call for black
people to begin to define their own goals, to lead their own organizations
and to support those organizations. It is a call to reject the racist institutions and values of this society.

The concept of Black Power rests on a fundamental premise: *Before a
group can enter the open society, it must first close ranks.* By this we
mean that group solidarity is necessary before a group can operate effectively from a bargaining position of strength in a pluralistic society. Traditionally, each new ethnic group in this society has found the route to
social and political viability through the organization of its own institutions with which to represent its needs within the larger society. Studies
in voting behavior specifically, and political behavior generally, have
made it clear that politically the American pot has not melted. Italians
vote for Rubino over O'Brien; Irish for Murphy over Goldberg, etc. This
phenomenon may seem distasteful to some, but it has been and remains
today a central fact of the American political system. There are other
examples of ways in which groups in the society have remembered their
roots and used this effectively in the political arena. Theodore Sorensen
describes the politics of foreign aid during the Kennedy Administration
in his book *Kennedy:*

> No powerful constituencies or interest groups backed foreign aid.
> The Marshall Plan at least had appealed to Americans who traced
> their roots to the Western European nations aided. But there were
> few voters who identified with India, Colombia or Tanganyika
> [p. 351].

The extent to which black Americans can and do "trace their roots" to
Africa, to that extent will they be able to be more effective on the political scene.

A white reporter set forth this point in other terms when he made the following observation about white Mississippi's manipulation of the anti-poverty program:

> The war on poverty has been predicated on the notion that there is such a thing as a community which can be defined geographically and mobilized for a collective effort to help the poor. This theory has no relationship to reality in the deep South. In every Mississippi county there are two communities. Despite all the pious platitudes of the moderates on both sides, these two communities habitually see their interests in terms of conflict rather than cooperation. Only when the Negro community can muster enough political, economic and professional strength to compete on somewhat equal terms, will Negroes believe in the possibility of true cooperation and whites accept its necessity. En route to integration, the Negro community needs to develop a greater independence—a chance to run its own affairs and not cave in whenever "the man" barks—or so it seems to me, and to most of the knowledgeable people with whom I talked in Mississippi. To OEO, this judgment may sound like black nationalism. . . .[1]

The point is obvious: black people must lead and run their own organizations. Only black people can convey the revolutionary idea—and it is a revolutionary idea—that black people are able to do things themselves. Only they can help create in the community an aroused and continuing black consciousness that will provide the basis for political strength. In the past, white allies have often furthered white supremacy without the whites involved realizing it, or even wanting to do so. Black people must come together and do things for themselves. They must achieve self-identity and self-determination in order to have their daily needs met.

Black Power means, for example, that in Lowndes County, Alabama, a black sheriff can end police brutality. A black tax assessor and tax collector and county board of revenue can lay, collect, and channel tax monies for the building of better roads and schools serving black people. In such areas as Lowndes, where black people have a majority, they will attempt to use power to exercise control. This is what they seek: control. When black people lack a majority, Black Power means proper representation and sharing of control. It means the creation of power bases, of strength, from which black people can press to change local or nationwide patterns of oppression—instead of from weakness.

It does not mean *merely* putting black faces into office. Black visibility is not Black Power. Most of the black politicians around the country today are not examples of Black Power. The power must be that of a community, and emanate from there. The black politicians must start from there. The black politicians must stop being representatives of "downtown" machines, whatever the cost might be in terms of lost patronage and holiday handouts.

Black Power recognizes—it must recognize—the ethnic basis of

[1] Christopher Jencks, "Accommodating Whites: A New Look at Mississippi," *The New Republic* (April 16, 1966).

American politics as well as the power-oriented nature of American politics. Black Power therefore calls for black people to consolidate behind
their own, so that they can bargain from a position of strength. But while
we endorse the *procedure* of group solidarity and identity for the purpose
of attaining certain goals in the body politic, this does not mean that
black people should strive for the same kind of rewards (i.e., end results) obtained by the white society. The ultimate values and goals are
not domination or exploitation of other groups, but rather an effective
share in the total power of the society.

Nevertheless, some observers have labeled those who advocate Black
Power as racists; they have said that the call for self-identification and
self-determination is "racism in reverse" or "black supremacy." This is a
deliberate and absurd lie. There is no analogy—by any stretch of definition or imagination—between the advocates of Black Power and white
racists. Racism is not merely exclusion on the basis of race but exclusion
for the purpose of subjugating or maintaining subjugation. The goal of
the racists is to keep black people on the bottom, arbitrarily and dictato-
rially, as they have done in this country for over three hundred years.
The goal of black self-determination and black self-identity—Black
Power—is full participation in the decision-making processes affecting
the lives of black people, and recognition of the virtues in themselves as
black people. The black people of this country have not lynched whites,
bombed their churches, murdered their children and manipulated laws
and institutions to maintain oppression. White racists have. Congressional laws, one after the other, have not been necessary to stop black
people from oppressing others and denying others the full enjoyment of
their rights. White racists have made such laws necessary. The goal of
Black Power is positive and functional to a free and viable society. No
white racist can make this claim.

A great deal of public attention and press space was devoted to the
hysterical accusation of "black racism" when the call for Black Power
was first sounded. A national committee of influential black churchmen
affiliated with the National Council of Churches, despite their obvious
respectability and responsibility, had to resort to a paid advertisement to
articulate their position, while anyone yapping "black racism" made
front-page news. In their statement, published in the *New York Times* of
July 31, 1966, the churchmen said:

> We, an informal group of Negro churchmen in America, are deeply
> disturbed about the crisis brought upon our country by historic dis-
> tortions of important human realities in the controversy about
> "black power." What we see shining through the variety of rhetoric
> is not anything new but the same old problem of power and race
> which has faced our beloved country since 1619.
> . . . The conscience of black men is corrupted because having no
> power to implement the demands of conscience, the concern for
> justice in the absence of justice becomes a chaotic self-surrender.
> Powerlessness breeds a race of beggars. We are faced with a situa-
> tion where powerless conscience meets conscienceless power, threat-
> ening the very foundations of our Nation.

We deplore the overt violence of riots, but we feel it is more important to focus on the real sources of these eruptions. These sources may be abetted inside the Ghetto, but their basic cause lies in the silent and covert violence which white middle class America inflicts upon the victims of the inner city.

. . . In short, the failure of American leaders to use American power to create equal opportunity *in life* as well as *law*, this is the real problem and not the anguished cry for black power.

. . . Without the capacity to participate with power, i.e., to have some organized political and economic strength to really influence people with whom one interacts, integration is not meaningful.

. . . America has asked its Negro citizens to fight for opportunity as *individuals*, whereas at certain points in our history what we have needed most has been opportunity for the *whole group*, not just for selected and approved Negroes.

. . . We must not apologize for the existence of this form of group power, for we have been oppressed as a group and not as individuals. We will not find our way out of that oppression until both we and America accept the need for Negro Americans, as well as for Jews, Italians, Poles, and white Anglo-Saxon Protestants, among others, to have and to wield group power.

It is a commentary on the fundamentally racist nature of this society that the concept of group strength for black people must be articulated— not to mention defended. No other group would submit to being led by others. Italians do not run the Anti-Defamation League of B'nai B'rith. Irish do not chair Christopher Columbus Societies. Yet when black people call for black-run and all-black organizations, they are immediately classed in a category with the Ku Klux Klan. This is interesting and ironic, but by no means surprising: the society does not expect black people to be able to take care of their business, and there are many who prefer it precisely that way.

In the end, we cannot and shall not offer any guarantees that Black Power, if achieved, would be non-racist. No one can predict human behavior. Social change always has unanticipated consequences. If black racism is what the larger society fears, we cannot help them. We can only state what we hope will be the result, given the fact that the present situation is unacceptable and that we have no real alternative but to work for Black Power. The final truth is that the white society is not entitled to reassurances, even if it were possible to offer them.

We have outlined the meaning and goals of Black Power; we have also discussed one major thing which it is not. There are others of greater importance. The advocates of Black Power reject the old slogans and meaningless rhetoric of previous years in the civil rights struggle. The language of yesterday is indeed irrelevant: progress, non-violence, integration, fear of "white backlash," coalition. Let us look at the rhetoric and see why these terms must be set aside or redefined.

One of the tragedies of the struggle against racism is that up to this point there has been no national organization which could speak to the growing militancy of young black people in the urban ghettos and the black-belt South. There has been only a "civil rights" movement, whose tone of voice was adapted to an audience of middle-class whites. It served as a sort of buffer zone between that audience and angry young blacks. It claimed to speak for the needs of a community, but it did not speak in the tone of that community. None of its so-called leaders could go into a rioting community and be listened to. In a sense, the blame must be shared—along with the mass media—by those leaders for what happened in Watts, Harlem, Chicago, Cleveland and other places. Each time the black people in those cities saw Dr. Martin Luther King get slapped they became angry. When they saw little black girls bombed to death *in a church* and civil rights workers ambushed and murdered, they were angrier; and when nothing happened, they were steaming mad. We had nothing to offer that they could see, except to go out and be beaten again. We helped to build their frustration.

We had only the old language of love and suffering. And in most places—that is, from the liberals and middle class—we got back the old language of patience and progress. The civil rights leaders were saying to the country: "Look, you guys are supposed to be nice guys, and we are only going to do what we are supposed to do. Why do you beat us up? Why don't you give us what we ask? Why don't you straighten yourselves out?" For the masses of black people, this language resulted in virtually nothing. In fact, their objective day-to-day condition worsened. The unemployment rate among black people increased while that among whites declined. Housing conditions in the black communities deteriorated. Schools in the black ghettos continued to plod along on outmoded techniques, inadequate curricula, and with all too many tired and indifferent teachers. Meanwhile, the President picked up the refrain of "We Shall Overcome" while the Congress passed civil rights law after civil rights law, only to have them effectively nullified by deliberately weak enforcement. "Progress is being made," we were told.

Such language, along with admonitions to remain non-violent and fear the white backlash, convinced some that that course was the *only* course to follow. It misled some into believing that a black minority could bow its head and get whipped into a meaningful position of power. The very notion is absurd. The white society devised the language, adopted the rules and had the black community narcotized into believing that that language and those rules were, in fact, relevant. The black community was told time and again how *other* immigrants finally won *acceptance:* that is, by following the Protestant Ethic of Work and Achievement. They worked hard; therefore, they achieved. We were not told that it was by building Irish Power, Italian Power, Polish Power or Jewish Power that these groups got themselves together and operated from positions of strength. We were not told that "the American dream" wasn't designed for black people. That while today, to whites, the dream may *seem* to include black people, it cannot do so by the very nature of this nation's political and economic system, which imposes institutional racism on the black masses if not upon every individual black. A notable comment on that "dream" was made by Dr. Percy Julian, the black scientist and director of the Julian Research Institute in Chicago, a man for whom the dream seems to have come true. While not subscribing to "black power" as he understood it, Dr. Julian clearly understood the basis for it: "The false concept of basic Negro inferiority is one of the curses that still lingers. It is a problem created by the white man. Our children just no longer are going to accept the patience we were taught by our generation. We were taught a pretty little lie—excel and the whole world lies open before you. *I obeyed the injunction and found it to be wishful thinking.*" (Authors' italics.) [2]

A key phrase in our buffer-zone days was non-violence. For years it has been thought that black people would not literally fight for their lives. Why this has been so is not entirely clear; neither the larger society nor black people are noted for passivity. The notion apparently stems from the years of marches and demonstrations and sit-ins where black people did not strike back and the violence always came from white mobs. There are many who still sincerely believe in that approach. From our viewpoint, rampaging white mobs and white night-riders must be made to understand that their days of free head-whipping are over. Black people should and must fight back. Nothing more quickly repels someone bent on destroying you than the unequivocal message: "O.K., fool, make your move, and run the same risk I run—of dying."

When the concept of Black Power is set forth, many people immediately conjure up notions of violence. The country's reaction to the Deacons for Defense and Justice, which originated in Louisiana, is instructive. Here is a group which realized that the "law" and law enforcement agencies would not protect people, so they had to do it themselves. If a nation fails to protect its citizens, then that nation cannot condemn those who take up the task themselves. The Deacons and all other blacks who resort to self-defense represent a simple answer to a simple question: what man would not defend his family and home from attack?

But this frightened some white people, because they knew that black people would now fight back. They knew that this was precisely what *they* would have long since done if *they* were subjected to the injustices and oppression heaped on blacks. Those of us who advocate Black Power are quite clear in our own minds that a "non-violent" approach to civil rights is an approach black people cannot afford and a luxury white people do not deserve. It is crystal clear to us—and it must become so with the white society—*that there can be no social order without social justice.* White people must be made to understand that they must stop messing with black people, or the blacks *will* fight back!

[2] *The New York Times* (April 30, 1967), p. 30.

19. VIOLENCE IN THE CITY—
AN END OR A BEGINNING?

THE MCCONE COMMISSION

Former Governor Edmund (Pat) Brown appointed John McCone, a prominent California business leader and former head of the CIA, and other leading Californians to examine the causes of the Watts Riot of 1965. McCone and his colleagues conducted extensive hearings and collected voluminous evidence on the problems of the urban ghetto. The result of their findings was a 101-page report that was widely acclaimed by government leaders when it first appeared. The following selection from the introduction to the report reveals the Commission's conclusions concerning racial unrest in Los Angeles.

Of Fundamental and Durable Import

As a Commission, we are seriously concerned that the existing breach, if allowed to persist, could in time split our society irretrievably. So serious and so explosive is the situation that, unless it is checked, the August riots may seem by comparison to be only a curtainraiser for what could blow up one day in the future.

Our recommendations will concern many areas where improvement can be made but three we consider to be of highest priority and greatest importance.

1. Because idleness brings a harvest of distressing problems, employment for those in the Negro community who are unemployed and able to work is a first priority. Our metropolitan area employs upwards of three millions of men and women in industry and in the service trades, and we face a shortage of skilled and semi-skilled workers as our economy expands. We recommend that our robust community take immediate steps to relieve the lack of job opportunity for Negroes by cooperative programs for employment and training, participated in by the Negro community, by governmental agencies, by employers and by organized labor.

2. In education, we recommend a new and costly approach to educating the Negro child who has been deprived of the early training that customarily starts at infancy and who because of early deficiencies advances through school on a basis of age rather than scholastic attainment. What is clearly needed and what we recommend is an emergency program designed to raise the level of scholastic attainment of those who would otherwise fall behind. This requires pre-school education, intensive instruction in small classes, remedial courses and other special treatment. The cost will be great but until the level of scholastic achievement of the disadvantaged child is raised, we cannot expect to overcome the existing spiral of failure.

3. We recommend that law enforcement agencies place greater em-

FROM "Violence in the City—An End or a Beginning?" A Report by the Governor's Commission on the Los Angeles Riots. Reprinted by permission.

phasis on their responsibilities for crime prevention as an essential element of the law enforcement task, and that they institute improved means for handling citizen complaints and community relationships.

The road to the improvement of the condition of the disadvantaged Negro which lies through education and employment is hard and long, but there is no shorter route. The avenue of violence and lawlessness leads to a dead end. To travel the long and difficult road will require courageous leadership and determined participation by all parts of our community, but no task in our times is more important. Of what shall it avail our nation if we can place a man on the moon but cannot cure the sickness in our cities?

20. WHAT THE McCONE COMMISSION DIDN'T SEE

FREDERICK J. HACKER, M.D.

The McCone Commission Report, widely acclaimed in some circles, was received more critically in others. Writing in Frontier *magazine, Frederick Hacker explains that there was positive value to the Watts riot. This is a fact that the white middle class finds difficult to understand, as the McCone Report reflects. Hacker, Clinical Professor of Psychiatry at the University of Southern California and the University of Kansas, is uniquely qualified to explain the psychological influence of the riot on its Negro participants.*

The Watts rebellion in Los Angeles has now been tidily swept into the 101 pages of the McCone Report. The report cost $250,000 and is obviously well-meaning and respectable. It suggests better education, more employment, and nicer relations between Negroes and the police department to avoid "the dull, devastating spiral of failure that awaits the average disadvantaged child."

It will also, in essence, be treated as a "white man's" report. It labels the rebellion "a formless, quite senseless, all but hopeless violent protest —engaged in by a few but bringing great distress to all." The McCone Commission, firmly on the side of God, country, and our present law and order, reached this judgment: "Yet, however powerful their grievances, the rioters had no legal or moral justification for the wounds they inflicted." What the McCone Commission fails to understand is that, from the standpoint of the lower-class Negroes living in Watts, the "disorderly and immoral" riots were neither senseless nor hopeless. The rebellion brought them enormous and immediate psychological benefits, or at least so they thought.

In all 101 pages of the report there is little consideration of the psychological reasons why the Negroes revolted and no appreciation of the psychological changes that occurred within the Negroes during the riots.

Frederick J. Hacker, M.D., "What the McCone Commission Didn't See," *Frontier* (March 1966). Reprinted by permission of *The Nation*.

As the only dissenting member of the commission, the Rev. Mr. James E. Jones, said in an interview, the report did not consider attitudes.

For the Negroes, what happened in southeastern Los Angeles last August *was* justified legally and morally. Where the police saw black criminals tearing apart law and order with a cascade of Molotov cocktails, the Negroes of Watts watched freedom fighters liberating themselves with blood and fire. The McCone Report says that only 2 percent of the Negroes participated in the rioting. It implies that the rest of the Negro community was cowering in darkened houses waiting for the forces of law and order to rescue them. Actually, the majority of the 400,000 Negroes in the area supported the riots. As one high school girl said afterwards, "Every time I looked out of my window and saw another fire, I felt new joy."

Not "Bad" or "Criminal"

The most distinctive generally shared feeling of the Negroes about the riots is that they were not criminal. To some, they were the explosion of a powder keg; to others, a rationally planned demonstration against sustained injustice; to others, a full-scale rebellion; to others an assertion of racial independence, a kind of racial identity struggle; and for others, a protest against intolerable poverty. For none of the Negroes, however, were the riots "bad" or "criminal" in the sense these words are used by the McCone Commission.

For the Negroes, there was no reason to feel guilt, shame, or regret. Although most of the rioters interviewed believe that it is wrong to "burn," "loot," "break down the law," they felt the looting and burning were merely excesses of a just cause and thus justified. In that respect, the Watts riots were psychologically analogous to the Hungarian Revolution and the Boston Tea Party, where the participants also did not try to excuse the single acts considered "bad" but felt fully justified by their over-all cause.

Some psychoanalysts tend to belittle violence as *sickness*. They—like the members of the McCone Commission—ignore the uncomfortable historical evidence that violence can unite, particularly if the violence occurs once and is not repeated. As in the mythology of bull fighting, violence—the ultimate violence that could or does lead to death—is the great unifier, the strange symbol of reality confronted with an ultimate truth. When one is nakedly facing one's destiny, presumably all falsehood and pretense falls away and one is—as described by rioters—"close to God."

"Alternative to Despair"

Conventional psychoanalytic theory says that resorting to violence, particularly collective violence, is a regression and a projection of inner feelings of panic and despair. This is undoubtedly true. What is overlooked is that violence is also an effective defense. In other words, violence is an alternative to despair. Through violence, you can rid yourself of a torturing feeling of helplessness and nothingness. Violence makes you feel good—at least for a while. And it could be argued that the "mental health" of the Negro community was much better after the riots than before, because the riots served as a safety valve against the feeling of apathy that was the strongest characteristic of life in Watts.

Life in Watts before the riots was not only deprived. It was dull. Anyone familiar with the psychology of modern crime knows that the search for novelty and the desire to escape monotony is by no means willful, arbitrary, or fanciful. The hunger and search for new experiences—popularly known as "kicks"—indicates just as legitimate a need as the search for food or sexual satisfaction.

The psychological climate of Watts last summer was one of apathy tangled with an acute sense of injustice. The Negroes felt that all the storekeepers were Jews and Italians, who, having suffered exploitation, were out to exploit Negroes. They felt all the policemen assigned to Watts were recent immigrants recruited from the South and therefore sadistic and brutal. Both reactions were serious misconceptions. But most of the carefully collected injustices did result from real deprivation and major suffering, although the suffering was often expressed in trivial terms.

It cost seventy-five cents to cash a check in Watts, while in nearby white communities it cost nothing. Food cost more in Watts. For example, canned peaches cost three cents more than they do in white neighborhood supermarkets. In Watts, there was no promise or possibility of real change. In Watts, there was no "action." In Vietnam people were dying; in Hollywood people were living the sweet life; in Watts nothing ever happened.

To the white Angelenos driving the freeways in their Monzas and Barracudas and Mustangs, Watts was invisible. By an accident of geography, it was underneath the freeway. It was underneath the freeway in the very center of their city, and the white Angelenos roared over it daily without noticing its existence. (Over and over again after the riots, the participants used the same words: "We put ourselves on the map." It was almost as though the riots had been planned as a tourist attraction and the inhabitants were now happy and proud that photographers and curiosity seekers were descending from the freeways to see where it all took place.)

In Watts, the police often reached for their guns if a Negro approached them even if he only wanted to ask directions. Few cared what happened to Negroes as human beings. To a great extent, only their women could get jobs—usually as servants. The police were continually harassing them—humiliating them by making them spreadeagle over a car hood to be searched, by mimicking their speech, by refusing to call them "Mister" and substituting the insults of "Hey, boy," or "Come here, monkey."

How Negro Men Saw Themselves

The Negroes of Watts were constantly degraded in the presence of their wives and children. Children need to see their fathers as strong and omnipotent. Negro children saw their fathers as helpless and frightened objects of the arbitrariness of white men in uniform. In school, the children were taught urban, middle-class, white values with their emphasis on aggressiveness, responsibility, and the assertion of masculinity. But adult Negro men were barred from responsibility and treated as though they were irresponsible children; and they were punished for aggressiveness. As a result, the children were contemptuous of their fathers. "Our dads didn't count," they said. "When we wanted anything, we asked our mothers." And the Negro men felt an even deeper sense of being victimized.

But the sense of injustice started to breed a feeling of hope. It is a curious and now often-discussed fact that riots occur precisely at a time when—objectively and subjectively—the situation is not only improving, but improving more rapidly than was believed possible.

Riots never break out when the situation is considered hopeless. Action then appears senseless, and the reduction of people to historical objects is so complete and internalized—and thus regarded as inevitable —that no resistance is possible. When black people or yellow people or white people think of themselves as born servants, helpless victims, there can be no rioting. People who say, "Give the Negroes a finger and they want the whole hand," and who blame the rioting on desegregation and liberal court decisions are, in part, right. So is Police Chief William H. Parker of Los Angeles when he blames *permissiveness* and the *over-regard for civil rights*. If the American Negroes were still slaves, there would have been little chance of rioting in the summer of 1965.

The trigger for the riots might have been anything. In fact, it was the arrest by the police of a drunken driver in the middle of a heat wave. For days the thermometer had stayed just under 100 degrees. The weather was as chronically muggy and oppressive as was the life of the average Watts Negro. In a heat wave, everyone feels like a helpless object battered by forces he cannot control. The riot started almost as a temper tantrum against the heat and the despair. In a short while, this feeling proved contagious. It spread to Chief Parker who had a tantrum against the liberals and to Mayor Samuel W. Yorty who had a tantrum against the state government. And, like a child's temper tantrum which has succeeded in attracting attention, the riot flowered under the attention of newspaper headlines and national television.

For the rioters, the riots were fun. The conventional explanation by middle-class parents to their children about sex skips over the important point that sex also can be fun. In much the same way, observers have not understood or have withheld the fact that the riots were fun. There was a carnival in the midst of carnage. Rioters laughed, danced, clapped their hands. Many got drunk. Violence was permissible. Children stayed out all night. Several children between the ages of ten and fourteen (who first asked the permission of their mothers to talk to a white man) later admitted defensively that it was "great fun." . . . "It was a little scarey but mostly it was great because everybody had a good time, sort of a ball." . . . "Nobody cared if we ever went to bed."

Contrary to the usual pattern of riots, there was hardly any sexual delinquency or increase in sexual activities. Usually rioting, and the un-controlled, unrestrained, and thus pleasurable descent into repressed and suppressed emotion and the release of all tension in the absence of ordinary inner and outer controls, brings with it sexual promiscuity. But when the lower-class Negro says he "wants to feel like a man," he is talking about status—not sex. The rioters constantly volunteered the information that "we never had to worry about sex." . . . "Sex is nothing to get excited about." . . . "Whitey makes too much of it." Sex has always been the lower-class Negro's one free pleasure. Homosexual and heterosexual experience starts young. And from the time a boy is ten or eleven, girls are always available. So the release of tension in rioting led not to sexual delinquency, but to looting.

Mixed Feelings About the Looting

The looting also was fun. There was great glee about the breakdown of a law-enforcement system identified with suppression and injustice. The objects looted from stores were often taken as a symbol of the Mardi Gras atmosphere of liberation from injustice. Some rioters said over and over again that they didn't need the things they stole and could not use them. In many cases, the stolen refrigerators, stoves, television sets and stereo sets were divorced completely from their utilitarian use. They had been coveted for a long time, but after they were stolen, they were often taken apart and abandoned. It was the ultimate in waste, in contempt for the white man's objects—a determined NO to acculturation, to the white man's world. Rather than useful instruments that had to be guarded and protected and cared for, the looted objects actually became toys.

During the riots there was, to paraphrase Coleridge, "a willing suspension of conscience." In rioting, one loses personal individuality by gaining collective individuality. One "becomes like the others" and this "makes you happy." . . . "I don't think any more." . . . "I had the good feeling that this was right and it was wonderful."

This liberation from conscience and from conscientiousness made possible for the rioters an involvement and an extreme commitment usually denied them. The most important resource the lower-class Negro lacks is the resource to get involved in something or committed to something, including the ordinary values of society that are unhesitatingly accepted by the middle-class white—and the middle-class Negro—American.

Bayard Rustin says that the black body has to be used precisely because democratic channels are denied to the Negro, and he has nothing but his body to fight with. During the Watts rioting, the apathy—which is a form of chronic mild depression—was swept away. Real feeling was restored to the Negroes by the full involvement of their bodies and by actual danger. There was ecstatic body involvement. ("It felt good all over." . . . "We were whole again." . . . "We were whole people, not just servants." . . . "We were new.")

Again and again one phrase was repeated: "At last we were where the action was." At last something was happening, and what was happening was extraordinarily important. It was the metamorphosis of the Negroes of southeastern Los Angeles from victims—historical objects—to masters. They were now men. As one explained the change: "It made our males men," and another said, "I saw children respect their fathers for the first time."

A Shared Feeling of Identity

The people of Watts felt that for those four days they represented all Negroes; the historic plight of the Negroes; all the rebellions against all injustice. They were doing the job that other Negroes were prevented from doing. They were setting an example; starting a pattern. Being able to watch themselves on television screens in store windows, even as they smashed the stores, reinforced their feelings of self-importance. In their simultaneous participation and watching their participation, they felt that the whole nation—black and white—watched them too. They felt the emotional involvement of the nation in the riot as a symbol. Like lighting the Christmas tree on the White House lawn, it was a shared experience.

There was an extraordinary religious—almost mystical—fervor. Economic and social injustices took on religious meaning. "All God's children got shoes," said one rioter, explaining his looting of a shoe store. The injustices had betrayed the promises of the Bible that all people should be equal and that the lowest is as good as the highest. Watts stood for every deprived Negro community. Frequently there was overt identification with Christ as a sacrificial being who by his suffering takes upon himself and atones for the sins of everybody. But the role of Christ was rejected in the next breath in favor of "being where the action is."

"A Strange Sense of Pride"

The emotionally liberating effects of the riots have not lasted, but they have been replaced by a strange sense of pride and accomplishment which is actually the finding of a national and racial identity. National identity, racial identity, and, often, religious identity are accepted ingredients of personality structure and seem to have been always present to those who have them. They forget that what now appears as given and predestined had to be taken and grabbed in the past. National identity is not a gift but an active and often violent deed. Were Americans not colonial Englishmen prior to their becoming Americans by violent action? Did not the Jews experience themselves as the arch-symbol of unwanted yet persistent guests in foreign countries until they grabbed their own country and forged their national identity in the assertive belligerence that had previously been considered "un-Jewish"?

There is an exhilarating feeling in the rioters that they have finally found and forged a new sense of identity. The riots welded them together, and now they feel capable of carving a new fate, not just passively enduring their present existence. Perhaps every national and racial identity derives from the fact—or at least the legend—of an aggressive rising. Is not every revolution a sudden and abrupt break with the past and the potential beginning of a new tradition? Destructiveness can lose its negative connotation when it has become successful in welding people together. The destruction of society becomes, by a change of function, the building of a new and different society. The rioters believe —and have to believe even if it isn't true—that a new era has started. The new era was foreshadowed by Montgomery and Birmingham, but they believe it really started with the violent uprising of Watts.

There is pride that now everybody knows *what* Watts is and *where* Watts is. Before, not even the people who live in Los Angeles knew. Now the whole nation knows. Before, nobody cared what happened to them. Now, by God, people have to care. Each of the rioters interviewed said something like, "You don't want to talk to my kind of Negro," meaning a proud, aggressive Negro who talks back. And each of the rioters interviewed assumed that the interviewer had had experience only with submissive Negroes.

The rioters now look upon themselves as self-respecting, fighting Negroes who would not be pushed around any longer, or, as they put it: "We're men now." . . . "We won't take any more from Whitey." . . . "It's finally happened. They can't get away with everything."

Assertive and masculine, the "new Negro" fights and does not necessarily wait to fight back. He fights first. And due to the easy manufacture of Molotov cocktails, there is now a constant threat of the repetition of violence. (Possibly, Molotov cocktails are more significant for our period, and, socially, a more important fact than the atom bomb.) To this "new Negro," the only good Negro is a destructive Negro. This feeling does not apply to the middle-class Los Angeles Negro who most often lives in an integrated neighborhood like Baldwin Hills, works with white lawyers or accountants, and pickets with white liberals for the Congress of Racial Equality (CORE). To him, this "new Negro" is enormously embarrassing. The middle-class Negro believes in passive resistance, in gradualism, in the melting-pot approach—the things which the Watts Negro calls "phoney hope solutions." Middle-class Negroes have tried to explain away the riots by saying "there are good and bad in every society." The rebellious, assertive Negro is—in their eyes as in the eyes of almost the whole community—the "bad Negro." They speak of him in the same stereotypes the whites use: "uncontrolled," "undisciplined," "childish," "close to the jungle."

"We Will Never Be the Same Again"

The rioters overemphasize the significance and importance of the riots: "The whole world knows and will never forget." . . . "Now we have something to remember." . . . "This is where our calendar starts." They have taken their fate into their own hands, and they feel that what happened is irreversible. "Our children and grandchildren will remember Watts." . . . "The world isn't the same." . . . "We aren't the same." . . . "We'll never be the same again." . . . "The world will never be the same."

To exactly the extent that the riots contributed to the enhancement of the self-image of the Negroes, it gave whites a furious feeling of impotence. Inwardly, they experienced the feeling of an inevitable surrender to Negro demands and the fear of "mongrelization," of "the black danger" which is so similar to "the yellow danger" of Spengler's *Decline of the West*.

Before the riots there were many subtle sociological and psychological distinctions within the white community, within the black community, and even within the police department. But the riots polarized everyone into two groups: black and white.

One of the functions of aggressive action is precisely this simplification. As the German kaiser once said, "I don't know any parties any more. I only know Germans." In Los Angeles, there was only white against black. This simplification and polarization relieves anxiety and solves moral problems by giving each party the same firm conviction in the justness of its fight. The line between good and bad is obvious to each side; nothing is blurred. Whoever is not on *our* side is either too stupid, too wicked or too depraved to be regarded as a human being. Why else is he not on *our* side, the side of the angels that has so obviously pre-empted all goodness, justice, and truth? All specific individual acts are justified and sanctioned if committed by the right side. *Our* side is idealized. The opponents, however, are satanized, made into devils. By their opposition to *us*, they have forfeited their place as human beings. They are less than human. Therefore, all laws respecting their human dignity can be suspended.

During the riots, the whites felt that Negro grievances did not have to be discussed or remedied. They feared the unleashing of uncontrollable forces that could sweep us all under. People who had previously been critical of Police Chief Parker rallied to his defense. Law and Order must be re-established and enforced. It did not matter what kind of Law and Order. As Chief Parker said, "They're on the bottom, we're on top," and he announced that he did not bargain with hoodlums. After the riots, some rioters were picked arbitrarily as culprits. They were treated as ordinary criminals. On the other hand, all police officers were cleared of charges. Their acts leading to deaths were declared justifiable homicide. *War crimes are committed only by the opponent.*

The rebels, during the riots, felt justified no matter what aggressive and destructive acts they committed because law enforcement itself was something evil and oppressive to them. Every act against the law or an officer of the law was, a priori, justified. (For a different example, remember the spy movies during World War II in which personally-innocent wearers of the hated Nazi uniform were killed to the applause of the audience.)

In a polarized situation, there is a common enemy, and the enemy is easily recognizable. In Watts, the Negroes were black, the police wore uniforms. Polarization melts away all inner conflicts. The participants feel free and guilt-free, while the external conflict is exaggerated, serving the purpose of eliminating inner turmoil.

When the riots were over, the polarization also receded. The old fronts within the Negro community and within the white community reappeared. There was name calling. Guilt distribution started according to a foreseeable and extremely repetitious pattern. There were immediate charges on every side of "playing politics," or "making hay out of the situation."

The "Delusion of Particularism"

In one sense, the rioters and the police stood together against the rest of the community. They shared a strange delusion of particularism. They believed their problems to be unparalleled, inconceivable to any outsider. Only someone with special understanding, long acquaintance and local participation could understand. For this reason the Negroes resented Dr. Martin Luther King's visit to Los Angeles, although they otherwise respected him as an effective Negro leader. The social agencies in Watts insisted on handling all reconstruction since they believed that only they knew the real situation and had the confidence of the Negroes. This attitude was strangely matched by the insistence of Chief Parker that the police did not need outside advice because they knew more than any outsider.

After the riots, Negroes of the area showed resentment because the white community sent middle-class Negroes to Watts as agents. There are two Negro assemblymen in Los Angeles and three Negroes on the fifteen-member Los Angeles City Council, but these five "Negro leaders" were ineffective in stopping the riots because the rioters considered any middle-class Negro submissive to white people and white values. They consider middle-class Negroes as "Uncle Toms" toadying to the white people and afraid to lose their positions with "Whitey."

The rioters had no particular desire for communication with the white community, yet they expected that the white community would and must help them and was actually compelled to help them to prevent further riots. They said that Black Muslims and Communists had not been involved in the riots, but, they added, who could say what might happen if the situation didn't improve. This hint of radicalization was a blackmail threat to the white community.

The ugliness of Watts had become intolerable, and they meant to burn the buildings partly as a kind of attempt at urban renewal. As they saw it, "The whites will now have to build better buildings because we don't have any." . . . "If we hadn't destroyed them, we would never get new ones." They believed the white community, and particularly the federal government, had to clothe them, feed them, and rebuild for them.

This magical expectation of full outside help to redress all the injustices that led to the outbreak was in strange contrast to the nearly unanimous insistence that all real improvement has to come from local leaders, local agencies, and people living in the community. Their insistence on "local leaders" reflects a resentment against middle-class Negroes who have moved from Watts, leaving the community with hardly any Negro lawyers, doctors or other professionals. ("How can we have pride when the successful Negroes don't stay?")

Shattering a "Negative Image"

Before the riots, the underprivileged and psychologically castrated Negro male of Watts had accepted and incorporated the contemptuous value judgment that considered him not quite human. He had actually seen himself as a negative copy of white values. He had prided himself on his lack of control, on his unwillingness to obey the rules of a game that he had not chosen. He had experienced himself as more real, more untamed, more natural than white people.

That negative image broke apart in the riots. Consciously and unconsciously, most of the rioters knew that the riots could not succeed and that they would have to pay for their defiance. The riots actually were an accident, the explosive coincidence of trivial events. Yet in the courage of a rebellion that attracted world-wide attention, the Negroes acquired a taste of autonomy. They were not any longer either positive or negative copies of the white man's values. They asserted a will of their own, no matter how little they knew what this will actually meant. Their rebellion left deep marks, even if it did not fully succeed. Perhaps the most amazing thing to the author was how often unsophisticated and uneducated rioters spoke about identity and about their pride in the national and international prominence they felt was gained by their rebellion.

What the McCone Commission didn't see is that the desire of Negroes for a proud image of themselves is as vital to them as the fulfillment of their economic needs. If the recommendations of the McCone Report are implemented by people who continue to think of the riots as only criminal and the rioters as ordinary criminals, the result will be disastrous.

A few days after the McCone Report, a committee of the Los Angeles Grand Jury, declaring that the riot was merely a crime spree, said, "There can be no extenuating circumstances to rationalize this ruthless outbreak of lawlessness and those who are convicted of leadership or participation in this riot should be punished to the fullest extent of the law."

Whatever the Grand Jury and the McCone Commission and middle-class Americans may think, the riot was *not* "equally abhorred and resented by all good, law-abiding citizens, regardless of race or status." For the overwhelming majority of the Negroes in Watts it was better to be feared than to be treated with contempt. What must be understood by the rest of America is that, for the lower-class Negro, riots are not criminal but are a legitimate weapon in a morally justified civil war. Already, the Watts riots have given the Negro a sense of personal and national identity. For the ghetto-Negro in the second half of the 20th Century, anything—even a new American revolution—is better than being invisible.

21. ON WATTS

ELDRIDGE CLEAVER

The rioting in Watts had a profound effect on black people that went far beyond the immediate community in Los Angeles. Evidence to support Dr. Hacker's conclusions in the previous selection can be seen in an excerpt from Soul on Ice, *written by the ex-convict and Black Panther Eldridge Cleaver.*

Folsom Prison
August 16, 1965

As we left the Mess Hall Sunday morning and milled around in the prison yard, after four days of abortive uprising in Watts, a group of low riders[1] from Watts assembled on the basketball court. They were wearing jubilant, triumphant smiles, animated by a vicarious spirit by which they, too, were in the thick of the uprising taking place hundreds of miles away to the south in the Watts ghetto.

"Man," said one, "what they doing out there? Break it down for me, Baby."

They slapped each other's outstretched palms in a cool salute and burst out laughing with joy.

"Home boy, them Brothers is taking care of Business!" shrieked another ecstatically.

Then one low rider, stepping into the center of the circle formed by the others, rared back on his legs and swaggered, hunching his belt up with his forearms as he'd seen James Cagney and George Raft do in too many gangster movies. I joined the circle. Sensing a creative moment in the offing, we all got very quiet, very still, and others passing by joined the circle and did likewise.

[1] *Low Rider.* A Los Angeles nickname for ghetto youth. Originally the term was coined to describe the youth who had lowered the bodies of their cars so that they rode low, close to the ground; also implied was the style of driving that these youngsters perfected. Sitting behind the steering wheel and slumped low down in the seat, all that could be seen of them was from their eyes up, which used to be the cool way of driving. When these youthful hipsters alighted from their vehicles, the term *low rider* stuck with them, evolving to the point where all black ghetto youth—but *never* the soft offspring of the black bourgeoisie—are referred to as low riders.

"Baby," he said, "they walking in fours and kicking in doors; dropping Reds[2] and busting heads; drinking wine and committing crime, shooting and looting; high-siding[3] and low-riding, setting fires and slashing tires; turning over cars and burning down bars; making Parker mad and making me glad; putting an end to that 'go slow' crap and putting sweet Watts on the map—my black ass is in Folsom this morning but my black heart is in Watts!" Tears of joy were rolling from his eyes.

It was a cleansing, revolutionary laugh we all shared, something we have not often had occasion for.

Watts was a place of shame. We used to use Watts as an epithet in much the same way as city boys used "country" as a term of derision. To deride one as a "lame," who did not know what was happening (a rustic bumpkin), the "in-crowd" of the time from L.A. would bring a cat down by saying that he had just left Watts, that he ought to go back to Watts until he had learned what was happening, or that he had just stolen enough money to move out of Watts and was already trying to play a cool part. But now, blacks are seen in Folsom saying, "I'm from Watts, Baby!" —whether true or no, but I think their meaning is clear. Confession: I, too, have participated in this game, saying, I'm from Watts. In fact, I did live there for a time, and I'm *proud* of it, the tired lamentations of Whitney Young, Roy Wilkins, and The Preacher notwithstanding.

22. FAREWELL TO INTEGRATION

W. H. FERRY

W. H. Ferry, author and social critic, formerly associated with the Center for the Study of Democratic Institutions, concludes that because American cities are becoming predominantly black, real integration is impossible. Thus, if the historic American experiment in democratic government is to continue to have meaning, Negroes must be allowed self-determination. Ferry's suggestions for this radical revamping of our social system are contained in his article "Farewell to Integration."

On many fronts the common denominators of poverty, ignorance, and neglect join black and white. I am aware of these intertwinings, as I am of the partial account I shall be offering when I write exclusively in terms of race. Poverty is a black problem, and a large one, but it is not *the* black problem. The same may be said about educational and cultural deprivation. Formulating the race issue in such terms comprises much

2 *Reds.* A barbiturate, called Red Devils; so called because of the color of the capsule and because they are reputed to possess a vicious kick.

3 *High-siding.* Cutting up. Having fun at the expense of another.

Reprinted, by permission, from the March 1968 issue of *The Center Magazine*, Vol. I, No. 3, a publication of the Center for the Study of Democratic Institutions in Santa Barbara, California.

of the conventional wisdom about the nation's most excruciating dilemma; and this is the heart of the problem.

The conventional wisdom is our way of kidding ourselves about realities, our way of putting a comfortable shoe over raw and ugly bunions. Often it does not matter that we disguise the facts from ourselves. A major import of this article is that it matters very much indeed if we continue to delude ourselves about the actual relations between blacktown and whitetown in the United States. Fooling ourselves about the future of this relationship is among the most dangerous games people play.

My argument moves on three propositions, which I shall set out in turn.

The first is that our major cities, already black, will become preponderantly black in less than a generation.

Philip Hauser's summary in the Fall, 1965 issue of *Daedalus* tells the story:

> The Negro has been transformed from a predominantly rural to a predominantly urban resident. . . . By 1960 the concentration of Negroes in [metropolitan areas] had increased to 65% . . . [B]etween 1940 and 1960, Negroes in metropolitan areas more than doubled, increasing by 109% as compared with 50% for whites.
>
> Even more striking . . . is [Negro] concentration *in the central cities of these areas* [my emphasis]. Between 1910 and 1920, the Negro population in central cities of metropolitan areas increased by 40%; between 1920 and 1940, by 83%; between 1940 and 1960, by 123%. Hence, by 1960, of all Negro residents in metropolitan areas, 80% lived in central cities. . . .
>
> Thus between 1910 and 1960, the Negro has been redistributed . . . from rural . . . to urban and metropolitan areas; but within the urban and metropolitan complexes [he] has become and has remained much more highly segregated than was true of white immigrants who flocked there before [him].

This speed-up toward blackening American cities has been accompanied by little discernible consideration—by whites, anyway—of what it will mean when a majority of America's central cities are inhabited by a majority—in some cases perhaps a large majority—of blacks.

One projection is that fifty of our largest cities will by 1970 have majorities of black inhabitants. Another projection says that by 1975 the fourteen largest cities in the United States will have black majorities of 60 to 80 percent. These projections may turn out to be wrong, but the evidence for them is mounting. Blacks have been moving steadily into the large cities since World War II. Mechanization of Southern farms is pushing them rapidly off the land. Starvation is being systematically employed by Southern whites as a method of chasing blacks from areas where their cheap labor is no longer needed and they become welfare burdens. In forlorn pursuit of community and jobs they go in larger and larger waves to the cities, south, north, east, west.

For the most part our cities are circular in shape, developed in rough concentric circles running outward from a core of offices and governmental centers. The most abject portions of these circles are blacktowns —areas that expand irresistibly with family growth and migrants from rural America. They expand, that is, until they bump into that green and leafy ring closing the circle on all sides, the suburbs. This is a barrier that is virtually unpassable except to a few blacks, a they-shall-not-pass miles thick and getting thicker. So blacktown, no matter how it grows, will have to stop at the signs reading City Limits. Thus, the growing blackness of our central cities is a result ordained by whites, like all major matters affecting blacks.

According to Frances Piven and Richard Cloward in *The New Republic*, blacks will be bilked of political control of the great cities by the rise of metropolitanism—by the emergence of the super-governments they see inevitably consolidating the chief functions and powers of megalopolis. The impetus toward super-government comes from many directions, of which the desire to maintain political ascendancy over black multitudes in the central city is only one. "Metropolitan government," Piven and Cloward say, "will help to [avert impending black control of the cities] by usurping many powers of the city."

They also believe that blacks may be too immature politically and too habituated to white dictation to convert even substantial voting majorities into economic or political power. This thesis is formidable, but it is not conclusive. Divided and unsophisticated the blacks may now be. But these conditions can change with the appearance of a leader or two and the self-confidence generated by a victory or two. I believe Piven and Cloward have also underestimated the capacities and ambitions of a contingent of blacktown not yet on the scene—the thousands now in Vietnam. Blacks may not be able soon to become effective governors, but they will have the numbers and perhaps also the growing will to prevent effective urban government by the traditional forces.

All American cities today, no matter what their ethnic proportions, are ruled by whites for whites. (Cleveland and Gary *may* prove exceptions; the evidence is not yet in.) I discount entirely the presence of token blacks in municipal offices, even in electoral positions. No harm is done by a black alderman who has little influence and no power; he can always be pointed to as an illustration of civic broadmindedness. The issue is not what it *looks* like but what it *is* like. One reads these days of concessions won for blacks by their representatives in City Hall or at the Board of Education. This seems to indicate that the democratic process is working. In reality it indicates only the grudging small price that whites are willing to pay for the large, if temporary, bargain of peace and quiet in blacktown.

No one can seriously maintain that blacktown ever has gotten or is now getting a fair shake from whitetown. Picayune is too strong an adjective to describe even the most advertised aspects of the so-called "progress" of the urban black. It might better be described as a thimbleful of water to a parched man, with another thimbleful promised for some time later, on the condition that he must behave himself.

The white middle-class view, compounded of self-righteousness and paternalism, leads naturally enough to the unbreakable habit of talking about "them" and "us." Thus whites glide smoothly to the conclusion that "we" will somehow rule "them" even when the cities, at least in terms of sheer population, become theirs.

This brings me to a second proposition which is the key to my understanding of the situation. I offer it tentatively even though I am convinced it is valid. If it is, it makes all of our present difficulties trifling and we have before us a problem in statecraft whose dimensions cannot now be imagined.

The proposition is that racial integration in the United States is impossible.

I set forth this proposition without qualification. There are no hidden unlesses, buts, or ifs in it. I shall not deny that in some remote future integration may come about. But I do not see it resulting from the actual present trends and attitudes in American society. It can only be produced by some event overturning these trends. There is no denial in this proposition that there will be a steady betterment in the material situation of blacks. This is even likely. My proposition does, nevertheless, contradict the words of President Johnson that "the promise of America" will be extended to all races and peoples in the nation's slums.

My proposition is sad. Like tens of thousands of other Americans I have supported, organized, and taken part in reformist projects, with integration always beckoning at the end of weary labors. Now such activities must be seen as nothing more than acts of good-will, rather like Peace Corps expeditions into an undeveloped country that look toward the welfare and material progress of the natives but not to their integration with the homeland.

My proposition, in short, smashes the liberal dream. It eliminates the democratic optimistic claim that we are finding our way to a harmonious blending of the races. It changes the words of the marching song to "We Shall *Not* Overcome," for what was eventually to be overcome was hostility and non-fraternity between black and white. My proposition dynamites the foundations of the NAACP, the Urban League, and similar organizations. It asserts that blacktown USA and whitetown USA, for all practical purposes and with unimportant exceptions, will remain separate social communities for as long as one can see ahead. I am not sure, but it may also mean that blacktown will become a separate political community.

The proposition, I am aware, lends support to Southerners who have been acting on it for hundreds of years. It would seem to place me in the camp of the bigots and locate me with the hopeless. It puts at ultimate zero the efforts of the tough and high-minded who are giving their lives, in the urban bearpits and rural hovels of America, to the dream of equality among men.

Yet I am convinced that integration in the United States is a sentimental, not a doctrinal idea. We came to the idea late in American history, and it disappears readily from the rhetoric of politics—though not from the list of sacred democratic aims—at the first sign of indocility, at the first showing of the rioter's torch. The vast fuss today about improvements in blacktown is not aimed at integration. Few are afflicting us any longer with such a tiresome lie. All these measures are primarily aimed at the prevention of civic commotions, secondarily at assuaging the conscience of whitetown, and finally at helping the blacks. Priorities tell the story. In the last seven years we have spent $384 billion on war, $27 billion on space, and less than $2 billion on community development and housing.

The United States is a white man's country, conducted according to white customs and white laws for white purposes. And it must be acknowledged that 89 percent of Americans are non-black. I would not even make the argument that whites should not run the country for their own interests. I would argue that whites do not see, except in perilous self-deceit, that racial integration is one of these interests. I believe that the white attitude toward blacks is generally benign except when black claims intrude on the majority's privileges or peace of mind. Whites have little objection to bettering the condition of black lives as long as it does not cost much, and as long as it leads to the continuance of blacktowns and so does not present the threat of genuine integration at any level. The white condition for black betterment is, to put it simply, separation.

Why is it so hard for us whites to say clearly that we do not want blacks living among us and sharing our world? There must be dozens of reasons playing on one another. One, I suppose, is that we are ashamed to admit we do not subscribe, after all, to a glorious myth. Another is the Christian message that binds us to brotherhood. But as something in our understanding of Christianity made possible the acceptance of slavery, it continues to make possible the shunning of blacks as less worthy than ourselves. Often enough this is accompanied by an aching conscience. So much must be conceded, but it is a conscience that aches amid widespread moral torpor.

Another reason, I suppose, is that after 400 years blacks are still strangers to whites. It is a rare white man who is acquainted with a black, except perhaps for the one who washes his car or shines his shoes. This is not accidental. It has been arranged that way by whites.

A commanding reason, I would guess, is to be found in the mystique of progress, in the belief that by nature everything must somehow improve all the time. Thus, the present degradation of a tenth of our people can be waved aside by referring to better things to come, as come they must to the deserving, perhaps in another century or two or three.

Scientific evidence of black and white likeness, in all qualities except skin color, does not perceptibly alter white attitudes, even among the educated. American liberal thought has, to be sure, on the surface accepted this evidence. Yet we cannot deceive ourselves that there has been any consequential movement of whites toward acceptance of blacks as neighbors, fellow-members of the country club, or potential members of the family. The backlash in the liberal community to ghetto eruptions has been almost as pronounced as that in the suburbs. A certain fragile chumminess has sprung up, notably along the margins of blacktown and whitetown, between the friendly and open-hearted and well-educated on both sides. But this involves a few thousands not millions of people, is far from equality and fraternity, and is no evidence of any important social change.

These encounters do not mark a road to integration but only the nervous response of a few well-intentioned persons either to idealism or to menacing conditions. On close inspection most examples of "successful integration" turn out to be candyfloss. To the vast majority, the black is perceived as belonging to a different order of humanity. This perception is not Southern or Northern but white in character. It is not a perception peculiar to one kind of whiteness, either, but to all kinds, from the lowest "trash" to those most highly situated in society. Hence the terrifying quality, even to the dedicated liberal, of the question, "Would you want your daughter to marry one?"

But I have not yet sufficiently set forth the grounds for my proposition that integration is impossible. In giving up on integration I am not giving up on the blacks but on the whites. Thus, my main evidence runs from the observations I have made about white hypocrisy and obtuseness. We whites cannot imagine what this country looks like from the perspective of blacktown. So we think it must look as it does to us. We cannot imagine the closed doors, the rebuffs, the despair, the second-placeness, the sheer separateness of blacktown. Often with the best of intentions, whites deal with blacks habitually as an inferior species. It is a kind of genteel banditry against the spirit of a people. Blacks are said to have profound psychological difficulties because of their antecedents in slavery. The white memory is similarly tainted; we cannot forget these beginnings either.

But this, it will be said, is what we are starting to get over. I wish it were so; but it just isn't. I fear that I shall not convince those who so insist, but I shall be satisfied to shake their confidence a little, for a great deal depends on getting the issues clear. The black-white situation remains as truly enigmatic today as it was 107 years ago, and the stakes, in my opinion, are the same: the preservation of the Union. If what is needful is to be done, we cannot proceed on illusions, especially illusions about an impossible goal. White America can no longer rationalize its treatment of blacks by "the art of forgiving generously those we have grievously wronged."

Several objections to this position from those who insist that integration is possible must be dealt with. The first points to the apparently successful programs of the armed forces. (I say "apparently" because all I know is that conditions for blacks are better inside the forces than outside, which is not to say much. *Commander's Digest* for September 13, 1967 reported that more than 40 percent of enlisted blacks said they were dissatisfied with their conditions.) The answer to this objection, in any case, is that we can integrate the nation any time we decide to organize it along military lines.

The second objection is that the young people now agitating on the

Vietnam and civil-rights fronts will eventually save us from disunity. The answer is that they will have as little success in achieving integration as they are having in preventing U.S. enormities and escalation in Indochina, and for the same reasons—the intractable quality of majority opinion.

The third objection is that multiplying affluence will make it possible, once an expensive war is out of the way, rapidly to raise U.S. standards everywhere, especially in blacktown. The answer is that such a program will not be aimed at integration. Anyway, reducing the taxes of whitetown is almost certain to be given a much higher priority by Congress than raising the quality of life in blacktown. Yet, money is not the problem; whitetown's attitude is the problem.

The fourth objection is that blacks and whites alike will settle for the desegregation of the community mainly through the gradual absorption of successful and well-known blacks. This sharply misunderstands the hot currents running through blacktown that show no signs of slowing down, and what actually happens. Sprinter Tommie Smith says, "On the track you're Tommie Smith, the fastest man in the world, but off it you are just another nigger."

The last and weightiest objection to my proposition is that, deep in their hearts, white Americans want integration. There is a national will toward it, these objectors say, which will finally prevail because it is rooted in a sense of Judaeo-Christian morality and responsibility to one's neighbors. The answer is that the contrary is the case. Who wants integration? Election results show consistently that at least 60 to 75 percent of American voters will endorse any proposition that is clearly anti-Negro. The best known example is the result of the Proposition 14 fight in California, where voters decided two to one that blacks should not be protected in their right to buy housing wherever they wished. And even if this customary two-thirds rejection of the black should change to 51 percent in his favor, would we then say that this showed the triumph of integration? Sadly enough, there is only one place where we have registered even a mild success: we have more or less integrated poverty.

Public and private policy in the United States with respect to blacks is hopelessly confused and ambivalent. Yet each face it shows is authentic in its own way. The howling white mobs in Milwaukee and Chicago are authentic. Programs to improve housing and education in blacktown are authentic. Spotlessly white comic strips are authentic. Lily-white unions are authentic, and so are lily-white corporation offices. Looting and burning in the stews of Newark and Detroit are authentic, as are the Sherman tanks of the Army and the carbines of the National Guard. The sharp cleavage between blacks and whites at the New Politics convention, the country's largest assembly of radicals for many a year, is authentic.

Particularly authentic is the sanguine liberal view of black progress. The liberal view is that patience and persistence will in the end perform the miracle. The enemy is ignorance. Whitetown's resistance, according to this viewpoint, is temporary—stubborn perhaps but penetrable by knowledge and association. The liberal view effectively dismisses what

400 years of subjugation have done to the psyches of both the subjugator and the subjugated, disregards the essentially unchanging positions of blacktown and whitetown, purrs over token accomplishments, and prattles of widespread black advances.

This is nearly the most disastrous myth of all; it is worth examining.

The myth is shattered the moment one looks into the real levels of black opportunity and social mobility; into the real quality of black life and health; into the real cultural and social circumstances of blacktown. The record is clear that after a decade in which integration became enshrined as the true hope of America, blacks are relatively worse off than they were when it opened. In the Fall, 1965 issue of *Daedalus* Rashi Fein showed that blacks consistently are about a generation behind whites. Three quotations are enough to make the point:

> In 1964, 16% of Negro males age 20–24 had one or more years of college—the same percentage as among white males age 55–64, most of whom received their college education 35 to 40 years ago. . . .
>
> . . . the Negro male child is born into a world in which his chances of reaching age 20 are about the same as a white's reaching age 37. A Negro girl at birth has the same chance of attaining age 20 as the white girl has of reaching 42 . . .
>
> Today the Negro faces an unemployment situation unknown to the white for almost two and a half decades. What is recession for the white—say, an unemployment rate of 6% —is prosperity for the Negro. He last saw an unemployment rate below 7.5% in 1953. . . .

Undeniably there have been steady gains in blacktown—decreases in infant and maternal mortality, more children attending school longer, and the like—arguments incessantly made by the liberals. It is painful to point out, however, that this is the same argument made by the government of South Africa in defending apartheid. The point is the constant time lag of twenty years, and often more, between advances in whitetown and blacktown. Though whites believe they should be, the absolute gains of blacktown are not conclusive. Again, the view from below is what counts, and that is of a whitetown gaining steadily on all fronts and leaving blacktown always behind.

Let me put forward the more general testimony in support of my proposition. The race situation in the United States today is marked by growing violence and expressions of hatred and fear on the part of both blacks and whites; growing disillusionment throughout all of blacktown's neighborhoods; increasing belligerency of young blacks and their leaders, and similar belligerency among a wide variety of white spokesmen and organizations; increasing isolation of the black middle class, from whitetown on one side and blacktown on the other; growing uselessness of "treaties" between blacks and whites as black demands become more basic and white resistance more determined.

These signs cannot be regarded as passing inflammations, brought on by irritants like Vietnam. Blacktown's deep discontents have not been provoked by Communists. The outside agitator is whitetown itself. It is important to recognize that separation—non-integration—is the way it has always been. The fostering of the illusion that integration is an achievable goal is bad enough in its effects on blacks, some of whom may still entertain a vision of their children foregathering in total equality under the white yum-yum tree. But the illusion is sinister in its likely consequence for whites. By engaging in it they are leaving themselves unprepared for the grand finale.

My third and final proposition is this: *The United States has at best a few years of grace to think through a political theory that will at once maintain democratic practice and institutions and provide for an ethnically separated minority community.*

Is this possible? From the point of view of history, the practical arrangements would not appear to be difficult. We have been running a separated country for a very long time. But we shall not be permitted to pretend any longer that integration is our end. We shall be relentlessly squeezed by numbers in the cities. No one can assume that blacks in a majority will permit our cities to be governed as they have been governed up to the present. Nor can anyone assume that blacks will automatically permit unofficial control of metropolitan affairs to remain in impregnable board rooms and remote suburbs, though it must be granted that this may happen.

These possibilities indicate some gaping holes in present political theory and practice. It would be more exact to say that they disclose the immense conundrums posed by majoritarianism when the majorities are black. Is whitetown yet ready to take the position that the political ascendancy of blacks must be frustrated, wherever it threatens? What price democratic theory? Blacktown will have something to say about it, since the consent of the governed will still, I would hope, have to be obtained. And it seems to me doubtful that whites, having gone to all the trouble of securing comfortable non-black enclaves, will be ardent to re-shoulder the problems they have gone to such trouble and cost to escape.

But even if metropolitanism is successfully invoked, it does not amount to a political doctrine for the governance of a separated nation. Nor does it signify integration. Plato and Aristotle dealt with the issue of a separated group—the slaves—by ignoring them in their constitutions. The ancient wisdom is plainly silly in our situation, for the clamant voices of blacktown, to say nothing of modern understanding of the rights of man, cannot be ignored. Yet a separated nation confronts us, and though I cannot think what a theory for its democratic government might be, I do not claim that it cannot be written. My argument is the contrary: such a theory must be composed. It is just another instance of the proposition that what is necessary has to be possible.

Here and there are some gropings. Milton Kotler, who is no advocate of disintegration, says:

> We cannot say that white America governs America for whites, but only for wealthy whites. The fact that poor or middle-class

whites may hate Negroes does not establish that they have political power themselves, since their class has no institutional share of state authority. The constitutional solution as it relates to cities is local government in the neighborhoods. These should be constituted with mixed government in which the many and the few share authority. . . .

Robert S. Browne of Fairleigh-Dickinson University, in *Ramparts* (December, 1967), espouses discussion between blacks and whites looking to partition—to separate states. He sees the urgent need to minimize "racial friction by suggesting some fair basis for the separation of the races." Black-white discussions . . . "may lead to two separate nations or it may lead us to some as yet untried type of human community superior to the present system of competing nationalism."

The intellectual task, for that is what it is, has barely been understood, much less undertaken.

There are certain directions which I believe it will be impossible for political theory to take. One will be to rely on science and technology somehow to bail us out of our difficulties, as some now believe technology will overcome the growing pains of mass public education. Thus, it has been seriously proposed that science may be depended upon sooner or later to figure out a way to change black skin to white; and hence we are advised to sweat out our tribulations until that happy day in the laboratory arrives and the nation may become all-white overnight. But what if the pigmentation genius discovers only how to turn white skin to black?

Another direction in which I think it will be impossible for political theory to turn is the establishment of colonies outside the borders of the nation. I place no importance on the tenuous alliances developing here and there between African nations and black Americans. Black resettlement, however, is a notion with respectable forebears, like those of Abraham Lincoln, who toward the end of the Civil War considered four or five schemes for colonization of the blacks, in Africa, the West Indies, and elsewhere. All were put aside with anguish and foreboding. Ours is the inheritance of a problem beyond the reach of the wisest President. It is in any case clear that there can be nothing to the idea of exporting millions of Americans to other shores.

I find equally distasteful, though some political theorists may not, the idea of formalizing the separateness of the races by establishing colonies of blacks within this country. It must be recognized that urban black towns already fit most descriptions of colonies. But the idea is blighted from the outset by the obsolescence of colonialism as a respectable political relationship.

Still another direction that political theory may not take is toward systematic repression and violence. There is little doubt that blacktown could be kept in a state of perpetual subjugation by the superior numbers and arms of whitetown. The theory we are seeking is not a plan of battle but a plan for peaceful coexistence. At a minimum the new relationship will have to be based on the understanding that it is aimed at the elevation and self-expression of the blacks, with unstinting white aid and cooperation as requested. It will have to achieve the consent of all parties and the acceptance of non-violent means as the ways of settling disputes.

The relationship must aim at co-respect equally with coexistence. The purpose is to reduce misunderstanding and enmities, not to foment them. The idea is finally for blacks to achieve the psychological sovereignty, individually and collectively, that whites take for granted. This assignment cannot be deemed impossible. Before the writing of the Constitution many learned men depicted the absolute folly of trying to bring together thirteen colonies of such disparate and competitive backgrounds.

Political theory will have to turn into radically new channels. Here is the ripest of opportunities for the "creative federalisms" of which we have lately heard so much from our Republican friends, though of course they were referring to new understandings among megalopolitan, state, and central governments. The creative federalists concerned about race will start from the fact that the major institutions of society are already arrayed, broadly speaking, on a basis of separation. This is the reason for FEPC's, civil rights laws, and the other legal paraphernalia of anti-discrimination. These legal arrangements assuredly ought not to be tampered with, at least until the creative federalists give us something better, for they provide a sort of demilitarized zone between blacktown and whitetown.

I raise the point about our major institutions, white-owned and directed, because they constitute a peculiar problem for the new federalists. These institutions penetrate and in many ways form the principal structure of blacktown. Supermarket, chain drugstores, gas stations, were, not by chance, major victims in the civil turmoil in blacktown. There is little reciprocal penetration of whitetown by black institutions. Enterprises owned by soul brothers are few and feeble. Without the economic and political structures of whitetown, blacktown would collapse; but removing black contributions to the structure of the community would have little effect, save perhaps in a few areas in which blacks figure prominently—in welfare departments, in the entertainment industries, and in the national football and baseball leagues.

Let me emphasize again that the theoretical object of this creative federalism will not be that of prescribing another and perhaps more imaginative program aimed at culminating in integration. Nor do I contemplate any form of apartheid (a mischievous word that might well be dropped from the debate), as is evident from my insistence on agreement by all parties to a contract of separation.

The separate state imagined here is not designed to make life easier for whitetown nor to lighten its load. Nor, in its long first stage, does it appear to make life smoother, except psychologically, for blacktown. On both sides the situation initially will be trying in the extreme. Blacks who are visible, equal, organized, and bargaining from positions of strength will for whites be a novel and annoying experience. Blacks will find an autonomous and self-governing community far harder to cope with than any of the ardent separatists have ever suggested.

While we are struggling toward the forms of official separation, probings in blacktown toward indigenous structures must be regarded sympathetically by whites—and from a respectful distance. Many such efforts are under way—foundations, cooperatives, corporations, school districts, self-policing schemes, social and cultural centers. That many are rudimentary is to be expected. Blacktown has had little of the delicious experience of self-determination. Mistakes will be made; but they will be home-made, not inflicted. The very innocence of many current approaches to black autonomy is tempting, especially to white liberals, whose impulse is to rush in, crying, "Let me help! I know how better than you!" And doubtless this may often be the case. But the stern advice to such well-wishers must yet be, "Stand back, stay away until summoned; and when you are summoned, give the help that is asked for and go away." For the essence is black striving toward selfhood, independence, dignity.

The discovery of the philosophy and machinery for democratic government of a separated country would at first appear to be a constitutional issue. Perhaps, however, it will be found possible to handle it without amending or revising the Constitution. Perhaps all that has to be done is to change the first line of the Constitution henceforth to read, "We, nine-tenths of the people of the United States, in order to form a more perfect Union. . . ." More seriously, it may be a matter for that constitutional penumbra called tacit consent. By this I mean that blacktown and whitetown may, by a series of unacknowledged steps, arrive at a mutual and unstated understanding of the main conditions for maintaining an ethnically divided society. It was tacit consent that until quite recently kept the situation relatively quiet and peaceful.

The first of these steps would be, of course, to let the idea of integration die; by common consent to banish it from the lips of whitetown reformers and politicians and from the expectations of blacktown. Another would be an agreement against humiliation on the one side and disturbance on the other. This would be a wide radiation effect of the agreements against discrimination already legislated. A third step would be increased political autonomy for blacktown, accompanied by markedly stepped-up subsidies from whitetown, which will see blacktown's needs for supplementary help to be at least as important as those of the shipping industry, the corporate farmers, and other veterans of the subsidy trough.

It is doubtless clear that there is next to nothing here about blacktown's reactions to my propositions. This is because I do not know what they are. I mistrust polls of black opinion. Until recently it has made no difference what blacks think. I have never known whether the idea of integration is attractive to blacks. I have idly supposed it was. I know that many blacks have said they wanted integration desperately; others have said that they want the right to integration, whether or not they choose to avail themselves of it. I would guess, without any way of knowing whether I am near the mark, that the attitudes in blacktown toward integration might be put in three classes:

The great majority might say, "Integration would be nice, but Whitey's not going to give it—that much is plain from our experience—so we will have to make do until a better arrangement happens."

The miniscule middle class might be saying, "We want integration very much indeed, and sometimes it seems to be coming close. But then it pulls away again, and meanwhile we are becoming more and more cut off from the rest of the blacks."

The young black leaders seem to be saying, "You know what you can do with your integration, Honkey Baby. We want no part of your society and culture; it is corrupt, hypocritical, and brutal."

The question in any case is not how relatively hopeless blacktown may feel about integration but what its outlook might be on the proposition of formal separation. I am impressed by the rising separatism in blacktown, exemplified by statements like those of Malcolm X and his successors. It appears to me to be the last and decisive development in blacktown's outlook on its situation. Along with everything else, events and ideas in blacktown are at an accelerating rate. Since 1954, the year of the *Brown* decision on the schools, the tempo has stepped up. We have passed in these thirteen years through desegregation and integration into nationalism, and now into separatism.

The requirement is to agree on the terms of peaceful coexistence. Unless we can find them, the second Civil War is inevitable. We shall make a great error if we seek these terms amongst the fragments of the integrationist dream. If we in whitetown had ever really wanted integration we would have rushed to achieve it, as we rushed to the moon. If ever integration had a chance, it has receded indefinitely into the clouds of acrimony and self-interest thrown up by urban violence and the promise of a great deal more of the same. For blacktown now will never accept the token of integration for the reality. It will not immigrate into whitetown with its passport stamped "conditional on good behavior as determined by white authorities." What it will do instead is unclear. Its options are limited. Its capacities are uncertain. What is certain is that it cannot any longer be expected to deceive itself.

A political theory that will embrace our dilemma and provide satisfactory terms for coexistence is not outside our reach. The penalty for failure will be rising violence and bloodshed, and at the end the showdown now being called for by reckless and vindictive men in both towns. And even after such a confrontation nothing will be decided. All the questions will remain. We have muddled through as far as we can go.

I am at the end of a morose tale. It is time to return to the great city, which we have chosen for the black as his habitat and thereby as the locale for the test of the Union. It is here that we shall have to find the replacement for the ideal of integration. Makeshifts may for a while suffice, and bribery has its temporary uses. But finally we shall have to learn how to run a separated society, without the sacrifice of freedom and justice for any man. Since we cannot have integration, we must have something.

23. THE FATE OF THE DR. MARTIN LUTHER KING MEMORIAL RESOLUTION

In the midst of the Negro civil rights movement, the late Dr. Martin Luther King, Jr., stands out as a moderate, nonviolent man. Many persons, sorely disturbed by racial and educational turmoil, are reacting in a negative way to the varied efforts by minorities to assert themselves. This "backlash" was evident when the California State Senate Rules Committee decided to reject a resolution sent from the lower house proclaiming April 4 as "Martin Luther King Day." This rejection by the members of the committee, all of whom are white, might suggest the great difficulty the Negro has in gaining recognition for his people.

Assembly Concurrent Resolution No. 15— Relative to the Proclamation of April 4, 1969, as Martin Luther King Day

WHEREAS, The brutal assassination on April 4, 1968, of Dr. Martin Luther King, Jr., the nation's leading advocate of social justice through loving, nonviolent action, brought grief and dismay to millions of people in the United States and around the world; and

WHEREAS, The dreams and ideals of this extraordinary man continue to touch the hearts of men of good will and inspire creative solutions to social problems that preserve and augment human values; and

WHEREAS, It is fitting that the memory of this man should be honored and that the principles for which he stood should be considered anew in these violent and uncertain times; now, therefore, be it

Resolved by the Assembly of the State of California, the Senate thereof concurring, That the members request the Governor to proclaim April 4, 1969, as Martin Luther King Day; and be it further

Resolved, That the Chief Clerk of the Assembly transmit a copy of this resolution to Governor Reagan and suitably prepared copies to Coretta King, Yolanda Denise King, and Martin Luther King III.

Legislative Counsel's Digest

ACR 15, as introduced, Warren (H.A.D.). Martin Luther King Day. Requests Governor proclaim April 4, 1969, as Martin Luther King Day.

California Legislature, 1969 Regular Session, Assembly Concurrent Resolution No. 15. Introduced by Assemblymen Warren, Brathwaite, Ralph, Bill Greene, Brown, Miller, Sieroty, and Waxman, January 14, 1969.

Memorial Resolution for Dr. King Defeated

A resolution memorializing Dr. Martin Luther King Jr. was defeated by the California Senate Rules Committee yesterday when a senator who is a member of the John Birch Society depicted the slain Negro leader as an associate of Communists.

The resolution, already approved by the Assembly, asked Gov. Reagan to proclaim April 4 as Martin Luther King Day in honor of the assassinated civil rights leader.

The resolution praised King as "the nation's leading advocate of social justice through loving, nonviolent action."

Committee members voted 3–2 against sending the measure to the full Senate after Sen. H. L. Richardson (R) Arcadia, a former coordinator for the John Birch Society, submitted a manila folder with written testimony denouncing King and his associates and supporters.

"Memorial Resolution For Dr. King Defeated," *Santa Barbara News-Press* (March 13, 1969). Reprinted by permission.

Chapter 6

The Quest
for Identity:
The Mexican-American

In the years following the discovery of gold, Spanish California was rapidly Americanized. Not only did the number of Anglos in the far West increase, but the political and cultural institutions that developed reflected the increase of American power. In the process, the *Californios* (including the Mexicans), who had enjoyed prominent positions in Old California, gradually found themselves relegated to second-class status on their own soil. In the early 1900s California experienced a "Spanish-Mexican renaissance," but it was a limited recognition of Hispanic heritage through such forms as architecture, social festivities, and a rediscovery of the history of the missions. Clearly, this respect for the past did not include the restoration of the *Californios* to their deserved place in California society. At the time when the old Spanish days were being romanticized, there was an influx of Mexican immigrants in the Southwest. These people were quickly made subordinate on the socioeconomic ladder in their newly adopted land.

In addition, a generalized image of the Mexican-American became popular. This stereotype portrayed him as being docile, without ambition, lethargic yet capable of great passion and greed, and obstinate in his refusal to accept "American culture." This legend persists in America today, largely as a result of his treatment in advertisements, stereotyped roles in the movies and on television, and subtle bias expressed in school textbooks.

Across the Southwest region of the United States, beginning in the late 1960s, there has been a concerted effort by younger leaders to awaken Mexican-Americans to their rightful place in American society. This effort has taken many forms. Attempts have been made to imbue in them a pride in their accomplishments, language, and past. A sense of kinship to the black "revolution" and new efforts at political organization are occurring. Within the Mexican community the term *"Chicano"* is used to emphasize the new sense of identity as a unique people; no longer do they wish to see themselves as hyphenated Mexican-Americans, unable to enjoy full participation in either culture. Implicit in this change in self-identity has been the rejection of the Anglo's stereotyped view of the Mexican. For some leaders an objective not yet realized is to change the limited economic role that traditionally has been the lot of the brown-skinned American.

The *Chicano* militant is now demanding an end to the perpetuation of old myths and his full share in the fruits of American society. *Chicano* intellectuals are exposing what they believe to be a fraud perpetrated on their people and are creating a literature that glorifies their race. *"Viva la Raza"* has been a clarion call not only to celebrate racial pride but also to create brown unity as a basis for increased economic and political power.

Californians should resist the temptation to minimize this "problem"; it will not go away. Indeed, in the decade since 1960 the population of those with Spanish surnames in the Golden State has doubled, whereas the general population has increased only 50 percent. With the rapid growth of this minority group, the Californian will finally come face to face with the concept of cultural pluralism. How should one regard this new development? Should the demands of the *Chicano* militants be interpreted as a healthy sign? Has there been a lessening of the Mexican stereotype in American culture? Are there significant differences between the movements of the *Chicano* and the black militant? These are some of the questions that the reader may consider as he examines the selections that follow.

24. THE MAN ON THE WHITE HORSE

CAREY MCWILLIAMS

Nowhere is the distorted image of Old California more aptly portrayed than in the city of Santa Barbara, a community with a history rich with Hispanic-Mexican traditions. Santa Barbara, along with many other California communities, stages a yearly historical pageant and festival that supposedly is an accurate reflection of its past. In the selection that follows, Carey McWilliams describes this fantasy heritage.

"Three hundred years," writes Tom Cameron in the Los Angeles *Times* of August 29, 1947, "vanished in an instant here in Santa Barbara today as the city and more than 100,000 guests plunged into a three-day round of pageants, parades, street dancing and impromptu entertainment. It is *La Fiesta*. Santa Barbara is a particularly bewitching señorita today. With glowing copa de oro flowers entwined in her raven tresses and with her gayest mantilla swirling above her tight-bodied, ruffled Spanish colonial gown, she is hostess to honored guests from near and far. It is a time when Santa Barbara gazes over her bare shoulders (*sic*) to a romantic, colorful era of leisurely uncomplicated living. . . ."

With one thousand beautiful, "gaily caparisoned" Palomino horses prancing and curveting along State Street—renamed for three days "Calle Estado"—the history of the region is dramatized in costly and elaborate floats. This year, 1947, the Kiwanis Club enters a float in honor of Juan Rodríguez Cabrillo; Rotary honors Sir Francis Drake; the Exchange Club pays homage to Sebastián Viscaíno. "A traditional wedding party of 1818, escorted by caballeros, canters along. It represents the wedding of Anita de la Guerra and Capt. Alfred Robinson." Following the *charros*, riders from San Gabriel and the Spanish grape carts drawn by donkeys with flower girls astride, come the Long Beach mounted police, the Del Rey Palomino Club, *Los Rancheros Visitadores* (headed by J. J. Mitchell of *Juan y Lolita Rancho*), and of course the Los Angeles sheriff's posse headed by Eugene Biscailuz, the sheriff, himself an "early Californian." The celebration comes to a finale with the presentation in the Santa Barbara Bowl of a pageant written by Charles E. Pressley entitled *Romantic California*—and very well titled it is.

"Spanish" food is served; "Spanish" music is played; "Spanish" costumes are worn. For this is the heritage, a fantasy heritage, in which the arbiters of the day are "Spaniards." The Mexicans—those who are proud to be called Mexican—have a name for these "Spaniards." They call them *"Californios"* or *"Californianos"* or, more often, *"renegados."* These are the people after whom streets are named in Los Angeles: Pico, Sepúlveda, Figueroa. It is they who are used by the Anglo-American community to reconcile its fantasy heritage with the contemporary scene. By

FROM Carey McWilliams, *North from Mexico* (Westport, Conn.: Greenwood Press, Inc., 1968). Reprinted by permission.

a definition provided by the *Californios* themselves, one who achieves success in the borderlands is "Spanish"; one who doesn't is "Mexican."

This fantasy heritage makes for the most obvious ironies. Cinco de Mayo is one of the Mexican national holidays which Los Angeles, now a Good Neighbor, has begun to observe. It is celebrated by parades, fiestas, and barbecues; speeches by the mayor and the Mexican consul constitute the principal order of the day. Invariably the parade winds its way through Olvera Street and the Plaza—sections of the old Mexican town now kept in a state of partial repair for the tourist trade—to the City Hall. Leading the parade through the streets, riding majestically on a white horse, is a prominent "Mexican" actor. Strangely enough, this actor, a *Californio* three hundred and sixty-four days of the year, becomes a "*Mexicano*" on Cinco de Mayo. Elegantly attired in a ranchero costume, he sits proudly astride his silver-mounted saddle and jingles his silver spurs as he rides along. The moment he comes into sight, the crowds begin to applaud for he is well known to them through the unvarying stereotypic Mexican roles which he plays in the films. Moreover, they have seen him in exactly this same role, at the head of this or some similar parade, for fifteen years. Of late the applause is pretty thin and it may be that the audience is becoming a little weary of the old routine. A union organizer of Mexican descent once remarked to me: "If I see that white horse once more, I'm going to spit in its eye."

Following the man on the white horse will be other horsemen, few of them with any pretensions of Mexican descent but all similarly attired, mounted on splendid Palominos, horses worth their weight in gold, decorated with their weight in silver trappings. At one time there were men in Mexico who dressed in nearly this fashion. The full irony of the situation dawns when one realizes that the men who lead the parade are dressed like the same class whose downfall is being celebrated. The irony would be no greater if the *Angelenos* put on the brilliant red uniforms of British grenadiers when they paraded on the Fourth of July. For on Cinco de Mayo blood was shed to rid Mexico of grandee landowners who threatened to suck it dry. Here, in Los Angeles, the men who lead the parade symbolically represent the grandees while the Mexicans line the pavements.

These *Californios* are in no small part responsible for the fact that the Mexican population of Los Angeles—the largest minority in the city—is so completely deprived of meaningful civic representation. Since it is impolitic for any Los Angeles official to ignore the Mexican vote completely, care is taken that the roster of civic committees shall always include at least one name which is obviously Spanish or Mexican. If a quick glance is taken of the list of names appearing on the civic committees devoted to housing, juvenile delinquency, racial, and welfare problems, these same names constantly reappear.

It has only been of recent years that the *Californios* have been elevated to this anomalous and largely factitious status. There was a time when they scarcely existed in the eyes of the Anglo-Americans. When the Native Sons of the Golden West were asked, in the early 1900's, to submit a list of "the men who had grown up with Los Angeles," for a civic memorial, they included only Anglo-American names. When the first "pioneer society" was formed in Los Angeles in 1896, not a single Mexican or Spanish name appeared on the membership roster and the by-laws expressly provided that "persons born in this state are not eligible to membership." Ignored throughout this early period, the *Californios* promptly acquired a new and spurious status the moment it became necessary to use them to maintain the subordination of Mexican immigrants in the general scheme of things.

Today the typical *Californio* occupies, in most communities, a social position that might best be compared with that of the widow of a Confederate general in a small southern town. On all ceremonial occasions, the "native Californians" are trotted forth, in their faded finery, and exhibited as "worthy representatives of all that is finest in our Latin-American heritage." In appointing *Californios* to civic committees, most officials realize that they have achieved the dual purpose, first, of having a Mexican name on the roster for the sake of appearances, and, second, that the persons chosen will invariably act in the same manner as Anglo-Americans of equal social status. Thus the dichotomy which exists throughout the borderlands between what is "Spanish" and what is "Mexican" is a functional, not an ornamental, arrangement. Its function is to deprive the Mexicans of their heritage and to keep them in their place.

In community after community, the Anglo-Americans genuflect once a year before the relics of the Spanish past. Just as Tucson has its annual *La Fiesta de los Vaqueros* so nearly every city in the borderlands now has its annual Spanish Fiesta. It is during *La Fiesta* in Santa Barbara that the annual ride of the *Rancheros Visitadores* occurs. This particular revival is based on a practice of former years, when the rancheros made the rounds of the ranchos to pay a visit to each in turn. "In May, 1930," to quote from the Santa Barbara *Guide* (WPA), "some sixty-five riders assembled for the first cavalcade. Golden Palominos and proud Arabian thoroughbreds, carrying silver-mounted tack, brushed stirrups with shaggy mustangs from the range. Emerging from the heavy gray mist of a reluctant day, they cantered with casual grace down the old familiar trails of the Santa Ynez, to converge on Santa Barbara. . . . Here, amid the tolling of the bells, the tinkling of trappings, and the whinnying of horses, the brown-robed friars blessed them and bade them 'Vayan con Dios.' . . ." This was the first ride of the *Rancheros Visitadores* whose president, today, is Señor J. J. Mitchell. Since this auspicious beginning, the affair has steadily increased in pomp and circumstance. Nowadays it is invariably reported in the Southern California society columns as a major social event of the year. A careful scrutiny of the names of these fancily dressed *visitadores*—these gaily costumed Rotarians—reveals that Leo Carrillo, "the man on the white horse," is about the only rider whose name carries a faint echo of the past that is being celebrated so ostentatiously.

Numerous institutions have been founded in the borderlands to keep the fantasy heritage alive. First performed at Mission San Gabriel on April 29, 1912, John Steven McGroarty's "Mission Play" was presented at over 2,600 performances and was seen, according to its modest author, by over 2,500,000 people. The Padua Institute, located at the base of the Sierra Madre Mountains near Claremont, is another institution which works hard to keep the fantasy heritage alive. Here, in a beautiful setting, the lady from Des Moines can have lunch, see a Spanish or Mexican folk play, hear Mexican music, and purchase a "Mexican" gift from the Studio Gift Shop. The Padua Institute is dedicated to "keeping alive the romantic life and music of Old Mexico and Early California." Olvera Street, in the old Plaza section of Los Angeles, is still another attempt to institutionalize the false legend.

Harmless in many ways, these attempts to prettify the legend contrast most harshly with the actual behavior of the community toward persons of Mexican descent. To the younger generation of Mexicans, the fantasy heritage, and the institutions which keep it alive, are resented as still additional affronts to their dignity and sense of pride.

Try as they will, the Anglo-Americans cannot quite enter into the spirit of La Fiesta. Compliments are exchanged between the mayor and the consul-general and the usual remarks are made about Benito Juárez and Abraham Lincoln; but, somehow, the emptiness of the occasion echoes in the platitudes spoken. This meretricious quality is always apparent in the gauche efforts of the press to whip up some semblance of enthusiasm. "Vivas and olas filled the air. . . . Los Angeles yesterday donned the festive regalia of her Mexican heritage . . . Cinco de Mayo Festival On, Si, Si"—are excerpts from the Los Angeles *Times* of May 6, 1947. On the Sixteenth of September, 1947, a Miss Frances Anderson was selected as the reigning señorita in one Southern California town; while, in another, a Miss Virginia Thomas was selected. Both towns have a large Mexican population.

In an editorial commending a program to teach Spanish in the lower grades, the Los Angeles *Times* (August 29, 1944) in a fervor of *españolismo* wrote: "we have missed learning the homey, friendly gossip of the little people who have big hearts even if lean purses. We have missed much, señores . . . Viva Mexico! Viva el Español!"

25. ¡VIVA LA FIESTA! OLD SPANISH DAYS? A DEBATE

Santa Barbara's gala celebration each summer is now being scrutinized closely by its Chicano citizens, who question the historical validity of "The Old Spanish Days Fiesta." A series of letters appeared in the local newspaper, the Santa Barbara News-Press, debating the issue. These letters reflect the new interest in this dispute by both the Anglo and Mexican elements in the community.

Fiesta Seen Offensive

Editor, News-Press: I hope it will not surprise Santa Barbarans when they learn that La Fiesta offends the pride of Mexicans and Mexican-Americans in Santa Barbara. Some of the participants know better, but the majority, I am convinced really do not know that they are offending Mexican-Americans. Space will not enable me to detail the main objections to Good Ole Spanish Days; the details, however, can be found in Leonard Pitt's "Decline of the Californios," Carey McWilliams' "North From Mexico" and also, his "Southern California Country"; the articles featured in the most recent issue of "Probe" are also excellent documented sources.

Mexican-American history rankles with injustice. Not too long ago, Santa Barbara was ruled by Mexicans who lived comfortably through the exploitation of Indian cheap labor. In the 16th century the Spaniards introduced Spanish institutions into the Southwest, but it was Mexicans and Indians which preserved Spanish institutions until the 19th century when the United States stole the Southwest from Mexico.

It would take volumes to catalog all the injustices which Mexican-Americans have experienced since the conquest, 121 years ago. One of these peculiar injustices is the defamation of the Mexican-American heritage. By 1890, Mexican-Americans were reduced to cheap labor, and to justify the conquest, subsequent acts of violence, dispossession, and racial discrimination Anglo-Americans began to pervert the heritage of Mexican-Americans by referring to the past as Good Ole Spanish Days. So vicious have the public schools and other indoctrinating media become that Mexican-American children refuse to call themselves Mexican, choosing rather to be called Spanish. The schools, communication media, and La Fiesta do tremendous harm to the minds of Mexican-Americans; they teach Mexican-American children to despise themselves.

Now why would the merchants in Santa Barbara wish to vulgarize and

"Fiesta Seen Offensive," *Santa-Barbara News-Press* (August 10, 1969); "Fiesta Needs Revisions," *Santa-Barbara News-Press* (August 17, 1969); "Two Basic Questions Raised on Fiesta," *Santa Barbara News-Press* (September 13, 1969); "Objection to 'Chicano'," *Santa Barbara News-Press* (September 23, 1969). Reprinted by permission of the *Santa Barbara News-Press*.

pervert the heritage of Mexican-Americans? To make a fast buck? Are these the very merchants who discriminate against Mexicans in housing, education, and of course, employment? The big question is of course whether Mexicans should continue to be pushed around each year? Surely, there are some men to be found in the Mexican-American community, a community representing close to 20 percent of the populace. Evidently, there are many Anglo-Americans who are also revolted by Good Ole Spanish Days. I would say most Santa Barbarans are losing interest in this silly masquerade.

In order to save La Fiesta, I recommend: (1) all receipts and profits go to Mexican-American scholarships; (2) change the name to Good Ole Mexican Days, or better still, just La Fiesta; (3) dramatize programs which eliminate discrimination against Mexicans; (4) plan activities which promote better or friendly relations between Mexican-Americans and Anglos in Santa Barbara.

JOSEPH NAVARRO

Fiesta Needs Revisions

Editor, News-Press: Santa Barbarans should carefully ponder Joseph Navarro's letter in the News-Press criticizing the character of the Fiesta. Do not take offense at it, if that is your inclination. It is a statement of major importance that should be seriously weighed, not brushed aside impatiently because the author has said things in bald ways. He speaks from those who have a legitimate and sobering grievance. This city has been creative in many ways. It remains to be seen whether it will now respond equally well to the issues Mr. Navarro raises—issues that will be raised again and again, make no mistake about it, until they are dealt with satisfactorily.

His main point is that it is absurd historically, and harmful socially, for Santa Barbara to speak of the "Old Spanish Days"; that the true heritage is Mexican, Santa Barbara having been originally Mexican in derivation and in governance. He speaks poignantly and accurately of the exploitation and mistreatment of Mexican-Americans and of the tendency among Mexican-American children to deny their Mexican heritage when surrounded by influences such as the Fiesta which exalt Spain and ignore Mexico. He calls upon us to begin rectifying the balance by altering the character of the Fiesta to highlight the Mexican heritage and direct attention to the deplorable conditions that Mexican-Americans have faced and face today.

There is good reason to argue with his historical point. California was founded and ruled by the Spanish government for half a century. The period of Mexican rule was half of that. Furthermore, California never did revolt against the Spanish crown when the Latin American wars of independence were going on. When California became part of Mexico after that country gained its independence, it looked upon the governors sent up from distant Mexico—California then was extremely remote from everywhere—as foreigners.

The period of Mexican rule, from about 1820 to 1846, saw frequent rebellions against Mexican governors. Californians insisted that the governor should be a Californian. Near-anarchy in the Mexican period led many to begin looking toward American annexation, or to the status of a British protectorate. The American "conquest" was almost without bloodshed; certainly there was none of the bitter, house-to-house struggle against the invader that was then going on in Mexico against the American armies.

With the best will in the world, it is hard, in short, to think of California as being genuinely a part of the Mexican nation. It is hard, too, to think of California as being genuinely "Spanish." The original settlers who came up from Mexico were highly mixed in their ancestry and later comers arrived from all parts of the world. There were British and Americans and Russians and Swiss and Hawaiians and Indians and Germans and Mexicans and Chileans; there were blacks, browns, whites and reds. Few came from Mexico after the original immigration.

As the years went by, this highly mixed population became, quite simply, Californios. That's how they thought of themselves. They lived in California, a remote part of the world where, decade after decade, they carried on their lives with very little reference at all to the outside world.

And then they were engulfed. The Gold Rush stampede wiped out that world overnight. They were shoved aside, faced with complex and fast moving economic and legal situations completely foreign to all their experience and within a brief period of time even the most eminent of them had lost their lands.

American society was made up of many mutually hostile ethnic groups. Prejudice against those who were "different"—especially in skin color—was a deeply-rooted characteristic in the American mind. The Californios found themselves detested and dealt with callously. Those later thousands who have since come up from Mexico have generally entered the secondary position in American life long since occupied by their predecessors. We are a long, long way from being a country where Mexican-Americans are given the same opportunities as everyone else. In housing conditions, level of education and income, recent studies have shown that those of Spanish surname are in a situation worse than that of any other ethnic group.

As a native-born Santa Barbaran, I have long felt that in important ways the Fiesta was built upon false assumptions. Adopting the Spanish architectural style was valid, for there were sound inheritances from Spain and from Mexico in the local region that provided justification. But making out that early Santa Barbara was a land of Spanish dons and senoritas always seemed a bit much. It was just not so. Old California was a blend of many things, many influences and it has become, since 1846, an even more complex land.

Why not make it a more real festival? Why not simply concentrate not on Old Spain but on Old California? And why should Old California stop at 1846? Why should not "La Fiesta" (as Mr. Navarro wisely suggests we call it) take in also that long period of Santa Barbara life before the turn of the 20th century, or even before the second World War, when it was a quiet, interesting, unique little community with many memorable people, qualities and problems, worth bringing into the parade? Walker Tompkins' [local historian] files are full of things that would make the parade fresh and interesting again, instructive to all and enjoyable. A walk around the photograph gallery in Harry's Restaurant is much more fun, and more revealing of Santa Barbara, than the present parade.

In sum, I agree with Mr. Navarro. We need to rethink the nature of the Fiesta and, in doing so, we need to stop blinking away the fact that the Mexican-American community in Santa Barbara has good reasons for feeling doubts about the genuineness of the whole proceeding.

ROBERT KELLEY

Two Basic Questions Raised on Fiesta

Editor, News-Press: Following this year's Old Spanish Days Fiesta a number of concerned citizens have publicly called attention to the need for a critical and comprehensive review of this annual Santa Barbara event. Various criticisms and objections have been raised, with one leading argument questioning nothing less than the historical and cultural authenticity of the events which Old Spanish Days Fiesta supposedly celebrates. This year, in fact, Chicanos in Santa Barbara questioned not only the historical authenticity of Fiesta but also the unrepresentativeness of an event advertised as a "community fiesta."

On Aug. 31 the News-Press attempted to survey the criticism of Fiesta, reporting, among other things, the Chicano argument. It was less than accurate, however, in presuming to explain the "facts" of the socalled "Brown Beret incident" by appealing to the interpretations of Messrs. Robert Rowe and Paul G. Sweetser exclusively. Nonetheless, the writer, a man steeped in Santa Barbara's historical lore, did provide readers with an extraordinarily revealing example of the confounded logic (not to raise the specter of racism) which guides the organizers of Fiesta by accurately reporting that, "The Chicanos were told that there was a need for Mexicans in the parade, but asked them to take the parts of Spanish soldiers or Mission Indians." . . . In other words, Mexicans were needed, not as Mexicans, but as Spanish soldiers or Mission Indians. Obviously there is no scarcity of Conquistadores or Indian Chiefs.

Our concern is not to deal with petty prejudices but to participate in this year's Fiesta postmortem by examining briefly two fundamental questions. First, what is the nature of Santa Barbara's Hispanic and Mexican past? Secondly, given the character of our contemporary community, how can the Fiesta truly represent the people of Santa Barbara?

Any attempt to discuss the Spanish or Mexican background of Santa Barbara, if it is to be productive, must begin by understanding the racial and cultural syncretism which characterized the society of New Spain (Mexico) for three centuries. Almost 30 years ago, Professor Carl Sauer pointed to the emergence of a distinctive Mexican racial type by the late 16th Century in the northern frontier regions of New Spain. Later, from this same northern frontier—in particular, Sonora, Sinaloa, and Baja California—came the earliest settlers of Santa Barbara.

Historically, of course, Santa Barbara was the last Royal Presidio founded in New Spain (Mexico). The expense of its founding was paid by the kingdom of New Spain, the largest and richest kingdom in the Spanish empire. The first commandant and all of his soldier colonists but one were natives of Mexico and as such, representative of diverse racial strains. The Spanish presence consisted mainly of the Spanish governors and assorted Franciscan priests from the different Spanish kingdoms. Even the noted Father Serra was in Santa Barbara only for a brief religious service and was not seen here again. Every commandant in the 50-year history of our Presidio except one was a native of Mexico, as was every soldier except two. The supply ships that supported early California all came from Mexico, none from Spain. In California, aside from the handful of Spanish governors and priests and soldiers, everyone was a native of Mexico. California was part of the Mexican empire and the Mexican republic.

Obviously the historical record (especially the references to Santa Barbara's Hispanic and Mexican past), as reported by Walker Tompkins in the News-Press, is in serious need of correction. A closer examination of the evidence does not support his view that Santa Barbara's Mexican experience was of short duration and for that reason of no great importance. Furthermore, to suggest, as he does, that Santa Barbara's heritage is largely Spanish owing to three centuries of Spanish political sovereignty, as against 20-some years of Mexican control, is not only simplistic but unhistorical.

If Santa Barbara is truly going to celebrate annually a community fiesta, then its history must be represented accurately with proper recognition of the role different groups have played in the growth and development of the city. What is more important, however, is that the Fiesta involve the people of Santa Barbara, not as passive onlookers or self-deceiving elitists, but as active, joyful participants. The young, the old, the different cultures and ethnic groups, the different races, must all contribute. A fiesta fundamentally celebrates the human spirit; it is an affirmation of community life.

JESUS CHAVARRIA
FERNANDO DE NECOCHEA
RUSSELL RUIZ
GUILLERMO VILLA

Editor's note: The News-Press article did not state that the Mexican period in Santa Barbara history was "of short duration and for that reason of no great importance." It gave the chronology of Spanish-Mexican-American sovereignty to put in perspective the statements that "Old Spanish Days" is an inappropriate designation for La Fiesta.

Objection to 'Chicano'

Editor, News-Press: Regarding, "Chicano Advice Given by Speakers": It is like using a shotgun to hit a cucaracha to take two widely divergent groups, the Brown Berets and the Union Civica Mexicana, the latter a responsible, sensible and well balanced group of United States citizens, who are proud of their Mexican-American heritage, and attempt to mix them together. The Union Civica Mexicana had gathered to commemorate Mexico's 159th Anniversary of Independence from Spain, and not to observe the advocated overthrow of the United States as preached by the Black Panthers, Brown Berets and other self-styled leaders of the poor little black, brown and red man. In my opinion, these groups are hate mongers.

Students taking part in a Mexican-American walkout from school on "stay away from education day" were told by Mrs. Virginia Aceves, "The key to our success is education," adding, "You can find new ways to solve the Chicano problem." I would imagine that the more days taken from school would increase the Chicano problem since the Chicano problem is brought about through ignorance and lack of education.

Who are they helping? Corky Gonzalez? What are they accomplishing? Is this progress?

How long is it going to take the teachers and this permissive society of ours to get some backbone and stop sanctioning these wholesale walk-outs and unauthorized absenteeism. It is a fine thing when a stranger from another state can cause your children to lose valuable time away from school. Suppose he had advocated a week, a month, a year? Where do you draw the line?

As an American of Mexican ancestry, I take exception to this Chicano label which is now being brainwashed by the Brown Berets into the minds of our younger generation. It is bad enough to have allowed our ethnic element to be branded "Mexican-Americans" when we know our loyalty as Americans comes first. If we preserve our cultural heritage, it is because by first being true to ourselves we become better citizens. This does not mean that we are willing to sacrifice the preparation needed to pave our way towards a more productive and brighter future by digressing precious time into the study of cultural backgrounds at taxpayers' expense.

Some say the schools are bad, but they have got to be better than no school at all. Why blame others for those evils which are within ourselves? Such as the fear of being unable to win. We pave the way for defeat by saying the cards are stacked against us, that we have no chance, that only the rich can succeed. Having laid this groundwork for failure we can now stay out of school and attack the establishment and demand college degrees without going through the formal process of obtaining an education.

RUBEN N. MARTINEZ

26. THE MEXICAN APPROACH TO UNITED STATES HISTORY

JACK D. FORBES

Mexico's impact on American society has never been adequately recognized by most historians. In fact, Mexican influences continue to pervade Southwestern culture in a variety of ways. Dr. Jack D. Forbes suggests that the Anglo-American should be more aware of the Mexican contribution to American culture.

The northward movement [to what is now the United States] was indeed Spanish-led, but on the other hand, its colonists, and by the eighteenth century even its soldiers, were usually natives or mixed-bloods. And herein exists another phenomenon of great significance, the gradual biological assimilation of both Spaniards and non-Mexican Indians into the Mexican mass. Europeanized partially though they may have been, the Mexicans were the racial victors. But they were more than that, for *mexicanismo* spread even under the very eyes of the Iberians and eventually Moctezuma was as important in the north as he had been in Anáhuac. The Yaquis of the 1820's and the Apaches of the 1840's were fighting, in their eyes, for the cause of Moctezuma, and at least the members of one Pima village south of Tucson were certain by the 1840's that they were of Aztec origin.

The culture introduced into the United States by the Hispano-Mexican advance was, from the earliest period, a blend of Iberian and American traits, with the Mexican influence dominant in everyday affairs. However, even the religion of the Spaniards was greatly modified by folk beliefs, and more especially by the Virgin of Guadalupe-Tonantzín cult.

Perhaps the most significant result of the Hispano-Mexicano northward movement was, however, the process of unification whereby many tribes were amalgamated into the hispanicized Mexican community. This amalgamation was as much a result of intermarriage and assimilation with Mexicans as it was the conscious policy of the Spanish Crown. Ultimately the non-Spaniard triumphed and since 1821 *mexicanismo* has gradually become the conscious ideal of an independent Mexican nation. As a result of this development the Mexican government can dedicate banners *"a Cuauhtémoc, Patriota Ejemplar"* and the newspaper *El Universal* of Mexico City can refer in headlines to *"Cuauhtémoc, el mas Alto y Limpio Símbolo de Mexicanidad."*

From 1821 to 1848 much of the Southwest was part of the newly founded Mexican republic and it should be obvious that internal developments in the region are pertinent to the overall synthesis of United States history. One could discuss at length such matters as the economic

FROM Jack D. Forbes, "Mexican Approach to United States History." Used by permission of the author.

importance of trade, the development of travel routes, developments in mining, the introduction of various mining techniques later used in the California rush of 1848–49, the founding of new towns and the growth of many others, the development of ranching, the range cattle industry and the cowboy, the introduction of quasi-republican or republican institutions, the continued absorption of local Indians into the general population, and to mention only one more, the Mexicanization of numerous individuals of Anglo-American origin.

In brief, the Mexican Southwest was not, as Charles Edward Chapman once put it, simply "waiting for Old Glory." It was a frontier region of Mexico which was slowly adapting to the modern world while at the same time participating in the development of a modern Mexican culture. And this latter development, incidentally, has become a part of the United States' heritage, as millions of Mexican-Americans and Anglo-Americans can testify.

The Mexican approach to United States history does not cease with "the Alamo" and the Bear Flag "Revolt." On the contrary, the movement of Anglo-Americans into the Southwestern states and the subsequent immigration of additional Mexicans into the same region has facilitated the Mexicanization of "Anglos" as well as the "Americanization" of Mexicans. It is not possible in this article to survey, even briefly, this process of Mexicanization, however, its scope can be indicated by noting that the range of Mexican influences extends from the cowboy and Mexican food, to marijuana smoking and the use of peyote or its derivatives, from the bracero to Congressman Henry Gonzalez of Texas, and from *mariachi* music to the *Ballet Folklorico de México*.

The Mexican-American population of the United States is today increasing very rapidly due to a high birth rate and continued immigration. Thus it seems clear that their influence will grow, especially as they become more vocal and politically active. On the other hand, it must not be forgotten that Mexico itself has had and will continue to have a considerable impact on the United States. And here one must go beyond such things as foreign policy and international economics to consider, for example, the impact of Mexican culture upon Anglo-American tourists and residents. Many of the latter return to the United States Mexicanized to varying degrees, and large numbers of Anglo-Americans have come under the influence of Mexican art, music, literature and culture in general although perhaps never having seen Mexico. In brief, Anahuac remains a dynamic center of both advanced and folk cultures and its impact will become stronger as the years go by.

It is to be hoped that this essay, merely suggestive as it is, will serve to bring greater recognition to the Mexican aspect of the North American heritage. Six thousand years of influence demand attention, not within some area of "exotic" foreign study, but as an integral part of United States history. The heritage of Anáhuac, whether seen in its indigenous, Hispano-Mexican, modern Mexican, or Mexican-American manifestations, is a living part of the past, and of the present, and of the future of the United States.

27. LET JUSTICE BE DONE

JOANNE GONZALES

Because the Chicano sees himself as the victim of a long history of oppression, he has concluded that the only means of self-protection is in unity. The following poem reflecting the need for solidarity is taken from La Raza Yearbook, *a Chicano publication in Los Angeles.*

On a bed in a shack a brown child lies
He tosses in anguish and restlessly sighs
His mother sits by him and helplessly cries
His father is broken, he knows his son dies

He must be in Calcutta, Ceylon or Bombay
No, he's in San Antonio, Texas, U.S.A.

In the land of the free and the home of the brave
He is dying of hunger, he cannot be saved
Come brothers and sisters and weep by his grave

This child is our child, we are all one
La Raza Unida—Let Justice be done.

28. BROWN BERETS

An example of Chicano power can be seen in the Brown Berets organization. This militant group is insisting that only by banding together and demanding more self-determination can Mexican-Americans begin to receive their just share in American society. The following declaration is taken from La Raza.

Today, under the pressure of warrants, two Brown Berets went on trial for disturbing the peace during a demonstration on Whittier Blvd. They faced a jury of twelve persons, seven of whom were Chicano. These seven brothers and sisters had much in common with the two Brown Berets. They were Brown in color, residents of E.L.A., and had parents who came from Mexico. They had much, much in common but they lacked the most essential element—EDUCATION. Education and feeling about being Chicano.

The Brown Berets were brought to trial because they know about the injustices which have been heaped on our people; they were brought to trial because they are attempting to better conditions for Chicanos all over; they were brought to trial because of the reputation they have gained as the "liberators of E.L.A." The Brown Berets are not seeking

Joanne Gonzales, "Let Justice Be Done," *La Raza Yearbook* (September 1968). Reprinted by permission.

"Brown Berets," *La Raza* (March 31, 1968). Reprinted by permission.

glory and publicity. They are seeking Chicano Power for our people so that we can have control over our environment; control over our schools so that our children can receive a better education; control over the agencies which are supposed to be administering to the needs of our people; control over the police whose salaries we pay but who continually brutalize our people.

Due to the activities of the Brown Berets even Anglos are beginning to wake up to the disturbing fact—which up to now they have refused to admit or face—that they are practicing racism, a racism that considers the Chicano a different kind of animal—an odd, inferior, and unworthy creature of close association with the superior white race. Some anglos are now aware that the contacts they have with us form nothing but the most superficial relationships. The Brown Berets are attempting to eliminate this. This and such "poetic" statements as:

"White is Right,
Brown can just stick around,
But Black must go back."

No, our black brothers will not go back and Hell no, we will not just stick around. We will act like a thorn in the establishment's side. That is the kind of sticking we will do. The Brown Berets have done more to shake up the establishment than any group could accomplish in three centuries. The Brown Berets have led the March for Liberation: liberation for our people, La Raza Unida, through Chicano Power. Despite their accomplishments, the Brown Berets were found guilty of disturbing the peace. The peace of mind of the Anglo establishment who wants to maintain the status quo. The peace of mind of the Anglo who eats three meals a day, lives in a comfortable home, and has a two car garage and can see only one color—white. The peace of mind of the Anglo merchants who overcharge our people for the items they buy and then sends his white kids to Harvard and Yale on our money. They were found guilty despite the fact that there were seven brown faces in that jury. We do not hold any malice or harbor any ill intent toward our people in that jury. All we have to say is, "Come home brothers and sisters. Come home and see where it's at. Come home and stand united and fight for liberation."

29. OUR PLURAL HERITAGE

JACK D. FORBES

Some people hold the view that real equality in the American
Southwest should include an educational system that reflects our
pluralistic society. In the article below, Professor Jack D. Forbes
suggests that the traditional Anglo educational philosophy has
contributed to the identity crisis that Mexican-Americans have
experienced in the United States.

The Treaty of Guadalupe Hidalgo, our southwestern heritage, and administrators of the Los Angeles City Schools came into open conflict recently when two teen-agers running for student office at Belmont High School delivered Spanish-language political speeches in the school's auditorium. The teacher who encouraged them, of Mexican ancestry, was transferred to another school, and the students, also of Mexican descent, were admonished by an administrator to give no more speeches in "foreign" languages.

Thus a long-smoldering contradiction flared into the open: on the one hand, there is the open policy of discouraging the use of Spanish by Spanish-speaking students and teachers in most Southwestern public school systems and, on the other, the provisions of the Treaty of Guadalupe Hidalgo, negotiated by the United States and Mexico in 1848, *guaranteeing* to Mexican Southwesterners equal rights with Anglo-Americans.

For many years Spanish-speaking educators led by Prof. George Sánchez of the University of Texas, Marcos de León of Van Nuys (Los Angeles) High School, and others have been urging that Anglo school administrators in the Southwest awaken to the bicultural and bilingual realities of the region. In order to understand their pleas, and the current efforts of such groups as the Mexican-American Ad Hoc Educational Committee of Los Angeles (headed by de León) one must briefly glance at the history of school policy in the areas ceded by Mexico in 1848.

Between the 1840's and the 1880's English language and Anglo-American procedures were substituted in Southwestern public schools for the Spanish language and Mexican procedures. This change was brought about because the incoming Anglo-Americans, as military conquerors, did not wish to be assimilated into the Spanish-speaking Southwestern culture. They wished instead to transform the region's way of life into a replica of Ohio, Arkansas or Maine. This rejection by the Anglo-Americans of assimilation into Southwestern life has had important consequences. *The burden of assimilation was removed from the shoulders of the Anglo and forced onto the backs of the conquered Spanish colonials, Mexican-Americans, and Indians.* Cultural pluralism was, in most cases, rejected and no fusion of Hispano and Anglo culture was promoted by the schools. Education was to be Anglo-oriented for *all* pu-

Jack D. Forbes, "Our Plural Heritage," *Frontier* (July 1964). Reprinted by permission of *The Nation*.

pils admitted to the schools, regardless of their linguistic and ethnocultural backgrounds.

This educational revolution has cut Anglo youth off from the rich Southwestern heritage and made public education very difficult for Spanish-speaking young people. Those who could not speak English could not, of course, be admitted into regular schools; and where they were provided with tax-supported instruction it was often in inferior, segregated facilities, at least for the elementary grades (and this segregation still continues in some regions, either in separate schools or separate classrooms). Spanish-speaking pupils who managed to endure several years of this type of schooling frequently were afraid subsequently to enter the Anglo school, or dropped out soon after entrance, or were segregated within the latter school either by their own feelings of alienation or by discrimination.

Thus education in the Southwest was "stacked" in favor of the Anglo pupil (who was already favored in terms of wealth). Is it any wonder that Spanish-speaking youth sometimes demonstrated anti-social attitudes? And of course this situation was complicated by the arrival of thousands of new Mexicans between 1900 and 1929. "Mexican schools" became overcrowded, discipline problems frequently exceeded education as the central theme of such schools, and all kinds of related problems developed. The Anglo educators were largely unable to cope with the realities of cultural pluralism in the Southwest. Instead they continued to operate as if they were in Iowa.

Consequently, the Mexican student suffered from an educational system that was oriented toward the favored sons and daughters of Anglo parents. In spite of the reforms of the 1940's and 1950's the situation remains much the same, especially in rural and semi-rural school districts. The schools still heavily favor the Anglo middle-class student and discriminate against the Spanish-speaking and other non-Anglo students.

The Southwest is a region with many diverse cultural and linguistic traditions that are worth preservation. Diversity of language and culture can enrich a region if healthy attitudes toward our composite heritage are adopted, and furthermore it is unjust to demand that cultural groups who were in the Southwest before the Anglo be forced, via the schools, to surrender their traditions. It may also be illegal, since the Treaty of Guadalupe Hidalgo is presumably still in force.

The Importance of Cultural Diversity

A number of things can be done to correct the problem. First, we must consciously encourage bilingualism as one of our most valuable assets. Even Anglo students can, with effort, do what every Spanish-speaking and Indian student is required to do: master a second language. This means that school districts should have signs prepared in English and Spanish for use in the schools, encourage bilingualism in the classroom, make sure that all teachers in areas where there are Spanish-speaking students acquire some facility in Spanish. Second, districts must insist that history instruction be handled in such a way as to illustrate the Hispano, Indian, Negro and other non-Anglo viewpoints. Ideally all schools should have courses in Southwestern history. Courses of this nature should be offered early in order to help develop interest among those students who might otherwise drop out because of feelings of alienation. But above all, teachers must be admonished to give attention to non-Anglo contributions *wherever* relevant to the subject-matter being considered.

Third, every effort should be made to see that Hispanic-American literature, music and art are a part of the school's curriculum. Mexican native dances, folk art, crafts, secular customs, mariachi music, *et cetera* should be taught by qualified instructors (perhaps brought in from the local *colonia*) as a living part of our heritage, and not as a quaint bit of "foreign" culture. And what an excellent opportunity this would present for establishing a close relationship between the school and the Spanish-speaking community.

Fourth, teachers of Mexican ancestry must be sought after, and they must be encouraged to retain, if they desire, their Mexicanism. This latter may be their foremost contribution to the school. Likewise, every school district should have someone on the staff who is especially trained in anthropology or sociology and who is prepared to work effectively with non-Anglo students. Administrators *must* be required to master the Spanish language if they are involved in any position necessitating personal contact with Spanish-speaking parents.

Fifth, information intended for parents, such as communications regarding the problems of a particular student or general programs of the school, should be made available in Spanish. If it is really important that a strong relationship exist between school and parents, as all educators seem to assert, then why overlook the only effective means of communicating with Spanish-speaking parents?

Broader Educational Opportunities

Finally, genuine efforts must be made to provide all low-income groups with meaningful educational opportunities. This means vocational training that is legitimate, and not mere "busy-work" shops where unwanted students are allowed to participate in "supervised activity" for a few hours. It also means encouraging minority group students to pursue college prep programs if they so desire. It means giving special attention to the needs of students from low-income families in terms of intensified remedial instruction and special counseling. It means recruiting *superior* teachers for such work in place of assigning the weakest or newest instructor to "dumb-bell" classes. It may mean extra-pay for such assignments in order to recognize the extra skill required for work with so-called problem and low-achievement students.

If we truly succeed in making our schools "Southwestern" instead of "Middle Western," and if we improve at the same time the excellence of our offerings, the "problems" of Spanish-speaking students will diminish considerably. There will still be problems, but at least we will have equalized the relationship of Anglo and Hispano pupils insofar as this can be done by the schools.

30. COMMUNITY PARTICIPATION AND THE EMERGING MIDDLE CLASS

PAUL M. SHELDON

The cry for "La Raza Unida" increased in volume in the Southwest during the 1960s. This idea of ethnic or racial unity has not yet been fully realized, however. Professor Paul M. Sheldon suggests that there are factors that make Mexican-American solidarity difficult to achieve.

The southwestern states have long been the home of a large minority population that is referred to by various descriptive names. In California and to a degree in Arizona and the Midwest, there is grudging acceptance of the term "Mexican-American." With apologies and with awareness of its inaccuracy and its distastefulness to many persons, the term Mexican-American is used here because it is the simplest and most inclusive term by which to describe this portion of the American population.

Factors Which Prevent Cooperative Action

The very inability to agree on an all-inclusive name is an example of the unique heterogeneity of the roughly 4,000,000 Spanish-speaking people who live in the five southwestern states. Heterogeneity is a major factor in their inability to get together, to develop strong leadership, and to form organizations through which this large group may express its needs and desires and make itself felt in the political, economic, and social life of the broader community. It compounds the problem of self-identification that occurs among all minority groups.

To start a long discussion among Angelenos of Spanish-Mexican descent simply introduce the subject of self-identification or throw out the question, "Who are we?" It will continue for hours. At a conference on problems of Mexican-American youth held at Occidental College in 1963, six discussion sections were announced for the participants. By far the largest number signed up for the section on self-definition. After meeting for several hours in the morning and again in the afternoon the section members reported that

> . . . (we) cannot agree on a single definition of Mexican-Americans. Objectively, it is determined by the attitudes of the dominant community; subjectively, it is the totality of each individual, of how

Paul M. Sheldon "Community Participation and the Emerging Middle Class," in Julian Samora (ed.), *La Raza: Forgotten Americans* (South Bend, Indiana: University of Notre Dame Press, 1966). Reprinted by permission of the publisher.

each person conceives of himself. . . . The discussion has raised
a number of interesting points and evoked many challenging ideas
warranting further consideration . . . the group should meet again
for further discussion.[1]

The often repeated complaint that "Mexican-Americans cannot get together on anything" could be explained by heterogeneity alone, without
any additional complications. It is not, however, the only separating
factor.

Persons of Spanish-Mexican descent in the United States are further
fragmented by differences in degree of acculturation. Their or their forebears' residence extends from the earliest sixteenth-century settlements
to those who arrived yesterday from Mexico. There are those who, after
several generations of exposure to the English language and to Anglo
mores and values, have become (at least outwardly) completely Americanized. They retain little of their linguistic or cultural heritage. Others
who have been here equally long speak only Spanish, follow Mexican
ways of life, eat only Mexican food. Many elderly people look forward to
returning "home" to Mexico.

There are differences among people who came from one or another
state in Mexico and among those who have migrated from various areas
of the Southwest; there are differences in religion and in a host of subtle
factors that make for lack of cohesiveness.

Social class differences are becoming increasingly significant as more
and more Mexican-Americans achieve higher levels of education and
move up the socioeconomic ladder without changing their identity; they
remain persons of Mexican descent instead of becoming "Old Spanish,"
as was formerly the custom when being "Mexican" carried greater
stigma.

The Mexican Tradition of Individualism

Individualism is a major characteristic of Mexican culture. Awareness
of personal differences, respect and admiration for individuality are
characteristic throughout Mexico, in urban as well as rural populations
and in all social classes. One student has called it ". . . a country often
described as 'many Mexicos,' where individual worth is held to be almost
sacred and admitted conformity to the group, *any* group outside of the
family, a cardinal sin." [2]

The Mexican tends to react differently toward each person, depending
on their interpersonal relationships. To the Mexican, all men are *not*
created equal. He may well say: "Juan is my brother, Carlos is my 'com-
padre,' José is my enemy, that fellow who came yesterday to my office
seeking a favor is totally unknown to me. How could I possibly treat each
of these the same?"

In the United States a certain amount of lip service may be paid to
individuality, especially if the individualist lived a hundred or more
years ago. In practice, however, conformity, the submerging of the indi-

[1] *Summary of the Proceedings of the Twelfth Southwest Conference, Occidental College*, April 1963, pp. 25–28.

vidual to the interests of the group, is a vital part of the American heritage. "In unity there is strength" is the accepted pattern; Anglo-Americans have accepted the British tradition of working together to achieve a common goal and rallying round a common cause.

This tradition takes on increased meaning as the population becomes more highly urbanized, more concentrated in the city. We foster it in our schools under the label "adjustment." The lone voice is seldom heard in urban affairs. A major characteristic of Western society is the proliferation of voluntary associations. Urban populations may indeed be heterogeneous, as Wirth pointed out, (but effective action in this country is possible only when individuals band together into political parties, labor unions, professional groups, luncheon or civic clubs.)

It is not surprising that Mexican-Americans have been unable to put to effective use the tool of the mass voice to promote the common good of their group. They are in fact *not* a group; they do not speak with a common voice; they do not have mutual agreement; they are fragmented first by their heterogeneity and second by the tradition of individualism.

Other and perhaps more subtle factors militate against their forming effective coalitions or developing strong leaders: the tradition of first loyalty to the extended family; the pattern of the double standard and of clearly defined male-female roles; the rural folk distaste for individual advancement at the expense of one's peers; these and other traditional values in opposition to the mores of the Anglo-urban society place the Mexican-American at a disadvantage. They also create value conflicts in the upwardly mobile middle class.

These conflicts, not easily resolved, are evident when one aspires to a position of leadership within his own community, and especially when he seeks to form the strong organizations that are necessary if Mexican-American needs and desires are to be brought effectively to the attention of those in authority in the broad urban community.

Immigrants from Mexico to the United States have been largely but not entirely from the lower class. The few remaining descendants of the early Californios claim descent from the Spanish-Mexican settlers who developed the ranchos in the late eighteenth and early nineteenth centuries. The Manitos of northern New Mexico take pride in similar but earlier ancestry. Fugitives from the 1910 Revolution included landowners, merchants, and professional people who, although they tended to be forced into considerably lower status in the United States, passed on to their children more urbane attitudes and values.

To understand their difficulties in accommodating to the Anglo-urban way of life, especially their problems of organization and leadership, it is necessary to consider all of these traditions and, insofar as possible, to compare each with the others as well as with the mores of the new Anglo-based society.

The design for the present study took account not only of the traditional values and mores of the rural folk culture of Mexico but also of

2 Ida Serena Lovey, "Certain Mexican Social Values: A Comparative Inquiry into Tradition and Change" (unpublished master's essay, Department of Social Science, Roosevelt University, Chicago, 1962).

traditional and emerging values of the urban upper and middle classes, especially as they are described by Beals and Humphrey[3] and Gordon Hewes.[4] These and a few other scholars have attempted to understand the personality of the modern urban Mexicans who most nearly approximate the rising middle-class Mexican-Americans in cities in the United States.

By far the greater part of the migration from Mexico has taken place within the past 50 years and continues today. The migration from rural areas to the cities of Mexico and the United States is even more recent— much of it within the last 20 years. A majority of the families or recent in-migrants to Los Angeles came originally from the rural border provinces of Sonora and Chihuahua, often by way of Texas.

Rural folk values and mores, therefore, are still helpful in trying to understand people of Mexican descent in this country. However, we must be constantly aware that, although broadly characteristic of the majority of immigrants from Mexico and from other areas throughout the Southwest, the Mexican rural folk traditions do not apply to all groups in the urban Southwest, that they have been influenced by rapid changes taking place in Mexico as well as in cities north of the border. Modern Mexico strongly influences Mexican-American residents of Los Angeles, not only because of continued in-migration, but also because of extensive visiting back and forth across the border.

We must be cautious, then, in generalizing about so heterogeneous a group as the Mexican-American population of Los Angeles. As one said wryly, in commenting on a paper written by a local Mexican-American leader, "He lists nine different types of people of Mexican descent living in Los Angeles, but I don't see myself or my friends as fitting into *any* of these groups."

[3] Ralph Beals and Norman D. Humphrey, *No Frontier to Learning: The Mexican Student in the United States* (Minneapolis: University of Minnesota Press, 1957).

[4] Gordon Hewes, "Mexicans in Search of 'The Mexican,'" *American Journal of Economics and Sociology*, 18 (January 1954), 209–23. See also the summary of literature relating to upper- and middle-class Mexicans in Ida S. Lovey's thesis, pp. 10–17 [see note 2].

Chapter 7

The Quest
for Identity:
The Indian

The treatment of Indians in American culture is an ignoble chapter in our national history. It constitutes a fairly constant chronicle of exploitation, cruelty, and neglect—if not by design, at least accidentally. It represents a tradition that has characterized not only California but all of America, from North to South and East to West, from the early settlements of the seventeenth century to the present.

For more than a century, official government policy toward Indians has been based on white paternalism, evidenced by the reservation system and the various programs designed to stimulate Indian assimilation into white American culture. The widespread assumption in recent years has been that progress was being made and that Indians were becoming part of the larger society. But in fact, the gap between Indians and the rest of America has increased. Why is this so? A major reason is that most Americans have been ignorant of the realities of Indian life in modern America.

These traditional efforts toward assimilation have not worked. Indians continue to be strangers in their own land. Like other minority groups who see themselves as the victims of oppression in the United States, some Indians are rejecting the old paternalism. A new generation of Indian leaders is demanding a release from what they regard as their colonial condition, and they want greater autonomy in making the decisions that affect their own lives. They are seeking a redress of past injustices and present inequities, including the expropriation of their land and

166

their subservience in the socioeconomic structure of American society.

If the "problem" has been ignored in the past, there is currently appearing a plethora of information that reveals the sordid condition of most Indians in the United States. There is a growing realization that Indian culture is not monolithic. A wide diversity of customs, language, and culture have divided the Indians, therefore preventing the unity needed to resolve their problems. Senatorial committees, governmental reports and statistics, and scholarly publications are now exploring these heretofore ignored facets of native American culture, and more popular journals are contributing to the American's awareness of the issue. Revelations of inadequate housing, mass unemployment, and other social inequities, however, are not enough to create the understanding and subsequent action needed to solve these problems.

Of greater importance is the broader and more intangible issue of cultural diversity. An apparent trend concerning Indians and other minorities is a belief that everybody cannot be measured by America's traditional white Anglo-Saxon standards. An interesting reflection of differences that exist in societal value systems can be seen in much of the contemporary Indian literature, with its emphasis on ethereal, spiritual, otherworldly ideals.

Since World War II the Indian dilemma in the Golden State has grown rapidly. As a result of immigration from reservations in other states to Western metropolitan areas, California today has one-sixth of the national Indian population. The Indian's presence has created a new set of problems which, combined with his previous historical plight, have stimulated a debate regarding his position in California and the greater Southwest. The readings selected for this chapter supply information about health and welfare conditions and educational and job opportunities available to the American Indian. The reader should consider some of the larger questions in this current debate as he examines these selections. What have been the pitfalls in the government's historic Indian policy? Is assimilation possible? on what terms? How is the notion of "Indian identity" important in understanding the issue?

31. INDIAN YOUTH SPEAK

The new generation of American Indians is expressing its
dissatisfaction with the traditional roles Indians have played in
America. The following selection suggests the growing awareness that
basic changes must be made in the government's official Indian
policy.

During the 1960's many young Indian college students began to question the effects that the non-Indian, western European cultural orientation in education was having upon their lives and the lives of their people. In order to find ways to protect themselves and their tribal communities from sure cultural death, they organized themselves into a small but effective voice known as the National Indian Youth Council.

As the membership and leadership in the NIYC has changed and developed, so has their outlook and approach in dealing with the problems which concern them. The following excerpts from a recent Statement of Policy are significant, and demand our attention and study.

"Since earliest contacts with Western Man, the American Indian has been considered unproductive, unprogressive and uncooperative. Because we have been classified as a culturally deprived people, we have been subjected to systematic study by foreign cultures resulting in the imposition of institutions and programs to "improve our condition." Millions of dollars have been poured into projects by the government to help the American Indian; somehow this money has by-passed the majority of the tribal communities and ended up in the pockets of administrators and so-called Indian consultants.

"Abandoning a program of militant extermination of the Indian, the government has tried to dictate, through the establishment of colonial structures, the direction of Indian life. Concepts of tribal integrity and cultural equanimity have been overlooked in favor of enculturating the Indian and assimilating him into the American mainstream as fast as possible. The failure of this policy can be evidenced by the existence of 400,000 Indians still living within a tribal system in reservations through the United States. Most of these people live in communities with economic levels well below the poverty criterion. . . ." "The unwillingness to submit to the government's system of cultural death by allowing oneself to exist under these living standards seems, to us, to be a fight as real as the Indian wars of the previous century. The weapons employed by the dominant society have become subtler and more dangerous than guns—these in the form of educational, religious and social reform, have attacked the very centers of Indian life by attempting to replace native institutions with those of the white man, ignoring the fact that even these native institutions can progress and adapt themselves naturally to the environment."

"The major problem in Indian affairs is that the Indian has been neg-

"National Indian Youth Council Issues Statement of Policy," *Indian Truth*, Vol. 45, No. 3 (Winter 1968–1969).

lected in determining the direction of progress and monies to Indian communities. It has always been white people or white-oriented institutions determining what Indian problems are and how to correct them. The Establishment viewpoint has neglected the fact that there are tribal people within these tribal situations who realize the problems and that these people need only the proper social and economic opportunities to establish and govern policies affecting themselves. Our viewpoint, based in a tribal perspective, realizes, literally, that the Indian problem is the white man, and further, realizes that poverty, educational drop-out, unemployment, etc., reflect only symptoms of a social contact situation that is directed at unilateral cultural extinction."

"Realizing the rise of ethnic consciousness and the dangers of policies directed at that consciousness, the National Indian Youth Council was formed to provide methods of action to protect the tribal communities through implementation and coordination of educational resources. The nature of this work has, basically, been directed into research, training, and planning and programming at community, tribal and national levels. Believing firmly in the right to self-determination of all peoples, we attempt to reverse the hierarchial structure of existing agencies such that "the People" directly determine the policies of organizations and bureaucracies established to serve them: therefore, we act as resource individuals to serve our people."

"The American Indian has been communicating for the past two centuries; it is time that someone listened. The era of the young Indian as spokesman for his people has, we hope, ended. Realizing that we are of a marginal nature, we are not qualified to act as representatives for a tribal people in voicing, deciding and judging issues relevant to these people. We are prepared to address our people, not as "potential leaders," but as resources. Leaders arise from the people; an Indian leader cannot be delegated by the BIA or manufactured out of the tribal community by American society through an education that largely ignores his native culture."

32. INDIANS DESERVE A BETTER BREAK

A centuries-old complaint of the Indian has been the expropriation of his land by the white man. There is some evidence that the present governmental administration of the Indian still cannot adequately safeguard his interests. A Los Angeles Times editorial offers a modern case study of the Indian as a victim of a fumbling and insensitive bureaucracy.

Already approved by Nevada, the California-Nevada Water Compact has been blocked in the California Legislature by opposition from conservation groups and the Paiute Indians from the Pyramid Lake Reservation in Nevada.

"Indians Deserve a Better Break," *Los Angeles Times* (July 16, 1969). Reprinted by permission.

The Indians point out that their lake is shrinking. They want it stabilized at its present size.

We suggest the solution lies not in stalling the interstate compact, but in a more enlightened approach on the part of the secretary of the interior and the governors of California and Nevada.

Water is available in sufficient quantity to slow shrinkage of the lake, but it is being diverted by the federal government to the Newlands Irrigation Project.

Even though Newlands is one of the oldest projects under the 1903 Reclamation Act, establishment of the Pyramid Lake Reservation predates that project by a quarter century.

Interior Secretary Walter J. Hickel has declared that Pyramid Lake is not a compact problem but one involving the Indians, Nevada and the federal government.

Hickel's latest statement to that effect is in marked contrast to his earlier position in opposing the compact because he supported the position of the Pyramid Lake Indians. And it makes almost incomprehensible his agreement now to a sharp reduction in the size of the lake in order to spur passage of the California-Nevada compact.

That agreement, put together in a closed huddle between Hickel and Govs. Reagan and Paul Laxalt, would stabilize the lake by reducing its size from 110,000 acres to 70,000 acres. The result would be vast areas of unsightly mudflats.

What could possibly motivate such thinking?

It can only give rise to a suspicion that once again the Indian is going to fare badly at the hands of the Great White Father in Washington—aided and abetted this time by two state governors.

Perhaps there is not enough water in the Truckee to stabilize Pyramid Lake, but experts say the Newlands project is getting more water than it needs. The federal government could ease the situation by reducing its diversion from the Truckee and increasing its draw on the Carson River, which also serves the project.

To propose instead a rapid drain-down of the lake to shrink it by 40,000 acres is fantastic. Whoever was responsible for dreaming up the idea should now have the decency to scrap it.

33. THE CONSTITUTION AND THE AMERICAN INDIAN

JACK D. FORBES

With the advent of Indian militancy in California, a number of Indians have begun to question their relationship with the federal government. Moreover, the inadequacies of Indian reservations and schools have shocked the general public. Jack D. Forbes, a professor of Indian descent, comments upon the Indian's legal position vis-à-vis the Constitution.

It is common knowledge that American Indian people have, for a long period of time, been deprived of many constitutional protections and have been subjected to a pattern of domination by the United States federal government in sharp contrast to the limited authority of the latter relative to non-Indians. *The federal government, in brief, has been able to exercise the powers of local and state governments in relation to Indian tribal territories while, at the same time, being constitutionally prohibited from exercising those kinds of powers in regard to the white population.*

Is this notion of federal supremacy in relation to Indian tribes firmly rooted in the Constitution or is it simply a bureaucratic side effect of conquest? What are the constitutional powers of the federal government relative to Indians? Are there any limitations to federal power over Indian territories?

The Constitution is a document which both awards and denies power to the federal government. To be more precise, the Constitution creates a "limited" federal government, that is, one whose powers are limited to those powers specifically enumerated. In addition, the Constitution also limits the power of the federal government by mentioning certain kinds of behavior totally prohibited to that government (as in the Fifth Amendment).

It would seem clear that those powers denied to the federal government by the Constitution cannot be exercised by that government as regards Indians who are subjects (or citizens) of the United States. Quite obviously, the limiting aspect of the Constitution would become meaningless if one or more classes of the population could be *arbitrarily* exempted from being protected by that document. Of course, it might be argued that the two examples of Negro slavery and Indian wardship (both of which violated the Fifth Amendment and other sections of the Constitution) can serve as precedents for the ability of the federal (and state) government to set aside or ignore the Constitution more or less at will. However, it should be noted that Negro slavery was, in fact, recognized by the Constitution (in regard to the apportionment of representation in the House of Representatives), although in a "back-handed"

Jack D. Forbes, "The Constitutional Powers of the United States Government in Indian Affairs: A Preliminary Sketch." Used by permission of the author.

manner. Indian wardship, on the other hand, arose as a part of a process of extra-legal military conquest and can be regarded as a bureaucratic, as opposed to a constitutional, development.

What are the *constitutional* powers of the federal government relative to Indians and Indian tribes? First, it is interesting to note that the only reference to federal power over Indians is found in Section Eight which states: The Congress shall have power . . . to regulate commerce with foreign nations, and among the several states and with Indian tribes . . .

This is the "Interstate Commerce Clause" which basically determines the relationship of the several states to the federal government. The language of this section is clear: the federal government possesses the authority to regulate commerce (relations as well as trade) with the Indian tribes.

What does this mean? Quite clearly, *the above section does not give the federal government any greater power over the Indian tribes than it has over the several states*, since states and tribes are covered by the same language in the same clause. The authority of the federal government as regards the *internal* affairs of a tribe or of a state is limited to the regulation of "interstate," "inter-tribal," "tribal-state," "state-federal," or "federal-tribal" matters, that is, those activities having a direct relationship to "commerce" across state and tribal boundaries.

The above section also means that *no state can exercise any jurisdiction over tribes* since states and tribes are mentioned as equivalent units and since the federal government is specifically granted whatever authority exists in this area. If the federal government does not choose to regulate "commerce" with the tribes it does not mean that a state can step into the breach, any more than a state can establish diplomatic relations with a foreign nation in the absence of federal diplomatic activity.

In this connection another important clause should be cited, to the effect that powers not granted to the federal government are reserved to the states *and to the people*. In brief, a power not granted to the federal government is not automatically possessed by a state but may be possessed by the people and "the people" must, it would seem, include people of American Indian extraction. Clearly, a multitude of Supreme Court decisions (especially *Worcester v. Georgia*) have held that Indian tribal territories are immune from state jurisdiction and cannot, in fact, be a part of any state without a process of formal merger (and this process has never been clarified, constitutionally speaking).

To return to the powers of the federal government, it is clear that that government possesses *only* the same powers in relation to tribes as it possesses in relation to states. But what about the status of Indian individuals?

Indian individuals, as citizens or members of tribal territories ("domestic dependent nations" as the Supreme Court once put it) would seem to be protected from excessive federal or state regulation by virtue of the arguments presented above. In addition, however, the Constitution contains a number of clauses (especially in the "Bill of Rights") *which specifically limit the power of the federal and state governments in relation to all classes of persons found within the jurisdiction of the United States.*

It is quite clear that Indian individuals residing outside of the boundaries of any tribal territory but within the boundaries of the United States are, and have been, covered by the above clauses of the Constitution (in spite of contrary practice on the part of whites) *since even resident "aliens" are covered by most such clauses.* But what about Indians residing within a tribal territory or (in more recent terminology) on a reservation?

Supreme Court decisions have made it quite clear that the Constitution is applicable in any region or territory which has been "incorporated" into the United States, that is, which is "a part of" the United States. Clearly, Indian tribal territories (reservations) within the continental United States and Alaska are "a part of" the United States, from the viewpoint of the United States government. Not only has that government made its jurisdiction and laws felt in those areas but all official publications and maps of the government explicitly assert that such Indian reservations are "incorporated," that is, are part of the "homeland" or the "national territory" of the United States.

To argue that the Constitution and its guarantees do not apply to reservation Indians and their organizations is to argue that Indian reservations are "foreign" territories only "temporarily" under the jurisdiction of the United States. This viewpoint, while perhaps favored by a very few Indian separatists, certainly is not the viewpoint of Congress.

Individual Indians, as citizens and subjects of the United States residing within the national territory of the United States cannot be denied the full protection of the Constitution. In addition, however, certain clauses of the Constitution, such as the Fifth Amendment, limit the power of the federal government without reference to the geographical area in which the limitation is to be effective.

To summarize the above arguments briefly:

1. *Indian tribal territories* (so-called reservations plus nonceded Indian lands) which have been incorporated within the external boundaries of the United States *are part of the United States but are not generally a part of any individual state.*
2. *Indian tribal territories exist as unique political units,* comparable to the District of Columbia and Puerto Rico. Therefore, when we speak of the *basic units* into which the United States is divided we must speak of a) states, b) tribal territories, c) federal district (District of Columbia), and d) overseas territories. *The United States is not composed solely of fifty states!*
3. Indian tribal territories, constitutionally, possess the same autonomy (local self-rule) in relation to the federal government as do the several states.
4. The term "reservation," although utilized generally by the federal government, technically refers only to the "reservation of lands" for Indian use and is not necessarily the correct name to be applied to each and every tribal territory as a political unit (any more than

the Commonwealth of Virginia becomes the "State" of Virginia merely because it is generally referred to as a "state" of the United States).

What does all of this mean, in practical terms? Very simply, it means that virtually all of the acquired powers of the Bureau of Indian Affairs and of the Secretary of the Interior over the internal affairs of Indian tribal territories *are without legal basis.* They are derived from the practice of treating Indians as conquered persons, and the Constitution does not (at least since the Civil War) recognize any class of conquered persons residing within the limits of the United States!

34. HEALTH PROBLEMS OF
THE CALIFORNIA INDIAN

HARRY NELSON

The Indian's plight in California is reflected in a study made by the State Health Department which pointed out that the Indian's life span is decades shorter than that of the average Californian. Harry Nelson, a Los Angeles Times *medical writer, reports some revealing statistics about the extent of the health problems facing the Indian in the Golden State.*

American Indians living in California live an average of only 42 years, according to a State Health Department report on the health problems of Indians.

The report says the health status of Indians is "immeasurably worse" than that of other Californians. The average life span for all Californians is 62 years.

The report paints a picture of widespread alcoholism, malnutrition, poor sanitation, birth defects and infectious diseases among the estimated 100,000 Indians who live in the state, including 35,000 on "bleak, unproductive reservations."

The situation has worsened during the last 14 years because health services terminated by the federal government in 1955 have not been replaced by the state.

Health workers visited rural and urban Indian communities and found that:

—25% of Indians who move to the city to get help do so because of alcoholism problems.

—Many Indian women living in cities return to the reservation to deliver babies because of unfamiliarity with city ways and difficulties in adjusting away from their families. But the reservations lack adequate medical facilities.

—Vitamin C "virtually nonexistent" in the diets of 100 Indians taking part in a nutritional survey on three Southern California reservations. Of the 100, including 38 children, only five had vegetables in the past three meals and only two had eaten fruit.

The combined effects of physical and cultural isolation and delays in getting preventive or early treatment for illnesses result in an average hospital stay two and one-half times that of other Californians, according to the report.

It estimates that probably fewer than 1% of Indians have health insurance, compared with almost 70% of the medium and higher income groups. Seventy per cent of reservation families earn less than $3,000 a year.

The report indicates that California's problem is worse than in some other states with Indian populations because health services formerly provided by the U.S. Public Health Service have not been replaced.

In the early 1950s Congress ended the status of American Indians as wards of the federal government and abolished all Bureau of Indian Affairs offices in California, Florida, New York and Texas.

In 1955 all federal health services for Indians in California were terminated. All these actions, the report says, were done with the approval of the Legislature and the State Health Department.

Between 1955 and the present, however, "no state funds were made available to continue any of the terminated health services, and the health of California's Indians has deteriorated," the report says.

In other states which did not terminate federal aid for health care for Indians, the appropriation has increased from $24.5 million in 1955 to $99.5 million in 1969–70.

California's share this year would be $1.6 million based on the 1955 ratio. But if the distribution of the federal funds were on a per capita basis, its share would be more than $15 million.

California has one-sixth of the nation's Indian population. Indians come to Los Angeles, San Francisco, Oakland and San Jose—most of them from other states—at the rate of 6,000 to 10,000 a year.

The report states that the federal government, "under pressure from various organizations in the state," has reinstituted educational services which were terminated about the time that health services were ended.

It says the Public Health Service is not willing to introduce new health programs without specific direction from Congress.

Last year the Legislature asked Congress to provide for full financial participation by California Indians in all federal programs, particularly in health, education, sanitation, and vocational training, but no action has been taken.

The Health Department said the State Board of Public Health will examine the whole problem . . .

35. WHERE INDIANS USED TO PLAY

SUSAN LYDON

The Indians' seizure of Alcatraz Island should be seen as something more than a rash act of retribution. The symbolic gesture of freeing a former federal prison represented for many Indians their attempts to break out of what they consider a prison that the Bureau of Indian Affairs and white America have created for them. The following article explores the symbolism and greater meaning of Alcatraz to red and white Americans.

PROCLAMATION
TO THE GREAT WHITE FATHER AND ALL HIS PEOPLE

We, the native Americans, re-claim the land known as Alcatraz Island in the name of all American Indians by right of discovery.

We wish to be fair and honorable in our dealings with the Caucasian inhabitants of this land, and hereby offer the following treaty:

We will purchase said Alcatraz Island for twenty-four dollars (24) in glass beads and red cloth, a precedent set by the white man's purchase of a similar island about 300 years ago. We know that $24 in trade goods for these 16 acres is more than was paid when Manhattan Island was sold, but we know that land values have risen over the years. Our offer of $1.24 per acre is greater than the 47¢ per acre the white men are now paying the California Indians for their land.

We will give to the inhabitants of this island a portion of the land for their own to be held in trust by the American Indian Affairs and by the Bureau of Caucasian Affairs to hold in perpetuity—for as long as the sun shall rise and the rivers go down to the sea. We will further guide the inhabitants in the proper way of living. We will offer them our religion, our education, our life-ways, in order to help them achieve our level of civilization and thus raise them and all their white brothers up from their savage and unhappy state. We offer this treaty in good faith and wish to be fair and honorable in our dealings with all white men.

We feel that this so-called Alcatraz Island is more than suitable for an Indian Reservation, as determined by the white man's own standards. By this we mean that this place resembles most Indian reservations in that:

1. It is isolated from modern facilities, and without adequate means of transportation.

2. It has no fresh running water.

3. It has inadequate sanitation facilities.

4. There are no oil and mineral rights.

5. There is no industry and so unemployment is very great.

6. There are no health care facilities.

7. The soil is rocky and non-productive; and the land does not support game.

8. *There are no educational facilities.*

9. *The population has always exceeded the land base.*

10. *The population has always been held as prisoners and kept dependent upon others.*

Further, it would be fitting and symbolic that ships from all over the world entering Golden Gate, would first see Indian land, and thus be reminded of the true history of this nation. This tiny island would be a symbol of the great lands once ruled by free and noble Indians.

—Indians of All Tribes

From San Francisco, as the light changes hour by hour, Alcatraz, little more than a mile offshore, changes color and shimmers like a giant jewel in the midst of one of the world's most beautiful bays. Inmates of the island's prison called it "The Rock," a barren and desolate place from which there was no escape. But the real agony of the Alcatraz prisoners, as anyone who has ever been there can imagine, was the heartbreaking beauty of the world they viewed from its confines. Bobby Kennedy closed the prison down in 1963, and since then the City of San Francisco has been trying to decide what use to make of the island. The Board of Supervisors promised a plastic mecca for tourists of exactly the sort that has made Fisherman's Wharf the most lucrative and congested area of the city. But on November 9th while the Supervisors contemplated an Alcatraz Space Tower, the fate of the island was suddenly and dramatically decided by fourteen young Indians, most of them militant students from colleges in the San Francisco Bay Area, who invaded the island and claimed it for their people. In 1964, a group of Sioux Indians, citing an 1868 treaty which gave them rights to surplus Federal lands, made an abortive attempt to take the island, but no one took their claim to the land seriously.

They hid out overnight on the island, inspecting the deteriorating old buildings and established squatters' rights. When the group voluntarily surrendered after a 19-hour occupation, Richard Oakes, a 27-year-old Mohawk announced: "We will construct our new nation here."

Two weeks later the Indians came back, more than 80 of them, including 6 small children. They were led by the original 14 and by other students from UCLA and the University of California at Santa Cruz. Landing on Alcatraz just before dawn, they proclaimed it "free Indian Land." They brought with them a supply of food, a ceremonial drum, and a large poster of Apache chief Geronimo. They spent their first night on the island with a victory pow-wow and ceremonial sing. "We won't resist arrest," Dennis Turner, a Mission Shoshone, said, "but how will they find us? We are the invisible Americans."

The Indians of All Tribes who occupy Alcatraz want the island as an Indian cultural center. They would set up a permanent center for the Native American Studies and a traveling university for gathering and disseminating knowledge on the reservations. They would create an American Indian Spiritual and Medical Center, which will practice our ancient tribal "religious and sacred healing ceremonies"; an Indian Center of Ecology; a Great Indian Training School offering contemporary vocational training and an Indian restaurant serving native foods. Lastly, the Indians on Alcatraz are talking about an Indian Museum. One part of the museum, "will present some of the things the white man has given to the Indians in return for the land and life he took: disease, alcohol, poverty and cultural decimation (as symbolized by old tin cans, barbed wire, rubber tires, plastic containers, etc.)."

The permanent landing party demanded that Secretary of Interior Hickel come to the island and turn it over to the Indians; that the island be governed by a popularly elected "Indian entity . . . without participation in its management by any agency of government"; and that the Government fund the building of the cultural complex. There were hassles at first: an on-again, off-again Coast Guard blockade, repeated urgings to leave and threats that Indians would be arrested for trespassing, and sabotage of electricity, plumbing, and water supplies. While Hickel has still not negotiated with the Indians, Alcatraz has been withdrawn from the for-sale market, and a constantly shifting population of Indians has been on the island for [nearly a year].

> Isn't it brutally ironic that the Indian would have to invade what was considered the most terrible federal prison to find a new sense of freedom for himself?   Adam Nordwall, Chippewa

All whites wanting to visit Alcatraz have to receive clearance through the San Francisco Indian Center, and only those with official business are allowed on the island. The Indian Center, a recreational and vocational guidance center for Bay Area urban Indians, is housed in temporary quarters. The Indian Center's permanent building burned down on October 29th, and provided the immediate impetus for the invasion. Inside there's total chaos: phones ringing, newly-arrived Indians waiting around to find out how they get to the island, piles of clothing, food and toys donated for the permanent residents, and white boat owners shouting offers of help. The whole scene is presided over by a strikingly beautiful Indian girl named Shirley Keith who had been studying in Paris before the invasion. Frantic, she tells me, "We're expecting 10,000 people on the island for a big pow-wow tomorrow, and no whites or press allowed."

I try again a couple of days later. The boat to Alcatraz—an old eccentric called "Cap'n Armstrong" has most consistently donated his services —leaves from a pier behind Fisherman's Wharf. There's been a bad storm for the last couple of days and a mean wind blows off the choppy water. Indian families, refugees in their own land, huddle together in blankets behind whatever small windbreakers they can find on the pier. Behind a mountain of cartoned supplies in the middle of the dock— electric heaters, blankets, warm clothing, food—two women laugh and joke with everyone there.

Stella Leach, one of them, has a fur cap tilted rakishly over to one side of her head. She's the nurse on the island and one of its acknowledged leaders. Half Sioux and half Colville, she grew up on the Pine Ridge

Reservation. She has four sons who have all fought in Vietnam, a married daughter, and two foster children. She runs an Indian well-baby clinic in Oakland, and as a nurse, as an Indian, and as a woman, she's seen a lot of suffering in her life. It shows on her face, which at 50 is weathered and tough and still strikingly good-looking. "Have you met Grace Thorp, our Jim Thorp's daughter?" she says. "She's come to help us with public relations."

Grace is a huge, amiable woman with a white puffy face. A halfbreed Sac and Fox from Oklahoma, she had been selling ads and real estate in Phoenix but decided she was needed more on Alcatraz. A middle-aged man, hearing Grace is Sac and Fox, begins chattering to her about people they might know in common. A shy teenage boy tentatively approaches Grace and Stella's carton bastion: "Do you give sandwiches to Navajo?" "Honey, we give sandwiches to everyone when we have them," Grace says, handing him a loaf of Italian bread. It is freezing cold and they have been waiting for a boat since 8 in the morning, warmed only by a feeling of community and kinship.

All supplies—food, water, firewood—have to be hauled to Alcatraz by boat. Some hippies drive in with a pick-up truck full of wood and unload it on the dock. Stella's telling stories in her deep voice: "Two guys came up to the clinic one day and said, 'We're from the LA Times.' They walked straight in and opened the medicine cabinet. 'This where you keep all your narcotics?' 'We don't have any narcotics,' I said. 'That's your hang-up, not ours.' 'What do you give people for pain?' they said. 'Oh, we're tough. We just grin and bear it.' They asked me all these questions, said they were interviewing me. 'Hey, next time you come here to do a newspaper story,' I said to them, 'You'd better remember not to wear your regulation shoes.' Man, we know cops when we see them; we've been surrounded by them all our lives."

We've been waiting for hours. Two vans arrive from the Indian Center to load up the supplies and take them back. "Oh no you don't," says Stella, "We're getting out there if I have to rent the boat myself." "We need a dance," says Grace, and a fiddler, one Dale Kindness, pulls a chair from nowhere and begins playing "Turkey in the Straw." At 5:00 Stella rented a fishing boat to carry the supplies and some 40 Indians to the island.

Next morning I hitched a ride to Alcatraz with Tom Caulfield, the skipper of the sloop "Saturna," the first boat to ferry supplies to the island during the blockade. It was a gloriously windy day, and we went under full sail. As we pulled up to the dock on the north side of the island the water was rough, and everyone on board had to fend off as the boat bobbed up and down. People jumped aboard from all directions. My sleeping bag, food and cigarette supply, and I got pulled up on a rubber tire, tied to a rope. Tom took off with new passengers.

We trudged up the steep hill, part winding driveway, part narrow stone staircase, past crumbling balustrades and over-grown gardens. Desolate, bleak, barren, the words the press has always used to describe Alcatraz have some truth, but the island is staggeringly beautiful. What grows there, besides the ubiquitous eucalyptus trees is wild and strange, and the remnants of gardens once lovingly cultivated with roses and marguerites make parts of the island lush with greenery.

The main cell block, administrative office, and two large houses are on top of the hill surrounding a cement courtyard. Down the hill on the west side of the island are some small frame houses and an apartment building where the caretaker, Thomas Hart, and his wife live. A game of basketball was going on in the courtyard. The silence of the island, broken only by occasional foghorns and the lapping of the water, made the surrounding cities fantastic faraway mirages. The atmosphere on the island itself was that of Indian reservations I've visited: not much work to do, people in houses listening to transistor radios or, when the electricity works, watching soap operas on television. A few men fished from the dock, catching rock cod. A group of kids rode around in the bed of a pick-up truck that sometimes works, picking up garbage from the cans in the main courtyard and taking it down to the dump to burn it.

About 150 people are living there now, but because of the storm many of the permanent residents are marooned on the mainland. Families with kids live in the caretakers' apartment buildings or the paint-peeling house that once belonged to the warden. Some of the small houses where groups of younger people live have been fixed up quite comfortably, with posters, decorations and furniture found in other buildings on the island. Stella's clinic is in a wooden Victorian house, furnished with cots and medical supplies, but without heat or hot water. There's a nursery school and a school for everyone else, from first graders to high school seniors, taught by Linda Arayanado, a half Creek, half Filipino student from Berkeley. In the same building a crafts center holds classes in beadwork and quill work. Here are the only hot showers on the island.

In the beginning of the occupation plumbers and electricians worked on getting minimal plumbing facilities and lights working. The electricity is off about half the time and mechanics work incessantly on the pickup trucks, refrigerator, and other cast-off paraphernalia of our culture. The lack of heat and electricity make conditions bleak, but almost all the Alcatraz residents say they're no worse off here than on their reservations or in the city slums where Indians on Federal relocation programs end up.

Meals are served in the mess hall in the main cell block. All work is done by volunteers rather than on a regular job schedule. There's one working faucet of water, one sink, one refrigerator, and three apartment-sized stoves run on propane gas. Water has to be boiled to wash dishes. Food is donated by various people on the mainland. "Our supplies are vast but out of balance," one of the cooks tells me. "We don't have enough protein and fresh vegetables, and milk and eggs are always short. Variety is not great, and we don't always have balanced meals, but there's enough food on the island to last indefinitely. For lack of food we're not gonna starve. When this is over I'm going to compile an Alcatraz cookbook with all the weird things we've done: squeezing grapefruit when we run out of vinegar, using worcestershire sauce for salad dressing."

They eat a lot of rice, beans and fried bread, and when food runs out at mealtimes, there's always peanut butter and jelly sandwiches. "How do you want your steak, well-done or medium-rare?" they joke at mealtimes, which are as noted for gossiping and exchanging stories about tribal customs as eating. We ate, and the cook, incredibly, prepared meals by the light of a few candles and flashlights. As we ate, people came down to dinner in an eerie procession, moving their flashlights up and down the three-tiered rows of cells that lead to the mess hall. After dinner one night they brought out the drum, and the soft sounds of songs in Kiowa and Sioux resounded through the dark cell block. There have also been occasional rock dances—"Big Rock on the Rock"—in the prison auditorium.

> Personally I'd like to rip off the whole United States of America, but I like to think my training as a social worker has made me a realist.
> Vicky Santana, 25, halfbreed
> Blackfoot from Montana

Indians of All Tribes, the name which the Alcatraz Indians have chosen for themselves, represents about 80 of the 250 American tribes. I met Sioux, Colville, Comanche, Klamath, Yurok, Apache, Navajo, Cheyenne, Creek, Blackfeet, among many others. Many on the island are urban Indians, students on EOP grants, involved in Indian Power movements at their schools. They came to Alcatraz for many reasons: for adventure, out of idealism, and some because, like many American Indians, they had nothing else to do. For older reservation Indians, Alcatraz has become a sacred land; they come from everywhere in the country just to touch their feet on it, filled with amazement at what their children have done. "The old people on the reservations were looking at their young people with mixed emotions, thinking they were losing their identity as Indians. Alcatraz has given them a new sense of hope," said Richard Oakes, former spokesman for the invaders.

Oakes has massive shoulders and a dimpled smile. He is a Mohawk and his wife Annie is a Pomo from California. As he sat talking to me in the dining room he turned to his youngest son and asked, "What tribe are you?" A pause, a smile and then "Pomahawk" loud and clear. Oakes led the first assault on Alcatraz, and was the elected spokesman for the Indians in the beginning, but the press talked only to him and played him up as "the President of Alcatraz," creating some bitterness among the others. Since a tragic fall that killed the eldest of his five children, he's moved back to San Francisco.

Except for big pow-wows where they wear their ceremonial costumes, the Alcatraz Indians wear their Indian-ness in small ways: a pair of intricately beaded gloves, a turquoise and silver watchband, a beaded necklace, or a fringed and beaded buckskin pouch. But one sees in their faces the dignity, pride and competence of old daguerreotypes—the prominent features, the copper-colored skin, the straight, glossy black hair that are the unmistakable signs of Indian beauty. The Indians see Alcatraz as their last chance for cultural survival; and the young particularly are determined not to lose.

Despite the apparent calm of life on the island, the Indians know they are involved in a desperate struggle. Stella Leach, sitting around the tiny gas heater in her clinic, served tea to her sons and their friends, and talked about the now-or-never feeling so prevalent on Alcatraz. "We can't lose this; if we do, why, there will never be another chance for the Indians. This took a great deal to do because it isn't in our nature to grab things. The earth to the white man means how many acres of timber can we get out of this, how many tons of ore can we get from this mine. The earth was our mother and she gave us everything we needed—she fed us and clothed us and kept us warm and kept us together—why should we take from her? Alcatraz has got us back together again, although it's a frail thread. And if we lose this, it will take us another 150 years to get it together again."

Their militancy is expressed in the signs they have painted on the island: "This Land Is My Land" on the main cell block, "Home of the Free Indian," "All Men On Mother Earth," on the water tower, and in the flag—a teepee and a broken peace pipe—that flies from the water tower. On the driftwood tree at the entrance to the main cell block hang the tops of tin cans painted in nail polish with the Indian's history: "Trail of Tears," "Wounded Knee," "Genocide," "B.I.A.," "Kinzua Dam," "As Long as the Grass Shall Grow."

Several weeks ago a Hopi brought a tape-recorded message to Alcatraz. It told of a 1200-year-old prophecy that the American Indian would be pushed off his land from the East to the West, and that when he reached the farthermost Western tip of America, he would begin to reclaim it. The Alcatraz invasion occurred at a propitious time: people speak of this year as the Year of the Indian, a time of cultural renaissance and revival of interest in the Indians. Books long out of print have been re-issued, new ones published, and the hippie subculture reveres and imitates traditional Indian ways. The white culture's growing horror at the rape of the land we took from Indians creates an atmosphere in which, as Stella Leach says, "My people can begin to grow again, and show, by doing our own thing in our own way, that we have something special to offer to the world."

"I think it's really poetic," said Leo Leach, one of Stella's three sons now living on the island. "The prison is falling down all by itself." The catwalks around the prisoner's exercise yard are rotting, and the barbed wire has come loose from the fence and twisted itself up in weird configurations that look quite beautiful. "Here we're free," David Leach said. "We govern ourselves; we live as Indians, and no one tells us what to do. Out *there* is the prison."

> The Indian's "plight" has always inspired recurrent orgies of remorse, but never has it forced us to digest the implications of a nation and culture conceived in genocide.   Peter Collier, Ramparts

White America, like Alcatraz, is falling down, and we are beginning bitterly to learn some lessons about the land that the Indians always knew. Most of the damage—to the Indians, to the land, to ourselves—is irreparable. Alcatraz has, to a certain extent, brought unity to the Indians, but it is a unity born of desperation. The Indians' tribal differences of a naturally factionalized people are the source of some tension on Alcatraz. There are bitter factional disputes among the leaders over power and over appropriation of the $11,000 bankroll. Some of the more traditional men resent Stella's leadership role and the prominence of the other women. "It is not the Indian way," they say about the women, just as they reprimand someone who has committed some infraction of the Council rules. Behind that saying, however, is the sad knowledge that the cultural genocide has been almost completely successful: that "the Indian way" is impracticable in most situations the Indian faces in contemporary society.

In alienating the Indian from his ancient culture and isolating him on reservations where he is completely at the mercy of the whims of the BIA, the white man has corrupted and ghettoized him. And the invasion of Alcatraz isn't a magic that can immediately eradicate the heritage received from the white man. The drunken Indian is not a joke stereotype but a bitter reality, and although the Council has outlawed alcohol on the island, it is still a major problem. There are thefts and fights and rumors of drugs—the problems of the ghetto, the manifestations of the despair of people who have nothing to do. The tragedy of the American Indian is evident on Alcatraz as it is on the Indian reservations, and all the noble savage romanticism in the world cannot balm the pain of this tragedy.

The young people sitting around the dinner tables in the main mess hall like to talk about their tribal customs and their hopes for Alcatraz, but that talk is counterpointed by the depressing stories they tell about their own lives. They talk about their experiences in the Government boarding schools where Indian children are confined and beaten for speaking tribal dialects. They talk about relatives serving long prison sentences for petty crimes, usually "just for being Indian"; about their tribes being terminated by the BIA and the confusing bureaucratic maze of the relocation programs; about the poverty and sickness in their childhoods, and the suicides on the reservations; about the constant land swindles in their own lifetimes and their grandparents' stories about the massacres and indignities they lived through. There is no comfortable way for most of them to live away from their reservations, for the only way they can have self-respect is to live as Indians. Yet they know that the reservations mean unemployment, alcoholism, and perhaps suicide, if they choose to go back.

The population of Alcatraz shifts constantly, not just because people get tired or have fights and leave, but also because Alcatraz is a movement. New people are coming to work there and the veterans take off for other battlegrounds. The other day I ran into three people I had met on Alcatraz. Two of them—David Leach and Judy Scraper—used to be Council members, and now they were hitchhiking to Washington. David was going up to the Colville Reservation because the tribe was having its final vote on termination; and Judy and another girl were going to Seattle to take over Fort Lawton. When the Indians first invaded Alcatraz

Senator George Murphy said he hoped the epidemic wouldn't spread, "because if you come right down to it, someone could claim the whole United States of America." During the time I spent on Alcatraz a poem we learned in grade school kept running through my mind—"Where we walk to school each day/Indian children used to play"—its horrifying implications clear for the first time. Unfortunately for George Murphy, the Alcatraz epidemic *is* spreading, precisely because, when you come right down to it, the Indians have every right to claim the whole United States of America. And the Indians on Alcatraz know that reclaiming their land is their only hope for survival.

36. INTERVIEW WITH AN INDIAN PULITZER PRIZE WINNER

N. SCOTT MOMADAY AND JOSE COLMENARES

The economic deprivation of the Indian demonstrates how poorly the traditional American "melting pot" theory has worked. N. Scott Momaday, professor of American literature at the University of California and Pulitzer Prize winner in 1969 for his novel House Made of Dawn, *has commented on the awareness of self-identity as the first necessary step toward becoming a full member of American society. Dr. Momaday's remarks in an interview with the California Teachers Association magazine,* The Valuator, *suggest the contrast between the Indian's ethereal and spiritual qualities and the practicality of Anglo society. Momaday, who is an Indian himself, claims that Indian culture contains ideas that could enrich American society as a whole.*

VALUATOR.   How closely do you identify with the Kiowa?

MOMADAY.   It's only been in the last few years that I have asked myself seriously what it means to have Kiowa blood flowing in my veins. I suppose in a sad way, that's true of many of the younger Kiowans today. The language is forgotten. It's not a conscious attempt, but an indifference, an absence of curiosity.

I've developed a marvelous pride in my people, in their cultural heritage. They have an extraordinary and fascinating history. Three hundred years ago, for example, they started migrating from Western Montana, to the Black Hills, and from there to Southwestern Oklahoma. My wife and I retraced those paths. That Kiowa journey is now fixed inside of me, in my blood. I love to wonder about it.

VALUATOR.   What characteristic of the Kiowa fascinates you most?

MOMADAY.   The reverence for language. This is true of all Indians. There is a strong verbal tradition. They exist through language. They perpetuate themselves through the stories and legends that are passed

By Jose Colmenares, *The Valuator* (Spring 1969), California Teachers Association/Southern Section. Reprinted by permission.

on to succeeding generations. Words have great power in themselves. Language is treasured, explored, delicately shaped because it is magic. And it is, you know. Words form ideas, and ideas, if they are valid, live forever.

VALUATOR.   What is there in the Indian view of life that could be valuable to the Anglo?

MOMADAY.   Patience. A commitment to life that is not abrasive. A willingness to flow with the nature of the universe. It's the idea, I suppose, of a circle. And this is a traditional symbol among many Indian tribes. All of history, time past, present, future, personal destinies, are all part of that circle, and it goes on without end.

Life is not a tragedy, a conflict between nature and man, a battlefield or a world to be conquered. There is no need for corrosive self-analysis. Indian people have a wonderful sense of humor. They have resisted the Western tendency to take itself seriously. They are serene.

VALUATOR.   How closely do Indians identify with American society?

MOMADAY.   You'd be surprised how much pride they take in being American. Patriotism is a very real thing. To be an Indian, is to be American. Some tribes, perhaps because of some warlike tradition, are very proud of the young men who go off to fight the wars of the nation. That's one of the great vocations among Indians: a career in the army.

VALUATOR.   What happens when the Indian confronts Anglo society?

MOMADAY.   The Indian is a very religious man. And Anglo society can be very cynical, very brutal in its attitudes toward unorthodox religions. The Indian is made aware that his religious and ethical values are inane outside the reservation. The reservation gods are dead. But then he's told the Anglo's god is also dead. God is dead! At this point you've stripped the Indian of all spiritual consolation. The results are tragic. Indians are profoundly religious in their outlook and relationships. They need their faith.

VALUATOR.   What about Christianity as an alternative religious experience?

MOMADAY.   I am a Christian, but I am very sceptical about the possibility of Christianity as a substitute. In times of crisis, the Indian doesn't go to the Protestant or Catholic church. He goes to his own gods. He only pays lip service to Christianity. When it really matters, Christianity offers little consolation.

VALUATOR.   In the novel, Abel, the leading character, becomes an alcoholic. Is this a common problem?

MOMADAY.   Alcoholism is a very serious problem among Indians. I imagine that men like Abel, who are suffocated by the city, frustrated by the lack of social opportunities, resort to alcoholism. If they can't beat the white man or function effectively in his cage, then they can at least drink him under the table.

VALUATOR.   Apparently in your novel you see the Indian as a tragic figure?

MOMADAY.   I sometimes think the American Indian is really the only tragic figure left in literature. He doesn't understand his situation. He is not equipped to live in society and no one will seriously help him. Quite simply, the world is going by without him.

In the novel, Abel is absurd. He's ridiculous, and his absurdity is entirely public. Everything he does is colored with a veil of pain. It's only when he leaves the city and returns to the reservation that he finds an opportunity to become a man again.

VALUATOR. Why has the Indian become a tragic figure?

MOMADAY. We have robbed the Indian of his pride. He has been a prisoner of war for generations, and we have not let him forget it. We've made him dependent on the generosity of the white man spiritually, psychologically, and often materially. The Indian has lost his dignity. He's been turned into a grotesque caricature, a pot maker, a bead salesman, a silly fool who chases John Wayne down the trail. He's been encouraged to prostitute his own skills, so that when he makes pottery for tourist consumption, he uses poor clay and nonpermanent colors. There are still people who take an Indian, dress him up in a fright war bonnet, and ask him to do a vaudeville routine for the matinee crowd.

VALUATOR. How involved are they in the civil-rights movement?

MOMADAY. There is no reluctance to support the movement. However, they wish to preserve their own identity. There is a problem of diversity in attempting to organize the Indian as a political force. There are over 100 living Indian languages in this country. The problems of the Navajo are not always the same as those of the Kiowa or the Apache. It's even been difficult to pass Federal legislation which would be practical for all Indian tribes.

VALUATOR. What is your opinion of the schools maintained by the government on Indian reservations?

MOMADAY. They are certainly more desirable than uprooting or relocating the Indian student. However, despite some excellent Bureau of Indian Affairs schools, there is still the problem of automatic segregation. The Indian has little exposure to the dominant society. When he finally collides with the Anglo world, it can be a tragic experience. That's the story, of course, of "House Made of Dawn."

VALUATOR. What can education do to improve the condition of the Indian?

MOMADAY. The whole concept of education can be changed so that the objective is to instill within the Indian a pride in being what he is. He can be taught his own history, which has never been done before. He can be educated into the conviction that his way of life is intrinsically valuable, and valuable to the dominant society.

Chapter 8

The Quest for Identity: The Confusing Presence of the Oriental

The post-war economic success of most Orientals* in California has made their roles as minority groups difficult for the white majority to understand; their situation is different from that of other minority groups. Although one might acknowledge that not all racial and ethnic minorities enjoy perfect equality in the United States today, frequently Orientals are pointed to as "proof" of America's open society. Those who espouse this "success story" point of view remember that Orientals temporarily occupied the least desirable positions in Western America. During the century following their arrival, these immigrants—the Chinese coolie labor force that helped build the railroads during the 1870s and 1880s, the Filipinos who came after the turn of the century, and the Nisei during World War II—encountered nearly unmatched antipathy and prejudice from Caucasian Americans. Yet in spite of this hostility, their hard work, tightly knit homes, veneration of education, and obedience to law have gained for many of them economic security and respect in American society. Thus, according to our traditional value system, Orientals have successfully joined the mainstream of society in the United States and are now enjoying the fruits of the so-called American Dream.

Although statistical measurements of economic success indicate that the income of the average Oriental in California ap-

* Many Americans categorize all persons of Asian background simply as Orientals. There are, however, significant differences in customs, values, and experiences among the major Oriental groups.

proximates that of the average Caucasian, there is a new mood developing that casts some doubt on the reputedly significant achievements of the various Asian-American groups. For some members of the third-generation Oriental community, there is a new tendency to question the virtue of the "melting-pot" concept. They reject the suggestion that "Americanization" should be measured by the degree of assimilation by the ethnic group into the already existing society. In this view, the individual's success is defined in terms of his ability to adopt the customs and mores of traditional America.

Part of this new generation of Oriental-Americans is now examining the wisdom of this interpretation of "assimilation." Their feeling is that to simply don a white mask and imitate an Anglo-Saxon life style is to pervert the concept of self-identity. They suggest that if assimilation is to occur, it must be on the ethnic group's own terms. Orientals consider it imperative that their own traditions not be totally sacrificed to the idol of American conformity. Such a sacrifice, they believe, is too high a price for admittance to American life.

Although this attitude of concern does not compare with the stridency of the blacks or even that of the *Chicano,* it is on the increase. This in a sense parallels the general "generation gap" in white middle-class America. Thus, most of the present generation of Oriental parents, products of the Depression, victims of prejudice and, in some cases, internment camps, do not share this view. After long years of adversity, they have achieved prosperity and public acceptance. The new view is a part of the new generation of recently affluent Oriental youth who are becoming aware of the problem of assimilation vis-à-vis the challenge of preserving their own sense of ethnic identity. They are looking at themselves in a new way and raising questions that may be of value to the reader. Should they assume that the security and acceptance that they have won is complete and irrevocable? Are there signs that this "success story" is becoming increasingly less certain for many urban Asian-Americans? Is there a legitimate basis for a "generation gap" to exist among the Oriental communities in America?

37. SUCCESS STORY: JAPANESE AMERICAN STYLE

WILLIAM PETERSEN

The search for self-identity is important, and it currently plays a significant part in the cultural life of minorities in America. A sociologist formerly with the University of California examines the factors that help to explain how the Nisei were able to surmount discrimination as severe as that encountered by any of the minorities. Of special significance is Professor William Petersen's opinion that the Japanese have been able to establish and maintain meaningful links with their cultural antecedents in their quest for self-identity. Perhaps the relevance and applicability of this search for oneself is crucial.

Asked which of the country's ethnic minorities has been subjected to the most discrimination and the worst injustices, very few persons would even think of answering: "The Japanese Americans." Yet, if the question refers to persons alive today, that may well be the correct reply. Like the Negroes, the Japanese have been the object of color prejudice. Like the Jews, they have been feared and hated as hyperefficient competitors. And, more than any other group, they have been seen as the agents of an overseas enemy. Conservatives, liberals and radicals, local sheriffs, the Federal Government and the Supreme Court have cooperated in denying them their elementary rights—most notoriously in their World War II evacuation to internment camps.

Generally this kind of treatment, as we all know these days, creates what might be termed "problem minorities." Each of a number of inter-related factors—poor health, poor education, low income, high crime rate, unstable family pattern, and so on and on—reinforces all of the others, and together they make up the reality of slum life. And by the "principle of cumulation," as Gunnar Myrdal termed it in "An American Dilemma," this social reality reinforces our prejudices and is reinforced by them. When whites defined Negroes as inherently less intelligent, for example, and therefore furnished them with inferior schools, the products of these schools often validated the original stereotype.

Once the cumulative degradation has gone far enough, it is notoriously difficult to reverse the trend. When new opportunities, even equal opportunities, are opened up, the minority's reaction to them is likely to be negative—either self-defeating apathy or a hatred so all-consuming as to be self-destructive. For all the well-meaning programs and countless scholarly studies now focused on the Negro, we barely know how to repair the damage that the slave traders started.

William Petersen, "Success Story: Japanese American Style," *The New York Times Magazine*, Vol. cxv, No. 39432 (January 9, 1966). © 1966 by The New York Times Company. Reprinted by permission. Professor Petersen is currently preparing a book on this subject.

No Parallel in U.S.

The history of Japanese Americans, however, challenges every such generalization about ethnic minorities, and for this reason alone deserves far more attention than it has been given. Barely more than 20 years after the end of the wartime camps, this is a minority that has risen above even prejudiced criticism. By any criterion of good citizenship that we choose, the Japanese Americans are better than any other group in our society, including native-born whites. They have established this remarkable record, moreover, by their own almost totally unaided effort. Every attempt to hamper their progress resulted only in enhancing their determination to succeed. Even in a country whose patron saint is the Horatio Alger hero, there is no parallel to this success story.

. . .

Education of Nisei

The key to success in the United States, for Japanese or anyone else, is education. Among persons aged 14 years or over in 1960, the median years of schooling completed by the Japanese were 12.2, compared with 11.1 years by Chinese, 11.0 by whites, 9.2 by Filipinos, 8.6 by Negroes and 8.4 by Indians. In the nineteen-thirties, when even members of favored ethnic groups often could find no jobs, the Nisei went to school and avidly prepared for that one chance in a thousand. One high school boy used to read his texts, underlining important passages, then read and underline again, then read and underline a third time. "I'm not smart," he would explain, "so if I am to go to college, I have to work three times as hard."

From their files, one can derive a composite picture of the Nisei who have gone through the Berkeley placement center of the University of California over the past 10 years or so. Their marks were good to excellent but, apart from outstanding individuals, this was not a group that would succeed solely because of extraordinary academic worth. The extracurricular activities they listed were prosaic—the Nisei Student Club, various fraternities, field sports, only occasionally anything even as slightly off the beaten track as jazz music.

Their dependence on the broader Japanese community was suggested in a number of ways: Students had personal references from Nisei professors in totally unrelated fields, and the part-time jobs they held (almost all had to work their way through college) were typically in plant nurseries, retail stores and other traditionally Japanese business establishments.

Their degrees were almost never in liberal arts but in business administration, optometry, engineering, or some other middle-level professions. They obviously saw their education as a means of acquiring a salable skill that could be used either in the general commercial world or, if that remained closed to Japanese, in a small personal enterprise. Asked to designate the beginning salary they wanted, the applicants generally gave either precisely the one they got in their first professional job or something under that.

Tenacity at Purpose

To sum up, these Nisei were squares. If they had any doubt about the transcendental values of American middle-class life, it did not reduce their determination to achieve at least that level of security and comfort. Their education was conducted like a military campaign against a hostile world; with intelligent planning and tenacity, they fought for certain limited positions and won them.

The victory is still limited: Japanese are now employed in most fields but not at the highest levels. In 1960, Japanese males had a much higher occupational level than whites—56 percent in white-collar jobs as compared with 42.1 percent of whites, 26.1 percent classified as professionals or technicians as compared with 12.5 percent of whites, and so on. Yet the 1959 median income of Japanese males was only $4,306, a little less than the $4,338 earned by white males.

For all types of social pathology about which there are usable data, the incidence is lower for Japanese than for any other ethnic group in the American population. It is true that the statistics are not very satisfactory, but they are generally good enough for gross comparisons. The most annoying limitation is that data are often reported only for the meaninglessly generalized category of "nonwhites."

In 1964, according to the F.B.I.'s "Uniform Crime Reports," three Japanese in the whole country were arrested for murder and three for manslaughter. Two were arrested for rape and 20 for assault. The low incidence holds also for crimes against property: 20 arrests for robbery, 192 for breaking and entering, 83 for auto theft, 251 for larceny.

Housing Conditions

So far as one can tell from the few available studies, the Japanese have been exceptional in this respect since their arrival in this country. Like most immigrant groups, Nisei generally have lived in neighborhoods characterized by overcrowding, poverty, dilapidated housing, and other "causes" of crime. In such a slum environment, even though surrounded by ethnic groups with high crime rates, they have been exceptionally law-abiding.

Prof. Harry Kitano, of UCLA, has collated the probation records of the Japanese in Los Angeles County. Adult crime rates rose there from 1920 to a peak in 1940 and then declined sharply to 1960; but throughout those 40 years the rate was consistently under that for non-Japanese. In Los Angeles today, while the general crime rate is rising, for Japanese adults it is continuing to fall.

According to California life tables for 1951–61, Japanese Americans in the state had a life expectation of 74.5 years (males) and 81.2 years (females). This is six to seven years longer than that of California whites, a relatively favored group by national standards. So far as I know, this is the first time that any population anywhere has attained an average longevity of more than 80 years.

For the Sansei—the third generation, the children of Nisei—the camp experience is either a half-forgotten childhood memory or something not quite believable that happened to their parents. They have grown up, most of them, in relatively comfortable circumstances, with the American element of their composite subculture becoming more and more dominant. As these young people adapt to the general patterns, will they also—as many of their parents fear—take over more of the faults of American society? The delinquency rate among Japanese youth today is both higher than it used to be and is rising—though it still remains lower than that of any other group.

Juvenile Delinquency

Frank Chuman, a Los Angeles lawyer, has been the counsel for close to 200 young Japanese offenders charged with everything from petty theft to murder. Some were organized into gangs of 10 to 15 members, of whom a few were sometimes Negroes or Mexicans. Nothing obvious in their background accounts for their delinquency. Typically, they lived at home with solid middle-class families in pleasant neighborhoods: their brothers and sisters were not in trouble. Yori Wada, a Nisei member of the California Youth Authority, believes that some of these young people are in revolt against the narrow confines of the Nisei subculture while being unable to accept white society. In one extreme instance, a Sansei charged with assault with the intent to commit murder was a member of the Black Muslims, seeking an identity among those extremist Negro nationalists.

In Sacramento, a number of Sansei teen-agers were arrested for shoplifting—something new in the Japanese community but, according to the police, "nothing to be alarmed at." The parents disagreed. Last spring, the head of the local JACL called a conference, at which a larger meeting was organized. Between 400 and 500 persons—a majority of the Japanese adults in the Sacramento area—came to hear the advice of such professionals as a psychiatrist and a probation officer. A permanent council was established, chaired jointly by a minister and an optometrist, to arrange for whatever services might seem appropriate when parents were themselves unable (or unwilling) to control their offspring. According to several prominent Sacramento Nisei, the publicity alone was salutary, for it brought parents back to a sense of their responsibility. In the Japanese communities of San Francisco and San Jose, there were similar responses to a smaller number of delinquent acts.

Sansei Generation

Apart from the anomalous delinquents, what is happening to typical Japanese Americans of the rising generation? A dozen members of the Japanese student club on the Berkeley campus submitted to several hours of my questioning, and later I was one of the judges in a contest for the club queen.

I found little that is newsworthy about these young people. On a campus where to be a bohemian slob is a mark of distinction, they wash themselves and dress with unostentatious neatness. They are most good students, no longer concentrated in the utilitarian subjects their fathers studied but often majoring in liberal arts. Most can speak a little Japanese, but very few can read more than a few words. Some are opposed to intermarriage, some not; but all accept the American principle that it is love between the partners that makes for a good family. Conscious of their minority status, they are seeking a means both of preserving elements of the Japanese culture and of reconciling it fully with the American one; but their effort lacks the poignant tragedy of the earlier counterpart.

Only four Sansei were among the 779 arrested in the Berkeley student riots, and they are as atypical as the Sacramento delinquents. One, the daughter of a man who 20 years ago was an officer of a Communist front, is no more a symbol of generational revolt than the more publicized Bettina Aptheker.

It was my impression that these few extremists constitute a special moral problem for many of the Sansei students. Brazenly to break the law invites retribution against the whole community, and thus is doubly wrong. But such acts, however one judges them on other grounds, also symbolize an escape from the persistent concern over "the Japanese image." Under the easygoing middle-class life, in short, there lurks still a wariness born of their parents' experience as well as a hope that they really will be able to make it in a sense that as yet has not been possible.

Immigrant History

The history of the United States, it is sometimes forgotten, is the history of the diverse groups that make up our population, and thus of their frequent discord and usual eventual cooperation. Each new nationality that arrived from Europe was typically met with such hostility as, for example, the anti-German riots in the Middle West a century ago, the American Protective Association to fight the Irish, the national-quota laws to keep out Italians, Poles and Jews. Yet, in one generation or two, each white minority took advantage of the public schools, the free labor market and America's political democracy; it climbed out of the slums, took on better-paying occupations and acquired social respect and dignity.

This is not true (or, at best, less true) of such "nonwhites" as Negroes, Indians, Mexicans, Chinese and Filipinos. The reason usually given for the difference is that color prejudice is so great in this country that a person who carries this visible stigma has little or no possibility of rising. There is obviously a good deal of truth in the theory, and the Japanese case is of general interest precisely because it constitutes the outstanding exception.

Meiji Era Emigrants

What made the Japanese Americans different? What gave them the strength to thrive on adversity? To say that it was their "national character" or "the Japanese subculture" or some paraphrase of these terms is merely to give a label to our ignorance. But it is true that we must look for the persistent pattern these terms imply, rather than for isolated factors.

The Issei who came to America were catapulted out of a homeland undergoing rapid change—Meiji Japan, which remains the one country of Asia to have achieved modernization. We can learn from such a work as Robert Bellah's "Tokugawa Religion" that diligence in work, combined with simple frugality, had an almost religious imperative, similar to what has been called "the Protestant ethic" in Western culture. And as such researchers as Prof. George DeVos at Berkeley have shown, today the Japanese in Japan and Japanese Americans respond similarly to psychological tests of "achievement orientation," and both are in sharp contrast to lower-class Americans, whether white or Negro.

The two vehicles that transmitted such values from one generation to the next, the family and religion, have been so intimately linked as to reinforce each other. By Japanese tradition, the wishes of any individual counted for far less than the good reputation of his family name, which was worshiped through his ancestors. Most Nisei attended Japanese-language schools either one hour each weekday or all Saturday morning, and of all the shushin, or maxims, that they memorized there, none was more important than: "Honor your obligations to parents and avoid bringing them shame." Some rural parents enforced such commandments by what was called the moxa treatment—a bit of incense burned on the child's skin. Later, group ridicule and ostracism, in which the peers of a naughty child or a rebellious teen-ager joined, became the usual, very effective control.

This respect for authority is strongly reinforced in the Japanese American churches, whether Buddhist or Christian. The underlying similarity among the various denominations is suggested by the fact that parents who object strongly to the marriage of their offspring to persons of other races (including, and sometimes even especially, to Chinese) are more or less indifferent to interreligious marriages within the Japanese groups. Buddhist churches have adapted to the American scene by introducing Sunday schools, Boy Scouts, a promotional effort around the theme "Our Family Attends Church Regularly," and similar practices quite alien to the old-country tradition.

On the other hand, as I was told not only by Buddhists but also by Nisei Christian ministers, Japanese Americans of whatever faith are distinguished by their greater attachment to family, their greater respect for parental and other authority. Underlying the complex religious life, that is to say, there seems to be an adaptation to American institutional forms with a considerable persistence of Buddhist moral values.

Role of Individuals

It is too easy, however, to explain after the fact what has happened to Japanese Americans. After all, the subordination of the individual to the group and the dominance of the husband-father typified the family life of most immigrants from Southern or Eastern Europe.

Indeed, sociologists have fashioned a plausible theory to explain why the rate of delinquency was usually high among these nationalities' second generation, the counterpart of the Nisei. The American-born child speaks English without an accent, the thesis goes, and is probably preparing for a better job and thus a higher status than his father's. His father, therefore, finds it difficult to retain his authority, and as the young man comes to view him with contempt or shame, he generalizes this perception into a rejection of all authority.

Not only would the theory seem to hold for Japanese Americans but, in some respects, their particular life circumstances aggravated the typical tensions. The extreme differences between American and Japanese cultures separated the generations more than in any population derived from Europe. As one Issei mother remarked to the anthropologist John Embree: "I feel like a chicken that has hatched duck's eggs."

Issei-Nisei Relations

Each artificial restriction on the Issei—that they could not become citizens, could not own land, could not represent the camp population to the administrators—meant that the Nisei had to assume adult roles early in life, while yet remaining subject to parental control that by American standards was extremely onerous. This kind of contrast between responsibility and lack of authority is always galling; by the best theories that sociologists have developed we might have expected not merely a high delinquency rate among Nisei but the highest. The best theories, in other words, do not apply.

One difficulty, I believe, is that we have accepted too readily the common sense notion that the minority whose subculture most closely approximates the general American culture is the most likely to adjust successfully. Acculturation is a bridge, and by this view the shorter the span the easier it is to cross it. But like most metaphors drawn from the physical world, this one affords only a partial truth about social reality.

The minority most thoroughly imbedded in American culture, with the least meaningful ties to an overseas fatherland, is the American Negro. As those Negro intellectuals who have visited Africa have discovered, their links to "negritude" are usually too artificial to survive a close association with this—to them, as to other Americans—strange and fascinating continent. But a Negro who knows no other homeland, who is as thoroughly American as any Daughter of the American Revolution, has no refuge when the United States rejects him. Placed at the bottom of this country's scale, he finds it difficult to salvage his ego by measuring his worth in another currency.

Barriers a Challenge

The Japanese, on the contrary, could climb over the highest barriers our racists were able to fashion in part because of their meaningful links with an alien culture. Pride in their heritage and shame for any reduction in its only partly legendary glory—these were sufficient to carry the group through its travail. And I do not believe that their effectiveness will lessen during our lifetime, in spite of the Sansei's exploratory ventures into new corners of the wider American world. The group's cohesion is maintained by its well-grounded distrust of any but that small group of whites—a few church organizations, some professors, and particularly the A.C.L.U. in California—that dared go against the conservative-liberal-radical coalition that built, or defended, America's concentration camps.

The Chinese in California, I am told, read the newspapers these days with a particular apprehension. They wonder whether it could happen here—again.

38. COMPATIBILITY OF JAPANESE AND AMERICAN MIDDLE-CLASS VALUES

HARRY H. L. KITANO

The similarities between the American and Japanese value systems have contributed to the Japanese-American "success story." Perhaps the most important aspect of this achievement of success is that it has not been necessary for the Nisei to sacrifice all the customs peculiar to his culture in order to be an American. Professor Harry Kitano of the University of California at Los Angeles explores the concept of cultural pluralism and suggests that the American "melting pot" might be stronger if each of the "ingredient" peoples were encouraged to retain the customs indigenous to their older cultures.

Caudill stresses the compatibility of Japanese and American middle-class values. For example, politeness, the respect for authority and parental wishes, duty to the community, diligence, cleanliness and neatness, emphasis on personal achievement and on long-range goals, a sense of shame concerning nonsanctioned behavior, the importance of keeping up one's appearance, and a degree of "outer-directedness" are values shared by the two cultures.

However, from our evidence it appears that the acculturation of the Japanese has not been because their culture and the American middle class are the same, but rather because of the functional compatibility and interaction between the two. The Issei have not acculturated, and

Harry H. L. Kitano, *Japanese Americans: The Evolution of a Subculture,* © 1969. Reprinted by permission of Prentice-Hall, Inc., Englewood Cliffs, New Jersey.

have retained most of the ways of the old culture. Even the Sansei retain
a certain degree of Japaneseness. However, the differences often facili-
tate rather than hinder their adjustment to American society.

For example, Iga notes that success-aspiration and obligation, both of
which the Japanese American values more highly than does the Caucasian, are ideal norms of an older Protestantism, and both values help the
group to become successful in America.[1] Some other characteristics in
which Japanese Americans are higher than Americans are conformity
and compromise. Therefore, a complex of patterns of Japanese-
American culture, wherein success-aspiration and regard for rapid socio-
economic success are coupled with deference, conformity, and compromise, may explain why the group at the present time is doing well in
America, but has not raised the hostility of the larger society.

An "Ethical" Culture

The American and Japanese cultures have different ways of viewing
norms and goals. The American appears more goal-oriented—efficiency,
output, and productivity are highly valued, and the primary object is to
win or to achieve success. The Japanese system appears much more
norm-oriented—the how, the style, and the means of interaction are
important, so that playing the game according to the rules is as important as winning it.

The norm-oriented culture may prove to be quite adaptable to external
changes (e.g., the Issei immigrant, or the behavior of the Japanese during the wartime occupation of Japan), provided that some social structure remains, because interrelationships have meaning in themselves.
How to interact with others—superiors, inferiors, and equals—can be
relatively easily transferred from one structure to another, so that such a
system may be less stressful to its members than one that is more suc-
cess-oriented in terms of goals. For when goals are blocked or are un-
reachable, or when the lack of success in terms of "output" are glaringly
apparent, the individual in such a position may be placed under very
high stress.

. . . The employer-employee relationship provides an example of the
possible difference between the two cultures. A Japanese firm will tend
to keep an inefficient employee, since Japanese norms encourage the notion of obligation; the *oyabun* (parent) and the *ko-bun* (child) relationship obtains between employer and employee, and is a goal in itself. Con-
versely, an American firm will not hesitate to fire an unproductive employee—the goals of the system are productivity, and can be summarized
in the familiar phrase, "I'm running a business, not a welfare agency."

In a similar vein, American baseball players who have played in Japan
feel that the Japanese will never be major leaguers until they develop a
greater will to win. By this the American means that Japanese pitchers
should throw at batters more often; Japanese players should slide with
spikes high, challenge umpires, and play a more aggressive game. There
is little question that if the worth of a culture is measured in terms of

[1] Iga, "Changes in Value Orientation of Japanese Americans."

efficiency and productivity, the American model is vastly superior, but one may also question the possible emotional cost of such a system to those who cannot "make it" there. However, there are indications that the modern Japanese business and economic world is rapidly moving toward the American model.

Assimilation of the American Culture

The present trend away from the Japanese culture in terms of norms, values, and personality means that in the near future there will be almost complete acculturation. For example, although Japanese and Americans have differed in the past in their collective and individualist orientations, the collectivity orientation has diminished among Sansei and at present is similar to that of Caucasian samples. Egoistic behavior and the importance of self over others has developed to such an extent that, in [one] study, on a question dealing with the family and the nation, the Sansei held a more individualistic position than did the non-Japanese American! Similarly, standards of discipline, paternalism, status distinction and other parameters of the "American" value system show that the Sansei are for all practical purposes completely acculturated. Iga states:

> Their [the Sansei] desire to be assimilated appears to be so complete and their knowledge of Japanese culture so marginal that we cannot anticipate their return to traditional Japanese cultural interests. The only factor which prevents them from complete assimilation seems to be the combination of their physical visibility, and racial prejudice on the part of dominant group members.[2]

But parts of the Japanese culture undoubtedly remain. The tea ceremony, flower arranging, ondos and other dances, sukiyaki and other Japanese dishes, have become firmly a part of the Japanese-American culture. Certain traditions are already lost. Nisei and Sansei remember fondly the public singing performances of their otherwise restrained Issei parents at festivals and picnics, but the self-conscious Nisei have not stepped in to fill the role. Some values—responsibility, concern for others, quiet dignity—will hopefully survive, but other less attractive aspects—authoritative discipline, blind obedience to ritual, extensive use of guilt and shame to shape behavior, and the submissiveness of females—will not be much regretted in their passing.

Finally, although most empirical tests indicate the similarity of the Sansei to his American peers, the groups are by no means identical. Hopefully, in a culturally pluralistic society, the Sansei will find an effective combination of Japanese and American values, a personal value system for maintaining a mature and responsible attitude toward themselves and the world.

．　　　．　　　．

2 *Ibid.*

Cultural Pluralism

This leads to a pertinent question: What has been the most significant factor in the Japanese acculturative process? The answer seems to
be the pluralistic development of a congruent Japanese culture within
the framework of the larger American society. If we may be permitted a
somewhat elaborate metaphor, this development may be envisioned as
two trees, sprung from different seeds but flourishing in the same soil, in
identical climatic conditions, the younger of them springing up by the
side of the older, so that although the two trunks, rooted in similar
values and aspirations, nourished by similar factors of education and
industry, are separate, their branches intermingle, and eventually, it
may be difficult to distinguish the leaves of one from the leaves of the
other. The organic and gradual nature of this metaphor is particularly
appropriate to cultural pluralism, yet it must be emphasized that this
mode of acculturation seems only to work when two cultures spring from
relatively similar seeds. The exotic plant of some cultures seems not to
flourish in American soil. For some groups it seems apparent that cultural pluralism hinders acculturation and assimilation simply because
the discrepancies between the cultures seem to lead to increased diver-
gence and intergroup tensions. In such cases, assimilation seems to require the dissolution of one of the cultures, and its substitution by more
"American" patterns of behavior. Such a process inevitably requires
more time, more conflict, raises critical questions of value, and creates
more difficulties for the individuals and cultures caught in the process.
Further, as we have mentioned in our opening chapter, there may be a
functional order so that the smoothest method of adaptation follows an
acculturation, integration, and assimilation sequence.

A comparison of cultural pluralism with other modes of acculturation
immediately involves one in the subtleties of possible modes of selective
cultural pluralism. For instance, a purely cultural-pluralistic development might imply, say, the retention of the native language as well as its
customs and values. Yet the Japanese have quickly and almost completely discarded the Japanese language, and artificial attempts to preserve it (e.g., Japanese language school) have largely failed. In other
dimensions, too, certain unwieldy Japanese customs were almost immediately supplanted by more efficient American ones. The potential inherent in cultural pluralism for retaining some elements of a distinctive
way of life and discarding others is one of its most attractive elements. It
is a cliché to say of America that it is a great melting pot, meaning,
presumably, that the disparate elements that comprise it are eventually
commingled in an amorphous brew labeled "the norm," and that this is
desirable. Yet, surely, the distinctive contribution of Oriental, of Mexican, of African, and many other cultures, could greatly improve the
savour of the bland American brew. The cultural-pluralistic development
of the Japanese-American group so far provides another example of
how the native and American may coexist.

Structural Pluralism

The problem of structural pluralism is a related issue. Followed to an ultimate extreme, it might describe a society with a vast number of independent groups maintained through restrictions on friendship, dating, and marriage. There is an obvious danger to the proliferation of such structures—the restriction of friendship and marriage to persons within one's own network could very well foster a strong "we" and "they" feeling, leading to less communication, more misunderstanding, more prejudiced attitudes and higher levels of discrimination.

The development of pluralistic structures for the Japanese was originally based more on necessity than choice—there was little opportunity for Japanese to enter into the social structure of the larger community. Currently, however, the matter of choice appears to be of a more voluntary nature—most Japanese can enter into the social structures of the larger society, although there is always the element of greater risk and possible rejection for those choosing this path. The continued existence of the ethnic structures, however, limits the opportunity for "risk-taking," and many Japanese who might otherwise have ventured into the larger society choose the easy way out through participation in the ethnic structures (even though these groups are as "American" as any). The comment of "being more comfortable and at ease with one's own kind" covers many situations. However, many Japanese still need the ethnic structures and the justification for the cradle-to-grave services (e.g., a Japanese doctor will be on hand at delivery; a Japanese priest will perform over the burial; and in between, one can live a life of friends, dating, and marriage primarily with other Japanese) provided by the ethnic community is important; however, the structures may be playing a negative role when their strength pulls back some who might venture into the larger society. This writer feels that social interaction based primarily on interest and achievement is healthier than one based on ethnicity.

Judged by most standards, the coexistence between the Japanese and American cultures has been successful. Education, productivity, and "Americanism" have been high, and crime, delinquency, and other forms of social deviance have been low. And if we remember that this has been accomplished by a nonwhite group, the progress appears even more remarkable.

Interestingly enough, the adaptation of the Japanese to the United States is similar to that of many European groups—what Park refers to as a natural history cycle.[3] A typical pattern of interaction between groups starts with contact, followed by competition, then by accommodation. Accommodation is usually acompanied by segregated ethnic islands, which eventually leads to the final stage of assimilation. When an observer takes a long-range historical view of the interaction between two cultures, the process as described by Park appears to have high validity. It must be added, however, that this model can function best

[3] Robert E. Park, *Race and Culture*, ed. E. C. Hughes, et al. (Glencoe, Illinois: The Free Press, 1950), pp. 138–151.

when there are equal opportunities (e.g., especially in education and employment) and where there is a willingness on the part of both cultures to accommodate to each other.

The unusual part of the Japanese adaptation is that it is being accomplished by a "nonwhite" group and a population heretofore considered to be "unassimilable." In fact, the adaptation has been of such a quality that it has been termed a "model American minority." [4]

But we must also be reminded that the judgment of Japanese Americans as the "model American minority" is made from a strictly majority point of view. Japanese Americans are good because they conform—they don't "make waves"—they work hard and are quiet and docile. As in a colonial situation, there tends to be one set of prescriptions for those in power and another for the subject people. But, ideally, members of the ethnic community should share in any evaluation of the efficacy of their adjustment. For if the goals of the American society include freeing an individual for self-expression and creativity, and if social maturity includes originality, participation, and the opportunity for individuals to function at their highest levels, then certain questions may be asked about the Japanese. It may be a disservice to some of them to continue calling them "good" and reinforcing their present adaptation. The kind of goodness that led them to accept the wartime evacuation can, in the long run, be a drawback as well as a strength. Perhaps this is one group where emphasis on the self—the development of individual self and the satisfaction of ego needs—can be more highly emphasized.

However, it would be tragic if some of the strengths of the Japanese culture were to be forgotten. The ability to look beyond self and to act in relation to others is an admirable quality, and the ethnic identity, whether in terms of a nation and manifested as pride, or in terms of a community, helped the Japanese achieve a degree of cohesion and group loyalty that appears important for a meaningful life. Without an abstraction that leads beyond self, life may regress to self-indulgence and to self-gratification so that the accumulation of wealth and power—often associated with "success"—may only be an empty victory. Hopefully, the next generation of Japanese Americans will integrate the best of the Japanese and the American cultures so that their lives will reflect the richness of both. But, at the risk of being unduly pessimistic, the probability that they may draw from the more negative elements of both of the cultures is also a realistic prospect.

We have described a group that has been effective in social organization, effective in socialization, effective in controlling deviant behavior, and effective in "becoming successful" in American terms. When we look back on the past prejudice and discrimination faced by the Japanese, we find that even their most optimistic dreams have been surpassed. Such a story may give us some optimism for the future of race relations in the American society.

[4] William Petersen, *The New York Times Magazine,* January 9, 1966.

39. NISEI, NISEI!

MARY TAKAHASHI

*That the Japanese-American has not always enjoyed economic success
and a sense of ethnic pride is evidenced by a poem written by
M. H. Constable, pseudonym for the Nisei writer Mary Takahashi.
Written in 1946, as the Nisei were being released from the internment
camps of World War II, the poem conveys the psychological
destruction of the camp inmate and the corresponding dislike of
those who allowed the tragedy of the camps to happen.*

I have no face—
This is a face,
(Nisei, Nisei!)
My face of astigmatic eyes,
Other eyes.

A composite of sneer and word,
The cherry blossom and the sword,
Where I hang as on gallows wood;
(Nisei, Nisei!)

Set in the island centuries
Of the mixed stocks Yamato breeds.
(And this is censored:
No one reads
Of our dissimilarities,
Nisei, Nisei!)

Is this so yellow?
Brown and plain
White are the skins of old Japan.

I have no face.

My sallow cheek
Is greenish in the subway light,
My parents' mild and patient eyes
Mocked in these narrow apertures;
Look, glasses make this low-built nose
The shadow of a caricature.
(Nisei, Nisei!)

Give me the eyes that form my face!
All outside eyes, all looking down,
The eyes of everyday that frown,
The starry world, the street, the job, the eating place—

All eyes I envy for their anonymity.
(Nisei, Nisei!)

Mary Takahashi, "Nisei, Nisei!" *Common Ground* (Spring 1946). Reprinted
by permission of the American Council for Nationalities Service.

This is mirage.
These are my twenty years of youth—
To look the thing I hate and what I am:
(Nisei, Nisei!)

Where is the heart to scour this enemy mask
Nailed on my flesh and artifact of my veins?
Where is a judge of the infernal poll
Where they vote round eyes honest and mine knave?

This is a dream.
These eyes, this face
(Nisei, Nisei!)
Clutched on my twitching plasm like a monstrous growth,
A twinning cyst of hair, of pulp, of teeth. . . .

Tell me this is no face,
This face of mine—
It is a face of Angloid eyes who hate.

40. MELTING-POT CONCEPT REJECTED BY SOME JAPANESE AMERICANS

DAN L. THRAPP

Some people feel that "cultural pluralism" is a concept that has not been fully realized. In spite of the Oriental-American's apparent success, there is a growing sentiment that the relationship between the white and Oriental communities is not based on equality. In the article that follows, the Religion Editor of the Los Angeles Times *explores the reluctance of the Japanese-American to be completely dominated by the prevailing white society.*

The hallowed American ideal seeing this nation as a vast melting pot of peoples and races has not been realized and may not even be desirable, in the view of one American who admits to being only semi-assimilated.

The Rev. Roy I. Sano concedes that in tackling this almost sacrosanct goal, minorities who desire to remain minorities may be seeking trouble.

But it is a fact of life, he said.

Domination Feared

The reason, basically, for the opposition of certain ethnic minorities to becoming homogenized into the American body is that "this means Anglo-Saxon domination" and little more.

Mr. Sano is a Methodist minister, associate pastor of Centenary

Dan L. Thrapp, " 'Melting Pot' Concept Resisted by Some Ethnic Groups in America if 'This Means Anglo-Saxon Domination,' " *Los Angeles Times* (December 1, 1968). Copyright, 1969, by the *Los Angeles Times*. Reprinted by permission.

Church, a Japanese American congregation. He is a second generation American of Japanese ancestry.

"I recognize that the Japanese, for example, are not likely to preserve their unique cultural traits, because they can quickly become acculturated," he said. "It is really more a matter of continuing with their own kind.

"Some of us are beginning to feel uncomfortable in a structure dominated by Caucasians. We have the same language as they, our interests are almost identical, yet we know that on some points we are not allowing that part to come out where we do differ.

True Acceptance

"I know this mostly through the church, where there is real effort and concern to make it work. However, the ability to truly 'accept' somebody really different, is the part I am trying to work out."

Many Caucasians, he said, are attracted to the Japanese, for example, "because they are quaint, or exotic—different in that sense of the word."

"But the kind of differences I am trying to raise are those differences we know are not attractive to the hierarchy dominated by Caucasian leadership. If it could accept them, we would be comfortable."

Mr. Sano spoke not only for the Japanese Americans, but for the multitude of other races and ethnic groups—Indian, black, Asian and others —that make up the American society.

He explained that "we may want to be like Caucasians, but we may not want to join them in marriage, for example, or we may prefer to remain with our own kind in religion.

"This disturbs the Protestant leadership, which holds ecumenism to be an ideal. It says that here comes a group of ethnic minorities, who desire to be like Caucasians in some ways, but who reserve the right to decide who are to be their ministers and how their ministries ought to move.

"It is at this point that I sense a letdown in most Protestant gatherings. It is this 'vague universalism of Protestant theology' that is really bugging us.

"This is because what it truly means is to become Anglo-Saxon, and we cannot do that."

Mr. Sano denied that the sense of what he was saying amounted to racial "arrogance," but rather to racial "pride."

"This is what black theology is trying to establish," he said.

"I have heard black leaders say that they must first create a sense of being a people among blacks, then talk of becoming Christian.

"People must belong to some social entity, or some union, or some other corporate structure first. Protestant theology tends to ignore this basic need; at any talk of 'race' it becomes edgy and uneasy. I notice this when talking of Japanese 'community.' I am sure it is also true in the case of other ethnic groups."

Yet Mr. Sano does not believe that this should lead to a fracturing of society or separatism, but rather a stronger, more viable whole because the various elements can work together, each with pride in his own heritage and culture and people.

He said that "the relationship between the Caucasian and the Japanese American has become a relationship between an inflated ego and a bloated head."

The Caucasian, he said, has the inflated ego; the Japanese American, and perhaps some ethnic groups, the bloated head.

Both characteristics are the result of superficialities, he said—the ego because of a lack of interest in, or understanding of the basic worth of other cultures, and the bloated head because of false pride in casual compliments.

Surface Aspect

He noted the superficial acceptance of Japanese Americans in American society.

"But this acceptance needs to be tested," he said.

"There are reasons to believe that it is superficial, and that their place in the larger community is still precarious."

Much of the "acceptance," he believes, might be because of Japanese eagerness to appear "like" Americans, and to fit in, and not because of the Japanese character or basic culture or nature.

"It becomes important to allow their full selfhood to come out and if, then, the Japanese American still is accepted, then we can truly say we are secure members of the community."

When an ethnic minister joins the larger church, he added, "we are called to end the fundamental feature of our ethnic make-up and join the existing structure.

"The assumption is that ethnic communities are going to disappear. In point of fact, however, these communities are persisting in American life. Despite acculturation, there is a serious resistance to assimilation."

The Caucasian, seeing the apparent disappearance of ethnic minorities at times, fails to see the ethnic person persisting still as the "invisible man" of society.

"The persistence of ethnic communities troubles Caucasians," he said. "But why should it?"

He predicted that "joining the American people might really mean forming power blocs of interest groups based largely on ethnic and color lines and having these power blocs participate in policy-making decisions which affect them.

"This is a serious, but noteworthy, departure from the melting pot notion.

"Since these ethnic communities are so persistent, the strategy of the Christian church should include structural manifestations recognizing them.

"It requires specialized structures to serve the peculiar realities of this generation. The unexpected persistence of ethnic associations calls for re-evaluation of our strategies and structures."

41. THE CHINESE FAMILY TRANSPLANTED

BETTY LEE SUNG

The Chinese are another group that has demonstrated its ability to adapt to American society. Not only have many Chinese achieved great financial success, but their adaptation to American social norms has been widely acclaimed. As acculturation continues, however, there are signs that this distinguished record of accomplishment is changing and that increasing numbers of young Chinese Americans, like their Anglo counterparts, are rebelling against the values of their elders.

Each year, while more than a million youths find their way into trouble with the law, American authorities, school officials, parents, law-enforcement agencies, and scientists have noted the conspicuous absence of Chinese children among the offenders. A municipal judge of New York City wrote to *The New York Times* to say that not in seventeen years on the bench had a Chinese teen-ager been brought before him on delinquency charges. The judge queried his colleagues and found that they, too, had never seen a Chinese teen-ager hailed before their court on any charges of depredation, narcotics, speeding, burglary, vandalism, stick-up, purse-snatching, or mugging.

Astonished by their own discovery, they checked with Chicago and San Francisco, where the judges confirmed their findings.[1] In further substantiation of the low incidence of juvenile delinquency among Chinese children, the Juvenile Aid Bureau of New York City reports that in 17,000 cases handled by the Bureau, only 12 involved Chinese, and these were for minor infractions such as marking a wall with chalk.[2]

In two school districts of Portland, Ore., and Seattle, Wash., where 71 to 90 percent of the students were Chinese, the rate of juvenile delinquency was markedly below that of adjacent areas.[3] A study undertaken by the California State Department of Correction revealed that out of 1,600 youth under custody, only one was Chinese-American.[4]

This commendable record brought praise by Congressman Arthur Klein of New York who read it into the *Congressional* Record on July 29, 1955.

Why do the Chinese children not succumb to the same evil influences

[1] "Why No Chinese-American Delinquents?" *Saturday Evening Post* (April 30, 1955), p. 12.

[2] [Milton L. Barnett, "Alcohol and Culture: A Study of Drinking in a Chinese-American Community," Ph.D. dissertation, Cornell, 1953], p. 215.

[3] [Norman Haynor and Charles Reynold, "Chinese Family Life in America," *American Sociological Review*, 2 (October 1937)], p. 636.

[4] Alvin Rudoff, "A Study by the California State Dept. of Correction," Sacramento, California.

that tempt their schoolmates and playmates? Why are they not affected by the same environmental forces that lead American youth astray? What factors in the Chinese upbringing enable parents to nurture their children into upright, law-abiding youths?

In probing into the backgrounds of Chinese children, social scientists found that the more common causes of anti-social behavior do not apply. Chinese children have more than their share of crowded, antiquated living quarters in Chinatown or in the cheaper rental areas of large cities. As a visible minority group they suffer economic and social discrimination. As marginal individuals, they straddle the fence between two cultures with resulting personal and cultural conflicts. With the majority of Chinese, the family income is never sufficient to cover the increasing needs of large broods. In families that were mutilated, the mothers and sisters lived in China while the fathers were both parents to the sons.

.   .   .

Although a large share of the credit for the low incidence of juvenile delinquency among the Chinese may be attributed to the family within the context of the old Chinese culture—the Chinese child learning early to respect authority and operate within the acceptable standards of society—there are other contributing factors. Until the recent liberalization of the immigration laws, there were few Chinese families and consequently few Chinese youths. As was pointed out in an earlier chapter, the Chinese kept to themselves and lived under their own code of rules and regulations. Any deviant behavior was handled within the community by the family elders, and the parents were called to task if the children got into trouble. A silver-haired lady who had already passed the half-century mark in age made this point doubly clear when she explained, "Even if I, at my age, did something wrong and got in the courts, Chinese people would be asking, 'Whose daughter is she?' "

The children were always kept busy. About a fourth of the children in the vicinity of New York's Chinatown attend Chinese school following American school from 5 to 7 P.M. daily. Homework and chores leave little time for mischief-making. Another cultural heritage—the Chinese love of learning and respect for scholarship—causes the parents to spur their children on to higher academic achievement. Therefore children have to work harder at their studies.

The Chinese go to great lengths to keep their "dirty linen" within the family walls. They regard it as a serious loss of face when the parents cannot keep an offspring in line or if a family quarrel becomes publicly known. Aunts and uncles, brothers and sisters, cousins and even distant kin exert great pressure upon the party or parties to adjust their differences or mend their ways. Even when trouble in a family is common knowledge throughout the Chinese community, there is a great deal of reluctance to reveal it to outsiders.

In recent years, however, evidence of creeping pre-juvenile delinquency behavior has become apparent. At the first, the Chinese dismissed the incidences and refused to believe their ears. "Impossible," they said. "Not our children." If they were concerned, they went home and tried to keep a tighter rein on their offspring by more stringent rules and sterner punishment, but somehow, these methods were not as effective as they used to be.

Increasing reports appeared in the Chinese press about unruly boys, truants, vandals, and gang fights in the Chinatowns of Honolulu, San Francisco, and New York. At teen-age dances the boys come in groups, dressed in tight levis, sporting Beatle hairdos, and toting their own beer supply. The skirts of their chicks are halfway up their thighs. It is hard to believe that these are Chinese boys and girls although they are no different from American boys and girls their own age.

.   .   .

The shades of opinion as to whether the Chinese youth will undergo the same demoralizing process as other minority groups on their path to acculturation varies, depending upon whom you speak to. There is consensus, however, that the authoritarian control which the family once exerted over the children has slackened. The garment, the costume-jewelry, the food-packing industries that have sprung up around Chinatowns are taking more and more women out of the homes, and the mother had always been the central figure in the discipline and character molding of the Chinese children.

"It is those Hong Kong teen-agers who have come over here and spoiled our good name," assert the native-born Chinese-Americans. They are the trouble makers. They think they are better than we are and refuse to accept jobs in the restaurants, laundries, and groceries. They are not used to work because their families just cashed the remittance checks sent to Hong Kong by the fathers. They have been living in a polyglot city like Hong Kong, which is not Chinese and not Western.

"They don't do well here in school because they have difficulty with the language, and they can't get decent jobs for the same reason and because of their stuck-up attitudes. They just hang around Chinatown and idle their time away."

.   .   .

On the other hand, the China-borns blame the native-borns for the disintegration of family discipline. The native-borns are accused of challenging the authority of their elders, of not learning how to speak Chinese, and of being devoid of Chinese culture. The contention is that native-borns are responsible for most of the trouble. A study by Rose Hum Lee, late professor and head of the Department of Sociology at Roosevelt College, titled "Delinquent, Neglected and Dependent Children of the San Francisco Bay Region" and published in the *Journal of Social Psychology* of August 1952, seems to corroborate this.

From information supplied by the Juvenile Court of San Francisco, Professor Lee found that of 170 delinquency charges against children of Chinese ancestry between 1943 and 1949, 145 were committed by native-born males and 18 by native-born females. In comparison, only 5 foreign-born males and 2 foreign-born females had police records against them.

However, the figures for this period pre-date and preclude to a large extent the huge influx of teen-agers who immigrated to this country after 1946. Moreover, delinquent behavior was no cause for consternation prior to 1960.

Professor Lee's study revealed that most of these cases resulted from: (1) cultural conflict between parents of foreign or mixed nativity and children of American birth; (2) the fact the most of these children came from broken homes; and (3) the longings of these children for self-expression. The children themselves provided illuminating insight toward a solution to their problems. They confessed that they did not know where to seek guidance, counsel, or sympathetic understanding when they thought their parents had failed them.

My own thoughts are that it is not the nativity but the individual background of the person or family involved. The fact remains that the Chinese family in the United States has undergone modification to reflect, for better or worse, the conditions in this country. In the process, some disorganization is inevitable.

In its new form, the family has shrunk in size. The extended kinship family is rare. Family stability has been shaken up by the peculiar situations created by the reunion of mutilated families and the mass importation of brides. Husband-and-wife relationships have been altered by the freedom and higher status accorded women. Parental authority, once absolute, has been undermined by comparison with more permissive attitudes in American families. Symptoms of the younger generation's protests are showing up in anti-social behavior.

Considering that the Chinese family has been battered by wave after wave of new ideas, the shock of physical transplantation from one continent to another, the process of integration into American life, the learning of a new language, and the acceptance of different roles by the members, it has survived the storm well.

42. DISCONTENT OF ORIENTAL YOUTH REVEALED

KUO-YI PAO, HENRY H. Y. TIEE, AND
GEORGE C. WANG

*There is growing evidence that the Oriental-American is not as
thoroughly ensconced in the security of the middle-class way of life
as is commonly supposed. In an article written for the* Los Angeles
Times, *three Chinese professors from Southern California universities
point out that the old structures of the home and the family are now
being eroded rapidly by the new forces of technology and
urbanization. They warn that even in the Oriental-American
community an extremely explosive situation is developing.*

Those of us who are genuinely concerned with the recent social disturbance and are increasingly alarmed by the ever-mounting racial tension
heartily agree with Dr. Theodore H. C. Chen (Topical Comment, June
8) that the plight of the Oriental-Americans demands imminent attention.

Dr. Chen vividly portrayed the awkward position of this ethnic community in the current struggle between the white majority and the black
minority for social justice and racial equality. It is indeed strange that
the *de facto* Chinese- and Japanese-American minority are *de jure* classified as non-minority; therefore, they are not entitled to share some of the
fruit borne out of the cataclysmic social movement. Nor have they been
accepted by the black minority as their "soul brethren" because neither
the Chinese nor the Japanese did join the blood baptism of racial upheaval. What then is their social identity?

No wonder there are increasing signs of restlessness in the Oriental
youth. As faculty members of UCLA and USC who are in a position to
observe the youth's movement, we have the obligation to call attention to
the fact that behind the facade of a seemingly peaceful and orderly Oriental community, there is a seething powder keg which may blow up one
day if the factors that build up the heat are not removed.

The ethnic community which once was held solidly together by family
ties and which once throve on individual frugality and industriousness
has been eroded by the ruthless advance of urbanization and social insti-
tutionalization.

Today, the Oriental ethnic community is plagued by the same social
malady of unemployment, juvenile delinquency, and poverty as those
that bugged their white and black brethren. Despite these troubles, the
adults of the ethnic community so far obstinately refuse to turn to the
government for help or to stand up to fight for their rights.

It is true that to a certain extent they have themselves to blame because if they do not voice their grievances no one will be aware of the

Kuo-yi Pao, Henry H. Y. Tiee, and George C. Wang, "The Oriental-American,"
Los Angeles Times (July 19, 1969). Reprinted by permission.

social injustice which they have been suffering. Furthermore, if they do not stand up and fight for reform, no one is going to fight for them.

However, we do not believe the old saying: "The squeaking wheel gets the grease." We believe in social conscience, justice, and fair play. In our society in which the majority are well educated and understand the causes of the racial crisis, the present plight of the Oriental-Americans can and will be alleviated, provided that both the white majority and the ethnic minority are willing to do something about it.

The Chinese- and Japanese-Americans should realize that in a modern society although individual efforts and family ties are still virtues, these virtues are not substitutes for social action.

In a democratic society in which there is no blue blood, no one shall hold any prerogative; but in a society where there is still racial discrimination, every one should be ready to defend his rights. Muteness and inaction will only invite contempt and dismay.

In our opinion, the solution lies in the cooperation of the liberal white and the moderate minorities.

43. SHADOWS IN THE ORIENTAL "CRYSTAL BALL"?

JEFFREY MATSUI

The feeling that all is not well in the Oriental-American community is mirrored by the disconcerting remarks of a columnist for the Japanese-American newspaper Pacific Citizen. *Jeffrey Matsui cautions his Nisei friends against assuming that their acculturation into American society is complete. The writer asserts that economic and political factors could alter the Oriental-American's position in the United States in the future as they have in the past.*

A few evenings ago I may have gotten a couple of Nisei upset by suggesting that our future may not be too bright, not too comfortable or secure.

Our discussion began when the two Nisei started wondering out loud about what the country was coming to—with all those punks, anarchists and communists allowed to run around loose to destroy the American way of life. They appeared to be a bit too "objective" and smug to my liking so I very matter of factly said, "Being a minority person, the actions of the left doesn't bother me. That's the worry of the majority community. What scares me is the super Americans of the right who are always looking for excuses to get at the 'foreigners.' "

After looking at me kinda funny, at first, they recovered and tried to save me by explaining in a sorta condescending way that we're all just plain Americans and there's no other kind, thanks to the 442 and our own personal sacrifices, etc.

Naturally, I didn't quite agree and told them that the "just plain Amer-

Jeffrey Matsui, "Today's Protest," *Pacific Citizen* (January 31, 1969). Reprinted by permission.

icans" thing ain't so yet but this is what much of the unrest of which the Nisei is critical of is all about—to make it so. This is why it's so important that the Nisei keep informed of what today's protest and dissent is all about—because it's about him, his family and future.

From there it's my regular harangue, which could be considered a more dignified "confrontation" if I were a bit more sober. Its purpose is to "shake up" the unshakeable Nisei. So you tell them not to worry about America's problem with the Black minority because it would have to be at least reconciled within 10 years so that a concerted effort can be made against Americans of Oriental ancestry.

"Why would Americans be made to hate Orientals again[?]" is asked. And why not? In the past, the white majority and their minority cohorts of the time have been made to hate any group at the will of the establishment institutions.

We've hated Indians, Chinese, Japanese, Mexicans, Blacks, Chileans and what have you. And nothing has really changed in this area because the hypocrisy in the application of our system has been allowed to live on under the guise of tradition.

Imagine 10 years from now how threatening China will look and what will the America-Japan relations be like after another decade of competition for business markets. And so Americans will be "told" to hate Asia.

But it may not be easy to hate anything so far away and impersonal. It's not enough to put a rock in the hands of the average man on the street, you've got to give him something to throw it at—something with which he can identify Asia and the hated Oriental.

Enter American of Oriental ancestry. But, of course, something must be done with your previous image of being the "good" minority. And so we'll also have to go through the painful and slow operation of having our image changed.

Both Nisei argued loudly that this would never happen and I was at first hopeful that they would be able to convince me with new thought that I was wrong. But as it turned out, the Nisei seem to think about it more until at the end they seemed to be thinking "Why not?" "Why couldn't it happen?"

In any event it's hoped that at least these two Nisei will listen closer to what many of these "crazy" youths of today are fighting for. The struggle may well be for him and his children.

Chapter 9

Law and Order

A popular theme in recent political campaigns has been the cry for "law and order." Against the backdrop of the general increase in crime and violence in the cities and on the campuses, the white middle-class majority in California, as across the nation, has given a resounding mandate to candidates who demanded that the law be upheld and lawlessness of whatever kind curbed. To these citizens from suburbia, law is seen as a means of protection and security.

From the viewpoint of some minorities and youth, however, the slogan "law and order" frequently has another connotation. To many ghetto dwellers, especially, the law is a symbol of the power of the white majority, who too often seem insensitive to the needs of others. Radical students see the law as a tool of the existing society. Although the government establishment has promised much, in accordance with the official American creed of opportunity and equality, many people of the minorities regard these promises as unfulfilled. Pronouncements of hope from government leaders have contributed to an attitude of disappointment that occasionally leads to anger, distrust, and general alienation of the minorities and youth from the mainstream of society.

This misunderstanding that has developed among the ghetto, the campus, and suburbia is reflected in the relations that exist between the police—the official arm of the law—and those who experience the most frequent contact with the law. Excesses are undoubtedly committed on both sides, but minority spokesmen

213

are especially vocal in the charge of "police brutality." Lack of
adequate police training and an inadequate community relations
program might help to explain this alienation, insofar as it
exists. Yet militants claim that repression by the "power structure" can only be alleviated when their people have the power
to control their own lives and communities. Thus, they feel that
they must have a greater voice in their local government, including the responsibility for law enforcement.

Another aspect of the law that is seen by some minority group
members and students as a threat rather than as an assurance
of justice and protection for them is the application of the law
in the courts. They feel that the mere fact of the defendant's being a member of a minority can affect the court's view of him,
causing a miscarriage of justice. Their indictment is even more
damning when they ask what advances have been made toward
the realization of justice. They point to the basic statements of
the American creed—the Declaration of Independence; the Pre-
amble to the Constitution; the Thirteenth, Fourteenth, and Fif-
teenth Amendments; recent decisions of the Supreme Court; and
official reports like those of the McCone and Kerner Commissions
—and ask for evidence of progress.

Some experts suggest that the condition of minorities in California is not appreciably improving and that unless law is accompanied by justice, the concepts of law and order will become
increasingly meaningless to those minorities who suffer from
deprivation. Certainly the statements of young dissidents reflect
this negative attitude toward law enforcement. And with justice,
to many people, not apparent, the alienation gap continues to
widen. Indeed, as a result of the reporting of communications
media and the rhetoric of minority leaders who broadcast their
versions of what they see as miscarriages of justice, the gap
may widen to become a chasm.

There are indications that the call for "law and order" may remain paramount in the minds of the majority in California for
some time. Can the reader suggest reasons why this might be
true? From the selections that follow in this chapter, these questions might also be considered: Are some people "more equal"
under the law than others? What steps must be taken to create
better community-police relations? How relevant is the issue of
"law and order" elsewhere in the United States?

44. THE POLICE

PAUL JACOBS

Part of the "systemic" violence purportedly practiced against the inhabitants of the urban ghettos and barrios *are the attitudes and actions of the police assigned to these areas. Paul Jacobs, radical writer and unsuccessful Peace and Freedom party candidate for the Senate in 1968, comments on this problem in his book* Prelude to Riot: A View of Urban America from the Bottom.

So it is that the very sight of the police car rounding a corner in a Negro or Mexican-American ghetto and cruising slowly down the street is enough to scatter the gang of kids standing in front of a house. Fear sweat-staining their shirts, the nervous police officers drive down the street, already convinced that those "studs" are up to no good; they show their distrust and suspicion by the very way in which they look the teenagers over: every Negro and Mexican-American kid has learned to see himself as something evil reflected in the cold, distrustful police stare, the blank look behind which lurks the policeman's knowledge that he is Authority, equipped by the state with the legal power to interrogate, arrest, and, if necessary, shoot to kill.

"They can stay away from me forever," says the young Mexican-American neighborhood aide in one of the anti-poverty projects in Los Angeles. "They look at you like you're dirt if you're a Mexican, and if they don't like the way you look back, they can arrest you. I saw it once on my own street, when a kid wearing boots and gloves, a sharp kid, was walking down the street and got stopped by the cops. He started to argue with them that they didn't have a right to stop him, and the one cop just got out of the car and hit the kid right in the gut with his fist."

"I guess maybe I hate the cops for what they did to me," says another Mexican-American youth. "When the cops come out of their academy and get assigned to a barrio, everybody tells them, 'Man, it's rough out there. Those Mexicans'll give you a bad time. Don't let them put anything over on you.' So if you're walking down the street the first night the cop is on duty in a barrio, it's just too bad for you, because you can get arrested for nothing. Maybe he's going to make you stand and look right into his badge and if you just lift your eyes, it's into the jail. Once you're inside, they put you right in a cell and they book you. The two police make up their report and they can put down anything. You go before the judge and he reads the report, all the time holding his hand on his chin, and you think to yourself, What did I do?, and then the judge says, 'Oh, you're a cop beater, huh? You resist arrest, huh? Hundred-and-fifty-dollar fine or twenty-five days.' If you haven't got the money, it's boom, into the jail. In the old days, it was even worse. What the police did then was to wear gloves and work you over so they wouldn't leave any marks on you."

"The old days" were those immediately before and during World War II, when the Negro community of Los Angeles was quite small and the predominant minority group was the Mexican-American community, against whom the police leveled the same kind of charges that they make today against the Negroes. (In June 1943 a Citizen's Committee appointed by Governor Earl Warren to investigate the so-called zoot-suit riots in Los Angeles found, among other things, that "most of the persons mistreated during the recent incidents in Los Angeles were either persons of Mexican descent or Negroes," and asserted that "Mass arrests, drag-net raids and other wholesale classifications of groups of people are based on false premises and tend merely to aggravate the situation." And in view of the committee's 1943 recommendation that "Law enforcement agencies should provide special training for officers dealing with minority groups," the still slight instruction in race relations being given twenty-four years later has a special note of bitter irony.)

It is true that there is much less physical brutality now than in the pre-Parker times when, according to one official, the walls of the interrogation room were sometimes spattered with blood; but in its place there have developed patterns of both psychological and non-verbal brutality very often not understood by the police themselves. When these two types of mistreatment are linked with the occasional real case of physical violence, a body of support begins to grow for the charge of "police brutality."

Judging the physical behavior of the police is difficult in any situation, and especially in the highly charged ones in which racial prejudice is involved. What the police officer learns in the academy about the use of force he must quickly unlearn in his work. Initially he may be no more disposed toward violence and brutality than is the community of which he is a part. But the potentially dangerous nature of his mission, *i.e.*, the repression of crime through the apprehension of criminals, the way in which he views this mission as more important than the preservation of individual liberties, and the skewed view he gets of the world from seeing it primarily in terms of relative rates of criminal activity, all combine to justify the police officer's use of violence. And since he is assumed, because of the character of his work, to be defending society against antisocial types, his use of violence has been sanctioned.

In recent years more and more limitations have been placed upon the police by the courts, and the characteristic police response has been to attack the courts. But the change in the nature of the law has also affected the way in which the police now do their work. As one high police official describes the problem, "Until recently if an officer saw a car that seemed suspicious, he could stop it on the pretext of making some kind of a check for a possible traffic violation. Then, if he could detect visually that there were guns or stolen merchandise inside the car, he could make a search and arrest. But the courts started throwing out these arrests because no traffic citations had been issued, which the courts took to mean that the original stopping of the car had no basis in fact. So now, if an officer sees a car that seems suspicious, he stops it and finds some reason to give it a citation. Then he can make his visual check without worrying that if he makes an arrest it won't stand up in court. But of course lots of times there isn't anything wrong and so somebody has gotten an unnecessary citation."

In some situations, a conflict exists between the legal and moral sanctions on the police. Is a police officer who kicks down a door to get at a suspected narcotics peddler carrying out his duty zealously or is he violating the rights of a private citizen? What is the measure of how much physical force a police officer should use in making an arrest? Many police officers bristle even at the question and have their usual simple answer about those who raise it: "An old tactic . . . an old Communist tactic," says a police lieutenant in a division accused of condoning brutality.

A Negro social worker described a typical incident involving the use of force after she called the police to a settlement house when she found a teen-ager sniffing glue: "As soon as the police-came into the settlement house and the boy realized he was going to be arrested, he got very frightened. I asked the officers not to be rough with him. They told him they were arresting him and he should come with them. But he just stood there and looked at them. Then one of them jumped over and put a headlock on him so that the boy started choking. He began to kick, so they threw him down on the ground and put handcuffs on him. All the other kids started crying as they saw what was happening, and one little nine-year-old threatened us with 'We're going to start a Watts riot.' I think the police should have handled it better. They could have done something besides choke the boy, who was really badly bruised. Maybe they were new, because they seemed inexperienced. I guess they were frightened, too."

Such stories of physical violence are repeated again and again, so that they have become part of the folklore among most minority groups. "My boy was picked up one day by the police in the schoolyard," says a Negro lady who lives in a housing project. "The police says he looked suspicious. They pushed a shotgun at him and said, 'Nigger, hit the ground. I give you one second to hit the ground and then you're a dead nigger.' My son said to them, 'I hate your guts,' and they hit him in his sex organ."

Is her story true or false? There's no doubt that her son was arrested, and it's entirely possible that the police did push a shotgun at him, for that's not an uncommon way of handling what the police believe to be dangerous situations. Did the officers call him a nigger and threaten to shoot him? Maybe. Did the boy say "I hate your guts"? Perhaps he did, and perhaps he may have added "you white motherfucker" to it, but not even that is enough to justify the use of physical violence by the police. Yet despite the dangerous potential of the use of violence in racial situations, despite the basic violation of individual dignity inherent in the unnecessary use of violence, and despite the fact that the use of unnecessary violence breaks down the society's commitment to principles of law, the police in America have generally been exempted from either moral sanctions or legal punishment when they do use violence, including unnecessary killing . . .

45. POLICE-MINORITY RELATIONS IN THE SAN FRANCISCO BAY AREA

One effort to improve police-minority relations was a 1964 California government report that studied this issue from all sides. The selection that follows focuses on the San Francisco Bay Area, explaining the differing points of view held by the police and the Negro community.

Introduction

The Bay Area comprises nine counties clustered around San Francisco Bay. Its total population is second in the State only to that of Los Angeles. The 1960 Census enumeration showed a total population in the nine counties of 3,638,939. Of this, 244,411 were Negroes and an additional 123,555 were of other non-Caucasian races. (This does not include Spanish-speaking Caucasians.) Over 238,000 of the Negroes, however, resided in the San Francisco–Oakland Metropolitan Area. There were 83,000 Negroes living in Oakland, nearly 21,000 in Berkeley, over 14,000 in Richmond, nearly 75,000 in San Francisco, and over 10,000 in San Mateo County. The only sizeable concentration of Negroes outside this Metropolitan Area was in Vallejo.

The foregoing statistics show that the Bay Area's Negro population is concentrated in a relatively small, but densely populated area. And, within this area, as in other cities of the North and West, an extremely high percentage of Negroes live in racially homogeneous neighborhoods.

Negro population growth in the past ten to fifteen years has been as phenomenal as in Los Angeles. In 1940 in Oakland, for instance, there were 8,462 Negroes, or some 2.8 percent of the population. In 1960, there were over 83,000 or 22.8 percent of the population. Similar growths were experienced in San Francisco, Berkeley, Richmond, and Vallejo. Many of the newcomers are from the southern part of the United States.

The Committee's reception by officials both in Oakland and San Francisco was gracious in contrast to its experience in Los Angeles. Mayor John Houlihan of Oakland and Mayor George Christopher of San Francisco appeared in person to welcome the Committee. Both presented statements relevant to police-minority group relationships. All of the police and other city officials who appeared seemed to be seeking solutions to a very difficult problem and were anything but hostile and suspicious of "outside" interference. In large part, their attitudes were echoed by Negro spokesmen who appeared before the Committee. Although, as will appear, there were disagreements between the police and Negro leadership, the overall mood was one of trust and cooperative pursuit of solu-

California Advisory Committee to the United States Commission on Civil Rights, *Report on California: Police-Minority Relations*, August 1963, pp. 20–24. Reprinted by permission.

tions. This led to an openness lacking in Los Angeles, and permitted the Committee to come to grips with many of the underlying problems.

The Problem

As Seen by Negro Leaders

Six persons representing Bay Area Negro leadership groups (among them the NAACP, CORE, and the Urban League) appeared before the Committee. They stressed the following points:

Many Negroes in the area dislike and distrust the police, whom they view as the tangible symbol of white authority. These Negroes feel isolated from the community at large. For them this leads to feelings of noninvolvement and the expectation of unfair treatment from police officers. Children are imbued with a "ghetto" attitude. They reject community group values of order. They are told by Negro adults (from Southern States and elsewhere) to expect unequal treatment and they consequently view any police action directed against them as discriminatory. Many Negroes see police saturation of their neighborhoods as a product of bias. These people interpret such police action as harassment rather than the maintenance of security.

According to these spokesmen, on numerous occasions police officers treat Negroes belligerently. All agreed that the belligerence was normally oral—uncivil language, profanity, the use of epithets such as "boy" when referring to a Negro adult. The use of physical force is relatively rare. When this does occur, it is usually at arrest and in response to resistance. This resistance is often the product of police insensitivity, such as name-calling or threats of intimidation. Police often do not understand the dynamics of the Negro community and hence act in a way which stimulates resistance. The fault, however, is not all on one side. Many Negroes fail to see the policeman's side, the difficulty he has in coming into a hostile area to effect an arrest. Moreover, many Negroes resist arrest forcibly when they should go quietly once it is apparent that the arrest is going to take place. Additionally, many complaints leveled by Negroes charging physical violence are untrue; nevertheless, these charges are believed by the Negro community.

Police are charged with some outright discrimination. One is the use of dogs in San Francisco. Dogs were recently introduced, mainly to aid police in quelling potential mass disorders. Negro spokesmen see this as directed against Negroes—or at least Negro "types" of crime. One spokesman charged that the dogs were introduced only to intimidate the large number of southern Negroes who recently have come to San Francisco. Others stressed Negro fears of physical harm from the dogs, their symbolic quality in view of their historical use against Negroes in the South, and their alleged use only in the Negro communities. A second charge, made against the Oakland police, is that Negroes are arrested for prostitution and gambling while whites are not. (The speaker agreed with a Committee member's observation that this was due in part to the fact that more white prostitutes than Negro operate clandestinely and that gambling by whites occurs most frequently in private places where detection is difficult.) A third charge was that police in both cities harass interracial couples and treat Negro juveniles more harshly than their white counterparts.

Interestingly, intermixed with the charges were statements of praise for the departments involved. The Oakland head of the NAACP, for instance, while stressing the continuing need for communications and understanding, said in response to a question concerning rapport between the Department and the NAACP: "I have the feeling that as a total police organization the Oakland Police Department is head and shoulders above any other law enforcement agency in Northern California. This is not to say that they are perfect, or that they have even begun to approach their responsibility. They have within their department many individuals who make these types of oppressive actions. But, at the same time, they also are enjoying an influx of new personnel . . . and the people within the Department are taking more of a professional attitude towards their responsibilities to the community." Similarly, the NAACP representative in San Francisco praised recent police efforts in community relations and indicated trust in the Chief of Police's investigations of citizen complaints.

As Seen by the Police

Six police officials from Oakland, San Francisco, Berkeley, Richmond, San Mateo County, and Menlo Park appeared before the Committee. They all agreed that police-minority group relationships are extremely important to sound law enforcement. They saw the problems as follows:

Four of the officials stressed the high incidence of assaultive crimes in Negro neighborhoods. Each of them, however, showed a sophisticated awareness that the problem was mainly one of socio-economic status, isolation, and general Negro-white relationships. All officials realized that higher concentration of police in Negro neighborhoods is taken as evidence of unequal treatment. But, in the words of the Berkeley Chief, they find themselves on the horns of a dilemma for they must concentrate police in these neighborhoods to maintain law and order—to give all parts of their cities equal law enforcement. Moreover, in their view, the large majority of Negro citizens are law abiding and many of them (for instance in Berkeley) demand additional officers to keep the peace. Interestingly, nearly all of the officials estimated that a relatively small number of Negro repeaters are responsible for the bulk of crimes committed by Negroes. This shows, of course, that a high percentage of the Negro community is law abiding.

Most of the police officials agreed that they are forced to deal with outspoken attitudes of hostility among many Negroes. They see this as a central problem of law enforcement. It affects actual arrests (recently mobs have gathered around officers attempting to arrest Negro suspects). It means also that often the police are afforded no cooperation in enforcing the law. Every officer in attendance stressed that sophisticated community relations programs are necessary to ameliorate this hostility.

Chief Cahill of San Francisco stressed especially that police must learn the whys of the hostility and must constantly work on programs which open channels of communication between the police and the minority communities. He believes, for instance, that the present resistance of Negroes to the use of dogs illustrates a lack of communication. Negroes are not aware, he argued, that the dogs are specially trained, are well-controlled, and are extremely effective police tools to avoid violence, especially in potential riot situations. Cahill told the Committee that just before the meetings dogs had been used to open up a pathway in a hostile crowd which permitted the extrication of a threatened officer without using physical force or violence.

Two officials confirmed the opinion of the Negro spokesmen in describing alleged "police brutality" as "verbal brutality." Although only one of the officials admitted directly that an officer had been guilty of uncivility and the like, the heavy stress by all on the necessity of training in the proper use of language, manner of arrest, and manner of treating minority group persons indicated that this is a recognized problem.

The police officials agreed that employment of Negro officers helps in gaining the cooperation of the Negro community. They pointed out, however, that there have been considerable obstacles to such employment. . . .

As Seen by a Criminologist

Professor Joseph Lohman, Dean of the School of Criminology of the University of California and former Sheriff of Cook County, Illinois, appeared before the Committee and analyzed the problem as follows:

The police today in the North and West often find themselves caught between pressures from the Negro and white communities. Negroes are fighting for a change. Whites often are resisting and call on police to aid them in their effort. For instance, if a Negro demands service in a bar or restaurant, is refused, and declines to leave, the white owner calls on the police to arrest the Negro. Or, if Negroes demonstrate in such a way as to invite violent white reaction the police must somehow cope with the potentially violent situation.

Lohman also stressed the police role as a symbol of white authority and the legacy of suspicion and distrust brought to the North by southern Negroes.

Lohman sees education and training of officers and the effective opening of channels of communication between the police and the actual leaders of the Negro community as amelioratives. He praised Oakland's efforts along these lines.

46. THE EMPTY-HEAD BLUES:
BLACK REBELLION AND WHITE REACTION

AARON WILDAVSKY

The political milieu of the late 1960s reflected the polarization
between the white majority and the ethnic minorities across the
nation. A keen analysis of this alienation gap and seeming trend of
lawlessness has been made by Professor Aaron Wildavsky of the
University of California at Berkeley. Perhaps the most interesting
aspect of the essay is his indictment of the white liberal.

Liberals have been moaning those empty-head blues. They feel bad.
They know the sky is about to fall in. But they can't think of anything to
do. Having been too sanguine and too self-righteous about their part in
the civil rights movement, they are too easily prey to despair when their
contribution is rejected by those they presumed to help. Torn between a
nagging guilt and a secret desire to turn on their black tormentors, white
liberals have become spectators watching with frozen horror as their integrationist ideals and favorite public programs disintegrate amidst violent black rebellion. How did this maddening situation come about?
What can be done about it?

How to Enrage Whites Without Helping Blacks

A recipe for violence: promise a lot; deliver a little. Lead people to
believe they will be much better off, but let there be no dramatic improvement. Try a variety of small programs, each interesting but marginal in impact and severely underfinanced. Avoid any attempted solution
remotely comparable in size to the dimensions of the problem you are
trying to solve. Have middle-class civil servants hire upper-class student
radicals to use lower-class Negroes as a battering ram against the existing local political systems; then complain that people are going around
disrupting things and chastise local politicians for not cooperating with
those out to do them in. Get some poor people involved in local decision-
making, only to discover that there is not enough at stake to be worth
bothering about. Feel guilty about what has happened to black people;
tell them you are surprised they have not revolted before; express shock
and dismay when they follow your advice. Go in for a little force, just
enough to anger, not enough to discourage. Feel guilty again; say you are
surprised that worse has not happened. Alternate with a little suppression. Mix well, apply a match, and run. . . .

The dilemma of liberal politicians is exquisite. Now they play only
"minus-sum" games in which every player leaves the contest worse off

Aaron Wildavsky, "The Empty-Head Blues: Black Rebellion and White Reaction," *The Public Interest* (Spring 1968). © National Affairs, Inc., 1968.
Reprinted by permission.

class differences

than when he entered. The first rule is to get yourself hooked on purely symbolic issues. This guarantees that if you fail to get your policy adopted you are revealed as impotent and useless to the deprived. If you win your policy objective, you are even worse off because it is soon clear that nothing has changed. A typical game played under this rule is called "Civilian Police Review Board." The objective is to force a racist response from the voters who are fearful of their safety on subways and in the streets. The game begins with a publicity campaign focusing on fascist police, various atrocities, and other lurid events. The police and their friends counter with an equally illuminating defense: nothing is wrong that a little get-tough campaign would not cure. The game ends with a ballot in which white voters are asked to choose between their friendly neighborhood policeman and the specter of black violence. The usual result is that the whites vote for the police and defeat the review board. If a review board is created, however, it soon becomes apparent that a few judgments against policemen have no effect on the critical problem of securing adequate protection for Negroes. But the game is a perfect loser: everyone's feelings are exacerbated and the conflict continues at a new height of hostility.

There are many similar games. In Milwaukee, for example, wave after wave of Negro demonstrators cry out for a fair housing ordinance. The certain result is that whites are made furious. The sad thing is that, if the punitive marches succeed in their immediate goal, only a handful of Negroes at most will be helped. Or consider the drive to achieve school integration by bussing children to different parts of the city. If such integration is accompanied by huge efforts to create equality of educational achievement among black and white, all praise is due. But if black children continue to read poorly, race hatred may well increase. Black radicals will then be certain to condemn the liberal integrationists who have again left them and their children holding an empty bag.

The liberal politician is damned if he does and damned if he doesn't. He breaks his back to get two historic civil rights acts passed only to find himself accused of coming in too little and too late. The rat control bill is a perfect example of the classic bind. When Congress originally failed to pass the bill, it was made into a bitter example of inhumanity. Yet it can safely be said that had the bill sailed through Congress it would also have joined the list of those liberal measures that are not good enough to do the job. Too little and too late. How much all this is like Groucho Marx's famous crack that any country club willing to have him as a member wasn't exclusive enough for him to join.

We have learned some hard lessons. Every time we try to deal with problems of race we end up with symbolic gestures that infuriate everyone and please no one. Why? The American dilemma is a compound of racism suffused with class differences. Since America appears to be richer in economic resources than in brotherly love, it would be natural to tackle economic problems first. Few of us expect a quick solution to the lesser problems posed by large class differences among white people. None is surprised that upper-class whites do not integrate with their economic lower-class racial cohorts. Yet we persist in following policies that attack racism before economic equality has begun to be established. The result is that neither poverty nor racism is diminished.

Disheartened by the magnitude of the change required in racial behavior, unwilling to recognize the full extent of the resources required to improve economic conditions, we are tempted to try a lot of small programs that create an illusion of activity, ferment, and change. But nothing much happens. Confusion is rampant because it looks to some (mostly white) like so much is being done, and to others (mostly black) that nothing is happening. Hence the rival accusations of black ingratitude and white indifference. It is apparent that we should abandon symbolic policies that anger whites and do not help blacks and should concentrate instead on programs that will materially increase the well-being of poor people in the United States. Programs should be large rather than small, and provide tangible benefits.

. . .

Would these employment, income, and education policies stop black rebellions? [One has to be careful not to commit semantic aggression. The word "riot" is too aimless to apply to a phenomenon that is national in scope and that is clearly directed at expressing rage against the conditions of life of black people. To use "revolt," however, would suggest far more leadership, organization, and concerted action than appears to have been the case. So we are left with "rebellion," an appropriate word to designate violence by people who wish to express their hostility toward prevailing conditions but who are not yet organized to attack the larger society.] That is bound to be the question. Alas, it is a mean-spirited question because it deflects attention from human needs. But it will raise itself insistently, so we had better attend to it, especially if (as I believe) rebellions are bound to increase for a time. . . .

. . .

A Response to Rebellion

There will be rebellions; that much we can take for granted. The question is not whether these things will happen but how Americans will choose to react. It is easy to win tactical victories—disperse mobs brutally—and lose strategic battles. In the midst of consummate gall and endless effrontery, there is considerable danger of committing strategic suicide. What we do should depend on what we want. The prevailing confusion makes it advisable to take the risk of restating the obvious.

Just as Lincoln put preservation of the Union above all else in his times, so should we put construction of a multi-racial nation as our major objective. Our goal is that we all consider ourselves Americans who pay allegiance to the same political symbols and participate as citizens in the same national life. In pursuit of this goal, we must reaffirm our dedication to integration of the races for all who wish it. Wholly white or black communities can be one mode of participation in a common life. But integration is the preferred way of life for those who believe that there must be a single nation in America. A surface integration, however, must not be pursued at the expense of equality of achievement among black and white, for then integration will become a barrier to the creation of a joint American identity.

If we do not wish white and black men to live as citizens in the same country, we will have no difficulty in finding policies appropriate to that end. We can continue what we are doing. Better still, we can let violence feed on violence. The early riots have largely been aimless affairs in which destruction has been visited by Negroes on their own neighborhoods. Mass repressions visited indiscriminately upon black people can give them new reasons for race hatred and further violence. White people can be turned into proto-blacks—people who fear destruction because of their color. The difference between the races is that whites possess more abundant means of committing mayhem.

Americans who wish to hold open the possibility of emerging as a single people should not engage in mass repression. The surest way for black bigots to get a following is for white racists to create it. We want to open and not to foreclose the possibilities of being American together. There will be riots, and they will have to be put down. But our aim should be to separate the actively violent from the rest of the black community. Force should be limited, specific, and controlled.

Capitulation to lawless behavior would be bad. The hunger for humiliation shown by the New Left can only succeed in demeaning everyone. The black man's dignity cannot be won by the white man's degradation; the bread of humiliation will feed few people. The most destructive elements will simply be encouraged to raise the level of abuse. White anger will rise. Acting out the ritual frenzy of hatred will close all doors.

Our program should be neither suppression nor capitulation, but affirmation of common possibilities in a civil society. Without promising what no man can deliver—an end to the rebellions that are the consequences of our past failures—we can try to do what we now see to be right and just: A massive employment program, a concerted effort to improve educational achievement, and then support for a process of self-generating growth in the urban ghettos.

47. "BLACK POWER"—ITS GOALS AND METHODS

NATHAN HARE

One aspect of the current black power movement could be seen at San Francisco State College. Black students on the campus issued a series of demands to the college administration for the inclusion of a program of black studies. Dr. Nathan Hare, formerly a militant black faculty member, played an important role in this student revolt. The feeling of black power that pervaded the recent campus turmoil was expressed forcibly in May 1967 when Professor Hare was interviewed by U.S. News & World Report.

Q. Dr. Hare, what do you mean by "black power"?

A. "Power" is the ability to influence another person—even against his will, if necessary. We know what "black" is. So "black power" means the exercise by black people of influence on the forces which oppress us. Those forces happen to be white, for the most part.

Q. How do you intend to exercise this influence?

A. By any means available.

Q. What is the philosophy of the black-power movement? What are its aims?

A. The philosophy of black power is to bring about equality—not just equality of opportunity; we want equality *and* opportunity.

The Declaration of Independence declares the right to life, liberty and the pursuit of happiness. The catch is that it doesn't give you the chance to catch up with happiness. We don't want the pursuit. We want the happiness.

We want equality, not equality of opportunity.

This is what we seek, by whatever means seem necessary as we go along. Our ways will be revealed as the time comes.

Q. Is this black-power movement a basic change in Negro tactics—a new approach to Negro problems?

A. At least I feel—and I sense that black-power people feel—that we have been using the wrong tactics in the past, that our old tactics have not worked. Assimilation has not worked. Indeed, it has hampered our struggle.

We've been singing when we should be swinging, maybe. As Malcolm X [the late Black Muslim leader] said, we've been praying when we should have been preying, or playing when we should be flaying —you know, skinning alive.

But certainly we are going to work on new means and new tactics for bringing about this equality—not equality of opportunity, but equality.

Q. Can you give us an idea of the direction in which the black-power movement is heading?

A. Well, it seems to be moving toward self-assertion, self-sufficiency by the black people. It is a product of the failure of assimilation and of the quest for assimilation, which has been a long struggle. We have come to see, we feel, that assimilation won't work, partly because it mortifies the ego or the self-respect of the black person who feels that the only way he can get salvation is by being mingled among white persons. So he chases white persons into one neighborhood after another, into one school after another, making very little physical progress either place.

There has been some token integration—which some of us have refused. But statistics show there has been no real progress, occupationally or what not.

So we have realized that integration and equalization are not synonymous. Moreover, equality is not synonymous with sameness. There is no necessity for us to take over all of the culture norms and values of the white society, and we are going to begin to test them and to pick out those that we regard as desirable, and reject those— such as the Vietnam slaughter—which we deem to be undesirable.

Q. Is this a turning from individual effort to a group effort by Negroes?

A. Look—suppose you have a wall, and imagine that the persons on this side are mainly black and the persons on the other side are mainly white, and the blacks are trying to get over the wall because it's better over there.

As each one climbs up he steps on the heads and backs of the others. Then as they get up they are pushed back, one by one—or maybe a few individual blacks are let across so they can help push the others back.

So—as I said way back in 1964, when Stokely Carmichael [Chairman of the Student Nonviolent Coordinating Committee] was a student of mine, even though he already had his ideas then—maybe the best thing that black people should do is to turn back upon themselves for a little while, get their *esprit de corps* together and build a big ramrod, then all of them together rush and batter the wall down. This seems better than the idea of individualistic assimilation—of trying to act like the people on the other side, trying to take over their clothing, manners, hair styles, color or what not, and trying to get up there one by one.

Q. Does this mean you are abandoning integration?

A. Yes, as an end in itself. I'm sure that there is no effort to reject all white persons. Some white persons—even though they are few, like one half of 1 per cent—are blacker than most black persons in their thinking.

On the other hand, you have a majority of black persons who think white—although that majority is decreasing rapidly. So we can't just put it on the basis of skin color any more. But we have, of course, to watch the white person. Basically we take a person at his word. Then when he falls back on his word you handle him as you handle any other traitor of any color.

So therefore we don't see integration as anything which is a desirable end in itself. I can imagine a utopian world in which everybody would be integrated. But this does not seem to be possible under the present thinking and structure.

Therefore, we at least want the chance to develop on our own—not pray to the white establishment for equal rights, but become self-sufficient and assert ourselves and build our own communities. Maybe we'll have to decide whether we want to let white persons into our institutions, and so forth.

Q. Have you abandoned integration as a means, as well as an end?

A. We're giving up on it as a means to an end. We don't see it as a means to an end. It started as at least an idealistic means to an end, but it had become an end in itself, until this sort of Black Muslim, black-power type of push began.

White people thought that we could not have any institutions which were basically black which were of good quality. This has the effect of a self-fulfilling prophecy, because if you think that black persons cannot possibly have a good bank, then you don't put your money in it. All the best professors leave black universities to go to white universities as soon as they get the chance. The blacks even do the same thing. And this makes your prediction, which wasn't true in the beginning, come out to be true.

Q. You say you want more than equality of opportunity—

A. Equality of opportunity is more than just the right to go to school. A colleague of mine has proposed that every Negro child be given scholarships through the Ph.D. level, if he desires. Of course, there has to be some catching up, and even equal opportunity at the present time would be putting us at a disadvantage, still.

Yet, we don't ask any special favors. We just want to get people off our backs, stop whacking us down every time we rise up, and let us go by ourselves.

We have depended on the white "liberal" reform for centuries, and it has made too little progress. We want to go mainly by ourselves—try our own way.

Q. How do Negroes—who are only about 12 per cent of the population —expect to gain power all by themselves, apart from whites?

A. Well, there are white allies. But I'd like to point out that the white man rules all over the world, even though he's in the minority in the world scene. The white man is in the minority in Rhodesia and South Africa, here in the District of Columbia, and in certain parts of Mississippi and Alabama. Yet he rules. This is something which we have to get rid of.

The blacks outnumber the whites 23 to 1 in Rhodesia. But they grumble in the dark, and then when a white person passes by they tuck their tails and fall silent. Why, they could have taken each a finger—10 of them a finger apiece, 10 a toe apiece, and 3 could take any other appendages which they desired—and pulled each white man apart, if they had been organized and determined.

Q. But here in the United States, where you are outnumbered 8 or 9 to 1, how do you expect to gain power?

A. It's sort of ludicrous for an enemy group to come here with microphones and cameras expecting their opponents to tell them what they intend to do. It's not wise for a group to reveal its plans to its enemy.

Q. Do you consider whites your enemy?

A. I'm an enemy of those whites who are enemies of mine, who are enemies of justice.

Q. How do you differentiate?

A. We take them at their word until they're proven to be traitors, and then we purge them from our midst.

Q. Is black power an antiwhite movement?

A. No. It is an anti-antiblack movement.

Q. Do you think most Negroes hate whites?

A. No. I think most white persons hate Negroes.

Q. So you will not reveal your plans for black power to white people—

A. No, I wouldn't—not to many of them, and certainly not to strangers, and not to the whites as a whole.

Q. Do you actually have secret plans to seize black power?

A. I would say "no comments" on that. We're working on that problem. I think people will find out when the time comes.

Q. Would you say, then, that white people are in for some surprises?

A. I would suppose that they are. In fact, I used to go around predicting a black blitzkrieg.

Q. How would you define a black blitzkrieg?

A. It's sort of like a thousand giant Watts riots sweeping the country. [Watts was the 1965 riot area in Los Angeles.]

Q. Do you still think that's a possibility?

A. Not a thousand Watts—that's exaggerating. But I think a great number of them. I still feel that it's possible, though I don't feel that it's wise or necessarily desirable to predict it.

Q. What is the atttiude of the black-power movement toward violence?

A. They feel that, whenever attacked, American law and mores dictate that a person fights back. And it eventually has become acceptable to do so.

Q. You talk about fighting back when attacked. But what if you are not attacked? Do you consider violence a justifiable means to gain what you call black power?

A. No. I don't think we need violence for that. We have our ways, which we aren't revealing to the whites.

Q. What is behind these riots that have been erupting in so many cities of this country?

A. They are trying to say to the power structure that they aren't getting what they deserve.

Q. Is this considered by the black-power movement an acceptable means of expressing their feelings?

A. We don't have any judgments about that. We try to withhold judgments. Killing is not bad or good in itself. It can be bad if you kill a person for no cause, but it gets you a Medal of Honor if you kill a person in a situation in which the establishment finds killing desirable. So it's a matter of cultural definition as to what is desirable or good.

Q. If it came to what you call a black blitzkrieg, do you think the Negroes could possibly win in this country?

A. I don't have any idea. I'm not a military strategist. But I understand that the Viet Cong have done a pretty good job while being outnumbered. Even in conventional warfare, we have great weapons such as atomic bombs that we don't use now. I don't think the United States can afford to be dropping atom bombs in its major cities. But this is a possibility.

Q. Do you think there is a serious possibility of guerrilla civil war between whites and blacks in this country?

A. I don't see why it is so impossible in this country. What's so different about this country? And what's so different about the blacks, as compared to other groups, that they would never come around to that if other means were not successful?

Of course, civil war would probably be harder here than anywhere else. But I don't think it's impossible.

Q. Where would you draw the line? Where would you stop in this battle for equality?

A. I'm not waging a civil war. I don't want you to get that impression.

Q. But you talk about it as a possibility—

A. As a sociologist, sure. As a sociologist I'm obliged to discern and communicate the truth, and these are things which I see, sociologically speaking. It's not something which I'm calling for. It's just an unfortunate fact.

Q. Would you personally advocate going as far as civil war, if necessary?

A. I would not want to make any comment in that regard, because I would not want to be regarded as advocating it on the one hand—but, on the other hand, I do not want to be an enemy of the civil-war people, the guerrillas, if they start. I don't want them to get me. So I'm not taking any stand. I'm just trying to be a sociologist.

Q. How real do you regard the possibility of civil war—and how soon?

A. I regard it as very real. But it would not happen all at once. There has to be so much organization—and, before that, so much discontent and loss of faith by so many persons. So, if it's comforting to you, it's going to be quite a while off yet—though not so far as to be outside of our life span.

Q. Suppose that, by whatever means, you do succeed in achieving black power. What would you do with it?

A. Black power does not mean the overthrow of white power. It is not a matter of replacing white power with black power. We'd set up institutions or even emerge as an important, significant part of the existent white institutions.

We would hope that it would not come to pass that black power would turn around and do the same thing that white power has done.

Of course, if that *should* come to pass, we would have to admit that turn about is fair play. But we don't envision that or desire it. We do not strive to take over. We just want to be right up there on an equal plane—either separately or integrated or by any means.

Autonomy for Negroes—

Q. Does the idea of a separate State for Negroes enter into your thinking?

A. Well, the District of Columbia is two-thirds black, and pretty soon we're going to have what amounts to a separate State here, if we gain some autonomy through home rule. So, I think we'll start with the District of Columbia and see how it works out.

Q. If you took over the District of Columbia, would you tell the Federal Government to move out?

A. We could let them stay here, if the Government is willing to operate in a black city— a black State.

The Federal Government could still have its White House. Now, there are some persons who want to move it to Howard University and call it the "Black House." But I think we could let it stay the White House.

Of course, we'd have to start charging people tolls, like other cities do, to come in here.

Q. Charge tolls to outsiders coming into the capital?

A. Yes, such as commuters coming in here to work. Because all the streets are made to their advantage—one way going out during rush hours at night, one way coming in during rush hours in the morning, parking here—and we can't even get in to use our own facilities. Yet they pay their taxes to another State. So we'll have to start charging tolls after we have got this.

Q. Would you charge the Government rent for the land that it uses?

A. All these things would have to be worked out by the administrative elements of the black-power movement.

Q. In Washington and a few other communities where Negroes are a majority they could, of course, take political power. Is that what you have in mind as black power?

A. No. As I said, power by any means available. Political power would be one thing. We also want some economic power. We want some social power.

Q. Can you take economic power by the vote?

A. No, not much.

Q. Then how would you get economic power?

A. We must insist that we have not abandoned such things as voting and legal remedies and things of that kind. On the other hand, we must insist on keeping our means to ourselves.

Q. As a minority, don't you worry about hurting your chances by antagonizing the majority?

A. We don't worry about that. We worried too long about what white folks think about us—about the white backlash. What we need to do is lash the white backlash with the blacklash. So we're going to stop caring about what white people think. We've tried to change white hearts and souls. We failed. It is desirable, of course, to have mass sympathy on your side. But we can't depend on that too much, especially since we are fighting tradition, and traditions are very hard to eradicate by appealing to people by reason. So there has to be some alteration of methods. You know, there's always this hang-up on numbers—the idea that you need the whole world with you to do anything. I understand that only 30,000 persons were actively involved in the Russian Revolution. I don't know how many persons Castro had in the hills with him in Cuba, but not a great many.

Some persons have all kinds of theories—such as, say, get a few pounds of this drug, LSD, and drop it in the water supply of each major city and disorient the city.

You don't need the whole world on your side any more, and people are coming to see that.

Q. You say you have found it hard to appeal to reason. What are you appealing to now? Fear?

A. No, no. We don't intend to scare anybody. But we want to indicate that we're not scared any more.

Q. This black-power philosophy that you have described—is it growing or spreading fast?

A. Yes.

Q. Where is it growing fastest?

A. On black-college campuses.

Q. Is this the result of Stokely Carmichael's activities—his speaking and organizing tour from campus to campus?

A. Recently he has been doing that. I think that it's a good thing, because the people in the slums don't really understand things, or they can't articulate.

Q. Is it your idea that campus leaders will become the leaders of the people in the slums?

A. Yes. All of them will not be picketing or marching in the streets. But once black universities have become part of the new trend, then everybody that comes through those universities will be touched.

Q. If black universities become known as centers of black power, how long do you think black universities will last?

A. I don't know. But the way they exist now, we want to give them to the white folks, anyway. If they are going to continue as they have, as brainwashing factories, putting out freak persons with black faces and white minds, then maybe they should be closed.

Q. Is Stokely Carmichael really the formulator of black-power philosophy?

A. There was an "organization for black power" formed in 1963 by Jesse Gray in New York. And Adam Clayton Powell, when he spoke at Howard University about a year ago, proposed what he called "audacious power." Then Stokely Carmichael made the phrase "black power" famous during the Meredith march in Georgia last summer.

Q. So Mr. Carmichael did not originate black power—

A. He is the most famous advocate of it.

Q. Do you see Stokely Carmichael as the Negro leader of the future?

A. Yes, for the near future, at least. You see, revolutionary change occurs in stages, and types of leaders accord with the various stages. So leaders change. And the Rev. Dr. Martin Luther King—some of the leaders are reluctant to retire, like fighters who hang on too long. When leaders have fulfilled their function, it's time for them to retire.

"Contempt for Uncle Toms"—

Q. Do you think the Negro movement is coming into an era of leadership by college professors, such as yourself?

A. They increasingly are going to have to do that. Otherwise they will not be able to teach black students very well, because the students at most black colleges have great contempt for their professors—regard them as Uncle Toms, or, rather, as "Dr. Thomases."

Professors won't be able to communicate with black students if they don't start taking an active role in black power. And many of them are beginning to do that.

48. HOW TO CHANGE AMERICA

HARRY EDWARDS

Reminiscent of the Biblical admonition "an eye for an eye . . . ,"
many minority spokesmen speak of the use of violence as only a
response to the physical and psychological destruction that have been
imposed upon them. Harry Edwards, sociology instructor at the
University of California at Berkeley and organizer of the black
boycott of the Mexico City Olympic Games, reveals the true origins of
violence in America in his poem, which originally appeared in the
New York Times.

> For openers, the Federal Government
>   the honkies, the pigs in blue
> must go down South
>   and take those crackers out of bed,
> the crackers who blew up
>   those four little girls
> in that Birmingham church,
>   those crackers who murdered
> Medgar Evars and killed
>   the three civil rights workers—
> they must pull them out of bed
>   and kill them with axes

in the middle of the street.
>Chop them up with dull axes.
>>Slowly.
At high noon.
>With everybody watching
on television.
>Just as a gesture
of good faith.

49. THE SDS VIEW OF CAMPUS UNREST: TOWARD A NEW SOCIETY

JIM SHOCH

*Part of the campus scene in recent years has been the growth of the
student "New Left." Among the demands of radicals is their
insistence that they play a larger part in determining the role of the
university. Unrest and violence at colleges throughout California and
the nation are, in part, a projection of student dissatisfaction. Jim
Shoch, a member of* Students for a Democratic Society, *outlines some
of the reasons for student discontent. He believes that the existing
framework of the university and of society must be changed before a
meaningful and just society can emerge. This essay is from a six-part
colloquium that covered a wide spectrum of viewpoints in the*
Stanford Alumni Almanac.

To detail SDS's analysis of American society and its flaws, as well as our
vision of the future, is a tall order in this short a space. Nevertheless it is
a worthwhile one, for an understanding of the politics and goals of the
radical left is an essential prerequisite for the comprehension of the
events occurring today in the ghettos and on the university campuses.

Our fundamental premise is that America is ruled by and for a single
class. This stratum—whether it is called the "ruling class," the "governing class," the "corporate bourgeoisie," or the "ruling elite"—is the sector
comprised of the .5 percent of the population that controls 25 percent of
the nation's wealth. From these ranks are drawn the leaders of the giant
multinational corporations that run the economy and the men who control the governmental apparatus. A survey of the backgrounds of the
higher echelon members of the executive branch of the government reveals a predominant number of ex-corporate chieftains and associated
lawyers as well as bankers. Through its control of the executive branch,
the regulatory agencies, and government expenditures, this ruling class
consolidates and extends its control and preserves the financial health of
its corporations.

The ruling elite's wealth, of course, is based on these great corporations and banks. American industry today is characterized by a few large

Jim Shoch, "Toward a New Society," *Stanford Alumni Almanac*, Vol. 7 (April
1969), pp. 11–12. Reprinted by permission of the *Stanford Alumni Almanac*.

producers in each branch of industry who agree to inflated price levels to ensure a high and constant rate of profit at the expense of the millions of American workers and consumers. Besides depriving the working man of the product of his labor, this great concentration of wealth and power naturally produces at the base of the economic pyramid some forty million people living below the poverty level defined by the U.S. government, and another forty million persons living below the level of income defined as adequate to preserve a standard of "health and decency." It has been estimated that the retransfer of some $11 billion of income each year would raise every family's income above the poverty line, but somehow this step just hasn't been taken yet. Clearly, the existence of poverty in America today is senseless and indefensible. .

Monopoly capitalism is also in part responsible for the oppression of black people in this country. It is mainly the big banks and insurance companies that own most of the wretched ghetto tenements for which the inhabitants pay such exorbitant rents. The inadequate job opportunities and job-training programs for black slum-dwellers are largely the fault of the corporations who find that giving hope and dignity to the unemployed is unprofitable. And besides, a black industrial reserve army helps depress the level of wages in these inflationary times. The Urban Coalition seems designed to buy peace in the ghettos with a token amount of funds, for the size of the investment that would be necessary to completely eliminate discrimination and inequality would clearly be found to be unappetizing by the major corporations.

Bombs or Schools

American businessmen and politicians are fond of citing our $800 billion Gross National Product as proof of the nation's prosperity. But a closer look at the composition of this figure can be quite disconcerting. Ten percent of this GNP as well as ten percent of the nation's employment is due solely to military expenditures. Ghetto redevelopment would provide a perfectly adequate outlet for government funds to keep the economy running in its smooth Keynesian fashion, but such projects would compete with private developers who have plans to build middle- and high-income housing units in former slum areas. Recently, a $40 million rat control bill was laughed out of Congress, while the proposed ABM system, in the face of almost unanimous opposition by the scientific community, may well be approved. Congress may pick the annual budget to pieces, but proposed Defense Department appropriations always seem to breeze right through. But then, bombs depreciate a good deal faster than schools. The huge war-based firms of the "military-industrial complex" exert a powerful lobbying force on government officials, and the result is a senseless and destructive arms race in the face of widespread domestic poverty. As rich as America may be, she cannot afford both guns and butter, as some would have us believe.

American monopoly capitalism is irrational in other respects, too. To support the great automobile firms in Detroit as well as the giant oil companies, the government builds miles of highways and expressways resulting in smog that is now becoming a real health hazard. The development of the electric car and good public transportation has been retarded; but, then, what would this country be without Standard Oil and General Motors?

To ensure an adequate consumer demand, vast amounts of money are spent each year on advertising and selling costs, on packaging, and on the marginal differentiation of products. In addition, obsolescence is now built into cars, nylons, razor blades, light bulbs, and who knows what else, all to preserve a high volume of sales. The poor of this country may need food and clothing, but as they don't have the money to pay for these items, the corporations, through the mass media, create the drive toward conspicuous consumption in the more moneyed sectors that leads them to purchase expensive luxuries as well as all kinds of useless gadgets.

An economic system with the productive potential that ours has, and yet which uses this capacity to produce bombs and useless goods, can only be described as monstrous and irrational.

The constantly growing American corporations and banks are not restricted within national boundaries. These firms are penetrating further and further into the underdeveloped world in search of raw materials, markets for surplus goods, and outlets for surplus capital. Direct private U.S. foreign investment today totals some $56 billion, and roughly 40 percent of this is located in the Third World. Europe has recently begun to decry the American takeover of the advanced sectors of its economies, but American control of the underdeveloped nations is far greater.

U.S. firms invest largely in the extractive industries—petroleum, mining, and agriculture. This has resulted in lopsided growth for the developing nations. The underdeveloped countries have become dependent on the export of a single commodity, such as coffee, bananas, or copper, and they must buy the great bulk of their manufactured goods from the advanced industrial nations. The terms of trade in this exchange are continually worsening for the nations of the Third World. As American firms shift more toward investment in manufacturing enterprises overseas, in order to more efficiently exploit the local market, they monopolize the technology and technical know-how. By tying up local capital, they prevent the development of an autonomous national bourgeoisie capable of independently developing the nation's resources for its own internal use. Profits that are badly needed for reinvestment to promote growth in the host country are largely remitted to the United States. Extensive foreign interests, in alliance with local commercial and landed oligarchies, guarantee a stunted and deformed growth for the emerging nations.

To maintain a favorable investment climate throughout the Third World for its multinational corporations, the U.S. government—in contradiction to its supposed ideal of supporting only democratic governments through its economic and especially military aid—backs dictatorial military regimes capable of repressing threats to American vested interests. These regimes are, in fact, able and willing to repress all movements to bring about social reform. Any movement or government that is somewhat socialist in nature and which seems to threaten American interests is immediately labeled as "Communist," and pressure is brought to bear against it by the United States government. This pressure may take the form of the approval of an impending right-wing military coup, as in Brazil in 1964; the use of CIA agents to bring down a reformist regime, as in Iran in 1953 and Guatemala in 1954; or the actual deployment of troops to suppress a nationalist social revolution, as in the Dominican Republic in 1965 and currently in Vietnam.

The American ruling class equates "free enterprise" with "freedom," and attempts to impose its socio-economic system on the rest of the world. Thus has America become the world's leading counterrevolutionary power, brutally trying to repress the great struggle of the Vietnamese who are attempting to work out their own destinies free from foreign domination and exploitation. This country, supposedly dedicated to freedom and self-determination, vitiates these ideals by denying their realization to the Vietnamese in the furtherance of the vested interests of a relative handful of Americans involved in the exploitation of Southeast Asia and in the military machine. The death and oppression that results *must* be intolerable to every feeling human being.

A system that subordinates human needs and dignity to the accumulation of profits, as does American capitalism, necessarily produces in its pursuit of misplaced priorities needless poverty and oppression at home as well as death and destruction abroad.

Capitalism & Universities

American universities are integral parts of American monopoly capitalism. As industry increasingly employs more advanced types of technology, it also requires a more skilled labor force. Since an individual scientist or executive may leave or be lured from one firm to a higher paying job with another firm, individual corporations prefer not to risk the large amounts of capital necessary to train completely all of their technicians and managers. And so, the universities have become the centers of production of skilled manpower, both technical and administrative, which the corporations utilize. In addition, costly research or research that may not be of immediate use is also done at the universities, the results of which are then eagerly pounced upon by the corporations. Universities do an important part of the Defense Department's war research in this country, which is of great benefit to the mammoth corporations of the "military-industrial complex." Finally, universities are powerful agencies of socialization, fostering on the part of the students values and attitudes leading them willingly to embrace the American "free enterprise" system as the only politico-socio-economic arrangement that can truly promote political freedom. Thus, American universities are vital links in the production process.

Stanford fits the above description like a glove. It produces a great number of engineers and administrators for the corporations, and the war research done both on the campus and at the Stanford Research Institute, whose board of directors must be approved by this University's

Trustees, has made Stanford the third leading defense contractor among universities. The Stanford Trustees are predominantly members of the American ruling class with connections to such war-dependent firms as General Dynamics, Lockheed, Northrop, and FMC, and these affiliations make it seem unlikely that the Trustees will ever willingly decide to terminate the war research done at Stanford.

SDS disrupted the Trustee meeting at the Faculty Club on January 14 mainly to expose to the community Stanford's exploitative involvement in Southeast Asia, an involvement that has developed to defend and extend the interests of the Stanford Trustees and men like them. We will continue to use whatever means we think are necessary and effective in shedding further light on and eventually eliminating Stanford's participation in American militarism and imperialism.

We're often told that, as a group, we're merely destructive, that we never have any constructive alternatives to offer to the status quo. While more often than not this charge is an attempt to evade the issues at hand, some ideas as to what the "new society" would look like are absolutely essential. The details will, of course, have to be worked out in practice, but there are some general principles that can be laid out.

The new society, of course, will be a socialist one. The means of production will be taken from the small number of capitalists who now own them and will be run collectively in one form or another by the mass of Americans. The first major result of this will be a significant retransfer of income and wealth and the speedy elimination of poverty. A general overall plan formulated by duly-elected officials and with plenty of give and take up and down the line will ensure the production of goods that satisfy real human needs and which will not include implements of destruction and useless products for the affluent sectors of the population. Specifically, there would probably be fewer cars and hence less smog and fewer gas stations; fewer country clubs and more parks; fewer bombs and more schools. Private foreign investment would be eliminated, also eliminating a major reason for brutal U.S. interventionism in the Third World. In addition, the ideological basis of the Cold War would be in great part dissolved, easing East-West tensions.

The Socialist Society

A prime concern of this socialist society would be, of course, the maximization of individual freedom. Those who say that any kind of planned society inevitably limits this freedom are forgetting the fact that major corporate directors and executives are the only men currently making decisions in the realm of the economy. Under socialism, much of this decision-making would be greatly decentralized. While such fields as communications and transportation probably would be centrally administered, other industries could be run on the state level, and the great bulk of American enterprise could be run at the local level. Workers in a particular factory will decide as to what methods of production will be used. Workers will actively participate in the investment planning in their factories. Workers and consumers, with the advice of the central planning agency, could collectively determine the price of goods to be sold on a local basis. The central bureaucracy will be restricted and carefully supervised by the electorate to prevent the emergence of an entrenched political elite. Far more than ever before would the average citizen participate in decisions affecting his life. This would be democracy in the true sense, not the "liberal" democracy we now know in which freedom is restricted to voting every few years for the mediocrities of someone else's choice.

Those who point out that a democratic socialism has never really existed in an industrial society are right—yet there is no reason to fear a Stalinist type of despotism here for three main reasons. First, unlike Russia, we have a tradition of *political* democracy and civil liberties which the American people simply would not see destroyed. Second, unlike the Soviet Union in the 1930s, the United States is already an advanced industrial society. The strict regimentation of economic and political life that is necessary to achieve rapid development would be unnecessary in this country. And third, the Soviet Union had to develop in the face of an often hostile West, which helped to produce a repressive militarization of the economy. This is a problem we would not have to face after the transition to socialism. Everything in the United States favors the construction of a truly democratic, participatory form of socialism.

Perhaps most important, through a reorientation of the educational system and the communications media as well as the restructuring of the economy, a new set of values would develop. The satisfaction of real needs and not the maximization of profits would become the goal of human endeavor. The competitive capitalist ethic would be replaced by the ethic of cooperation. Individuals would work collectively to advance their own welfare and the welfare of all mankind. Self-realization would be achieved not through isolated, individual toil, but in a community, with all members as full and active participants. Human relations would cease to be mere market transactions entered for individual gain. As Eldridge has written, "Competition is the law of the jungle; cooperation is the law of civilization." It is to the construction of this truly human, humane civilization that we are dedicated.

50. THE PEOPLE'S PARK

RONALD REAGAN

The fires ignited by the Free Speech Movement of 1964 in Berkeley,
by the rhetoric of the New Left and the radical minority,
continue to smolder, and periodically they flare up again. One
example of this inflammatory situation was evident in the spring of
1969 when hundreds of young people, including many nonstudents,
attempted to take over a university-owned property and establish the
"People's Park." This confrontation is a kind of case study in the
problem of law and order. In a speech delivered in San Francisco,
Governor Ronald Reagan offered his analysis of the issue.

Many speakers of world renown have recognized this Commonwealth
Club as one of the Nation's preeminent sounding boards. You are a distinguished forum, and any speaker invited to address you gives great
consideration to his choice of subject, and certainly, I have no intention
of being an exception.

My problem, however, is how to choose between a number of tempting
topics. There are a number of state issues all vital and all more or less
controversial—such as California's crying need for true tax reform
which, incidentally, would give me a chance to explain why it should not
be based on compulsory withholding.

There is one subject, however, which stands out as probably the most
vexing and the most frustrating, not only to government, but to the
people of California: the "People's Park" controversy across the Bay in
Berkeley.

The volume of words already spoken and written on this subject have
not resolved a number of confusing aspects. Many questions remain un-
answered.

Is the University properly cast in the role as a greedy land baron,
ousting the poor homesteader? Did the University arbitrarily and unreasonably interfere with the citizens' volunteer effort at beautification of
an unused vacant lot? Did the forces of law and order precipitate the
violence and engage in massive but unnecessary "overkill"? Were there
no efforts on the part of the University to negotiate, conciliate or reconcile the differences between the people? And, even more basic, was this
just another episode in the nationwide wave of violence swirling about
our campuses and, if so, do we just continue reacting, restoring law and
order after the fires start and the rocks begin to fly?

Of greatest importance: Is the nationwide campus ferment that is
going on monolithic in nature? Is it a widespread youthful dissatisfaction with things as they are that is only occasionally triggered by the
more emotional into violence? Or are there, indeed, two separate groups
each with its own cause? Is there a silent majority, non-violent, but with
truly legitimate grievances? And, is there a separate rebellious minority

Address delivered before the Commonwealth Club, San Francisco, June 13,
1969.

promoting a real revolutionary cause—seeking whenever possible, by deception, to enlist the aid of the majority group?

Proper Perspective

I would like to attempt in this forum to try to find the answers to some of the above questions and to attempt to put into proper perspective the "People's Park" controversy.

In discussing this episode, two facets will have to be avoided. One, the case of James Rector who died of shotgun wounds. At this moment, the precise circumstances regarding his death have yet to be established officially by a coroner's inquest. I feel it would be improper for me to comment.

The other has to do with the numerous charges of non-demonstrators suffering injuries and arrest, and the allegations of mistreatment in the detention facilities at Santa Rita. Certainly the possibility of this must be recognized. There is no question but that part of the mob on that first day of violence intended only to be vocal and was caught in the crossfire as it tried to escape. Since all of this is under investigation, comments by me at this time would be improper.

But I can say, unequivocally, that if any citizen's rights were unjustly violated, if officials were guilty of misconduct, then justice must be done and the guilty must be punished.

The cause of the controversy is a city block, roughly 450 by 250 feet, purchased by the University two years ago for $1,300,000.00 as an eventual site for residence halls and research facilities. In the interim, it was to provide playing fields and recreation facilities very much needed on the Berkeley campus because the previous area devoted to this purpose has been used for a new campus building.

"A Political Freak-Out"

The land has lain idle for more than a year, during which time no one thought of using it as a park. On April 4, it came up on the University's priority list approved for immediate development. On April 18, that classic example of four-letter-word journalism, the "Berkeley Barb," issued a call for its readers to gather on the coming Sunday, April 20, equipped with tools to convert for their own use the University property into, "a cultural, political freak-out and rap center for the Western World."

It was made very plain: they were aware of the University's plans for immediate use of the property. We have to depend on leaflets, the *Barb* and the official campus paper, *The Daily Californian*, for word as to their intentions, but they were pretty explicit.

The *Barb* said, "We will police our own park and not allow its occupation by imperial power."

A handbill read, "We take a solemn oath to wage a war of retaliation against the University if it begins to move against the park. If the University attempts to seize $1,300,000.00 worth of land, now claimed by the people, we will destroy $5,000,000.00 worth of University property."

Another handbill bluntly warned that even sending surveyors or post-ing "No Trespassing" signs would be the signal for instant retaliation.

As a matter of fact, when the University did get around to posting "no trespassing" signs—51 of them—they were instantly torn down and burned.

The *Daily Californian* published an article by 27-year-old non-student, Arthur Goldberg—his name is familiar in the free and the filthy speech movements of a few years ago. In that article he praised the riots at Howard University and the University of Wisconsin and complained that not a —— thing was happening at Berkeley, although he didn't use "blanks." (That's a change in college publication since some of us were in school.) His article then went into a tirade against Chancellor Roger Heyns in connection with the University's plans for development, wind-ing up with this arrogant and insulting demand of the chancellor, "Who in the hell does the chancellor think he is? It is our park."

Ultimatums of this kind were the only answer the University received to repeated efforts to enter into dialogue with these people. The chancel-lor had appointed staff members to make overtures, whether rightly or wrongly, but probably because it was apparent that a number of legiti-mate citizens and some students had joined in the work on the vacant lot, by this time under the impression that it was just a volunteer com-munity project to pretty up an unused vacant lot.

The real leaders, of course, were Goldberg and a number of others whose records include participation in the Oakland Induction Center riot, seizure of Moses Hall, the Chicago riots and last summer's bloody riot in Berkeley when many of these same people demanded that Tele-graph Avenue be closed off and turned over to them as a park—perhaps "play-pen" is a more appropriate word. The names are all on the police blotter: Mike Delacour, Stuart Edward Albert, Paul Glusman, William Miller and Frank Bardacke, to name a few. None of them are students of the University.

The chancellor repeated several times his willingness to discuss the design of—and the development and the possible use of—this area by the adjacent community. At no time did the squatters even designate an individual or a committee with whom he could communicate. The Uni-versity's position actually was untenable.

The Legal Liability

Not enough has been said about the very real problem of legal liabil-ity. As owner of the property, the University was liable in the event of injuries to anyone in using this property as a park, or if it should become a public nuisance. The importance of this can be judged by the recent announcement that the City of Berkeley itself is in danger of losing its own liability insurance because of the recurring disturbances in the streets and in the neighborhood around the campus. The property, inci-dentally, had already become something of a public nuisance. Police had been responding to frequent complaints of nightly rallies, mass singing, shouted obscenities, bonfires throughout the night, and the gathering of unsavory characters who had so frightened many of the housewives in the neighborhood that they wouldn't even walk down the street to go shopping.

And, now it has been learned that part of the lush greenery that was planted to make the lot a so-called sylvan glade turned out to be marijuana.

One hundred and thirty-two residents of the neighborhood petitioned the University to end the use of the park by the squatters, and to go ahead with the University plans. In addition to the complaints I have already mentioned, there was one that the property was being used as a garbage dump and a toilet. Again, a measure of the risk of liability is the record of arrests that had already taken place.

It involved once a 21-year-old man, picked up for indecent exposure after the police found him sitting in the park, completely nude, in full view of the occupants and the passers-by. There were arrests for narcotic violations, armed robbery, a number of juvenile cases, some for drunkenness—including one 14-year-old, loitering and sleeping in the park— and four cases of juvenile runaways, one coming from as far away as Wisconsin.

The Right of Private Property

We all continue to use the term "park" but the issue had never been one of whether there should be a park or even whether a park was needed. There are no shortages of parks in Berkeley, and by the end of this summer, as a matter of fact, the City will have completed a new park only two blocks from the disputed site. By their own statements, the leaders of the property take-over have made it plain their purpose was political. They were challenging the right of private ownership of land in this country. They referred to the University's deed as a piece of paper that did not give the University the right to use this land.

All of the events I've mentioned—the attempts at communication, ultimatums by the dissident group—took place in the short period from April 20 through the second week in May—around three-and-a-half weeks. D-Day came on May 15. Before dawn, at 4:45 A.M., campus police led about 65 law enforcement officers to the site. There had been threats that the group was going to camp in and occupy the site, and forcefully prevent the University from going ahead with its own plans. About 75 individuals were found sleeping in the park and were warned they were trespassing. Only three refused to leave and had to be arrested. The building of the fence began at 6:20 A.M., and optimism reigned—there was no opposition. It began to appear that the police on hand were an unnecessary precaution. But, can anyone deny that the University would have been less than responsible had it not notified law enforcement of its intentions in view of the repeated threats of violence?

History of Riots

Now what about the police themselves? What did they have in mind when confronted with this call for their services? Were they deliberately provocative, looking for trouble, trigger-happy? Hardly!

In the past 11 months there have been four major riots in Berkeley. All of them involved militants from the south campus area of Berkeley. This neighborhood has become the most serious crime problem in that city. In these 11 months there have been eight major bombings or attempted bombings, nearly 1100 drug arrests, 750 in the south campus area alone. They've confiscated nearly 1,000 sticks of dynamite, more than 200 rifles, pistols and shotguns, dozens of molotov cocktails and materials for making more. There have been dozens of arson attempts resulting in more than $800,000.00 damage, including the gutting of Wheeler Hall. One policeman has been ambushed and shot, a dozen others have been fired upon.

In last summer's Telegraph Avenue riot, two California Highway Patrol officers were the victims of fire bombings. Molotov cocktails were exploded on the pavement at their feet; they were engulfed in flames; suffered burns that hospitalized them, and one of them has just recently been released and is now able to do a few hours non-physical work in the office each day.

Attempted bombings involved a Berkeley police car in the official police parking lot. A homemade bomb failed to go off; had it gone off it would not only have destroyed the car and driver, but would have destroyed several nearby buildings. It was a highly sophisticated weapon.

In another attempt—dynamite was placed against the side of two vats of highly flammable liquid. The dynamite exploded, but didn't rupture the tanks. Firemen in Berkeley said that had the tanks been ruptured, probably all of west Berkeley would have gone up in the holocaust.

All of this had to be taken into account by the police as they were called into action again. By noon on May 15, a total of 150 officers had been assigned to the area, 75 held in reserve, 75 on duty at the park site.

Incitement to Riot?

In the meantime, back on the campus, a noon meeting had been scheduled at Sproul Plaza to hear a lecture on Israel and the Mideast crisis. This isn't unusual. Permission is obtained through a student organization for meetings and then, sometimes, the sponsors forget the purpose for which they asked the meeting. The crowd in the Plaza numbered more than 2,000—some of them were obviously anticipating more than routine rhetoric. A group of medics dressed in white uniforms, wearing Red Cross symbols, mingled in the crowd. This has been normal procedure whenever a riot is planned or probable.

There were nine speakers at the rally—no one mentioned Israel—the ninth was Dan Siegel, University of California's student body president-elect. To use a trite phrase, it could be said that he appeared before an already-inflamed audience. Before he finished, they were screaming, raising clenched fists above their heads. He has been charged with inciting to riot.

He wound up his fiery speech saying, "Let's go down and take over the park!"[1] The crowd began to move. It moved on the line of 75 Berkeley police and Highway Patrolmen. Someone kicked in the glass door of a bank on the way down the street, the window of an automobile was smashed. Rocks, bottles and other missiles started to fly. Sheriffs' deputies fell in behind the crowd; from past experience they know that when the missiles start going, they are usually thrown from the rear ranks. But not today—this was a mob.

Sticks, bricks and prepared jagged pieces of pipe and steel—some 18 inches long—rained down, thrown from rooftops in end-over-end fashion, thrown into the police ranks. The force with which they were thrown can be judged by one that went through the door of a police car. Cherry bombs exploded in the street, some with BB shot glued on to act as schrapnel. Officers went down under the barrage . . . and were overrun.

This was no spontaneous eruption. The rooftops had been stockpiled with rocks and other missiles. There were similar stockpiles in nearby alleys. Heavy steel reinforcement bars—construction steel—had been cut into short, throwable lengths.

Sheriffs' deputies resorted to tear gas, but the barrage from the rooftops and the street continued. The small contingent of police and patrolmen had been broken up into little groups which were then surrounded. A thrown knife struck a patrolman in the chest and penetrated to the bone. One officer had his helmet shattered by a chunk of broken concrete thrown from a rooftop—others were hit in the face. Many suffered injuries that made it impossible for them to get up—let alone walk or even defend themselves.

Out of Control

Out on the fringes of the battlefield, a police car was overturned and set on fire. Those who did it discovered a Berkeley police reserve officer, a member of that volunteer group for 20 years, who had been assigned to traffic duty. They surrounded him, throwing rocks at close range. Backed against a building, he went down. He was literally being stoned to death, in the ancient biblical sense. Lying on the ground, he drew his revolver

[1] According to U.C. police reports, Siegel said: ". . . if we are to win this thing, it is because we are making it more costly for the university to put up its fence than it is for them to take down their fence. What we have to do then, is maximize the cost to them, minimize the cost to us. So what that means, is: people be careful. Don't let those pigs beat the —— out of you, don't let yourself get arrested on felonies. . . . Let's go down and take over the park."

—he did not fire it. The mob fell back, momentarily, at sight of the weapon and the people inside a locked building opened the door far enough to drag him in to safety.

The field commander of the Sheriffs' Office made his decision: the riot was out of control. Deputies armed with shotguns were ordered into action. When they arrived, they literally had to step over the bodies of injured officers who couldn't be helped or moved because the few left standing were under severe assault—and literally fighting for their lives.

Now, to all of those who are so quick to charge police brutality or over-reaction, let me call your attention to something else that hasn't been mentioned—with the one exception of the reserve patrolman. All of these officers, including those beaten to the ground, were armed with regulation .38 revolvers. Not one of them used his weapon, or even drew it from his holster under this assault. And yet, they stated that only the arrival of the deputies and their use of shotguns prevented the outright killing of isolated police and patrolmen.

As the afternoon went on, gas-dispensing vehicles spread tear gas in an effort to disperse the crowd. One of these was put out of action by the mob. They even captured a U.S. mail truck[2] . . . militants overturned more vehicles and turned in false fire alarms—and then stoned the firemen when they arrived.

The National Guard

At the start of the noon rally, a total of 150 police were on the scene; by the end of the day, the total had reached 791 . . . and they weren't enough. The sheriff said he could no longer guarantee the safety of the city. The city manager, the chief of police, the mayor and the sheriff joined in a request that the National Guard be assigned to prevent further violence.

Three battalions of the 49th Infantry Brigade, with supporting units, were ordered to Berkeley and I signed emergency proclamations banning outdoor public assemblies and prohibiting loitering in the streets.

A total of 48 persons had been arrested. On the basis of casualties alone, it would seem that the street people were out in front: ninety-nine officers had been injured—18 requiring hospital treatment; the total for the street people—43.

And yet, faculty groups in Berkeley, and on distant campuses, have publicly denounced the police and the use of the Guard. Others have chal-

[2] Berkeley police logs reported that a U.S. mail truck, later identified as an International Scout model, was stopped and seized at 2:06 p.m., May 15, at the corner of Bancroft and Telegraph Avenue in Berkeley. Berkeley Police Capt. Tom Johnson reported that the red, white and blue vehicle was surrounded by militants, doors were opened and demonstrators were going in and out of it. Pieces of what appeared to be letter-size paper were being strewn about on the street. Berkeley police logs reported mail was being taken from the truck. The truck's tires were deflated and dirt was put into the gas tank. It was 4:38 p.m. before the disabled vehicle could be towed away. Postal inspectors later reported they could not say whether there had been any loss of mail.

lenged what they term "overkill" and taking their cue from these supposedly reasonable mature adults, students have demonstrated in protest against the use of police and Guardsmen on the campus.

No one can take pleasure from bayonets in an American community or on a college campus. But the arrival of the Guard—with bayonets—brought an almost total de-escalation—an end to the hand-to-hand fighting and violence: there were a few skirmishes, false bomb reports, maneuvers by the Guard and police, and the dispersing gangs of militants.

For four days, the Guard successfully kept the crowds moving and dispersed, and then, on May 20, a large crowd made a stand in Sproul Plaza. Repeated warnings failed to move them. The situation was tense. The Guardsmen were being assaulted from the upper floors of one of the buildings. Chairs were being thrown down on their heads. The balcony of the Associated Student building was stockpiled with rocks and chunks of broken concrete.

All warnings failed. There was every indication that an imminent assault was at hand. The field commander made a battlefield decision and called for a helicopter to make a tear gas drop. The mob was told this had been done. Some left, but most remained.

There's no question but that innocent people suffered the distress that goes with tear gas. But there is no question, also, that tales exaggerated this episode beyond any resemblance to the facts.

There also can be no question that the alternative to the tear gas was hand-to-hand combat between the mob and the Guardsmen, and this could have provided real tragedy.

By May 24, the arrests had totalled 763—and 496 were non-students. Forty percent of those arrested weren't even from Berkeley. Finally, on June 2, University and local officials decided that order had been restored and asked me to withdraw the Guard. It was withdrawn. The Guard had put in 17 days at a cost to the taxpayers of $760,000.00. There is no way to assess the cost in damage, injuries, and loss of business to the community.

Thirteen-Point Manifesto

The issue is not closed. A "People's Park" negotiating committee has finally surfaced to declare there will be no real peace in Berkeley until the fence comes down. If we are to judge by past history, when it suits their purpose, an incident will be found or created as an excuse for intimidation, and more demonstrations and more violence.

They have issued a 13-point manifesto. Some of the points are very revealing.

—"Young people leaving their parents will be welcome with full status as member of our community.

—"We will turn the schools into training grounds for liberation.

—"We will shatter the myth that the University of California is a sacred institution with a special right to exist.

—"We will protect and expand our drug culture.

—"Through rent strikes, direct seizures of property and other resist-

ance campaigns, large landlords, banks and developers who are goug-
ing higher rents and spreading ugliness will be driven out.

—"Space will be opened up and living communities and revolutionary
families will be encouraged.

—"We will demand direct contributions from business, including
Berkeley's biggest business—the University, until a nationwide assault
on big business is successful.

—"The people of Berkeley must arm themselves and learn the basic
skills and tactics of self-defense and street fighting.

—"We shall attempt to bring real criminals to trial; where this is
impossible, we shall implement revolutionary justice.

—"We will create a soulful socialism in Berkeley.

—"We will unite with other movements throughout the world to
destroy [unprintable word] 'racistcapitalism' of the imperialist system.

—"We will create International Liberation Schools in Berkeley as a
training center for revolutionaries."

Bucolic Beautification?

I opened my remarks with some questions.

You can decide for yourselves whether the University arbitrarily and
unreasonably interfered with an innocent, bucolic beautification project.
And if it was the University that arrogantly refused to meet or conciliate.

I'll leave it to you to decide if the forces of law and order precipitated
the violence.

Should the University—having invested 1.3 million dollars for the
purpose approved by the administration of the University by its own
Capital Outlay Review Board and the Board of Regents—turn this investment over to some newly created corporation organized to put the
property in the hands of those who sought to take it by force? Or should
the University get on with the business of providing facilities for the
education of our young people?

And that brings me to the final question. Is there a revolutionary
movement involving a tiny minority of faculty and students finding con-
cealment and shelter in the disappointment and the resentment of an
entire college generation? A generation that is justifiably resentful of
being fed into the knowledge factory with no regard to their individualism, their aspirations or their dreams?

The answer is an obvious "Yes." The challenge to us is to establish
contact with these frustrated young people, to join in finding answers for
their problems before they fall to this mob by default.

Too Busy to Teach?

And at this moment in California the danger of this happening is very
real. And why not?

When Chancellor Heyns was meeting with law enforcement officers
and joining in their request for police and National Guard protection,
some of his fellow chancellors were endorsing the protests and the

hunger strikes. Faculty groups were passing resolutions deploring police tactics without so much as making a phone call to find out the facts.

I am firmly convinced these represent a minority, but they are the active minority. The majority of faculty are scholars too busy with their own research and writing to engage in such extra-curricular activities. But are they also too busy to teach?

Young men and women go to college to find themselves as individuals. They see the names of distinguished scholars in the catalogue and sign up for courses with the belief that they will learn and grow and be stimulated by contact with these men. All too often they are herded into gigantic classes taught by teaching assistants hardly older than themselves. The feeling comes that they're nameless, faceless numbers on an assembly line—green cap at one end, cap and gown and an automated diploma at the other. They want someone to know they're there. They aren't even missed and recorded as absent when they aren't there.

This generation—better informed, more aware—deserves much more. They are hungry for things of the spirit. They're filled with an idealism —a willingness to invest their energy in a truly creative effort, to make this world better.

The symptoms of rising rebellion have been evident for some time. They no longer bother to vote in student elections; so, that other tiny little group with its revolutionary purpose elects the student body officers and the editors who proceed to speak in the name of the University.

Those who administer and teach must make it plain that they will not be coerced by threats of force from that little group that is commanding so much of their attention. They must spell out in advance to that tiny minority the kinds of misconduct they will not tolerate and that there will be no negotiation with anyone who threatens violence. That's for the revolutionary part of the movement. Then, I say, if they will follow this and stand firm—the University can dispose of that kind of revolution within the week.

Communications

The greater problem has to do with the others—the majority—and it begins with communication. We must hear and understand their legitimate grievances . . . and solutions must be forthcoming. "Publish or perish" as a University policy must be secondary to teaching. Research, a vital and essential part of the educational process, must not become the standard by which the University rates itself as for excellence. The function of the University is to teach and its record must be established on the quality of the graduates it offers to the world—not on the collecting of scholarly names in its catalogue.

The few subversives on our campus will be much easier to handle if the so-called great silent majority has inner convictions, beliefs and confidence in our society and in us as adults. If we will turn our attention to them and their legitimate problems, and solve them, I guarantee you: you will have a great majority which will be an ally in handling the little dissident minority that only wants to break windows and cause trouble.

51. HIGH DANGER AREA

ROBERT M. HUTCHINS

Not all Californians agreed with Governor Reagan's handling of the
People's Park episode. Another viewpoint, more sympathetic to the
student, is offered by Robert Hutchins, former president of
the University of Chicago and now Chairman of the Board of the
Center for the Study of Democratic Institutions.

Education is becoming an extra-hazardous occupation. It is dangerous to enter a campus because the police or the National Guard may assume that you are a dissident student or professor and visit upon you the contempt they feel for these lesser breeds without the law.

It is even dangerous to live near a campus; for gas dropped from helicopters over the university may seep into your home. This happened the other day in Berkeley, Calif., during one of the most absurd and perilous phases of the war that Gov. Ronald Reagan is waging against the students and professors of his state.

It is hardly too much to say that the systematic program of overkill that the governor is following, in which escalation inevitably leads to further escalation, must end the brilliant career of higher education in California.

The Governor and his troops are now in a state that can only be described as hysterical. First a couple of thousand unarmed people marching quietly along the street are suddenly assaulted by officers in full battle dress with guns and various kinds of highly unattractive gases. One man was shot.

The next day the campus is surrounded and the same kinds of gases are sprayed all over the place from the sky. The troops had not learned the elementary lesson taught by World War I, that gas is a most unreliable weapon: it has a way of going where the wind carries it, and the wind is unpredictable. On this occasion the gas covered friend and foe indiscriminately, penetrating the hospital, classrooms and neighboring homes.

If we have got to the point where we can't attend college, or teach in one, or live near one without gas masks, we might as well call the whole thing off.

But before doing so we might take a sober look at the situation to see where we are and why we are there. Obviously the repressive measures employed in Berkeley can have only one effect: they will unite the students, the professors and the community against the forces of "law and order." This is something the radical students have not been able to do. Gov. Reagan has played into their hands.

A small group of students is intent on nothing but disruption. Everything turns on how this group is handled. They cannot get anywhere unless they can convince the other students that they have legitimate

Robert M. Hutchins, "High Danger Area," *Santa Barbara News-Press* (June 1, 1969). Copyright, Los Angeles Times. Reprinted with permission.

grievances. Indifference on the part of the administration to legitimate grievances, of which many administrations have been guilty, leads to demonstrations. If at this point the radicals can provoke the administration and the government into some ill-considered act of suppression, then they are on the path to victory, for they will unite with them students and faculty who beforehand were apathetic or hostile to them. The more repressive the acts they can provoke, the more successful they will be. Now in Berkeley everybody has a legitimate grievance. Respectable middle-class citizens who formerly despised the long-haired, shoeless students are now at last their allies.

I do not take seriously the prospect of a revolution in this country. Those students who want a revolution are few. They are a negligible threat to society. Students cannot accomplish revolutionary aims without the support of other aggrieved elements in the population. Everywhere in the Western world students have found it difficult to gain such support. In this country white revolutionary students have not even succeeded in getting black students to join them.

If Gov. Reagan wants a revolution, he has chosen the right road to it. At least what he has brought about in Berkeley bears a marked resemblance to civil war.

52. RUDENESS, WEAPON OF THE FANATIC

ERIC HOFFER

The words and actions of the radical left have alienated large
numbers of people. Eric Hoffer, the longshoreman-philosopher and
occasional lecturer at the University of California at Berkeley,
asserts that the irresponsible spokesmen are planting the seeds for
a violent rightist reaction in America.

Rudeness is the weak man's imitation of strength. Nothing so illustrates the incurable insecurity of the fanatical mentality as the affinity between fanaticism and rudeness. The family likeness between fanatics of diametrically opposed persuasions, such as the Nazis and the Communists, is partly due to the homogenizing effect of rudeness.

It is of course true that rudeness bolsters the fanatic's intolerance. It throttles the soft amenities which would dovetail him with others, and blur his uncompromising stance. Thus it is generally true that eras of blind faith are areas of bad manners. On the other hand, as Francis Bacon observed, "the times inclined to unbelief are civil times."

Right now the paragons of rudeness are found on the campuses and among people who fancy themselves in the vanguard of society. Obscenities have become a mark of sophistication, of idealism, and of attained manhood. Rudeness is now serving as a substitute for power, for faith, and for achievement.

To me the present escalation of rudeness is an indication that the apocalyptic Stalin-Hitler madhouse is by no means behind us. The yammering, screeching, obscene student hoodlums and Black Power murder boys who demand instant power and instant bliss are "final solutionists" of the Stalin-Hitler brand.

Sen. Ribicoff displayed historical illiteracy when he accused Mayor Daley and the Chicago police of being Gestapo. It was precisely because the Weimar Republic had no Daleys and no Chicago police to fight its battles in Germany's cities during the 1920s that the Nazis and their Gestapo came to power. It is never the police who start a police state. The opposite has been true; the "final solutionists" serve their apprenticeship fighting the police.

There is no getting away from it: if the mass of people in this country are not ready to strengthen the hand of their police or find some way of reacting quickly and forcefully against those who are determined to disrupt and destroy our institutions, we shall be heading toward a Fascist state and eventual holocaust.

The middle has up to now remained silent and inert. One is conscious of a dark resentment welling up in the majority. But, so far, no one has tried to channel the pent-up resentment into active resistance. It might perhaps be better for this country if the middle were to burst out in anger now and then, than that it brood impotently, and wait and pray for a Hitler.

Chapter 10

Jobs, Welfare,
and Housing

The interrelated problems of jobs, welfare, and housing are particularly vexing issues for minority people. There is an abundance of statistical data to suggest that employment for California's minority groups has followed a general pattern of little status and opportunity. It is not enough solely to explain this matter by pointing to the disparate levels of education, income, and employment between whites and nonwhites; something must be done to change it.

Of course, employment opportunities are being created today for some of the unskilled minorities, but such programs are available to only a small fraction of the people who need them. The inadequacy of these training programs is increased by the annual migration of thousands of Mexicans to the United States. Moreover, the recent movement of minority people from rural areas to the city has heightened the problems of those who are not acquainted with the urban job market. Thus, employment of minorities is not simply a class or regional problem; rather, it is a problem of the agricultural worker and the urban dweller, of both blue collar worker and professional.

Not only do these job realities have profound social effects upon these people (see Chapters 5, 6, and 7), but also it appears that the institutional agencies designed to cope with these problems may be failing. Welfare programs are expanding at explosive speed to meet the needs of the jobless while the number of unemployed is increasing. Governmental services straining to meet this challenge are unable to achieve their goals, as is evi-

denced by the overworked welfare agencies and the soaring costs
to the taxpayer. An alternative approach to minority social and
economic problems may be that black and other minorities
should engage in a capitalism of their own. The problem in this
approach has been inadequate capital, and as yet neither the
private nor public sectors of the economy have supported minority capitalism. Indeed, many commentators feel that the proposal for black capitalism made during the 1968 political
campaign will do little for those who have heretofore suffered
from economic deprivation.

It should not be assumed that the problems of employment and
welfare affect only their immediate victims. There is growing
evidence to suggest that these minority problems have many ram-
ifications—psychological and economic—with regard to society
as a whole. When blacks or other minorities are denied equal-
housing rights, the white man is automatically implicated. When
increasing numbers of people are jobless and subsist on the public welfare rolls, the whole society pays the costs. Moreover, it is
generally acknowledged that only the immense network of de-
fense-related industries prevents the unemployment rate from
climbing even more drastically.

Thus, the vague assertion is being made that our societal value
system itself must be updated to meet the needs of modern society. A new vocabulary is entering our lexicon today; for the
first time, Americans in the 1960s encountered such terms as
"cybernation," the "guaranteed income," and the "military-industrial complex." Advocates of this new thought argue that what is
at stake is nothing less than the survival of our way of life and
that to incorporate all people into the mainstream of our economy
would be to enrich the meaning of democracy and to increase our
prosperity.

Are such ideas realistic? Is it possible in our time for all of
society to reap the benefits of its affluence? Why have some states
and the Congress already launched experimental programs with
the guaranteed income? How have other industrial democracies
coped with the concomitant problems of jobs and welfare? What
other questions might be posed as the reader considers the con-
tents of this chapter?

53. MINORITY GROUPS IN CALIFORNIA

The following article from the Monthly Labor Review, *a publication of the U.S. Government, discusses the employment situation of minorities in the Golden State. The author cites certain factors that influence the likelihood of obtaining employment. This information provides the reader with a statistical measurement of the minorities' economic role in California.*

"South and East Los Angeles are literal islands of poverty and deprivation that have grown more depressed over the past 5 years." So said C. L. Dellums, chairman of the California Fair Employment Practices Commission, in introducing an analysis of a special survey of Negroes and Mexican Americans in ghetto areas of Los Angeles. The study,[1] comparing 1960 census data with that of a special census taken in November 1965, is the latest in a series of reports issued by the FEPC, and summarized here.

Two Communities

South Los Angeles, which includes Watts, is a predominantly Negro area (in 1965, 81 out of every 100 residents). Between 1960 and 1965, the total population of the area fell almost 10 percent; the Negro population expanded by 5 percent. In East Los Angeles, 76 out of every 100 residents in 1965 were Mexican American; here the total population declined by 8 percent from 1960 to 1965, while the Mexican American population increased by 6 percent.

In both South and East Los Angeles, population was relatively stable; 87 and 85 percent, respectively, of the residents in 1965 had lived in the area for at least 5 years. In both districts, the population was young; more than a third of the residents were age 14 or younger. The Federal Government estimates, Mr. Dellums noted, that by 1975 one-half of the U.S. population will be under age 25. These minority communities have already reached that proportion: in November 1965, 50 percent of the residents of South Los Angeles and 53 percent in East Los Angeles were less than 25 years old.

In both districts, too, the quality of housing deteriorated sharply while rental costs rose and the number of owner-occupied dwellings fell. In

---

[1] *Negroes and Mexican Americans in South and East Los Angeles* (San Francisco, Calif., State Department of Industrial Relations, Division of Fair Employment Practices, 1966). This and earlier reports in the series were prepared for the FEPC by the Division of Labor Statistics and Research. Single copies of the report are available from the Fair Employment Practices Commission, Box 603, San Francisco, Calif. 94101.

"Minority Groups in California," *Monthly Labor Review*, Vol. 89 (September 1966), pp. 978–983.

1960, 82 percent of the dwellings in South Los Angeles had been declared "sound" by the census takers; in 1965, only 67 percent were
"sound."

Purchasing power or "real" income of the average family in both areas
dropped nearly $400 over the 5-year period. One reason for this, Mr.
Dellums suggested, is that "Those families who manage to get ahead—
and whose breadwinners are able to advance educationally, economically or socially—those are the families that move out. They leave behind the subpoverty-level group—the uneducated, the unemployed,
those most discriminated against."

"But the fact that men employed in good jobs leave the South or East
Los Angeles areas in no way alleviates the serious problem for those who
remain," he continued. "Many of these remaining men, who have given
up hope of finding a job, have in a sense been dropped from the labor
force." Although some of the marked decrease in labor force participation rates (chart 1) can be attributed to increased enrollment in school,
the core of the problem appears to lie in the increasing proportion of
"labor force dropouts."

These persons—probably the least able to become fully participating
members in an urban economy—are likely to be left behind in the ghetto
areas as families with rising incomes move out. Another indication of
this is seen in the continuation of high unemployment rates. As the [ac-
companying] tabulation shows, in South Los Angeles the rate for men
fell only slightly, and the rate for women rose.

| | Unemployed persons as a percent of the civilian labor force | | | |
| | Men | | Women | |
	1965	1960	1965	1960
South Los Angeles	10.1	11.3	11.5	10.4
East Los Angeles	7.7	8.5	6.8	7.3
Los Angeles-Long Beach metropolitan area	[1] 5.2	5.6	[1] 5.2	6.0
California	—	5.8	—	6.6

[1] Men and women combined (rate compiled by the California Department of
Employment).

In East Los Angeles, although the situation improved somewhat, unemployment rates were still higher than in the Los Angeles metropolitan
area as a whole—this in spite of the increasing proportion who had
simply taken themselves out of the labor force.

The proportion of women in South Los Angeles who were married and
living with their husbands fell from 53 to 48 percent during the 5 years.
Among East Los Angeles women, the drop was from 55 to 51 percent.
The number of households headed by women increased, so that in 1965,
26 percent of all persons in South Los Angeles families were in households headed by women (up from 19 percent in 1960). In East Los Angeles, the proportion in 1965 (17 percent) was only slightly higher than

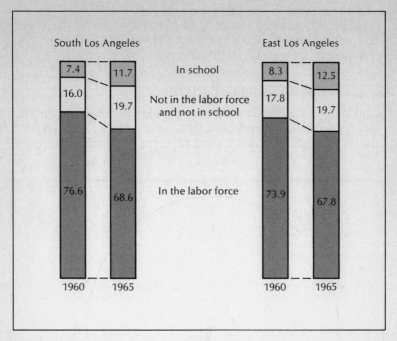

South Los Angeles East Los Angeles

In school

Not in the labor force
and not in school

In the labor force

Note: In both districts, in 1965, almost a fifth of the men were neither in school nor in the labor force.

in 1960 (16 percent). Largely because of the lower earning power of women, more than half of these households headed by women had incomes below the poverty level (59 percent in South and 50 percent in East Los Angeles).

In both districts young families—those with heads under 25 years—were in grave economic difficulties. Almost half of such families in South Los Angeles, and a third in East Los Angeles, had incomes in 1965 below the poverty level [see tabulation].

| | Percent of families with income below poverty level | | | |
| | South Los Angeles | | East Los Angeles | |
Age of family head	1965	1960	1965	1960
All families	26.8	23.9	23.6	21.7
Under 25 years	46.3	39.9	32.1	32.3
25–54 years	26.4	22.7	23.4	20.5
55–64 years	18.7	17.5	16.8	16.1
65 years or over	26.3	28.8	27.5	29.8

The Los Angeles report, summarized above, measured changes that have taken place between 1960 and 1965 in two particularly depressed areas. Earlier reports in the FEPC's ethnic series dealt with the population, employment, income, and education of the several minority groups, as portrayed in statistics from the 1960 Census of Population. The following summary presents highlights from the four reports.[2]

A Kaleidoscope of Racial Patterns

The makeup of California's minority population (chart 2) differs considerably from that of other States. Its largest minority consists of "Californians of Spanish surname," most of them of Mexican ancestry;[3] it

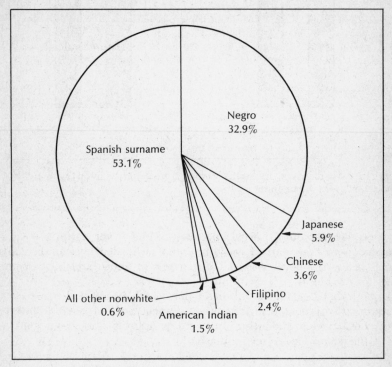

Note: In 1960, California's non-Anglo population numbered 2.7 million (out of 15.7 million). More than half were Mexican Americans.

[2] *Negro Californians*, June 1963; *Californians of Spanish Surname*, May 1964; *Californians of Japanese, Chinese, and Filipino Ancestry*, June 1965; and *American Indians in California*, November 1965. Charts and tables used with this summary were constructed in BLS from the tabular material in the reports.

[3] The terms "Mexican American" and "population of Spanish surname" are used interchangeably in this summary, although the data does include relatively small numbers of persons of other national origin or ancestry: Cuban, Puerto Rican, Central and South American, Spanish. The data relate only to white persons of Spanish surname; nonwhite persons of Spanish surname were excluded.

also has the largest Chinese population of any State, and is second only to Hawaii in the number of Japanese and Filipinos.

Before the coming of the first Europeans, it is estimated, from 130,-000 to 150,000 Indians lived in what is now California. By 1900, only 15,000 remained. During the next half century, the Indian population in the State grew slowly, reaching 20,000 by 1950. In the next decade, however, an upsurge in population growth and resettlement in California of Indians from other States brought the figure to 39,000.

Although tribal and allotted lands in the 83 Indian reservations and rancherias in the State total more than a half million acres, only 19 percent of the Indians live on or adjacent to the reservations. The majority reside on private property among the general population. During the 1950's, accompanying the rapid increase in Indian population, there was a decided shift from rural to urban living, so that by 1960 more than half of California's Indians lived in urban areas. The proportion living in rural areas was still greater among Indians, however, than among persons of any other ethnic group. (See table 1.)

The Spanish surname population also grew rapidly during the 1950's (by 88.1 percent) and continued as California's largest minority group. A very large proportion (80 percent) were native born, and 46 percent were also of native parentage. Among the 20 percent foreign born, 16 percent had been born in Mexico.

The Mexican American population was not as highly urbanized as some of the other ethnic groups, a fact probably related to the higher-than-average proportion employed as farm laborers. Persons of Spanish surname made up a larger proportion of the total population than did Negroes in all areas except the San Francisco-Oakland metropolitan area, where 8.6 percent of the total population in 1960 was Negro, compared with 6.4 percent of Spanish surname.

In 1960, more than one-third of all U.S. residents of Japanese, Chinese, and Filipino ancestry lived in California. Of all Japanese Americans in 13 Western States in 1960,[4] 82 percent were native born. The proportion of native-born Chinese was considerably lower—69 percent. Among Filipinos, 52 percent were American born. Between 1950 and 1960, the three Oriental groups participated in the general movement of population from rural to urban areas. The proportion of Japanese living in urban areas rose from 70 to 87 percent. The Chinese, already overwhelmingly concentrated in cities and towns (94 percent in 1950), made a further shift, to 96 percent in 1960. The shift was greater, however, among Filipinos—from 60 to 80 percent.

The Negro population, which in 1960 constituted 70 percent of the State's nonwhite population, is predominantly urban. In 1960, only 5.6 percent lived in rural areas. In the two largest metropolitan areas (Los Angeles–Long Beach and San Francisco–Oakland), Negroes in 1960 constituted respectively 6.9 percent and 8.6 percent of the total population.

[4] Data not available for California alone. States included were: Alaska, Arizona, California, Colorado, Hawaii, Idaho, Montana, Nevada, New Mexico, Oregon, Utah, Washington, and Wyoming.

TABLE 1
Population and Size of Family, by Ethnic Group, California, 1960 [1]

Characteristic	Total	White (except Spanish surname)	Spanish surname	Negro	Japanese	Chinese	Filipino	American Indian
POPULATION								
1960	15,717,024	13,028,692	1,426,538	883,861	157,317	95,600	65,459	39,014
As percent of total population	100.0	82.9	9.1	5.6	1.0	0.6	0.4	0.2
As percent of white population	—	90.1	9.9					
As percent of nonwhite population			—	70.0	12.7	7.6	5.2	3.1
1950	10,586,223	9,156,773	758,400	462,172	84,956	58,324	40,424	19,947
Percent change, 1950–60	48.5	42.3	88.1	91.2	85.2	63.9	61.9	95.6
Percent residing in urban areas	86.4	86.0	85.4	94.4	86.5	96.4	79.6	52.9
In-migration since 1955: [2]								
From other States	14.8	14.6	7.1	15.2	10.3	5.2	7.1	17.5
From other countries	—	—	5.1	1.0	10.3	7.4	13.8	—
SIZE OF FAMILY [3]								
Percent of families numbering—								
2 persons	35.4	37.2	21.1	32.1	20.5	19.1	21.2	17.5
3 persons	21.1	21.3	18.6	21.0	20.5	20.1	17.2	16.2
4 persons	20.3	20.5	20.0	16.2	23.1	22.1	17.5	15.4
5 persons	12.6	12.2	16.2	11.6	17.6	17.8	14.6	14.0
6 persons	6.0	5.5	10.6	7.8	10.3	11.4	12.0	11.5
7 persons or more	4.5	3.3	13.5	11.3	8.0	9.5	17.5	25.4

1 Dashes indicate data not available or not applicable. Detail may not add to totals, due to rounding.

2 In-migrants 5 years old and over, as percent of 1960 population.

3 For total, white (except Spanish surname), and Spanish surname populations, data relate to California. For nonwhite populations, data relate to 13 Western States; data on size of family not available for California alone.

Age and Size of Family

Indians exceeded all other ethnic groups in size of family in 1960, followed by those of Spanish surname and Filipinos. More than a fourth of the Indian families numbered seven persons or more.

Indians were younger, on the whole, than members of other minority groups in California; 45 percent of both Indian men and women were under 20 years of age in 1960. However, the Spanish surname and Negro populations were also concentrated in the younger age brackets. In 1960, 70.4 percent of the Mexican Americans and 65.2 percent of the Negroes were less than 35 years old. The senior citizens of California, on the other hand, were predominantly Anglo.[5]

In all three Oriental groups, the men were older, on the whole, than the women. The difference was greatest among Filipinos: 48 percent of the men were 45 or older, compared with 10 percent of the women. The age disparity, as well as the larger number of men, reflects the immigration of single Filipino men following World War I. Japanese, Chinese, and Filipino women were comparatively young. The under-35 age group accounted for 78 percent of Filipino women, 70 percent of Chinese women, and 65 percent of Japanese women.

Education

There were striking differences in the educational attainment of the three Oriental groups in 1960. Japanese, both men and women, were well ahead of the white population in the level of education achieved. For the Chinese, the picture was one of extremes; a relatively high proportion of both men and women had completed at least some college education, but approximately 40 percent had not gone beyond the eighth grade, and many of these were reported as having had no schooling at all. More than half the Filipino men and almost one-third of the Filipino women had not gone beyond the eighth grade. Filipino women achieved a higher education at all levels than did Filipino men, and had the highest proportion among women of all racial groups with at least 1 year of college.

For other nonwhite groups, educational levels were low. Only 3.3 percent of Negro men had completed 4 years of college, compared with 10.2 percent of all men in the State. Among the Indians, 43 percent of both men and women had not gone beyond the eighth grade, and less than 2 percent had completed college.

Educational attainment of the Spanish surname population was considerably below that of the total population, and of the nonwhite population as well. In all metropolitan areas for which 1960 figures were available, the median number of school years completed was lower for the Spanish surname population, male and female, than for either the total population or the nonwhite population.

[5] There is no precise definition for this term as used in the Southwest. Generally speaking, all white, English-speaking persons are included.

Income

Men in all the minority groups had median incomes in 1959 below that of men in the white population. Filipinos and American Indians were well below those of other minority groups. Among women, the 1959 median income of both Japanese and Chinese women exceeded that of women in the white population. (See chart 3.)

To exclude students and inexperienced workers, income figures were also compiled separately for men 25 years and over. Only among the white population did more than half these men earn $5,000 or more in 1959. Three-fourths of the Indians, and an even higher proportion of Filipinos, earned less than that amount.

Unemployment

In 1960, the unemployment rate was higher among Indian men than among men of any other ethnic group. Among women, Filipinos had the highest unemployment rate. As the tabulation shows, unemployment

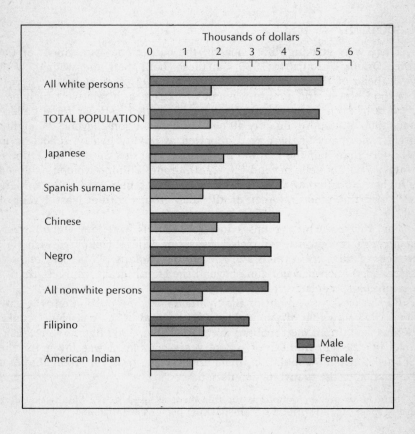

rates for both Japanese and Chinese men and women were considerably below those for white men and women.

	Unemployment rates, California, 1960	
Ethnic group	Men	Women
American Indian	15.1	11.4
Negro	12.7	11.4
Filipino	7.8	13.6
Spanish surname	7.7	11.2
White (including Spanish surname)	5.5	6.3
Chinese	4.9	5.1
Japanese	2.6	3.1

Unemployment rates were higher among Filipinos than other Oriental groups, perhaps in part because the Census count was taken during April, outside the peak employment period for farm workers, a sizable occupation group for Filipino men. (See table 2.)

The unemployment rate for nonwhite men was approximately twice that for white men. More than one-fifth of the nonwhite male teenagers in the labor force were jobless, as were 16.1 percent of the nonwhites age 20–24.

Occupation

An analysis was made of the racial composition of various occupational groups. Spanish surname men (8.7 percent of all employed men in the State) were 41.9 percent of all men employed as farm laborers and foremen. Spanish surname women (6.5 percent of all employed women) were 28.6 percent of all female farm laborers. Nonfarm laborers also included relatively high proportions of Mexican Americans— 18.1 percent of the men and 18.8 percent of the women.

Of all employed males in the State in 1960, 9 percent of the whites and 10.1 percent of the Negroes worked in the construction industry; Negroes represented 5.1 percent of all males working in the industry.

Thirteen percent of the State's employed male laborers (other than farm or mine) were Negroes; this represented 17.8 percent of the Negroes. Only 5.6 percent of the white male workers were in this category.

Among the men employed as craftsmen, foremen, and kindred workers, 3 percent were Negroes. This represented 13.3 percent of employed Negroes; 20.9 percent of employed white men were in this occupational group.

The agricultural background of Japanese and Filipino workers in California was evident in their 1960 occupational distributions. In each case, close to a third were in farm occupations. Among the Japanese, farmers and farm managers predominated; of the Filipino men, most were farm laborers and foremen. More than half of all Filipino men were either farm laborers or service workers.

Professional and technical occupations accounted for a sizable propor-

TABLE 2

Selected Characteristics of Population, by Ethnic Group and Sex, California, 1960
[Percent distribution]¹

Characteristic	Total		White (except Spanish surname)		Spanish surname		Negro		Japanese		Chinese		Filipino		American Indian	
	Male	Female	Male	Female	Male	Female	Male	Female	Male	Female	Male	Female	Male	Female	Male	Female
AGE																
Under 5 years	11.4	10.9	10.7	10.1	15.0	15.4	14.9	14.4	12.8	11.7	11.2	13.5	10.3	18.0	15.2	15.9
5–9 years	10.4	9.9	10.0	9.4	12.6	13.3	12.3	11.9	10.2	9.8	11.6	13.3	8.9	15.3	11.4	11.8
10–14 years	9.2	8.9	9.1	8.6	10.3	10.7	9.4	9.3	7.6	7.6	9.2	10.7	8.0	13.3	9.4	8.7
15–19 years	7.3	6.7	7.3	6.5	8.0	8.5	6.8	6.6	6.3	5.9	4.5	4.8	4.7	7.6	8.5	8.2
20–24 years	6.4	6.1	6.2	5.9	7.6	7.6	7.3	7.2	6.2	7.1	6.0	7.3	4.5	6.7	10.3	8.4
25–34 years	13.7	13.4	13.2	12.9	16.4	15.4	15.1	15.3	18.6	22.9	16.3	20.1	9.6	17.1	14.1	12.9
35–44 years	14.4	14.6	14.6	14.8	12.7	12.0	14.8	14.9	18.2	17.7	14.6	13.6	6.4	11.9	9.9	10.5
45–54 years	11.5	11.4	12.2	11.9	7.8	7.8	10.2	10.1	6.9	5.8	11.6	8.9	24.9	6.4	8.0	8.3
55–64 years	8.1	8.6	8.5	9.1	5.6	5.2	5.6	5.8	5.7	6.3	8.8	4.9	17.9	2.9	8.1	9.8
65 years and over	7.6	9.6	8.3	10.7	4.0	4.1	3.6	4.5	7.5	5.2	6.2	2.9	4.8	.8	5.1	5.5
EDUCATIONAL ATTAINMENT²																
No schooling	1.8	1.4	—	—	8.3	6.3	1.8	1.4	2.6	2.9	15.8	18.7	7.8	2.3	4.4	4.8
1 to 8 grades	26.1	23.6	—	—	43.2	41.7	36.1	32.6	16.9	17.2	25.0	20.0	45.3	28.3	38.9	38.5
High school: 1 to 3 years	24.4	24.6	—	—	24.8	26.6	28.8	29.3	17.4	16.0	13.9	13.2	18.1	23.2	30.0	29.0
4 years	24.3	30.1	—	—	14.9	19.2	20.6	23.1	34.3	43.3	16.1	24.9	15.4	21.9	19.1	20.4
College: 1 to 3 years	13.2	12.9	—	—	6.0	4.6	9.4	10.3	16.9	14.9	15.9	14.3	9.5	15.1	5.8	5.3
4 years or more	10.2	6.5	—	—	2.8	1.6	3.3	3.3	11.9	5.7	13.3	8.9	3.9	9.2	1.8	2.0
OCCUPATION³																
Professional, technical, and kindred workers	13.5	14.0	15.0	15.2	4.5	5.2	4.4	7.6	15.0	10.1	16.9	11.1	3.6	12.8	3.8	5.8
Farmers and farm managers	2.0	.3	1.9	.3	1.9	.1	.5	(4)	21.4	3.2	1.2	.3	2.9	.6	1.5	.1

	1	2	3	4	5	6	7	8	9	10	11	12	13	14	15	16
Managers, officials, and proprietors, except farm	11.9	4.9	13.3	5.4	4.2	2.3	2.3	1.3	7.9	2.8	14.3	4.5	2.0	1.7	2.0	2.8
Clerical and kindred workers	7.0	35.0	7.2	37.4	4.7	24.3	7.8	14.1	6.8	32.3	9.2	33.5	4.5	30.0	3.1	14.3
Sales workers	7.7	8.0	8.5	8.7	3.2	6.0	1.8	1.7	5.9	4.4	9.0	8.5	1.0	3.6	1.1	3.0
Craftsmen, foremen, and kindred workers	20.2	1.2	21.4	1.2	16.3	1.5	13.3	1.0	10.4	.9	6.6	.8	6.7	.4	16.2	.5
Operatives and kindred workers	16.5	11.6	15.5	9.6	24.0	32.4	21.9	14.6	9.1	16.4	12.1	25.8	10.8	16.4	23.1	15.3
Private household workers	.1	6.1	.1	4.6	.1	5.2	.6	27.2	1.1	11.6	1.4	1.6	1.0	3.4	.4	14.9
Service workers, except private household	6.4	12.0	5.7	11.5	6.4	11.6	16.4	20.7	3.5	6.8	20.6	6.8	26.2	16.8	5.2	16.9
Farm laborers and foremen	3.3	.7	1.8	.4	15.7	3.1	1.9	.4	9.2	7.0	.8	.8	27.5	4.9	10.2	2.4
Laborers, except farm and mine	6.2	.4	4.9	.3	12.8	1.2	17.8	1.1	5.9	.9	1.9	.3	5.0	.2	17.3	.9
Occupation not reported	5.1	5.8	4.7	5.3	6.2	7.1	11.3	10.3	3.8	3.6	6.0	6.0	8.8	8.3	16.1	23.1

INDUSTRY [4][5]

	1	2	3	4	5	6	7	8
Agriculture, forestry, and fisheries	4.6	3.4	14.9	2.0	25.1	1.9	28.5	10.7
Mining	.5	.5	.2	(4)	(4)	(4)	.1	.5
Construction	6.3	6.4	6.8	6.1	1.7	2.0	1.0	5.6
Manufacturing	24.1	24.0	29.8	17.5	15.7	16.0	13.0	24.6
Transportation, communication, and other public utilities	6.8	7.0	6.3	6.7	2.9	3.4	4.4	6.6
Wholesale and retail trade	18.8	19.4	15.9	11.1	18.8	38.9	15.8	9.1
Finance, insurance, and real estate	5.1	5.5	2.6	1.9	3.9	4.4	2.7	1.1
Business and repair services	3.4	3.6	2.6	3.5	3.1	1.8	1.0	1.7
Personal services	5.7	4.9	5.2	17.6	9.7	8.0	8.1	9.4
Entertainment and recreation services	1.4	1.7	1.1	.9	.5	.8	2.2	.9
Professional and related services	12.5	13.2	5.4	12.0	10.2	10.1	8.3	7.3
Public administration	6.1	6.1	3.7	10.7	5.1	7.4	6.8	4.8
Industry not reported	4.7	4.2	5.7	9.9	3.3	5.3	8.1	17.7

1 Dashes indicate data not available.
2 School level completed by persons 14 years old and over.
3 Of employed persons 14 years old and over.
4 Less than 0.05 of 1 percent.
5 Data not available by sex.

tion of both Chinese and Japanese men, reflecting their higher levels of educational attainment. The concentration of Chinese workers in urban centers was also reflected in their occupations.

Because of limited employment opportunities (particularly on reservations), low educational attainment, and lack of job skills, labor force participation rates among Indians are lower than among other ethnic groups (in 1960, only 68 percent of the Indian men and 31 percent of the women were at work or seeking work). Of the Indian men who were employed, a fourth worked in manufacturing industries, a proportion exceeded only by the Mexican American group.

54. THE STATE EMPLOYMENT SERVICE

PAUL JACOBS

One of the crucial problems facing the unemployed minorities is finding a job, which is generally done through the state employment agency. Paul Jacobs critically examines the operation and the administration of the state employment service in the following selection from his book Prelude to Riot: A View of America from the Bottom.

The basic assumption on which the employment service functions—that it is part of a "nationwide network of public employment offices that find jobs for people and people for jobs,"—is useless to the task of solving the unemployment problem of the "unskilled," especially the minority "unskilled." In fact, it does *not* find jobs for people or people for jobs if these people are the unemployed who have never worked. Indeed, as it has been operating, the service *cannot* perform that function. Instead, it has been helping those people find work who least need help and who might have found jobs without any assistance.

The failure of the California State Employment Service is not due to lack of good will either at the top levels in the federal government, which supplies the funds and the over-all direction, or at the high state levels, which direct the administration of the program. Many of the program's top administrators know that the way in which the organization has operated is wrong; many know that their institution has not been responding to the new demands upon it, especially at the lower administrative levels, and some of them even know what ought to be done. But even if they know, they cannot do what needs doing, for what needs doing lies outside the area of possibilities for the employment service as it is today. Whatever merits it once had as a social tool, it is no longer a useful instrument, because today's unemployment problem has dimensions and qualities that did not exist when the service was created.

The employment service, naturally enough, originally reflected in its internal organization and psychology the dominant views of a laissez-faire America about jobs and unemployment: a willing man could find a job, and unemployment was a sign of laziness or vice. The first public employment offices in the United States were municipal ones set up during nineteenth-century recessions; by the early part of the twentieth century the federal government had entered the field through the Immigration Service, which tried to spread immigrant workers all over the country. In World War I the federal operations were expanded, only to die out after the war, when it was again assumed that anybody who wanted work could find it without assistance. It was not until the Depression that Congress passed the Wagner-Peyser Act (1933) establishing the United States Employment Service. In 1935 the Social Security Act, which financed the unemployment insurance program on a federal-state basis, was tied into employment service operations; and in 1936 the state employment services were established, to work cooperatively with the United States Employment Service but with local control as a basic concept.

Over the years, in and out of the agency, its primary function—employment placement—became subordinated to its providing of unemployment insurance, especially during recessions, when it had to compete with private agencies for the few available jobs. And so the operation became known as the "unemployment" rather than the employment office, a name it still has to most of the unemployed today.

And since unemployment insurance, which is paid for by a payroll tax on the employer, is given only to those people actively seeking work, the "unemployment" became an often formidable barrier, which had to be got around in order to receive the benefits. First, the applicants for unemployment insurance benefits had to prove that they were unemployed through no fault of their own. Then they had to prove that they were continuing to seek work in order to continue receiving their weekly checks. Since the two functions of job placement and unemployment insurance were carried out until 1960 in the same physical location, it was easy for the unemployment insurance personnel to learn from their colleagues in placement whether or not the applicant was actively seeking work and therefore entitled to receive the benefits.

"The unemployment insurance system was always based too much on a worker's ability to get a job from the employment service," says one official of the agency. "A man would come in and the placement people would talk to him about taking a job. Then the unemployment insurance personnel would know about it and would disqualify the man if he didn't take the job. If he went out and applied for the job but didn't get it, there was always some question about whether he really tried for it. The heavy concentration of the offices was always on trying to get the man off unemployment insurance by getting him any kind of a job, instead of trying to help him get the best kind of job."

The federal government's method of financing the employment services long ago became another handicap to their being of use to the unemployed, unskilled worker. Basically, financing is determined by the *number* of placements. If fewer placements are made by an office, its staff is cut, and so the managers inevitably tend toward making fast and easy placements. And since placements in short-term jobs can be made more quickly than permanent placements, which require more interviewing and counseling time, the long-term jobs get neglected.

The unskilled workers' attempts to find jobs through the state employment services are also hindered because the size of the grants made by the federal government to the state offices is based on the unit-time system, a method of judging productivity borrowed from industry. Fixed amounts of time are established as the norms for the employment service personnel to carry out various assignments. Thus, in 1959 and 1960, 162.9 minutes were allowed for making a professional or clerical placement, while only 52.7 minutes were allocated for getting an unskilled worker a job, and a mere 22.8 minutes for making a placement in day or casual work. Forty-five minutes were allowed for each counseling interview.

This system of administrative piecework obviously went against the interests of the unskilled and minority workers. Helping such workers to get jobs which might raise their skill levels obviously demands a great deal more counseling and interviewing time than does helping a worker with readily salable skills and appearance. But because the federal policy emphasized making skilled, professional, and clerical placements by allowing them more time per placement, the people seeking work in those categories were favored over all the others.

In addition, the norms became maximums; the staff learned how to beat the system, as workers always learn how to get around piecework standards; the operations became routinized, and the need for filing daily reports on the filling of the unit-time quotas also helped to sacrifice the minority workers' interests to the piecework quotas. The forty-five minutes allocated for counseling is an apt illustration of how useless such a system is if the norms are actually used: the California State Employment Service discovered that proper counseling of a single unemployed teen-ager took at least fifty-eight hours!

Naturally enough, too, the prejudice patterns of American life existed within the service, and so for many years discrimination against members of minority groups was widely practiced. "Everybody in Los Angeles had heard or everybody assumed that there was a certain amount of prejudice with the employers and that the state was no exception," states a Negro official of the department in describing his experiences when he entered the employment service in the 1950s. "And frankly, when I took the written exam, I passed it and I honestly believed that I would be flunked on the oral. And I was. It was given by an all-white panel. Now maybe the reason I flunked was because I believed I was going to when I went into the orals, and so I failed. But anyway I appealed, and when I took it again, I passed it.

"One thing I noticed right away was that in the office where I worked the few Negroes who were there had been on the job for five or ten years. They were very quiet and some of them told me that I was on trial, that I shouldn't talk up, that I was marked because I had appealed from being turned down for the job."

Over a period of years the discriminatory practices of American business and unions were not only accepted within the state services but were translated into discriminatory placements. And even though some of the personnel may have doubted the correctness of these policies, they believed they had to accept discriminatory job orders in order to compete with the private agencies, which could more easily serve prejudiced employers even though they might be prohibited legally from doing so.

"Let's face it," states the manager of an employment service office. "In the past, employment service was completely employer-oriented. An employer would call me up and tell me that he wanted someone and that he would pay him a dollar an hour. I didn't question this. If he said he didn't want any Negroes, I wouldn't argue with him. I just assumed that if we wanted that employer's business, we had to do business his way."

55. THE GRAPE STRIKE IN DELANO: A THREE-PART CASE STUDY OF LABOR PROBLEMS IN CALIFORNIA AGRICULTURE

JOHN BERGEZ

The issue of the grape strike at Delano and other, subsequent, farm strikes has been a matter of continuing concern in the state and nation for several years. This strike, or huelga, *had definite implications for minority identity and unity, because most of the farm workers involved were Mexican-Americans or Filipinos. The two sides in the strike had contrasting views as to the causes of the problem. John Bergez wrote a three-part article for the student newspaper* El Gaucho *of the University of California at Santa Barbara reflecting a youthful view of the grape strike.*

Delano: Profit Purgatory

Delano is a singularly unremarkable interruption of Highway 99, situated in the San Joaquin Valley about 200 miles north of Los Angeles.

The town is unpretentious; it boasts two movie theatres, a single bowling alley, a thrice-weekly "community" newspaper, and a population that occupies all of 11 pages in the Kern County telephone book.

Delano bears none of the trappings of empire. Only if one knows that this somnambulant town is the center of a billion-dollar industry does he

John Bergez, of College Press Service, "Delano: Profit Purgatory," *El Gaucho*, Vol. 49 (May 6, 1969); "Delano: Living in the Past When Employers Were Kings," *El Gaucho*, Vol. 49 (May 7, 1969); "Delano: Spirit of 'La Huelga' Undiminished," *El Gaucho*, Vol. 49 (May 8, 1969). Reprinted by permission. (The grape strike referred to in these selections has been settled.)

begin to notice the subtle signs which set it apart from other small towns: the rusty railroad tracks that sever the town in two; the monotonous miles of grapevines, twined about bleached wooden crosses for as far as the eye cares to look; the blazing, uncompromising sun that makes the place a most profitable sort of purgatory.

Delano today is more than the heart of a huge grape industry; it is also the unlikely battleground for a struggle that could permanently change the nature of agriculture in the United States.

Yet despite the national significance of the grape strike and boycott in Delano, it is the nature and history of the town itself that has made the struggle between the United Farm Workers and the Valley grape growers the prolonged, bitter, tragic affair it has become.

The most obvious feature of Delano is that it is split in two by the railroad tracks and the more recent freeway. On the west side of the tracks in housing which a prominent city official privately admits is "blighted," live the chicano and filipino farm laborers, and a scattering of blacks.

On the east side, in moderate middle-class dwellings, live the "Anglos," the predominantly white residents who work in the banks, stores, motels and coffee shops. On the west side are the filipino national church, filipino hall, and the shabby headquarters of the United Farm Workers Organizing Committee, directed by Cesar Chavez.

The division could hardly be more graphic.

Tension and distrust run deep in Delano. Many shopkeepers refuse to discuss the strike, maintaining with dubious credibility that "we don't know anything about it." A stranger asking directions to the union headquarters, in the middle of the day, will find no one who will tell him. Students from Los Angeles who visited the union headquarters learned their car had been searched twice during their stay.

While many of the townspeople seem reluctant, or even afraid, to discuss the strike with strangers, some are less reticent. One outspoken citizen is Captain Gilbert, a young, earnest official of the 26-man police force.

"Cesar and his group aren't liked here at all," Gilbert explained. "They bring in all these outside groups and professional agitators and spread hate literature just to stir up trouble. Nobody's hungry here. Chavez is just trying to create turmoil and unrest with his propaganda."

The growers contend that there is no need for a strike because their workers are sufficiently paid and live in reasonable comfort. Gilbert has a slightly different view.

"A lot of these Mexican workers want substandard housing. They're used to it—that's their way of life. You and I wouldn't change 'em. The father goes out and spends all the family's money on booze and cards— no wonder they're poor. Not all of the Mexicans are that way. Maybe 10 percent. You could pay 'em $10,000 a year and they wouldn't live any better," Gilbert added.

It is a short walk from the police department through the downtown area to the freeway. Along the way, one notices that many cars sport antistrike bumper stickers. "Eat California Grapes—The Forbidden Fruit" is a favorite. "All the Cadillacs have them," a Mexican of about 20 explained.

The Delano Chamber of Commerce is on the fringes of the business district, just across the freeway from the West Side slums. On its wall hangs a plaque bearing the motto, "Wealth comes through understanding."

Delano: Living in the Past When Employers Were Kings

Delano today faces a sticky dilemma. The realities and rising aspirations of the 1960's clash with the town's mentality and structure, which apparently are nestled somewhere in the 1930's.

The problem is the exclusion of the agricultural industry specifically from legislation that guaranteed workers the right to organize and bargain collectively in unions. Farm corporations, consequently, enjoy relative freedom in their treatment of workers. Rural communities like Delano continue to live in a serene past when employers were kings.

It is this anachronistic vision that Chavez and the United Farm Workers are challenging in Delano. Farm workers have the lowest wage rates and the highest unemployment in the United States working force, according to the National Advisory Committee on Farm Labor.

The Delano grape growers contend that conditions in California are the best in the nation for farm workers. No one on the union side disputes that fact, but they derive little comfort from it. The average annual income of a grape worker in Kern County is $2,024—well below the national "poverty line" established by the federal government. Housing is also inadequate.

Delano growers, in answer to union charges, say they provide free housing for their workers; however, most of it is barracks-type, for males only, with no provisions made for families.

The Governor's Advisory Committee on Housing studied the situation and concluded, "Fewer than 20 percent of the California farm workers covered in our study lived in dwellings which could be considered adequate . . . For 33 percent of the dwelling units occupied by general field workers, the only toilet facilities were pit privies. Thirty percent of the dwellings had no bathing facilities, and 25 percent lacked even so basic a necessity as a kitchen sink with running water."

The union also charges that working conditions are substandard for farm workers. Although the growers point to state legislation insuring such benefits as minimum wages, sanitary working conditions and disability insurance, the union says these laws generally go unenforced.

A particular point of contention is the lack of facilities in the fields. As a result, it has become a comic ritual in Delano that the growers make a point of taking visitors on tours of the fields and showing off an outhouse. "They've been rushing like hell to make those things since it became an issue," a union member observed.

The union is currently most concerned with the use of pesticides, the general lack of knowledge about their possible effects upon both workers and consumers, and a number of cases of alleged pesticide poisoning.

Last January Chavez offered to meet with the growers to discuss the "urgent" pesticide issue alone, leaving all other differences aside for the moment. The growers refused. A local court has issued an injunction prohibiting the union to see the "public" records of pesticide use.

The union organizers also stress the fact that of all the benefits the workers are supposed to enjoy, the one most conspicuously absent is unemployment insurance. According to an independent study, the average grape worker in Kern County works 119 days out of the year.

Economic and working conditions are not the workers' only scourge. California's farm labor force is comprised largely of impoverished foreign immigrants—primarily Mexicans and Filipinos—who lack the educational, language, and job skills to break this vicious circle of poverty. And the whole picture is muddied by the prejudice he faces.

A doctoral thesis completed in 1966 for Stanford University relates the prejudice in an elementary school in the area, whose enrollment was at the time 58 percent Mexican. One teacher, asked why she chose an "Anglo" to lead five Mexicans in "orderly file" out of the classroom, replied, "His father owns one of the big farms in the area, and one day he will have to know how to handle Mexicans."

The president of the local chamber of commerce has nothing but praise for that school's principal.

The principal in question adds an anecdote that capitalizes the plight of the Mexican-American.

"Once we let a Mexican girl give a talk of some kind and all she did was mumble around. She had quite an accent, too. Afterwards we had several complaints from parents, so we haven't done anything like that since."

Delano: Spirit of 'La Huelga' Undiminished

After more than three years of strikes, boycotts, invective and violence, the camps on either side of Delano freeway seem as firmly entrenched as ever.

The table grape growers, for their part, continue [officially] to deny even the existence of a boycott or a strike, though they [privately] admit readily enough that there is indeed a boycott.

On the west side, the spirit of "la huelga" is undiminished. Union meetings are still jam-packed, foot-stomping, hand-clapping affairs. They sing Nosotros Venceremos—We Shall Overcome—with all the fervent sincerity of the eve of the first strike.

At the ramshackle cluster of buildings that serve as the union headquarters, banners, posters, buttons and bumper stickers abound; in the midst of them, invariably, are the likenesses of the two slain Kennedys, Gandhi, and Martin Luther King.

While both sides are standing firm, there has been a change in the growers' strategy. At first, they thought they could import workers to break the strike and simply ignore the union until it went away. That tactic succeeded in an earlier decade, against a different opponent. But the impetus of the civil rights movement and the awakening of the nation to the realities of poverty gave Cesar Chavez the weapons he needed to wage a different sort of war.

Chavez' appeal to churches, students and liberal organizations brought a flood of "outside agitators," the ones Delano is so fond of maligning. They made the difference, Chavez says, in the early days.

It was the idea of a boycott, however, that thrust the local issue into the national limelight. Originally the boycott was directed only against the Guimarra Corporation. As other companies loaned their labels to Guimarra, however, and all the table grape growers stood firm against union offers for elections, the boycott was extended to all California table grapes.

While bands of farm workers left their homes in Delano to seek support in strange new cities, the growers formed the South Central Farmers' Committee to churn out counter-propaganda and to escort visitors around the grape fields. The California Table Grape Commission announced this year that it has also retained a professional public relations firm.

Meanwhile, the union's boycott expanded in late February to include the huge Safeway chain, which has refused to stop selling grapes. Less than two months later, the union counted 30,000 consumers who had signed petitions saying they refused to shop at Safeway.

The war of attrition continues to grow in scope as both sides prepare for a possibly decisive harvest this year. Whatever the outcome, however, the UFWOC has vowed to continue the strike for as long as is necessary.

Chavez' dream in large part made "la huelga." If the small man with the large vision has his way, he'll have a great deal to say about what happens to la causa in the years after Delano.

56. A NEGRO NEWSPAPER TAKES A HARD LOOK AT "NEW SOLUTIONS" FOR GHETTO UNEMPLOYMENT

When racial problems became headline news in the 1960s, many political leaders offered "solutions" to the problems of ghetto unemployment. Although the political rhetoric sounds impressive, many minority leaders are concerned with what they believe is an inadequate response to the economic problems of the minorities. In two editorials in the Negro newspaper the Los Angeles Sentinel, *the issues of black capitalism and racial balance in hiring are criticized.*

Black Capitalism: An Empty Promise?

Last Sunday night, President and Mrs. Nixon returned from a trip that touched several eastern nations and heard the President promise aid in several different forms.

So be it.

In the meantime, we should like to question our honorable leader about the state of OUR nation. At the opening of the 1969 Watts Festival, a keynote speaker pointed out that the United States should attempt to feed and house its indigenous people before reaching for Mars.

We concur.

Since the inauguration, there have been promises of "Black Capitalism" but except in a few isolated cases, none has been forthcoming. The few men who have benefited from the present program are those men who could have perhaps qualified under normal conditions.

Black communities need meaningful programs that encompass a large segment of the community to the extent that they can feel the effects of such a project.

We need no more empty promises.

The past few months have seen several possible answers go down the proverbial drain. The veritable junking of one of the youth programs could prove to be disastrous.

We disagree completely with Vice President Spiro Agnew's recent statement to the effect that we need to use the spirit of our space program to alleviate hunger and suffering as opposed to the space program funds.

Perhaps we do need the spirit.

But at the same time we need the means with which to fight the existing problems. We need to replace President Nixon's "Black Capitalism" program with a project that would bring real jobs into the ghetto and at the same time inject that needed financial spark.

As a whole, the black community has had its fill of conversation and

"Black Capitalism: An Empty Promise?" *Los Angeles Sentinel* (August 7, 1969); "Same Old Shell Game," *Los Angeles Sentinel* (May 29, 1969). Reprinted by permission.

idle promises. Those people virtually locked into the ghetto must have economic means and the promised "Black Capitalism" has not given it to them.

There is an old adage that says, "Charity begins at home and spreads abroad."

We have not listened well.

We have begun our charity abroad while home is being neglected. This is a despicable act. We have chastised our neighbors and offered to give them help and we have left our own house unclean.

The kind of "Black Capitalism" we need is the kind that gives men jobs and provides education for our young, and keeps our families healthy. We don't need promises of grandeur and dreams of what could be ours if only we had the "capital."

The kind of capital we need can be found in warm clothing for the naked, food for the hungry, and rest for the weary; but not in empty words that smack of "Black Capitalism."

Same Old Shell Game

The report of an ethnic employment study released Tuesday confirmed the broad suspicion that Los Angeles County is still playing the old shell game on visual minority employees it was playing in 1964.

Negro employment by the County increased .004 percent.

Mexican-American showed the same rate of increase.

County officials make great to do about the fact that slightly more than 25 percent of their employees are black.

Negroes drop to 3 percent of the employees at the $1,000 to $1,500 level and to zero above that level.

The County employs less than 5 percent Mexican-American and 2.6 percent Orientals.

Orientals hold 3.8 percent of jobs over $2,000 per month with whites holding the rest.

It would seem that with a fair merit system and such a broad base of black employees, Negroes would fare far better in the advanced positions.

The fact is that the merit system, except on the entrance level, is a farce.

Under the leadership of COA Lin Hollinger and Personnel Director Gordon T. Nexvig, the County rigs promotional examinations up to 85 percent with subjective standards that are easily manipulated.

In addition to at least a 35 percent oral examination the County has a gimmick called "promotability" which can count as much as 50 percent on the total score.

A combination of oral and promotability scores can control the employment complexion of any wage level.

Where ability to score high on objective tests counts, Negro employment is exceptionally high. Where the personal opinion of interviewers and immediate supervisors comes in, as it does for promotional examinations, Negro employment drops off drastically.

That is the crux of the discriminatory employment practices of Los Angeles County.

As far as Negro employees are concerned, intensive recruitment is not needed.

What the County needs to do is to quit playing its old shell game of subverting the spirit and letter of the merit system and promote people on their ability rather than their skin color.

Until county administrators and supervisors prove they are capable of such color-blindedness, subjective portions of promotional examinations should be limited to 15 percent of total scores. Along with that they need to drastically modify the one in three role of selection.

Only then will ethnic employment figures reflect the true ability of citizens who work for the County of Los Angeles.

57. MINORITY FRUSTRATIONS IN SEEKING EMPLOYMENT

PAUL JACOBS

Since World War II there has been a high level of employment for whites in California and throughout much of the nation. The same favorable job market does not prevail for minorities, however. Paul Jacobs comments on the frustrations of minority job seekers who suffer unemployment or marginal employment in the midst of a period of white affluence.

To become an adult in America means to have graduated from high school and gone on to college, or to have left school, perhaps before graduation, to take a job or to learn a trade. To be an adult in America means to have work, to hold down a job, to have an occupation, to be a professional, or to be married to a man who fits into one of those categories. Work, a job, an occupation, a profession, are central to America conceptions of masculinity; it is as true for the whites in America as it is for Negroes and other minorities.

But in the case of the Negroes, and to a lesser extent the other minorities, the cities are now truly paying for the sins of the fathers. Since racism kept non-whites from decent jobs or the prospects of decent jobs for hundreds of years, the nearly permanent absence of employment has created an increasingly large pool of men and women unable to meet the standards of adulthood because they do not have the basic requirement of adulthood—a job.

The young men and women, searching for some other identity to substitute for their lack of occupation, turn to devices which make it even more difficult for them to get jobs. The young Negro's "do-rag," which makes the employment service official turn away from him in disgust, is there to protect his "process," the hair style he has adopted to give him some sense of individuality. Since the young Negro has no identity derived from work, he uses another means of establishing his identity, a means which in turn keeps him from getting a job and so further deepens his sense of bitterness toward society. And all of this is happening at a time when society's technological advances make scarcer and scarcer any kind of unskilled or semi-skilled job at which the young man might begin a life of working.

This is the dilemma confronting the Employment Service official; its dimensions are enormous and frightening. Every few years another generation is produced of young men and women who literally cannot speak or write English, though they may even have graduated from high school. Their perception of the world is so limited that events outside the narrow confines of their own lives have little or no significance for them. To get up in the morning, get dressed, go to work, come home, work in the garden, visit friends, earn enough money to buy a house in the Valley, spend a weekend at Lake Arrowhead, have babies who grow up to become teen-agers attending the senior prom, visit Hawaii for a twenty-fifth wedding anniversary, and never get arrested, never go to jail, hear about venereal diseases but never know anybody who gets them, have credit cards and play bridge, shop downtown before going to the PTA fashion show, learn to ski at Sun Valley, take scuba-diving lessons at Hermosa Beach, and on and on and on—these, the life patterns of middle-class Los Angeles, and comparable patterns in other cities, are unknown to these generations of unemployed, underemployed, and low-paid workers.

One link between them and the world outside is the TV. The TV is on all the time, its sounds a continuous undertone to the life of the house. While they are very young the TV is a combination pacifier and babysitter; as they get a little older it becomes a device for inducing euphoria, and so the kids watch the cartoons for hours. Everything they see reinforces that hatred of themselves for being born black which was once so widespread but which is now being replaced by hate of Whitey: they are exhorted to buy a certain detergent and "Think White! Go White! Stay White!" or to buy "flesh-colored" Band-Aids like the one being put on a little white boy's scratched white arm by his blond, beautiful, white mother.

The TV teases them, too, with its visions of what they as adults should have—the new cars, watches, dresses, electric shavers, sewing machines, radios, freezers, and all the other goods that pour out of the American cornucopia—but since they are without jobs, none of what they see on the white American TV is available to them. The only way they can get the newest-model anything is to steal it; and in their truncated society there is no strong moral sanction against theft, only the fear of getting caught.

So in place of any other occupation, some learn about crime. As kids they start by stealing from the dime store or supermarket. Then they serve an apprenticeship in purse-snatching. After that, perhaps, they try muggings and stickups, attempting to "score" at a gas station or liquor store out of their own neighborhood. Or perhaps they opt for the career line of the hustler, beginning with selling marijuana to their school-mates. From that they can graduate to pushing narcotics or handling stolen goods, specializing in the accessories stripped from cars in the housing project parking lots, and possibly developing this business so well that after a time they can take advance orders for specific accessories and make delivery within forty-eight hours. They can also expand into other areas of hustling, like buying cheap merchandise from jobbers in downtown Los Angeles and selling it in the ghettos as guaranteed stolen goods. (After the events of August 1965 the Los Angeles ghettos were flooded with allegedly looted merchandise; but much of the "loot goods" had actually been bought in order to cash in on the high demand for loot goods.)

The unskilled young men who do not become criminals take the menial jobs, which is all they can do, but reluctantly, for they know they will be sneered at by their peers. They know, too, that they will not keep the jobs, for they never had or have lost long ago the discipline of a daily routine. Perhaps they will pick up a smattering of some trade, but more often their hands and minds will be completely untrained in the skills needed in the cities today. The white newspapers' fat want ads sections, imploring aircraft engineers to come to Douglas Aircraft, electronic engineers to look at Litton Industries' pension plan, and chemical engineers to report tomorrow to Shell Oil mean absolutely nothing to them. After all, eight of the ten jobs most short of workers in the cities require either college graduation, some kind of special license, or more training than is obtained in four years of high school.

Many of the unskilled become parents very young, but the young men, unable to cope with their wives and families in a state of permanent joblessness, will drift off into some other section of the country, to repeat the same set of actions again and again. The mothers of their children know from their own childhood how to "get on the county," and soon the welfare department pattern becomes the life history of another generation.

The streets of the minority ghettos are filling up with these men and women, caught in a trap from which there is no escape.

Computers can predict, within fractions of a second, the time at which two space ships will rendezvous, but no one knows the exact number of totally unemployed men and women who live in America. No one knows how many men, women, and teen-age Americans work only part of the time, or how many are working at jobs that pay them so little that even when they put in forty hours or more, they still don't earn enough to bring them up to the basic poverty minimums set by the government. And no one knows how many Americans do get jobs but seem incapable of keeping them for more than a few days. All that is known about the number of unemployed, underemployed, low-paid Negroes, Puerto Ricans, and Mexican-Americans is that it runs into the many thousands. Estimates of the Negro unemployment rate range from a minimum of two and a half times to six times that of the whites; for Mexican-Americans the range is somewhat narrower but still very high.

A great many people know how widespread unemployment is among the minority groups and even understand something of its awful consequences. What is not understood is how ineffective such institutions of government as the state employment services have been in changing the situation, and why they have been so ineffective.

58. RACIAL PREJUDICE IN HOUSING

WILLIAM H. GRIER AND PRICE M. COBBS

In their book Black Rage *the black authors Drs. William H. Grier and Price M. Cobbs examine California and national attitudes concerning racial discrimination in housing. They suggest that white prejudice is the result of an irrational fear of minorities. In a period when some minorities are reassessing the desirability of integration, this selection might help to explain why militants believe integration has failed.*

In 1964, California citizens were allowed to vote on a proposition which in effect would have repealed an existing "fair housing" law.

The issue was widely publicized, the proposal was heavily financed, and it was voted into law.

During the campaign a wealthy white woman produced a series of rationalizations explaining why she was voting for the proposition. Although she lived in a large area of expensive homes and although her own home cost $150,000, she said she was most afraid of black people taking over her neighborhood.

The outrageously irrational quality of racial prejudice is evident in many aspects of the phenomenon. Housing bias is an example of a more far-reaching and influential effect. White people have a deep and abiding feeling that the races are supposed to be separated and that the preferential places should be reserved for themselves.

To live near blacks or to eat with blacks is to jeopardize one's status. White people are supposed to eat and live in better places than black people.

The following example may help to illustrate how central is the attitude of white superiority in this country.

The value of a home has come to be determined neither by the quality of the structure nor by the value of the structures around it. It can be sharply devalued by the proximity of a family of blacks. It is devalued because few other white families would purchase it, and unless it is sought by other black families, the owner finds its market value very low indeed.

FROM *Black Rage* by William H. Grier and Price M. Cobbs, pp. 187–188, © 1968 by William H. Grier and Price M. Cobbs, Basic Books, Inc., Publishers, New York. Reprinted with permission of Basic Books, Inc. and of Jonathan Cape, Ltd.

We know of no other ethnic group which by its mere proximity can so certainly make a man's home repugnant to him.

The wealthy woman in the example above was so troubled by the prospect of blacks moving into her neighborhood that she took a passionate stand for restrictive legislation in the hope of barring them more effectively. She seemed completely unaware that the number of black people in the market for $150,000 homes is very, very small and surely presents no threat to her affluent neighborhood.

Such attitudes suggest not only that proximity to blacks lowers a white person's status but that some of the low status of blacks "rubs off" on whites.

About the Authors

GEORGE E. FRAKES is Associate Professor of History at Santa Barbara City College. His published work includes *Teachers' Manual for Patterns in American History* (1968), of which he is coauthor, and *Laboratory for Liberty: The South Carolina Colonial Committee System, 1719–1776* (1970).

CURTIS B. SOLBERG, Associate Professor of History at Santa Barbara City College, has been visiting lecturer in American history at Northeastern University and, for the academic year 1970–1971, at the State Teachers College in Elverum, Norway. He is coeditor with George E. Frakes of *The Pollution Papers* (1971). He is also lecturer in a Scandinavian seminar series concerning environmental problems, sponsored by the United States State Department.